Niue 1774–1974

LAIFONEMAIPUKA

Niue 1774–1974

200 Years of Contact and Change

MARGARET POINTER

For the people of Niue-Fekai

Printed in 2015 in the United States of America by

University of Hawaiʻi Press
2840 Kolowalu Street
Honolulu, HI 96822
www.uhpress.hawaii.edu

20 19 18 17 16 15   6 5 4 3 2 1

This edition of Niue 1774–1974 is published by arrangement with
Otago University Press, Dunedin, New Zealand.

Library of Congress Cataloging-in-Publication Data

Pointer, Margaret, author.
Niue 1774-1974 : 200 years of contact and change / Margaret Pointer.
pages cm
Includes bibliographical references and index.
ISBN 978-0-8248-5586-4 (pbk. : alk. paper)
1. Niue—History. I. Title.
DU430.N5P65 2015
996.2'6—dc23

2015008631

The author gratefully acknowledges receipt of a Writer's Award from Copyright Licensing New Zealand

Design and layout by Fiona Moffat

Frontispiece: Niuean Hiapo. Gift of Sydney Aris. Auckland War Memorial Museum, Tāmaki Paenga Hira, AM30088.

Front cover photograph: People gather on the wharf at Alofi in 1900 as the governor's party prepare to come ashore (detail). Ranfurly Collection, Alexander Turnbull Library, Wellington, New Zealand, PA1-q-633_035-bottom

Contents

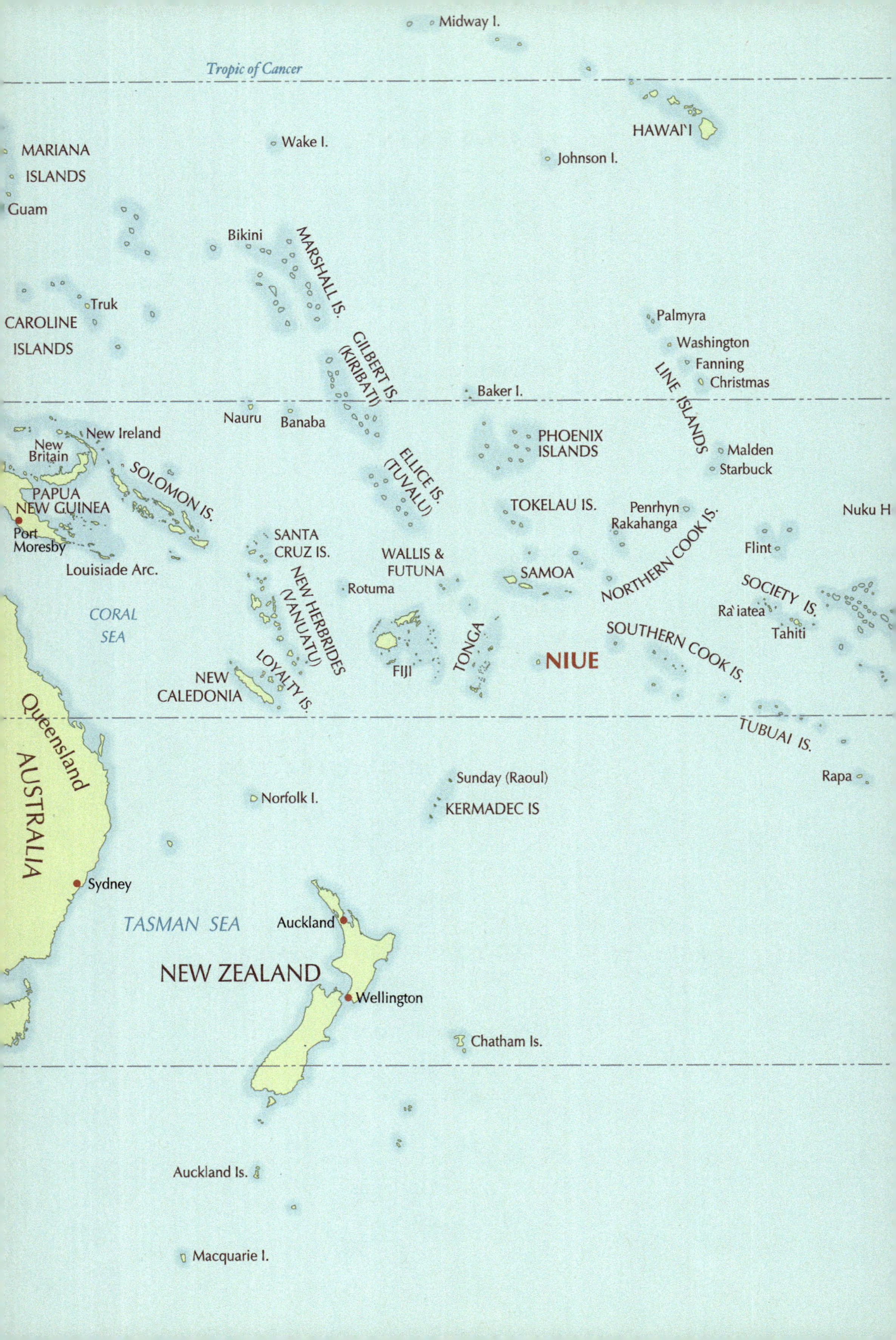

Midway I.
Tropic of Cancer
HAWAI'I
Wake I.
Johnson I.
MARIANA ISLANDS
Guam
Bikini
MARSHALL IS.
Truk
CAROLINE ISLANDS
Palmyra
Washington
Fanning
Christmas
LINE ISLANDS
GILBERT IS. (KIRIBATI)
Baker I.
Nauru
Banaba
New Ireland
New Britain
PHOENIX ISLANDS
Malden
Starbuck
ELLICE IS. (TUVALU)
SOLOMON IS.
PAPUA NEW GUINEA
Port Moresby
TOKELAU IS.
Penrhyn
Rakahanga
Nuku H
Louisiade Arc.
SANTA CRUZ IS.
WALLIS & FUTUNA
Flint
NORTHERN COOK IS.
SAMOA
Rotuma
SOCIETY IS.
Ra'iatea
Tahiti
CORAL SEA
NEW HEBRIDES (VANUATU)
FIJI
TONGA
NIUE
SOUTHERN COOK IS.
NEW CALEDONIA
LOYALTY IS.
Queensland
AUSTRALIA
TUBUAI IS.
Rapa
Sunday (Raoul)
KERMADEC IS
Norfolk I.
Sydney
TASMAN SEA
Auckland
NEW ZEALAND
Wellington
Chatham Is.
Auckland Is.
Macquarie I.

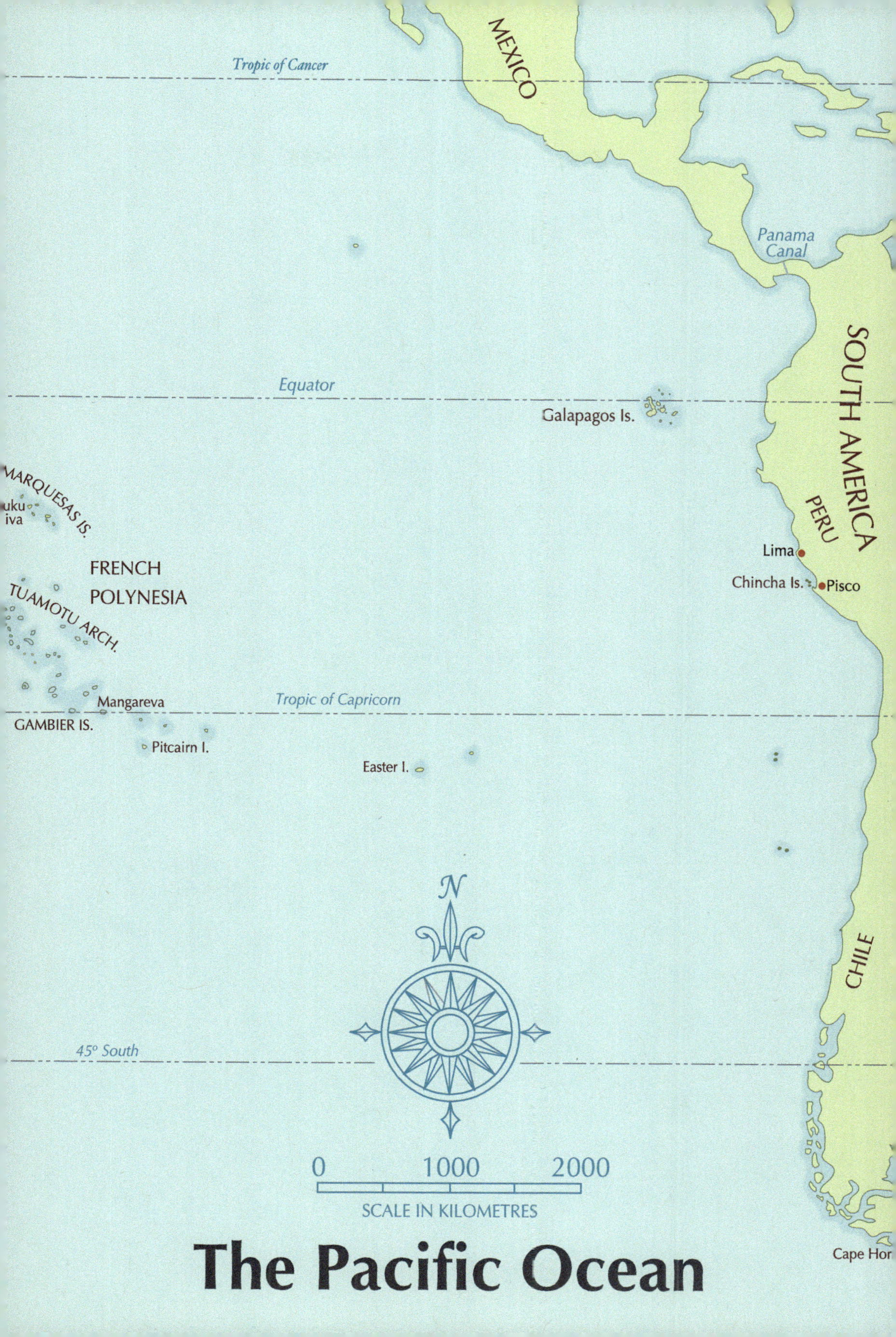

The Pacific Ocean

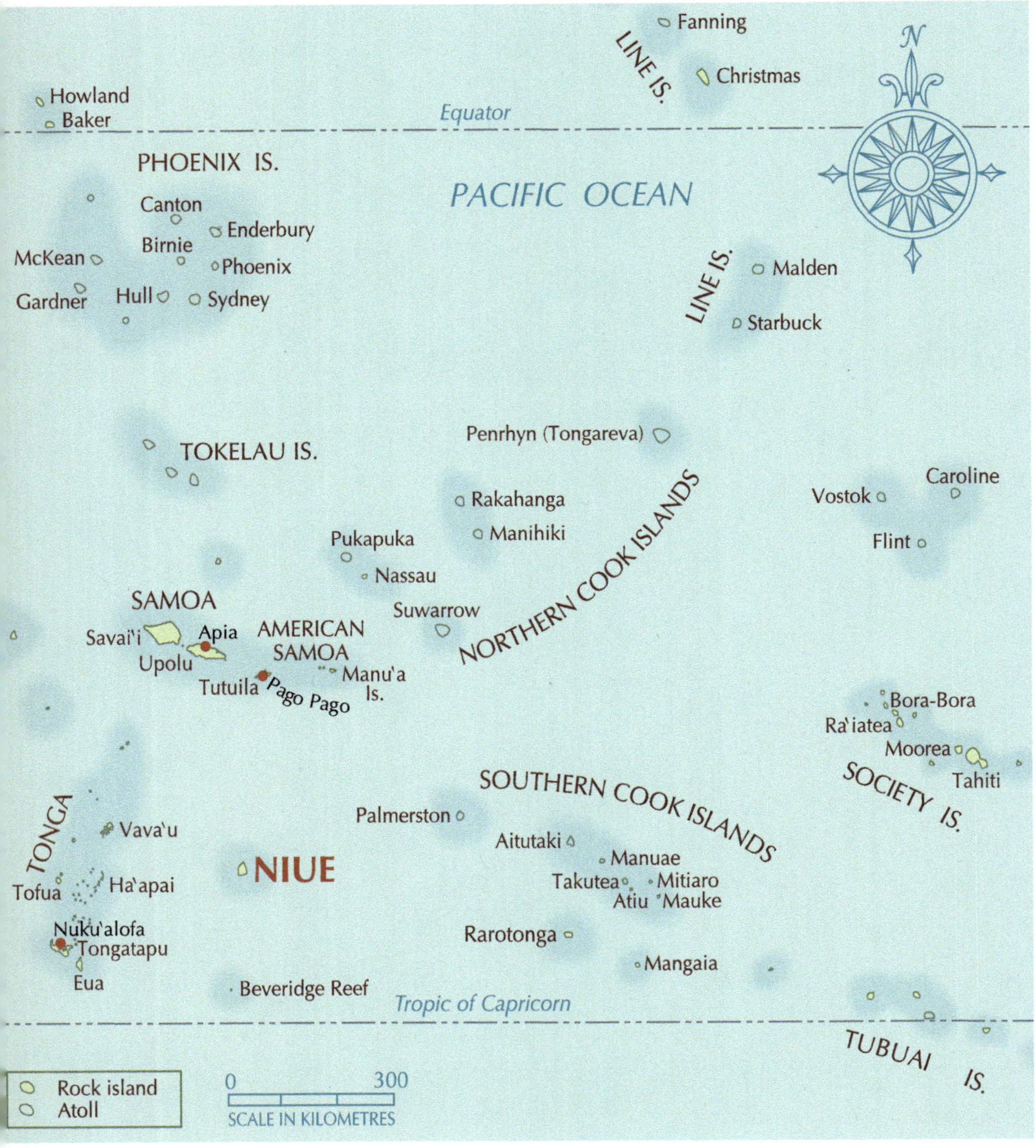

Fanning
LINE IS.
Christmas
N
Howland
Baker
Equator
PHOENIX IS.
PACIFIC OCEAN
Canton
Enderbury
Birnie
McKean
Phoenix
Gardner
Hull
Sydney
LINE IS.
Malden
Starbuck
Penrhyn (Tongareva)
TOKELAU IS.
NORTHERN COOK ISLANDS
Caroline
Vostok
Rakahanga
Manihiki
Flint
Pukapuka
Nassau
Suwarrow
SAMOA
Savai'i
Apia
Upolu
AMERICAN SAMOA
Manu'a Is.
Tutuila
Pago Pago
Bora-Bora
Ra'iatea
Moorea
Tahiti
SOCIETY IS.
SOUTHERN COOK ISLANDS
TONGA
Vava'u
Palmerston
Aitutaki
Manuae
NIUE
Tofua
Ha'apai
Takutea
Mitiaro
Atiu
Mauke
Nuku'alofa
Tongatapu
Rarotonga
Eua
Mangaia
Beveridge Reef
Tropic of Capricorn
TUBUAI IS.
Rock island
Atoll
0
300
SCALE IN KILOMETRES

Acknowledgements

While research and writing appear to be lonely activities they are in fact filled with other people, and in a project that has extended over five years there are so many to thank for their help and encouragement.

The institution where I have spent the greatest amount of time over this period is the Alexander Turnbull Library, within the National Library of New Zealand, in Wellington. Turnbull holds the research collections of the National Library and is an amazing source for Pacific history, both written and visual. My sincere thanks go to all the staff in this wonderful library.

Many other institutions were vital in my search for Niue material. Archives New Zealand was my main source for official papers covering the period of New Zealand's administration of Niue. Te Papa Tongarewa Museum of New Zealand had valuable image collections and a wonderful artefact collection. At the Auckland War Memorial Museum staff were very obliging in helping with my search for images and in accessing manuscripts, in particular Percy Smith's private diary. Auckland University Library Special Collections staff helped me access the archives of the Western Pacific High Commission, and Auckland City Libraries were extremely obliging in my search for images. The Hocken Collection at the University of Otago and the J.C. Beaglehole Room at Victoria University of Wellington both yielded useful material. In Sydney the Mitchell Library made available the diary and letter-book of the missionary William George Lawes.

No history of Niue could be written without visiting the island itself and I was fortunate to be able to make two research trips there, for five weeks in total. A huge fakaaue lahi to Moira Enetama, Director of Tāoga Niue, and her staff. Moira was a never-ending source of help: arranging weeks beforehand for the archival files I needed; driving me out to look at old sites and search for stone walls, graves, plants and even coconut trees; answering the endless email enquiries I sent her. At Tāoga Niue, staff have worked in very difficult conditions since cyclone Heta destroyed the

Huanaki Museum and Cultural Centre in January 2004. I hope that before too long they will again have a permanent building where their tāoga can be safely stored and displayed.

In addition to libraries, museums and archives, my research has been greatly enriched by help from many individuals. On Niue I value the long discussions I had with Young Vivian and I thank him for his ongoing support of my work. I also remember very useful discussions with Frank Lui, Hafe Vilitama, Justin Kamupala, Sifa Ioane and Hula Funaki at the Niue Language Commission, Hima and Pat Douglas, Ernie and Hine Welsh, Stafford and Salome Guest and Noga Bray. Thanks to the many others who gave words of encouragement and plates of umu kai. In Auckland Marion McQuoid generously gave of her time to talk with me. In Wellington I have been cheered along by the warm support of Rev. Falkland Liuvaie, Rev. Tom and Akele Etuata and H.E. Mrs O'love Jacobsen, Niue High Commissioner to New Zealand.

I was privileged to sit and talk with Jock McEwen shortly before he died in 2010. His son Andrew and Andrew's wife Mary have continued to support my project and I am grateful for family letters and photos shared with me. I was very pleased when Bill Larsen and his sister Alison agreed to meet me in 2012. They have been generous in sharing their memories and family photos and I thank them sincerely for being prepared to discuss what must still be a painful episode for their family. Selwyn Wilson, a former resident commissioner to Niue, was a treasure I found through the phone book. I acknowledge the help of Selwyn's late wife Cecily and I thank Selwyn for his thoughtful reflections during our long discussions.

There have been two very special contacts in London: Jonathan Lawes, great-grandson of Rev. Frank Lawes, and Anthony Aris, great-grandson of John Arundel. Others who have assisted generously are Lesley Edgeley-Page, Bill Graham, Tony Johns, Tim Lawson, Caroline McDonald, Doug Munro and Damon Salesa.

Historical research proved to be expensive and I am extremely grateful for three sources of funding to help make the project a reality. The Ministry of Foreign Affairs and Trade granted me a New Zealand History Research Award in 2010 which enabled me to spend time in Auckland. Special thanks to Neil Robertson for facilitating my access to restricted ministry files. In 2012 I was awarded a Ministry for Culture and Heritage New Zealand History Research Trust Fund Award which took me back to Niue and began funding the cost of images. My special thanks to Neill Atkinson, Chief Historian, for the support and advice he gave me. Finally in 2013 I won a Copyright Licensing New Zealand non-fiction Writers' Award for the project.

This very generous award has seen the project to completion and I am very grateful for the trust placed in me by CLNZ. These awards helped fund the work but, most importantly, they encouraged me to believe that the project was worthwhile.

Research and writing are only part of the process. Someone has to be prepared to publish the work and for this I give grateful thanks to Rachel Scott at Otago University Press who has guided me gently through the whole process. I thank her for her faith in this project. Dr Malcolm McKinnon reviewed the manuscript and I am grateful for his careful consideration, pertinent questions and wise counsel. Rachel has a great team around her and I thank them all for the part they have played in bringing this work up to publication standard.

I cannot finish without thanking my family, in particular my husband Mike. He was responsible for taking me to Niue in his capacity as New Zealand High Commissioner. He has patiently listened to me talking about Niuean history ever since. While he has left the history to me, he has been extremely helpful on the technical front and on constitutional and political questions. Our time on Niue was special and it was great to share it with our boys, Simon and Tom.

I thank everyone most sincerely but I accept sole responsibility for the ideas and any errors in this work.

Introduction

When people in New Zealand learned that our family was going to live on Niue for three years in the late 1990s they were frequently astounded, invariably confused. It was in the days before the island featured on the evening weather map in New Zealand and it really was an unknown location. Perhaps we meant Nauru. That island was widely known. A search of the public library failed to provide reassurance. The Cook Islands, yes, Tonga, Samoa, Fiji, Pitcairn, certainly, but nothing on Niue. We left with our boys and our cat and a large measure of apprehension.

Flying in to Niue requires considerable faith in the wonders of modern navigation for there appears to be nothing below but ocean. A mighty expanse of ocean. Then the plane begins its descent and through the window, as the wing dips, comes the first glimpse of a large, flat expanse of uplifted rock, covered in dense green vegetation, bush in some places and forest in others, with the sea breaking directly onto the narrow fringing reef. No looming volcanic peaks, no sparkling azure lagoon, no tiny atolls, just one large piece of flat rock less than half the size of Lake Taupo. We have arrived.

The airport is busy. People crowd near the exit to see who has arrived on the flight. Others sit beneath the flame trees, chatting and exchanging news. They are in no hurry. This is plane day, it comes only once a week and it is to be enjoyed. Before long there is the roar of engines and the smell of aviation fuel and the plane departs. People gather up their children and their visitors and the cars and trucks drive off.

We had been taken from the airport to our new home before the plane left for the return flight to New Zealand. We stood in our living room together and we listened to the plane go out over our roof. Then there was silence and later darkness, total darkness.

But gradually new sights and sounds and smells became familiar: long-tailed tropicbirds wheeling overhead, fruitbats squealing while feeding in the trees just before sunset, brightly coloured cotton dresses, roosters crowing at all hours of the day and night, the pungent smell of coconut fronds being burned, frigate birds appearing occasionally when forced in to land by a storm at sea, old trucks climbing the hill beyond our property, dogs barking, crocuses suddenly blooming across the lawn, humpback whales surfacing and blowing loudly, a night sky such as we had never seen before, village show days, feasts with trestle tables groaning under the weight of the umu kai, warm friendly Polynesian faces. Occasionally we saw a container vessel on the horizon; in the winter a trans-Pacific flight path brought a tiny silver bird overhead and we watched as it crossed our sky and disappeared. And we grew to love our new home.

Niue lies alone in the vast Pacific, an old uplifted coral atoll. The centre of the island is saucer-shaped and marks the ancient lagoon. There are two terraces, old fringing reefs, marking two periods of tectonic uplift. Thirty metres below the lower terrace is the newest fringing reef and beyond that the land drops steeply to the deep ocean. There is no anchoring, no harbouring and no protection. From the sea, the first uplifted terrace presents a formidable barrier – rocky cliffs broken by chasms and crevices and caves, vegetation clinging on bravely in the face of the saltwater onslaught. Across the island the surface is extremely rocky, the hard, weathered coral forming an unlikely base for vegetation. But in little hollows there are pockets of fertile soil and, miraculously it seems, plants grow. There are no streams or rivers on the island, but there are pools of brackish water and, less frequently, fresh water in the limestone caves. Beneath the island lies a lens of water which percolates through the coral rock above, pure and fresh and sweet.

This isolated island was settled approximately 1000 years ago from Samoa to the north and Tonga to the west. The people who came developed their own language and culture. The earliest name for their home is said to be Nukututaha, the island that stands alone. It came to be known by the people as Niue or Niue-Fekai, a name now used in formal situations and in song and legend. There were two main divisions on the island. The larger Motu division covered the northern part of the island and the Tafiti division, thought to be peopled by a later migration, the southern part. Between these two there was constant enmity; and while they were not always in a state of war, conflict was common. However, when faced with outside threats such as Tongan invasions, there was greater unity and for a time a patuiki, chief of chiefs, might be recognised.[1]

On Niue, history has been passed down orally through the generations. The contact history is no exception: stories are told of the arrival of the great English explorer James Cook, of men working on whaling vessels and on guano islands, of the Peruvian slave traders. Names such as Malden and Sunday Island, Peniamina

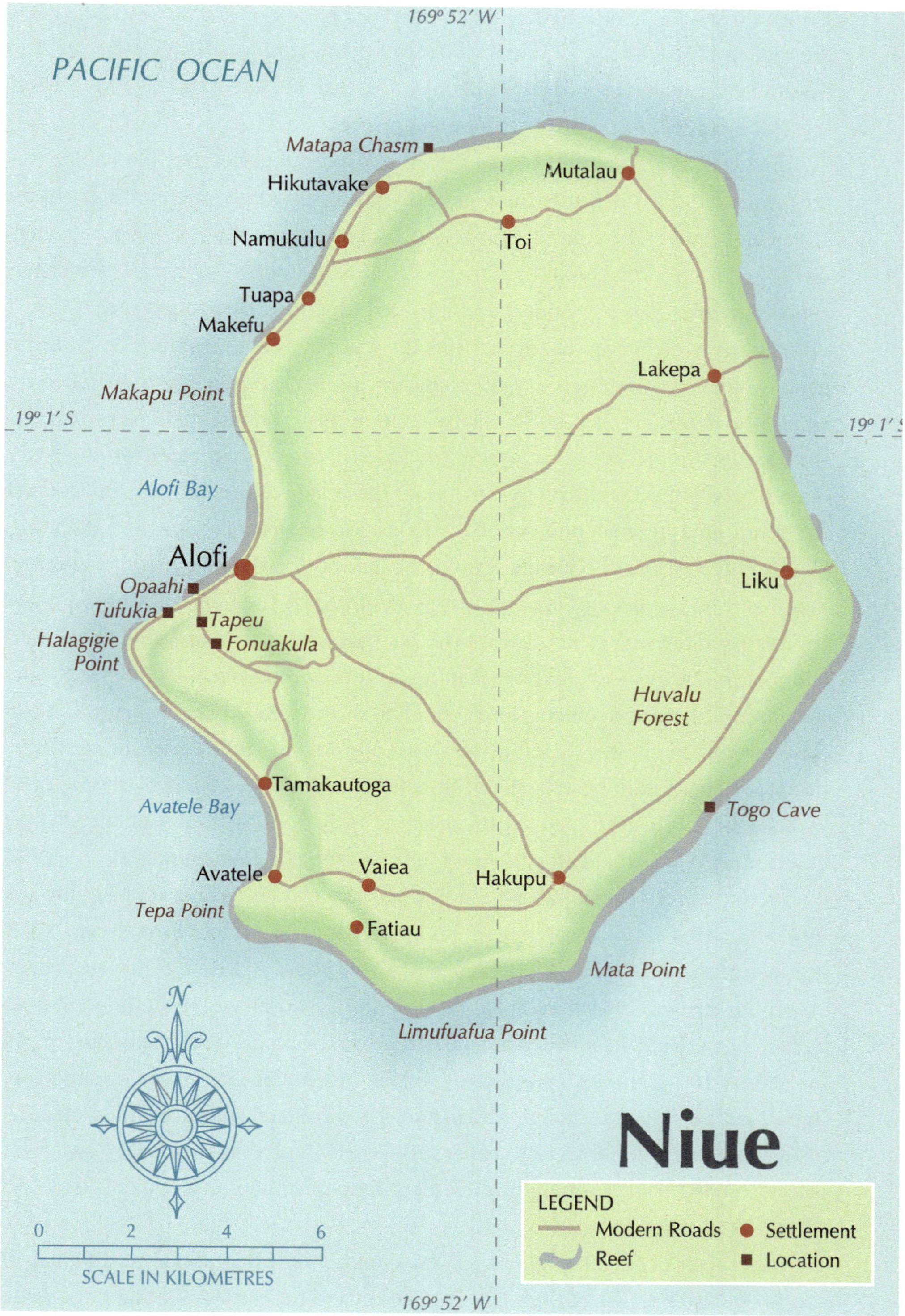
PACIFIC OCEAN
169° 52′ W
19° 1′ S
Matapa Chasm
Hikutavake
Namukulu
Tuapa
Makefu
Makapu Point
Mutalau
Toi
Lakepa
Alofi Bay
Alofi
Opaahi
Tufukia
Tapeu
Fonuakula
Halagigie Point
Liku
Huvalu Forest
Tamakautoga
Avatele Bay
Togo Cave
Avatele
Vaiea
Hakupu
Tepa Point
Fatiau
Mata Point
Limufuafua Point
N
0
2
4
6
SCALE IN KILOMETRES
Niue
LEGEND
Modern Roads
Settlement
Reef
Location

and Paulo and the revered name of Lawes of the London Missionary Society (LMS) are spoken of still today. The story of Niuean men going to war in Europe in 1915 is retold each Anzac Day. The Head family, Captain Bell, the murder of Mr Larsen, Jock McEwen and Robert Rex are all remembered.

This work is an attempt to take the events and the places and the people that are recalled in the oral history of Niue and weave them into a written history of the 200 years between the arrival of Cook in 1774 and the granting of self-government in 1974. It is also an attempt to place events in Niuean history into a wider Pacific context in order to better understand how and why things happened as they did.

In some ways Niuean history reflects the main themes of Pacific history: European exploration and discovery, missionaries and the introduction of Christianity, whalers and traders and settlers with their money and their diseases, imperial rivalry and colonial rule, decolonisation and self-determination. However, events often played out differently here because of the isolation, the difficulty of access to the island, and the small population the island was capable of supporting. Although Cook's encounter with Niueans was on the land, the majority of early encounters took place on the deck of passing vessels as they rode the tides and the wind and tried to avoid the jagged reef. It was easier for the Niueans to launch their small vaka and paddle out to a sailing vessel than it was for a sailing vessel to attempt to land men on the island and remain close enough to shore to pick them up again. The cultural meeting place[2] was therefore on the sea and not the land, and encounters were necessarily brief and individually of little lasting significance. But over time there was change and Niuean men began travelling away from the island on the whaling and trading vessels that had paused off the coast for a brief encounter.

The LMS was responsible for the first settlement of outsiders on Niue but not until the 1850s – late compared to other parts of the Pacific. First a very small number of Samoan mission teachers arrived on Niue, and then a European missionary and his wife were landed. Niue became a laboratory for the London Missionary Society and its position as sole church on the island would be unchallenged for almost 100 years. As such the role of the individual missionary became very important. Fortunately the first who came – two brothers who gave almost 50 years of service – were humble men, generous of spirit and wise of counsel, and their role in steering Niue through the difficult process of contact with the outside world cannot be underestimated.

The process of contact and change was slow, not only because of the difficulty of access but also because of the small population and the division of that population into tiny enclaves in different parts of the island. The advantage of this was that when outsiders did arrive the introduction of disease, which was to be such a feature of settlement in other Pacific locations, was sporadic and often geographically contained in one part of the island. European disease is a feature of the Niue story, but it was to be migration in the twentieth century rather than illness in the nineteenth century that produced the most dramatic decline in the population of the island.

Isolation and harshness of environment produce a fierceness and independence of spirit that make the Niueans survivors. They learned to cope with the resources they had. When cyclone or drought struck they had survival techniques. When strange vaka appeared on the horizon, they learned to embrace these visits and to benefit from them. At several pivotal moments in their history – the introduction of Christianity, the annexation of the island to New Zealand, the decision to move towards self-government – the Niuean people have shown a determination to play at least some part in how these events would unfold.

This is the story of 200 years of contact and change for the people of Nukututaha, Niue, the island that stands alone.

PART A.

Early Contacts

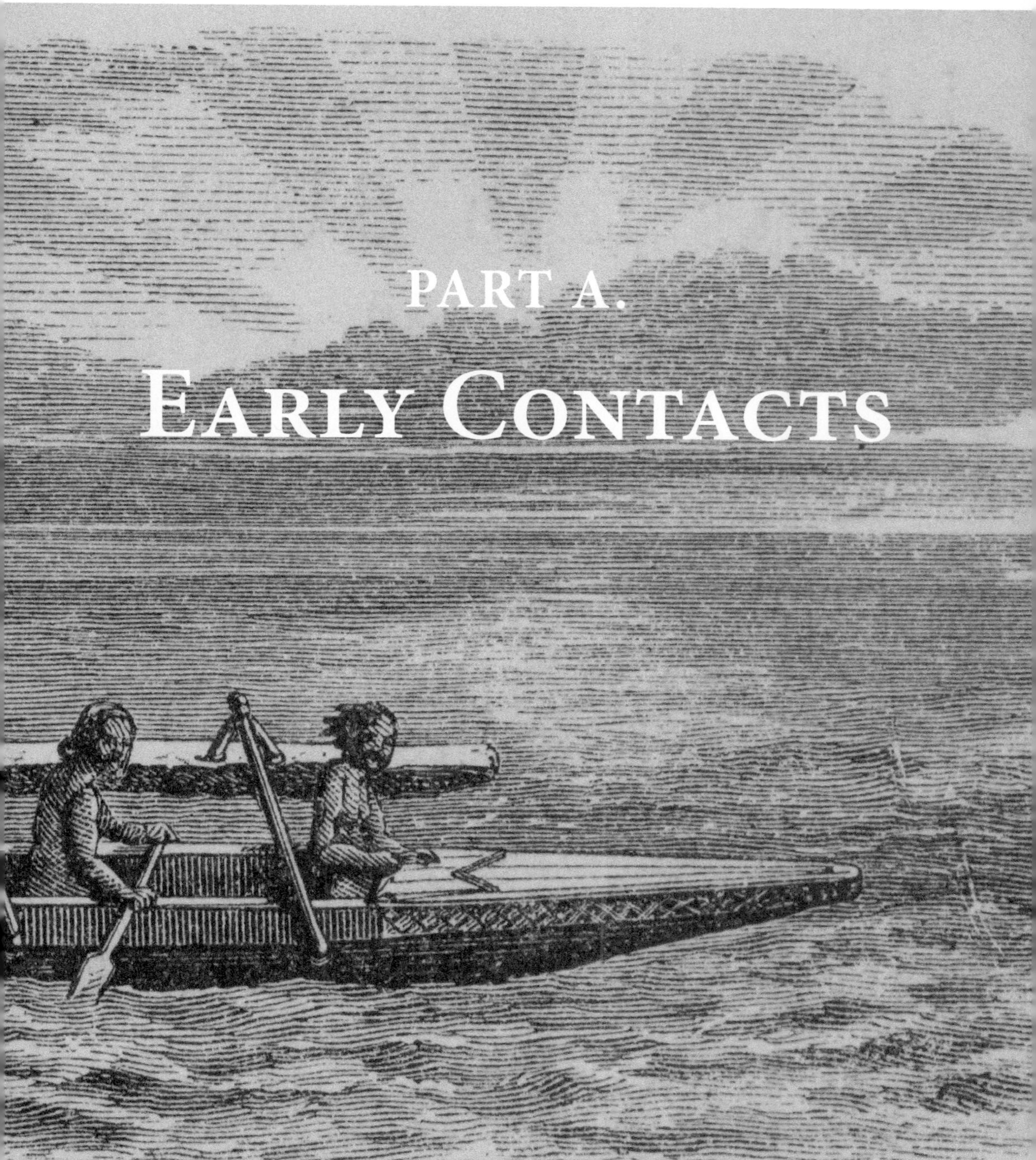

1. First encounters

The conduct and aspect of these Islanders occasioned my naming it Savage Island

When Captain James Cook sailed from Ra'iatea in the Society Islands on 4 June 1774 he and the men on board His Majesty's sloop *Resolution* had been away from home for nearly two years. They were into their second winter in the Pacific, waiting for the next summer which would allow a return to the southern oceans to continue their attempt to prove once and for all the existence or otherwise of a southern continent. The men were in high spirits. They had spent two months in the Society Islands, paradise to them after the frigid and dangerous conditions they had endured in Antarctic waters. They had eaten well and recovered from their latest bout of scurvy. They had traded and had enjoyed much social activity with the locals, in particular the women.

Cook was more reflective in mood. The departure from Ra'iatea marked a watershed for him. He had spent much time in the Society Islands during his first voyage on the *Endeavour* and again on this second voyage. He had formed close bonds with local chiefs, had exchanged names and been included in important ceremonies. During this latest visit he had enjoyed an improvement in his health after very severe and recurring intestinal problems during the voyage north from Antarctic waters. But now he believed he was departing from these islands for the last time. He refused to allow any Islander to take passage with him on the *Resolution* from this point on as he could not guarantee being able to return them to their original home. Hitihiti, who had been travelling with Cook for the previous season, left the ship at Ra'iatea after a very emotional farewell. There were final exchanges of lavish gifts, much weeping and waving, and the *Resolution* edged out through the reef and headed west.

The course now set was determined by Cook's aim to map the Pacific and chart as many islands as possible for the future use of navigators. He was a skilled surveyor and mapmaker and, using earlier reports of Pacific voyages, he decided to look first for the northern islands of the Friendly (Tongan) group, earlier visited by Dutch explorers, and then to head northwest in search of a group of islands visited by the Spanish in the early seventeenth century. These islands Cook was to name the New Hebrides (Vanuatu). The previous winter Cook had visited Tongatapu for the first time, so now he adjusted his westerly course from Ra'iatea a few degrees with the aim of finding the more northerly Tongan islands.

Twelve days out in light breezes and fine weather, land was sighted from the masthead. As the *Resolution* bore down on the island it was seen to be 'a low reef Island or rather a number of small Islots connected together by sand banks and breakers'.[1] The large numbers of seabirds, especially frigate birds, convinced the naturalists on board that this land was uninhabited, and while there was the promise of new plants to be discovered, the absence of an entry point through the reef or a suitable anchorage meant no landing was attempted. Cook 'looked upon it to be a new discovery and named it Palmerston Island, in honour of my Lord Palmerston one of the Lords of the Admiralty'.[2] The westerly course was continued, aided by easterly breezes and fair weather.

The men on watch again thought they saw land early afternoon on Monday 20 June 1774 but it was soon revealed to be cloud and Cook maintained a steady passage towards the west. An hour later another cry went up from the masthead and this time it proved to be correct. By 4 pm 'a tableland of good extent and covered with trees'[3] could be seen from the quarterdeck. By 5 pm Cook estimated the island to be due west at a distance of 5 leagues, and he shortened sail and prepared to tack to windward for the night.

At daybreak the *Resolution* came in close to the northern point of the island and then ran along the western shore at a distance of one mile from it.

> *[The shore] appeared steep and rocky, with here and there a narrow sandy beach at the foot of the rock. It was nearly level everywhere, and its greatest height seemed not to exceed forty feet; but it was covered with woods and shrubberies along the summit. About ten o'clock, we perceived seven or eight people running close to the water's edge. They seemed to be of a blackish colour, and were naked; something white was wrapped about their heads and loins, and each had a spear, a club, or a paddle in his hand. In several chasms between the rocks, we observed a few small canoes hauled upon the shore. We now likewise took notice of some coco-nut trees, of no great height, which stood on the slope of the rocks.*[4]

With these words, Georg Forster, the young naturalist on board, recorded the first European impressions of Niue. At the same time, Niueans were getting their first glimpse of a strange and wondrous vaka, unlike any they had previously encountered. They watched and waited, weapons at hand, to see what move this huge vessel might make next.

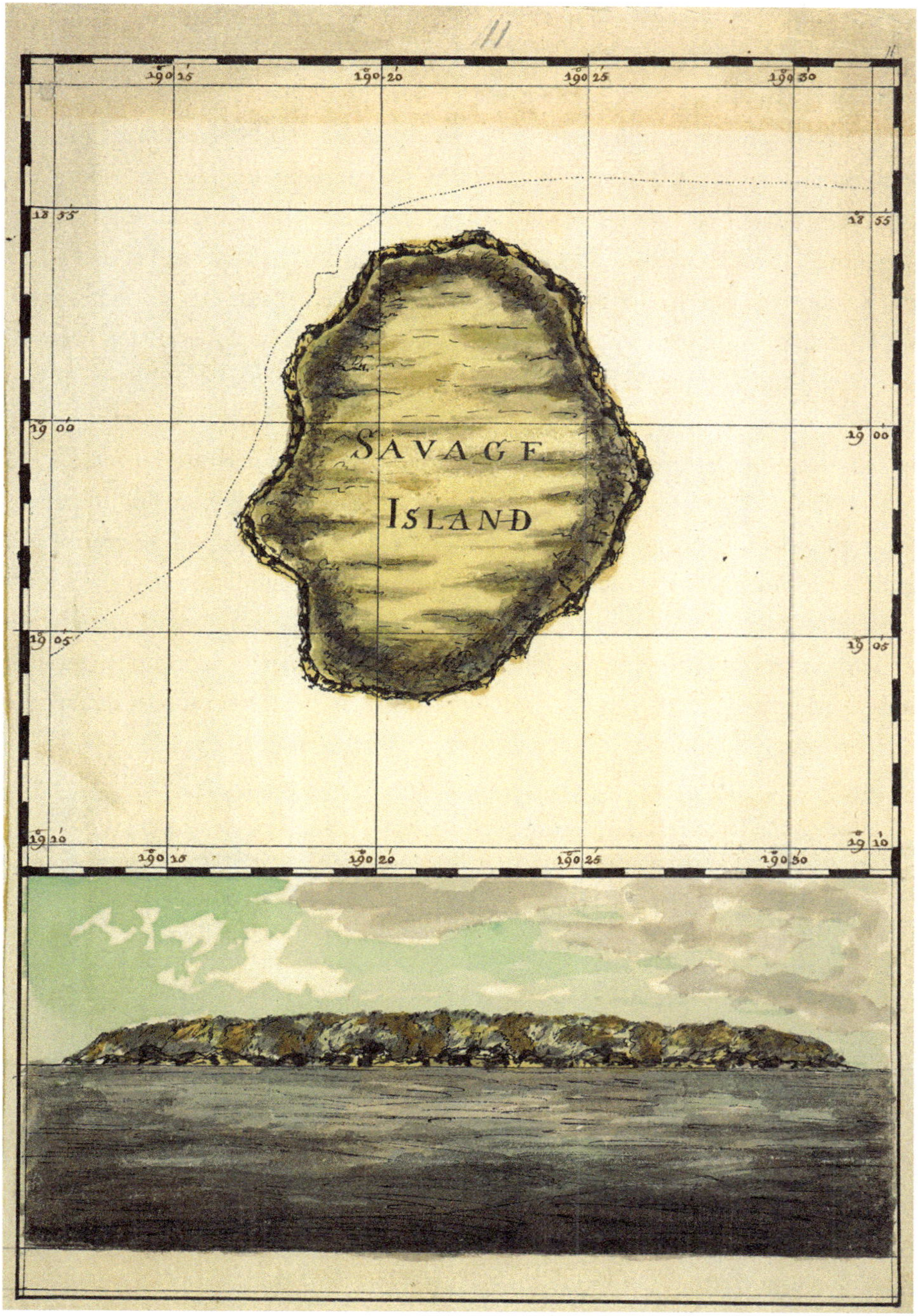

A chart of Savage Island in 19°S latitude, drawn by Captain James Cook in June 1774. Included on the chart is Cook's route from east to west and, below, another view of Savage Island, probably drawn by Hodges. British Library Board, Add MS. 15.500.11

From the side of the *Resolution* two boats were lowered. In one sat Captain James Cook. He was accompanied by the three naturalists – father-and-son team Johann and Georg Forster, and Anders Sparrman; the artist William Hodges; and the Forsters' servant, Ernst Scholient. In the second vessel sat Third Lieutenant Richard Pickersgill and a detachment of marines. Both boats were manned by sailors and both were armed. As they approached the island the people who had been seen on the shore 'retired to the woods'. Georg Forster observed the coral reef surrounding the whole coast but 'having found an opening, where the surf was not dangerous, we landed, and climbed up one of the adjacent rocks, where we posted some of our sailors and marines'.[5] The first encounter between Europeans and Niueans had begun.

The party under arms was posted to 'a high rock to prevent a Surprise'.[6] The others dispersed in two groups: the naturalists began eagerly scouring the rocks for examples of new plants, while Cook took two men and followed the course of a gully which he guessed would give access further into the interior of the island. It is difficult to estimate how long these explorations lasted before events forced both *Resolution* groups back to the lookout party. Anders Sparrman's account suggests it was very leisurely, as he refers to the naturalist group 'strolling and botanising'.[7] He wrote a description of the coastal area that remains accurate today.

> *We ... found this island to consist of a mass of coral raised above the sea level, formed into a wonderful variety of shapes by the wash and breaking of the sea against it, and upon which, by means of decomposition and bird-droppings, a certain amount of vegetation had, with difficulty, gradually taken hold, after which increasingly better roothold had been prepared for successive plants.*[8]

Georg Forster noted that while many of the small, shrubby plants were common to other low islands they had already visited, they also found some new species, 'all of which grew between the crevices of the coral, without the least atom of soil'.[9] The naturalists also commented on the presence of curlews, snipe, white-tailed tropicbirds, frigate birds and a grey heron. There were several smaller birds that could not be identified 'as we could not come near enough to shoot or distinguish them'.[10]

The leisurely botanising was suddenly interrupted by a call to return to the rocky lookout where the marines were keeping guard. Cook's exploration of the gully had been halted by sounds up ahead, including what appeared to be someone falling from a tree. Both groups retreated to the rocks facing the gully. They called out in 'those South Sea dialects' which they knew, explaining they had come as friends, and they heard shouting and calling among the Islanders. Presently 'the natives

Drawing of *Portlandia* by William Hodges. This was one of four new plant specimens collected on Savage Island in 1774 by the botanists on Cook's second voyage. Johann and Georg Forster, the botanists, drew the specimens themselves but Hodges often did additional drawings. Alexander Turnbull Library, Wellington, New Zealand, E-104-007

Tiale feutu, the Niuean name for *Portlandia*, growing on the coastal cliffs of the lower terrace of Niue today. Courtesy of Moira Enetama, Tāoga Niue

appeared at the entrance of the Chasm … and we began to make all the friendly signs we could think of to them, which they answered by menaces'.[11] In many previous situations like this, Cook and his men had been assisted by the presence in their group of a Polynesian who had been able to communicate to some extent and also read the cultural nuances of gestures and actions and in this way interpret for the Europeans. On this occasion the Europeans had no such assistance.

The Niuean group does not appear to have been very numerous but from among them one man stepped forward. He was 'dressed on his head with upstanding feathers and blacked over on his body as far as the waist, with a lance or Spear in his hand'.[12] He was soon joined by a younger man, 'to all appearance without a beard … [and] like him blackened … and [he] had a long bow, like those of *Tonga-Tabboo*,

Maka or throwing stones. These were made from stalactite material found in the many caves along the coast and in the inland forests. They were shaped and polished and were thrown by hand, usually as a first defence against an enemy. During the first encounter with Cook and his party, maka were thrown, resulting in some return musket fire. This collection includes the earliest Niuean item in the Te Papa Tongarewa collection, a highly polished calcite maka (top left) collected in 1859 by Reverend Inglis. The others were collected in the early twentieth century by Sir Joseph Kinsey, a member of the Polynesian Society. Museum of New Zealand Te Papa Tongarewa

in his right hand. With the left he instantly flung a very large stone, with so much accuracy, as to hit Dr Sparrman's arm with a violent blow, at a distance of forty yards.'[13] Sparrman confirms in his journal that this did indeed happen, but he makes no comment on the severity of the blow.

The upshot of the incident was that a musket was fired in the direction of the Niueans. Georg Forster suggested that the pain of being hit by the stone 'irritated' Sparrman so much 'that he let fly at his enemy'. Sparrman explains that the stone continued on and nearly hit Lieutenant Pickersgill, who was standing close behind him and was carrying no musket; he therefore ordered Sparrman to fire. It seems unlikely that Pickersgill would be unarmed, and this explanation by Sparrman is more likely to be an attempt to disguise his own instinctive reaction to the stone throwing, as he soon discovered that Cook was displeased at the musket incident. 'He believed that, with more patience, some reconciliation could have been reached.'[14] However, the damage was done. The shot from Sparrman prompted Johann Forster also to fire and the Niueans fled to the cover of the trees and were seen no more. The small-shot from the musket was thought not to have harmed the Niueans, but merely to have whistled past their ears, although Sparrman conceded that 'a few may have pierced the skin'.

During the ensuing wait to see if anybody would re-emerge from the bushes the *Resolution* party performed what Georg Forster described as 'the idle ceremony of taking possession'.[15] Cook makes no mention of this event, although it was standard practice when he landed, for what he believed to be the first time by a European, to take possession on behalf of the monarch. William Wales, astronomer on the *Resolution*, did not go ashore on Niue but spoke with William Hodges afterwards; he made comments in his journal to the effect that on first landing Cook took possession of the island, 'erecting the English Colours as is usual on these Occasions'.[16] He suggested the stone-throwing incident occurred during the actual flag-raising act, and he wondered if the Islanders had been offended by it. One other source refers to a ceremony but places it before the stone-throwing incident. A publication attributed to John Marra, gunner's mate on board the *Resolution*, recorded that Cook 'landed and took possession of the island for his Britannic Majesty King George the Third; hoisting at the same time an union jack, and giving it the name of Prince Frederic's Island, in honour of the Prince of Wales'.[17] Those ashore at the time make no mention of this name and perhaps Cook omitted it from his journal, as subsequent events on Niue gave him cause to search for a new name. If this was the case, it was certainly not the only time Cook made a decision to alter a name following closer inspection or reflection.

There was still no sign of the Islanders who had earlier appeared. Cook made the decision to embark and continue along the coast in the hope of finding a more favourable landing site and a more friendly welcome. This trip south along the western side of the island was made in the two small boats, under sail rather than oar power, while the *Resolution* stood off, tacking in the wind and following the progress of the shore party. Johann Forster commented that once they had embarked and were at a good distance from their first landing place, men appeared back on that beach. As they moved along the coast they spotted the occasional canoe pulled up on the rocks but they saw no people. Cook observed the cliffs along the shoreline and the caverns in the coral rocks, beaten into curious shapes by the action of the sea.

Cook and his companions eventually 'doubled a point and [we] saw a kind of bay open and went on along shore, which was everywhere an *Iron bound coast* and high surf ran along of it'.[18] The Europeans had rounded Makapu Point and were heading into Alofi Bay. The sails were taken in and the sailors began rowing as the men searched for a suitable landing place. Thinking they had found such a location, they edged the boats near the reef and, 'at the hazard of our necks',[19] three or four men landed, wading through the water then climbing the steep coral rocks. Johann Forster noted the discovery of another interesting plant, but the botanising was interrupted by shouts from those in the boats – apparently they had seen or heard Islanders higher up on the rocks – and the men made a hasty retreat. Cook makes no mention of any sighting of Islanders but suggests rather that the withdrawal was due to the impenetrable nature of the terrain.

At this point Cook decided to return directly aboard the *Resolution* but he changed his mind when 'a small beach on which lay four canoes' was sighted and some among them were of the opinion that they heard voices in the vicinity. Cook decided to attempt another encounter. Although the location of these two landings is not absolutely certain, the timing of Cook's decision to embark and the subsequent sighting of the beach area place them close together and they can only have been in Alofi Bay, a short distance from each other. Cook provides the best description of the third and final landing site.

> *The situation of this place was to us worse than the former; a flat rock lay next to the sea, behind it a narrow stone beach, this was bounded by a perpendicular rocky cleft of unequal height whose top was covered with shrubbery, two deep and narrow chasms in the cleft seemed to open a communication into the country.*[20]

He was describing what most agree is Opaahi, not far south of the present-day wharf at Alofi.

The four canoes that had been spotted lay at the entrance to one of these chasms. Cook realised that by approaching the canoes, the men would expose themselves to attack from above, so he positioned armed men on the flat rock from which they had a view of the heights. Cook went forward to get a closer look at the canoes with the four 'gentlemen' – the Forsters, Sparrman and Hodges. Hodges began sketching the canoes while the others examined their construction and contents. Georg Forster noted that they were 'very nearly of the same structure with those of *Tonga-Tabboo*, and had some carving, but were not so neatly wrought. They were single and had strong out-riggers. Some were covered with coarse mats, and contained fishing lines, spears and pieces of wood, which appeared to have served as matches for fishing at night.'[21]

Cook now performed a ritual he had carried out many times before in first encounter situations: he placed items in each canoe 'to induce the Natives to believe we intended them no harm'. These items consisted of nails, found to be universally acceptable in the South Seas; blue glass beads, prized for their curiosity value; and shiny medals, produced in England specifically for this second voyage of discovery. These medals were known as the '*Resolution* and *Adventure* medal'; 2000 were made to be left 'upon new discovered countries as testimonies of being first discoveries'.[22]

This whole process lasted 'but a few minutes', according to Cook, when Georg Forster saw a 'troop of natives' coming down the chasm. He called to the other men, and they quickly retired towards the rocks and faced the approaching Islanders. Attempts to speak with them failed, and Cook famously observed that 'one of them with the ferocity of a wild Boar advanced ahead of the others and threw a dart at

Opaahi, the site of Cook's third landing on Savage Island: Cook described the landing site with its flat rock on which he positioned armed men. This photo was taken by Percy Smith in 1901, during his three-month stay on Niue as New Zealand's first resident agent. Smith went down to visit the site, accompanied by his assistant, Lagiholo, and the Council member for Alofi South, Tatagata, and his family. They stood on the same flat rock while Smith photographed them.

Alexander Turnbull Library, Wellington, New Zealand, PAColl-7081-51

us, two or three musquets discharged in the air did not hinder him from advancing still further and throwing another'.[23] The first dart (spear) narrowly missed Cook – some say he avoided it by ducking – and the second grazed the side of Georg Forster, marking his clothes with a 'black colour with which it was daubed'. Muskets were fired. More Islanders appeared down a different path until one observer estimated there were approximately 30 of them. Weapons were 'brandished in defiance' and the visitors were 'challenged … with war-songs and dances'.[24] Cook noted that had his musket not misfired, the man who threw the spear could have paid for his courage with his life 'for I was not five paces from him when he threw his spear and had resolved to shoot him to save myself, but I was glad afterwards that it happened

Katoua or clubs were used after the initial throwing of the maka. Made of wood with a sharp ridge along each side of the blade, katoua were sometimes wrapped with sennit made from coconut-husk fibre and decorated with feathers, cowrie shells and braided human hair. They were held at the tapered end and the wide blade was used to strike the enemy. In this collection the top example has sennit binding and the centre example has sennit binding and cowrie shell decoration.

Museum of New Zealand Te Papa Tongarewa

otherwise'.[25] Eventually the firing sent the Islanders 'into the woods from whence they did not return, we had reason to believe none were hurt. Seeing no good was to be got of these people or at the isle we returned on board hoisted in the boats and made sail to WSW. The conduct and aspect of these Islanders occasioned my naming it Savage Island.'[26]

The first encounter between Europeans and Niueans had ended badly, and in the succeeding years both sides adapted, embellished, told and retold the story so an encounter myth evolved that suited the purposes of both groups. Cook's description of a single man advancing 'with the ferocity of a wild Boar' became plural and we suddenly have a different scene of these gentlemen facing an onslaught. Journals from the *Resolution* are vague about the amount of musket firing that occurred. Some report that many of the muskets were aimed but did not go off, a common problem with these weapons. Some recorded that there were no injuries, while others report hearing loud howls from the bushes, suggesting someone at least was wounded. One witness reported that the firing 'was incessantly kept up for some time, during which some of them were observed to drop, and the rest fled into the woods, and were no more seen, making, however, a dreadful howling and yelling'.[27] Another witness, recording his thoughts nearly 40 years later, suggested that 'Cook's life had been in most imminent danger'.[28]

A view of Savage Island drawn by William Hodges, official artist on HMS *Resolution* during James Cook's second voyage to the Pacific. Hodges often sketched and then painted later during the voyage. He has included HMS *Resolution* in the painting off the west coast of Niue in June 1774.

British Library Board, Add MS. 15.743.5

Those involved from the *Resolution* agreed that the decision to withdraw was actively taken by Cook. Georg Forster noted that 'we now embarked, and resolved to abandon a set of people, whom no entreaties could prevail upon to become our friends. The nature of their country … seems to have contributed to make their tempers so unsociable.'[29] As John Marra described it: 'The Captain finding nothing to be got here without a great deal of bloodshed, and without hazarding the lives of his people to no good purpose, thought proper to embark, and to continue his course in search of a more hospitable people.'[30]

Stories that have been passed down from generation to generation on Niue give a different perspective on events. The Niueans were simply offering the traditional challenge to visitors and their intentions were misconstrued. A story developed that the challengers had adorned their lips with a scarlet dye, the juice of the hulahula banana, and Cook had jumped to the conclusion that they were cannibals, dripping with the blood of their victims. Another scene is now painted in which the visitors are being forced to retreat back through the surf to the boats, hotly pursued by ferocious Islanders. Such a fanciful story has been thoroughly discredited by the Niueans themselves,[31] but it is easy to see how such storytelling would have appealed to Island audiences just as written accounts of Cook's brave deeds appealed to an eager readership in Europe.

The main reason for Cook's decision to 'quit this inhospitable shore'[32] lay in the purpose of the voyage. There was one overriding aim: to search the southern seas and determine once and for all the existence or not of a southern continent. Because this was only possible during the short summer period between December and February, Cook had suggested a second aim: to map and chart as much of the South Seas as possible for the future use of navigators. This would be done during the southern winter and Cook would return to New Zealand waters in plenty of time to make repairs to the ship, rest the crew and take on supplies for the journey south. During the winter of 1774 Cook aimed to make a large circuit of the Pacific; and in fact he journeyed from Easter Island in the east to the western Melanesian groups, which he named New Hebrides and New Caledonia. The discovery of Niue en route to the northern Friendly Islands was useful in allowing him to map another island, but he was in a hurry to move on.

His ship was well stocked with food, for his time in the Society Islands had coincided with the season of plenty; and besides, he knew he was not many days' sailing from the Friendly Islands, where supplies had been easily obtained the previous year. His observations on the nature of this new island convinced him that there was no suitable harbouring and he was able to estimate that the island supported but a small population and food supplies would not be plentiful, especially now that the winter solstice marking the season of scarcity had arrived.[33] He had an obligation to allow the naturalists on board to make as many visits ashore as possible for the purpose of collecting and observing, but this was at Cook's discretion, and Johann Forster's constant complaining and whingeing in this regard made the captain less inclined to accommodate the wishes of the naturalist.

Cook was anxious to return on board and continue his westerly course. There is an element of frustration and bad temper in his journal comments about the landings on Niue, especially regarding his decision to name the place Savage Island rather than his first choice, Prince Frederic's Island. Perhaps he was regretting his decision not to carry a Polynesian interpreter on board. Perhaps he was contrasting this first encounter with Islanders since departing the Society Islands with the reception he had become accustomed to receiving there. Perhaps his gut was once more troubling him. Perhaps he was merely anxious to keep to his timetable and cover as much ocean as possible before returning south.

For the Niueans, the event must have been alarming in the extreme, but at least it was short-lived. Two groups experienced an encounter with strangely clad men from this great vaka: they heard strange words, saw sticks that could kill or at least injure, and when these men had returned to their ship and sailed away, they wondered if this was the last they would see of them. Because each small community on the island was separate from and antagonistic towards the other communities, people in some parts of the island may have been unaware that these encounters had even occurred. It was, however, obviously a topic for much discussion in the localities where the Europeans had landed; and at a later time in Niue the stories would become part of the collective storytelling of the people.

It would be at least 50 years before another encounter with Europeans took place on Niue, but Cook's visit had two long-term implications for the history of the island. First, and most importantly, Niue was from this time on accurately located on the map. For the first time on any voyage of discovery, the men on board the *Resolution* had the means to accurately record not only latitude – distance north or south from the equator, but also longitude – distance east or west around the globe. During Cook's first voyage to the Pacific a timepiece had been designed in England to work specifically at sea and enable accurate calculations of distance based on difference in time between location at sea and at Greenwich, downstream from London. Cook was entrusted with this chronometer and was able to show its accuracy in the course of his second and third voyages. Niue was now drawn on the map at Latitude 19° 1'S, Longitude 169° 37'W, and from this time on it was known – by Cook's name of Savage Island – to other sea captains.

The second impact of Cook's visit to Niue was that there was now a surprisingly accurate account of the island's formation and topography. Georg Forster wrote:

> *The whole island is a coral rock, like that of the low islands, on which we saw very few coco-palms, and no useful trees. I have therefore formed a conjecture, that the interior parts are not so barren, but fit for the culture of nutritive vegetables. The general resemblance of this island to a coral ledge raised out of the water, almost leads me to suspect that it includes a fertile plain, which was once a lagoon. Whether a convulsion of the globe, or any other cause, lifted such a large piece of coral rock forty feet above water, is a point that must be left to future philosophers to determine.*[34]

Cook continued this line of reasoning when he asked: 'If these Coral rocks were first formed in the sea by animals, how came they thrown up, to such a height? Has this island been raised by an Earthquake or has the sea receded from it?'[35]

The encounters allowed time for only a fleeting glance at the inhabitants, but Cook was able to use his extensive knowledge of the Pacific to make some assumptions and comparisons. The Savage Islanders were compared to the Friendly Islanders because of the similarities seen in their canoes, which led Cook to decide they were 'full as ingenious'. Using the French explorer Bougainville's description of the inhabitants of the Navigator Islands (Samoa), Cook and his companions believed the Savage Islanders to be racially similar. John Marra described them as 'a fierce looking race … nimble and active, stout and resolute'.[36] And although the *Resolution* did not circumnavigate Niue, Cook was able to estimate its size, and a map prepared on board was published in London in 1777 and was extremely accurate.

On reflection, the visit by HMS *Resolution* to Niue was benign, Cook's footprint light. The Islanders had experienced more aggressive invasions from Polynesian voyagers in the past, and in the future there would be more unfortunate visits by European vessels. James Cook followed the enlightened principles of exploration given him by the president of the Royal Society, the Earl of Morton, when he first set out in the *Endeavour*. Remember, wrote Morton in his 'Hints' for Cook and his companions,

> *the Natives of the several Lands where the ship may touch … are the natural, and in the strictest sense of the word, the legal possessors of the several Regions they inhabit. No European Nation has a right to occupy any part of their country, or settle among them without their voluntary consent. Conquest over such people can give no just title; because they could never be the aggressors.*[37]

A month after leaving Niue, Cook was in the New Hebrides, where he experienced a more frightening and ferocious repulsion trying to land on Erromango. After a more successful encounter on Tanna, Cook reflected in his journal on the reason for the antagonism from Islanders:

> *… when one considers the light in which they must look upon us in, its [sic] impossible for them to know our real design, we enter their Ports without their daring to make opposition, we attempt to land in a peaceable manner, if this succeeds its [sic] well, if not we land nevertheless and maintain the footing we thus got by the Superiority of our fire arms, in what other light can they than at first look upon us but as invaders of their Country.*[38]

He could well have come to the same conclusion on his departure from Niue waters.

When he returned to the Pacific on a third voyage in 1777, Cook passed Niue but did not attempt another landing. He had collected the data he wanted and it was published and widely circulated in Europe. Until well into the nineteenth century this material would provide the basis for future decisions by Europeans as to whether they should avoid or engage with Niue Islanders.

2. Whalers

At daylight, Savage Island in sight

The first of the American whaling ships rounded Cape Horn into the Pacific in the early 1790s. They headed to the whaling grounds off the coast of Chile and Peru and gradually worked their way up the coast of North America. Demand for whale oil was increasing, money was being invested in the industry, and shipbuilders were producing larger vessels that could tackle the open Pacific and stay away from their home port for up to five years, until the approximately 3000 barrels in the hold were filled with the precious oil. During this time a whaler would cover the whole Pacific, moving with the seasons, the known migratory habits of the whales, and the need to repair the ship and take on replacement crew and supplies. By 1830 the American whalers out of New England dominated the Pacific whaling industry, with up to 700 vessels at work in any one year.

A typical whaler was a three-masted vessel purpose built for the job. It had to have a large bulbous hold for storage of the oil barrels and a long uncluttered deck where huge pieces of whale blubber could be cut and boiled to render the oil. There had to be space for the brick furnace over which two or three trypots – huge 200-gallon cauldrons – would hang. Four whaleboats used for the chase would swing from the sides of the vessel, ready to be lowered as soon as whales were sighted. The ships were well maintained, but they were foul-smelling, cramped and often dangerous places to live and work. The ship's master, assisted by his first and second mate, maintained strict discipline with the use of flogging and clamping in irons. There was a steward and cook, a carpenter and cooper. The rest of the 30-man crew were the labour force of the ship, providing the brute physical strength needed for whaling.

As the whale fleet in the Pacific grew, the task of filling the complement of crew on each vessel became more difficult. Various ports were known as places where new crew could be signed on, but they were also places where crew deserted. Honolulu and Lahaina in Hawai'i and Kororareka (Russell) in the Bay of Islands in New Zealand were major recruiting ports, but smaller ports in the South Seas such as

'Head out'. When undisturbed, whales will surface to breathe on a regular basis. Used air is forced out through the spout and the whale inhales approximately 50 times. The fluke or tail will then lift out of the water and the whale will dive vertically into the depths again. When a whale is disturbed, such as by a whaleboat, the pattern of breathing changes: some air will be taken in, the whale will sink horizontally a short depth below the surface, move a short distance and rise again. Moving in this way was known in nineteenth-century whaling jargon as 'going head out', and it enabled the whalers to position their boats and launch their harpoons when the head emerged. This illustration appeared in *Life and Adventure in the Pacific* by 'A roving printer', published in 1861.

Alexander Turnbull Library, Wellington, New Zealand, B-K-1094-168

Rotuma, Vava'u, Rarotonga and Apia also provided labour. Pacific Islanders were often taken on as crew for a period of one to two years before being returned to their home island. They were valued for their physical strength and their ability to work the whaleboats even in the roughest of conditions.

Once the master had a full complement of crew and his vessel was stocked with food and water and firewood for the furnace, he would stay at sea as long as possible to maximise the chances of taking whales and to avoid the possibility of losing crew ashore. In the South Seas the marine charts, dating from the explorations of the eighteenth century and particularly from the voyages of James Cook, showed the multitude of islands known as Polynesia. The whaling masters tried to avoid calling at these islands because of the risk of desertion, but they often wanted fresh fruit and water or just a break from the monotony of shipboard life, so they lay to offshore and allowed an exchange to take place on the deck. Islanders would come on board with fruit and vegetables, pigs and fowls, and exchanges would take place. Crew members might exchange small items for local handcrafts, and Islanders would entertain them for a short time before the whaling vessel moved on.

Cook's chart showed Savage Island lying alone to the east of the Friendly Islands. The name, and Cook's description of his encounter there in 1774, were enough to instil fear in many a whaler's heart, and the Islanders' reputation persisted well into the nineteenth century. In 1828, when a report was prepared for the American Congress to give as much information as possible relating to the geography of the Pacific, Captain Richard Macy, a Nantucket whaling master, was reported as saying that at Savage Island 'the natives are warlike; great caution is necessary in landing'.[1] Whether he was speaking from personal experience or retelling other stories it is impossible to tell. A whaling logbook notes in relation to Savage Island, 'they have been represented as being a savage race and it is not deemed safe and prudent to land'.[2]

In spite of this reputation, it is certain that by 1828 some whalers were pausing offshore and engaging in trade with Savage Islanders. In January 1828 the whaling ship *Independence* lay on and off the island for three days, adjusting the sails to suit the winds and currents, and the logbook records that canoes came out and trading occurred. In September 1828 a landing took place from a British whaler and the event was later recounted. Captain Hindson, master of the whaling brig *Lord Rodney*, arrived in Sydney harbour in late October 1828 with a tale of adventure to tell and a dire warning to offer other sailing captains.

The *Lord Rodney* was reported as departing the Bay of Islands in May 1828, heading for Tahiti. On the return voyage from Tahiti towards Tonga and then Sydney, Captain Hindson reported calling at Savage Island. He told a reporter for the *Sydney Gazette*:[3] 'The island is sixty miles in circumference, and thinly populated by a fierce and savage race of people, who go perfectly naked, are generally painted black and armed with bows and arrows, and spears. The Island lies low, with a perfectly iron bound coast, and there is no harbour; so that the difficulty of landing at any part is more than ordinarily great.'

Captain Hindson made the decision to go ashore in order to barter for fresh supplies of breadfruit, coconuts and bananas, which he believed were in plentiful supply. He took six of his men and came ashore by whaleboat. They were met by 'such demonstrations of hostility that it was found necessary to fire over them, when they made an effort as if to catch the balls as they bounded along the beach;

even when they comprehended the purpose of [my visit], it was found necessary to carry on the barter, pistol in hand'. The barter appears to have been successful; Captain Hindson recorded that the Islanders were mainly interested in acquiring glass beads. As each exchange occurred, Hindson said the Islanders let out a howl but there were no signs of smiling despite every effort to make them do so.

The *Lord Rodney* continued on to Tonga, where a story was related that filled the men with fear. Captain Hindson reported that some time previously an American whaler had called at Savage Island and a boat had been sent ashore with four men for the purpose of trading. 'They were met on landing by a large concourse of these savages, who, horrible to relate, dragged two of the unfortunate sailors out of the boat, tore them limb from limb on the spot, and devoured them in an instant.' The other two men managed to escape. The whaler subsequently put in at Tonga and the men recounted this tale of murder and cannibalism. It was noted in the newspaper report that the Islanders possessed no iron instruments whatsoever, and that it was extremely probable that the visit by the American whaler was the first by a European vessel since Captain Cook. Captain Hindson concluded his account to the *Sydney Gazette* with a warning to other sailing captains: 'Captains of vessels … who may have occasion to visit this barbarous people, should on no account trust themselves or their crews onshore unless well-armed, and in sufficient numbers to repel an attack from so ferocious a race of beings.'

The first missionary account of a visit to Savage Island in 1830 also refers to an earlier visit by a whaling vessel during which the Islanders seized a boat belonging to the vessel and 'murdered all the crew'.[4] No mention is made of cannibalism. When Captain John Erskine visited Savage Island on board HMS *Havannah* in 1849, he made reference to this report of murder but stated 'no record of such an event could be found in Sydney'.[5] While it seems that an incident between whalers and Islanders did occur during the 1820s, there is no evidence to support Hindson's allegation of cannibalism. In the telling and retelling, the story had acquired various embellishments that seemed to fit with images of a 'savage island'. A passing whaler noted in 1869: 'the island is Savage Island inhabited by cannibals [and] they came very near having us for their breakfast'.[6]

Besides its reputation for being unfriendly or downright dangerous, there were other, more practical reasons why Savage Island was not frequented by whaling vessels. The most obvious reason for simply passing by and noting the island in the logbook while making no effort to call there was the lack of natural harbouring for ships. As Captain Hindson had noted – and Cook before him – the island had an 'iron-bound' coast, rugged and rocky cliffs, with no entrances in to safe harbouring. In addition, the sea off the coast was too deep for any possible mooring. The best a ship could do was to make use of its sails, the tides, the currents and the winds to lay on and off the island, coming in closer to shore and drifting back out again. This was a dangerous activity for a ship that depended solely on wind power for movement; many a vessel was lost in the Pacific when it drifted too far inshore and a change of wind sent it onto a reef. As a consequence of this coastal geography, and with a circle of other islands within a few days' sailing that offered safe mooring, whalers noted simply: 'Savage Island to East … crew employed in ships duties' or 'saw Savage Island bearing East … all crew employed at boiling' or 'Employed in ships duties at 3 pm we saw the land called Savage Island inhabited by savages. We passed within 5 miles of it.'[7]

However, the presence of so many whalers in the South Seas led inevitably to some contact with Savage Island; and in the period from 1828 until the late 1860s, when whaling was on the decline, there were infrequent but slowly increasing numbers of visits. These were usually conducted between the whaling vessel and canoes on the open sea; to a much lesser extent, whaleboats went ashore to trade on the island. There are also reports that the occasional passing whaler sometimes grudgingly took a Savage Islander or two on board and deposited them in Samoa, possibly into the care of the London Missionary Society. This was often easier than trying to return a man to the island if wind and current were against them.

The stories of Cook's visit to the island would still have been fresh in the collective memory of the Niue people when the first of the whalers appeared on the horizon; there may well have been elders still alive who had witnessed, as children hidden in the rocks, the first European arrival. Now they watched as another vessel, huge in comparison to their vaka, approached the island, lowered its sails and lay offshore, riding in and out as the winds and currents dictated. The first encounter with such a vessel might have ended badly, but the fear did not remain for long. The appearance of sails on the horizon soon became a signal to prepare the vaka. Coconuts, bananas, yams and taro were loaded, along with any fowls there were to spare. When the whaler was nearer the coast the vaka were launched and the welcoming party headed out. One vessel noted the vaka came out a distance of 14 miles, but most encounters between whaler and vaka took place much closer to the coast. One early encounter was related by an American at the completion of a whaling voyage and return to New England in the late 1830s:

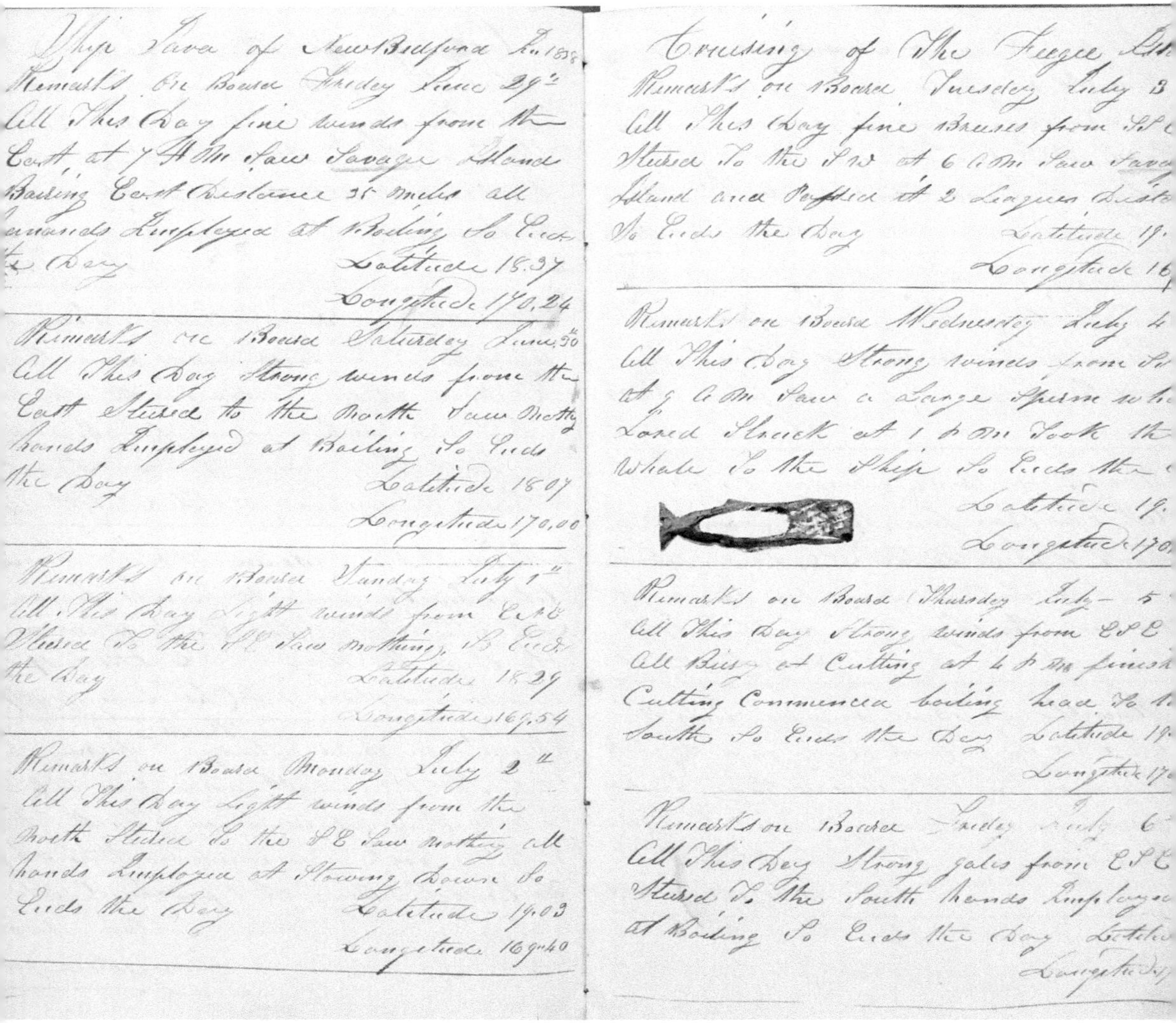

Ship Java of New Bedford ... 1838
Remarks On Board Friday June 29th
All This Day fine winds from the
East, at 7 AM Saw Savage Island
Bearing East Distance 35 miles all
hands Employed at Boiling So Ends
the Day Latitude 18.37
Longitude 170.24

Remarks on Board Saturday June 30
All This Day Strong winds from the
East Steered to the North Saw Nothing
hands Employed at Boiling So Ends
the Day Latitude 18.07
Longitude 170,00

Remarks on Board Sunday July 1st
All This Day Light winds from E&E
Steered to the N Saw nothing So Ends
the Day Latitude 18.29
Longitude 169,54

Remarks on Board Monday July 2d
All This Day Light winds from the
North Steered to the SE Saw nothing all
hands Employed at Stowing Down So
Ends the Day Latitude 19.03
Longitude 169.40

Cruising of The Feegee ...
Remarks on Board Tuesday July 3
All This Day fine Breezes from SE
Steered to the SW at 6 AM Saw Savage
Island and Passed it 2 Leagues Distant
So Ends the Day Latitude 19.
Longitude 16

Remarks on Board Wednesday July 4
All This Day Strong winds from SE
at 9 AM Saw a Large Sperm whale
Lowered Struck at 1 PM Took the
Whale to the Ship So Ends the
Latitude 19.
Longitude 170

Remarks on Board Thursday July 5
All This Day Strong winds from ESE
All Busy at Cutting at 4 PM finish
Cutting Commenced boiling head to the
South So Ends the Day Latitude 19.
Longitude 17

Remarks on Board Friday July 6
All This Day Strong gales from ESE
Steered to the South hands Employed
at Boiling So Ends the Day Latitude
Longitude

A typical logbook showing location, weather conditions and, most importantly, the capture of a whale. The whaling vessel *Java* is in the vicinity of Savage Island throughout the week from 29 June to 5 July 1838. On Friday 29 June Savage Island is noted to the east as the crew work on boiling down, so a whale has recently been taken. Savage Island is again noted on Tuesday 3 July and the following day a large sperm whale is sighted and caught. A stamp in the logbook for 4 July shows the capture. By Friday 6 July the *Java* is sailing south, still boiling down from the latest catch, but the latitude and longitude readings show it has now left the vicinity of Savage Island. As well as the whale stamp, another typical feature of this logbook is that every entry begins with the words 'Remarks on board' and finishes with 'So ends the day'.

Courtesy of New Bedford Whaling Museum, Massachusetts, ODHS 296

> *It was not long after ['land ho'] was announced from aloft, before a low, dark, uneven outline was seen stretching along for a space just above the horizon: it appeared indistinctly at first, but on nearer approach began to assume the hues, ridges and stability of land … When our ship approached within a mile or so of the shore … we saw a dozen or more canoes leaving the shore and rapidly approaching the ship. When quite near, one of the natives held up to view a bunch of bananas, which we conjectured to be a signal for trade; in answer, a few strings of beads and some fish hooks were displayed from the ship … [and] they quickly paddled alongside … Our visitors seemed rather distrustful at first, but some beads thrown into the canoes removed their fears, and a general traffic soon commenced … the trading [was] in pantomime, for neither party understood a word of the other's language … among other things that attracted the attention of our visitors, were the carved and gilded imagery of the ship's stern … [especially] two neatly carved and nicely proportioned human figures … As night drew on, the islanders got into their canoes and paddled away for their island home. We spread our sails again to the breeze and were once more moving over the waters …*[8]

The occasional newspaper report gave a full and possibly embellished tale of encounters in the South Seas, but the whaling ship logbooks were much more concise and matter of fact. The main purpose of the logbook was to record wind direction, weather conditions, latitude and longitude readings and the number of whales captured. A crew member was assigned the task of keeping the log – usually the first or second mate, or the master of the whaler; occasionally it was the master's wife, for sometimes not only his wife but also his children were on board for the long voyage. It depended on the whim of the recorder as to what else was noted beyond the basic details. Some logbooks are exceedingly brief, avoiding any personal comment. A murder on board might not be recorded;[9] the death of the master's child may be mentioned only in passing, between the wind direction and rainfall. Other logbooks are much more expansive and might include descriptions of encounters at various South Sea islands and sometimes sketches of places and ships. Many used a whale-shaped stamp in the log to mark a capture, and at the back there was usually a running tally of the number of barrels filled with oil. Crew lists sometimes appeared.[10]

Entries relating to Niue, always referred to as Savage Island, are infrequent but over a period of 40 years from 1830 it is possible to build up a picture of encounters. There are sightings and/or encounters every month of the year, but most visits are in December to February and also in July. About the same number report merely sighting the island as mention interacting offshore with the Islanders. Sending boats ashore was rare until the 1860s and it was not until this date that any ship records taking Savage Islanders on as crew.

> *SUNDAY 9 OCT 1836 Commences with strong breezes from southward at 6am saw Savage Island the canoes came off with bananas taro and spears. The inhabitants are a wild looking race.*[11]

> *TUESDAY 3 JAN 1837 at daylight saw Savage Island and at 11am canoes came off and brought a few bananas and sold them for fish hooks … on the west side of the island … the Natives were as naked as ever … for they had not so much as a fig leaf to cover the loins.*[12]

> *FRIDAY 17 FEB 1837 This day light winds from SE and calms. At 9am went on shore at Savage Island at 1pm came on board … found the Natives very friendly … could get nothing.*[13]

> *MONDAY 6 JULY 1840 1pm in with the SW part of Savage Island. Had a visit from the Natives very savage looking people bought a few bananas and some war spears, clubs etc [on Wednesday 8 July] running down SW side of Savage Island looks pleasant wish I could go on shore but dare not at night shorten sail.*[14]

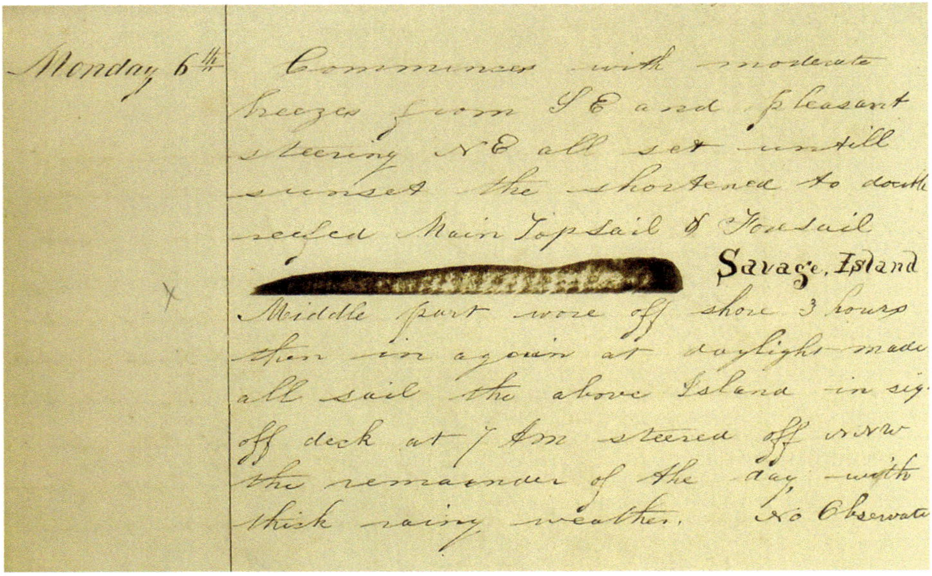
Monday 6th Commences with moderate
breezes from SE and pleasant
steering NE all set untill
sunset the shortened to double
reefed Main Topsail & Foresail
Savage Island
Middle part wore off shore 3 hours
then in again at daylight made
all sail the above Island in sig
off deck at 7 Am steered off NNW
the remainder of the day with
thick rainy weather. No Observati

An entry from the logbook of the whaling vessel *Janus*, dated Monday 6 July 1840, with a sketch of Savage Island. The entry for the day reads: 'Commenced with moderate breezes from SE and pleasant steering NE all set untill sunset the[n] shortened to double reefed Main Topsail & Foresail [sketch of Savage Island] Middle part [were] off shore 3 hours then in again at daylight made all sail the above Island in sight off deck at 7 Am steered off NNW the remainder of the day, with thick rainy weather No observations.' Courtesy of the Trustees of the New Bedford Free Public Library, Massachusetts, Ship *Janus* 1839–1841

27 August 1843 saw Savage Island and were boarded by some of the Natives from whom we obtained a few bunches of taro … in exchange for a few fish hooks, pieces of iron hoops etc.[15]

Tuesday 12 Dec 1848 This day light winds from the east and fine weather. The ship headed in shore at 3pm sent 2 boats in shore to do what trade these savages had. The boats lay off shore some time but got nothing but spears and war clubs. They came off to the ship in canoes 40 of them. They were savage looking fellows. I was glad to see them off at 5pm.[16]

Wednesday 21 Nov 1860 This first part steering for Savage Island at 4pm came up with it. Several canoes came off with some chickens and pigs and a few bananas … the natives appear to be very friendly … there are several missionaries on the island … we had several Natives onboard overnight. Ship laying off and on later trading for hogs and chickens … two Natives from island begged me to take them.[17]

Tuesday 11 Dec 1860 at about 8am the Natives began to come off to the ship and we began to trade with them for chickens hogs etc. [Wednesday 12 Dec] We have about 25 hogs 150 chickens and some fruit. This pm dressed 30 chickens and 1 hog … put 4 Natives on shore that we took from there last spring and took one new one with us.[18]

Wednesday 24 July 1861 Light airs from south … at 2pm 6 canoes came to us and we were 14 miles from land. We got 8 hogs from them and some fruit and had hard work to make them leave the ship.[19]

Sunday 22 Dec 1861 the canoes came off and commenced the trade and the larboard boat ashore again to get some old coconuts for the hogs and got a few bundles of arrowroot.[20]

Sunday 3 August 1862 Still laying off and on Savage Island the Captain went on shore and came off in the evening … ship laying off the west side of the Island, it being Sunday there was no trading going on. [Monday 4 August] stood in to the lea side of the island and traded with the Natives.[21]

Monday 25 June 1866 Savage Island in sight, at noon any quantity of canoes alongside trading fowls, yams, coconuts, pigs, arrowroot, canoes, shells, spears, tapa, bananas, oranges, mammy apples, war clubs and swords, laying off and on, mate went ashore, at sundown came back. [Tuesday 26 June] Morning strong breeze, foggy weather with light rain … larboard and waist boats went ashore to trade, laying off and on, plenty of canoes alongside trading, at 11am double reefed the topsails, killed a pig, bought 17 pigs and 790 yams, the Natives are thieves, at sundown all on board, squared away for Navigator Islands.[22]

Most whalers paused at Savage Island to trade then moved on; but in late 1838 the *Benjamin Rush* worked in the vicinity of Savage Island for almost two months. During this time at least five whales were caught and many others sighted. The weather was frequently rough, with gales and rain squalls, and during one storm 40 barrels of oil were lost overboard. Savage Island was often within sight for up to a week at a time and if the weather was bad the captain might bring the ship in to the lee of the island and allow trading to take place offshore. These exchanges were limited, as there was much work to do cutting, trying out and stowing the oil. In addition there were arguments among the officers and general dissatisfaction on board the ship. In the final weeks of December 1838 frustration mounted as many sperm whales were sighted but none taken – partly, it seems, because of First Officer West's refusal to take one of the boats out for the chase. The *Benjamin Rush* was brought in one last time to trade with the Savage Islanders, and then it set sail for New Zealand. The whaler visited the island again the following year as it was heading towards the Navigator Islands, and it made a final visit in August 1839 when it was noted that the 'natives came alongside but brought little or nothing to trade'.[23]

Such entries give us a glimpse of the interaction between New England whaling men and the Islanders, and the impressions formed by the Europeans from these brief encounters. Unfortunately many questions are unanswered, for there are no corresponding records of what the Islanders thought of these foreign visitors. We can only surmise what impressions the Islanders formed, and what impact these visits had on island life.

The Niueans were cautious at first and may have reacted in a way considered 'ferocious' by foreigners, but they soon overcame any fear of these new ships and seemed eager to engage in trade. If the whalers were surprised by the nakedness of the Islanders, the Islanders would have found the boat crew equally novel: strangely dressed, tattooed – something not practised on Niue – and foul-smelling due to their consumption of meat, something unknown in the Niuean diet until pigs were introduced in the 1850s. Even then, their revulsion towards meat meant that to begin with they kept pigs purely as a trade item.

Once a mission presence had been established in the northeast of the island in the late 1840s, more whalers came ashore but only after sighting the paper of credentials with which all mission teachers were issued before being left on an isolated island. This document confirmed that the bearer was working in the service of the London Missionary Society and could therefore be trusted. One American whaler stopped off the Niue coast in around 1847. Peniamina, the first mission helper left on the island the previous year, went out to the vessel and presented his credentials. On the strength of those, the captain decided to land with two boats in order to cut

'Cutting in' was the process of cutting the blubber from the whale carcass and hauling it on board. The first and second mates, suspended over the side of the ship with long spades, are cutting the blubber and peeling it off the body with the aid of heavy ropes and hooks attached to the main mast. When the blubber had been hauled onto the vessel, a fire was lit under the trypots and the next process, trying out or boiling, was commenced to render the valuable oil. This illustration is from *Life and Adventure in the Pacific* by 'a roving printer', published in 1861.

Alexander Turnbull Library, Wellington, New Zealand, PUBL-0161-002

firewood for the furnace. Night fell and it became too dangerous to attempt to leave the island, so the men slept in a cave near the landing place. Peniamina stayed with them, and they left again safely the next day.[24]

Although the visits were infrequent compared with some other South Sea islands, they were opportunities for the Niueans to practise the art of bartering, and they soon learned how it was done. When one Niuean tried to escape with his fish hook before handing over the spear as agreed, he got more than he bargained for. 'After getting a hook into his possession, for which he agreed by signs to give a spear, with a dexterous use of his paddle he slipped with his canoe away from the ship's side, carrying both hook and spear, and smiling at the apparent success of his treachery. The report of a musket and the ball whizzing past his ears, however, acted like a charm, for the canoe was paddled alongside at double quick time and the contested article forthwith delivered.'[25]

As visits by passing whalers – and other vessels – became more commonplace, the Niueans learned what trade items would be in demand, and they expressed clear preferences for the items they valued in return. It is not certain whether they deliberately produced more crops to meet the demand of passing whalers or whether they simply traded what they had at the time. Two clues suggest the latter. First, the infrequency and erratic timing of the visits would have made it difficult to produce crops specifically for trade, although they may have begun making more handcrafts that could be stored for trade with passing whalers. Second, a number of whaling logbooks noted that although they stopped to trade at Savage Island they could get nothing but a few spears. Famine was not uncommon on the island; drought would seriously damage the taro and yam crops, and cyclones would periodically wipe out reserves of coconuts. At such times the Islanders showed only what few handcrafts they had and little or no trading took place.

The first trade items secured by the Niueans from the Europeans appear to have been glass beads, probably for their novelty value. It did not take long, though, for the Islanders to insist on another trade item: the fish hook. On an island with no volcanic rock such as obsidian for fashioning hooks, and few beaches where shells might be found, or stranded whales to provide bone for this purpose, the Niueans depended on wood from a shrub known as mailē. One writer on pre-European Niue said the roots of the mailē were used;[26] another source says the mailē sometimes had hook-shaped branches and these were used.[27] Much of the fishing was done using nets, which could be made from plant material. But the arrival of whalers with metal hooks to trade was an opportunity not to be lost.

One result of the large number of whaling ships in the South Seas, and the conditions on board, was that men often deserted when the opportunity arose. They escaped into hiding until their vessel left and then became what were known as beachcombers. On Niue, however, there was little opportunity for this because of the isolation and the difficulty in landing. There are only two recorded instances of men attempting to come ashore from whalers, and in both cases they were unsuccessful.

In 1837, as the American whaler *Beaver* passed Savage Island, one crew member was brought ashore by whaleboat and left on the island. When the vessel returned to New England three years later, the master of the vessel, Captain William Rogers, was arrested on a charge of abandoning one of his crew. The captain promptly published his version of the story in a Boston newspaper. The crew member in question, John Brown, had 'repeatedly been guilty of mutinous and disorderly conduct' for many months. He was anxious to leave the ship and when Savage Island was reached in October 1837, Brown requested that he be set on shore. Captain Rogers stressed that whaling vessels were 'in the habit of stopping for refreshments and supplies' at Savage Island so there would have been opportunities for Brown to get off the island. The case against Rogers was discharged in June 1840.[28] As for John Brown, stories on Niue tell of him being given a vaka and some food supplies and being sent off the island; he is said to have sheltered in a cave along the coast until he was able to go out to another passing whaler and be taken on board.[29]

The second attempt to come ashore from a whaler occurred in May 1863, after the arrival on the island of the first European missionary. A group of 'eight sorry looking sailors appeared and said they had come to stay on shore until they could get off in some other vessel'.[30] They were immediately escorted back to their boat. When the voyage of the *Grecian* was later reported in the Australian and New Zealand press, the captain was reported as saying that the men had requested to be put ashore at Savage Island 'but the mission would not have them stay, and gave their reasons, that such a lot of unruly whalers would do more harm in one week to the natives than they could recover in seven years. The men returned on board very much dissatisfied at not being allowed to remain.'[31]

The whaling ships in the Pacific provided the people of Niue with their first encounters with Europeans since the visit by Cook. The encounters were tentative to start with, but gradually they appear to have become more relaxed. Both parties benefited: the whalers with fresh food and a break from the daily grind; the Islanders with a chance to barter for desirable items.

Shortly after the whaling visits began, other Europeans appeared on the horizon, some of whom were to have a much more lasting impact on Niuean life. However, it was the whalers who began the process of interaction and change on Niue.

3. Missionaries

A wonderful work is that which God has wrought on Savage Island

Within a few years of the first whalers moving into the Pacific another group of fishermen arrived, this time in search of men's souls. The newly formed London Missionary Society (LMS) sent the first batch of eager mission workers on board the *Duff* in 1796 to establish themselves in Tahiti. It was 20 years before a mission was successfully established but from that point on, the mission workers spread out to the Marquesas, the Hervey and Cook groups and, by 1830, to the Navigator Islands (Samoa).

The first missionaries of the LMS were members of evangelical congregations within the Church of England, people who lamented the decline in church standards and sought to return to a stricter form of Christianity that emphasised obedience, abstinence, self-improvement and moral correctness. They put great stress on the study of the Bible, and believed part of their mission was to spread the gospel as far as possible. The evangelicals studied the works of the great eighteenth-century explorers such as Cook and Wallis, and through these writings they came to see there was a great swathe of the earth's surface awaiting enlightenment. For the first time, Europeans other than explorers and whalers began to consider the possibilities of the great South Seas.

Many of these evangelical congregations consisted of men who were part of the newly emerging 'mechanic' class that was expanding as the industrial revolution gained momentum. They were ironworkers, builders, stonemasons, joiners, printers and binders, boat builders, cotton factory workers, candle manufacturers, buckle and harness makers, wheelwrights, druggists' apprentices and clerks.[1] They combined practical skills with religious zeal, and they began to see missionary work to other parts of the world as a highly desirable and God-driven vocation. They were young and often, especially in the early days, they were not ordained ministers when they left for the Pacific. Many completed their training and were ordained in Tahiti, the Cooks or Samoa.

The LMS was one of the most successful of the Protestant mission groups that entered the Pacific, and by 1830 it had already established several mission stations. In England, Scotland and Wales, men were being trained to take on the missionary life. Wives were being carefully chosen, too, for they were an essential part of the formula for success. Evangelical congregations throughout Britain were educated about the work of the missionaries and encouraged to contribute financially to their success. Like a well-oiled machine, the LMS was humming.

In the South Seas, the first mission workers had begun to comprehend the sheer vastness of the region they were hoping to Christianise. The distances to cover and the number of islands involved called for special measures. A purpose-built mission vessel was needed – not a ship that could bring men and their families from Europe to the Pacific, but one that could provide interisland travel, that could manoeuvre the narrow reef passages into the lagoon or ride the tides and currents off the coast where there was no natural harbour. A vessel that could be the floating office of the LMS – moving men and supplies from one area to another, checking on staff left on isolated islands, distributing the Bibles, prayerbooks and instruction manuals that were rapidly being translated into indigenous languages and printed, and collecting local produce that could be sold on the open market to help pay for the mission work.

The vastness of the territory produced another response that was especially embraced by the LMS. It became apparent that there were too few missionaries for the number of islands involved, so a new group of 'native mission teachers' were given some education and training in Christian teachings and then placed on other islands. They became the spearhead of the movement, the bridge between the local population and the new European arrivals, the point of first contact for the introduction of this new faith. They became fluent in the local language and sensitive to cultural nuances; and because they themselves were Polynesian, they were often seen as less threatening and therefore more immediately acceptable to the indigenous population. They worked hard and prepared the ground for the arrival of European missionaries who, as ordained ministers, were the only ones able to conduct the essential rites of the church: baptism and communion. Over the course of the nineteenth century, hundreds of Polynesian mission teachers were instrumental in assisting the spread of Christianity in the Pacific. They do not feature nearly as prominently as the European missionaries in the church literature, but the success of the LMS was to a very large extent due to their work.

Like the whalers, Reverend John Williams read the charts and noted Savage Island as mapped and named by Cook, and in 1830 he determined to call there en route from Rarotonga to Samoa. Williams was an adventurous man, as much explorer as missionary, 34 years old when he set out for Samoa but with 13 years' experience already in Tahiti and the Cooks, and eager to take every opportunity to extend the sphere of influence of the LMS. He sailed with two native mission teachers from Aitutaki, intending to leave them on Savage Island to begin the mission work there. The attempt to gain a foothold on Savage Island failed, however; and it would be 10 years before a second attempt was made, by which time Williams had been killed on Erromango in the New Hebrides while trying to introduce the gospel there.

The arrival and settlement of the LMS on Savage Island followed a pattern that was repeated throughout the Pacific, although the process took much longer there than in many other islands and was often used later by LMS writers as a case study in the rewards of perseverance. Williams' visit in 1830 was mirrored in a number of ways by further visits to Niue through to the late 1840s. Williams visited but did not land on the island; it would be 27 years before a European missionary accomplished that feat. After Williams' failed attempt to settle native mission teachers on the island it was 16 years before a Niuean mission helper was returned to settle there, and 19 years before a Samoan mission teacher was accepted in one district. Williams did, however, succeed in enticing two Niuean men to travel with him to Sāmoa to learn more about the mission work. This practice was repeated with each successive visit by the LMS, and as these people were returned to the island, it was hoped they would encourage their fellow Islanders to accept mission teachers.

John Williams first saw Savage Island from his ship, the *Messenger of Peace*, early in the morning of 19 June 1830. As they approached the shore he observed

> *a number of caverns of different sizes opening towards the sea which made it appear that the island had undergone some great concussion in nature. We perceived natives on shore in and near the caverns above mentioned. We made signs for them to come off by holding up a piece of white cloth as a flag. The people on shore did the same ... A boat was immediately let down and several of our natives went in towards the shore. The natives on the shore showed hostile motions, having each three or four spears or clubs in readiness, besides smooth stones in a belt round the body.*[2]

The native visitors landed successfully near Tuapa. They exchanged presents with the locals and encouraged them to visit the mission ship. Three canoes were

Messenger of Peace was the first vessel used by the missionary John Williams to visit other Pacific islands from his base in Rarotonga. It was constructed on the beach in Rarotonga by local labourers working under the direction of Williams. He confessed he knew little of shipbuilding and had scarcely any tools to work with but, being of the 'mechanical class' and fired with a passion to spread the gospel, he was determined to succeed. The locals had of course many useful skills to contribute to the task. Trees were split in half with wedges and adzed down with small hatchets. Wooden pins were used to bind planks together and as a substitute for oakum, used to waterproof the hull, a mixture of coconut husks, dried banana stumps, native cloth and other substances was used. Ropes were made from the bark of the hibiscus and local mats were quilted together to make strong sails. The vessel was tested on a voyage to Tahiti before setting out on the longer voyage to the Navigator Islands (Samoa), via Savage Island, in 1830.

Alexander Turnbull Library, Wellington, New Zealand, B-K-505-165

launched but only one old man agreed to go on board. 'On reaching the deck he was almost frantick with surprise and leaped about … using the most vehement exclamations at everything he saw as being wonderful beyond description.'[3] Presents were offered but 'he did not appear to value anything so much as a fish hook' and when he had 'satisfied his curiosity he was taken on shore to the great joy of his wife and children.'[4] Later versions of this story would suggest the old man was held hostage on the ship for some time but Williams does not suggest this in the journal he wrote at the time.

The visit was then marked by an incident that was to prove common during visits to the island and helps explain the length of time involved before the mission became established. When another boat went ashore, once again with only native teachers, they were sharing food with the locals when a chief with a number of men following him arrived from another part of the island and expressed a desire to visit the mission ship. These people were from Makefu and they were not allowed to launch their vaka from the Tuapa landing site. Consequently they made signs to the visitors 'to go round to another part of the Island'. The missionaries soon learned that every district of the island was separate from, and often hostile to, every other district and – as whalers had noticed – as soon as the ship drifted along the coast, canoes that had approached from one area returned home rapidly before canoes came out from the next.

Williams sailed further down the coast in the hope of being able to land the native mission teachers; but although the Aitutakians went ashore and were entertained with an umu kai, an earth oven of food, and some sugarcane, 'the two native teachers and their wives we intended to have left were so much alarmed at the frightful appearance and savage gestures of the natives that we could not prevail upon them to remain'.[5] Furthermore, when the chief who had wanted to visit the mission ship did so, it was remarked that hanging from a girdle around his waist was part of the handle of a clasp knife. One of the seamen on board the mission ship had heard the story of a whaleboat crew being murdered on Savage Island and it was supposed that this was where the knife handle had come from. This information made Williams more cautious and he agreed to carry the Aitutakians on to Samoa, even though he personally 'did not apprehend their lives would have been in danger'.

The failure to establish native mission teachers on Savage Island left Williams with only one other means by which

> *we might accomplish in some measure the object of our voyage [and that] was to try to get a native or two to accompany us and teach them the word of God, and treat them kindly and after the lapse of a few months bring them back with a native teacher. Three canoes soon approached the vessel and … we tempted two youths to stay on board by holding out to them fish hooks and pearl shells, articles they hold in great estimation. And while they were gazing at the wonders they saw we sailed away with them.*[6]

Later accounts talk of these two men, Niumaga and Uea, spending several days terrified as they watched those on the mission ship cook and eat pork, which they believed to be human flesh. Williams himself makes no further mention of the Niueans, although in a journal two years later,[7] when describing food sources in Polynesia, he refers to fruitbats which on Savage Island were 'numerous and eaten by the natives with great delight'. Some bats had perished on board the ship after it had left the island in 1830, and were cooked and eaten by the Niueans. They offered some to Williams who, although he was prepared to taste most things, declined these; in the margin of his journal he wrote a note referring to the creatures as vampire bats and equating them with heathenism and a representation of the devil. The eating habits of each party were obviously a source of amazement and concern to the other.

Williams kept to his word in trying to return the two Niueans to their own island two months after sailing away. His journal records the voyage south from Samoa in August 1830, but calms and light breezes for almost a fortnight prevented them from getting close to Savage Island and, with water supplies almost exhausted, the decision was made to head for Rarotonga. Niumaga and Uea spent several months with Williams on Ra'iatea[8] in the Society group and on Rarotonga. A voyage by the *Messenger of Peace* to transport a missionary family to Sydney in late 1830 or early 1831 provided the opportunity to return the two men to Savage Island, and this time the weather favoured them.

Niumaga and Uea were at first welcomed ashore with rejoicing by their families. However, an epidemic outbreak later resulted in Uea and his father, as the probable bearers of this illness, being killed. Niumaga somehow escaped, managed to board a passing whaler and eventually made his way back to Samoa.

The LMS workers made no further attempt to visit Savage Island until 1840, when a voyage took place from Samoa for the sole purpose of establishing a mission on the island. A very small vessel of 20 tons, the *Samoa*, was chartered for the journey. The expedition was led by Reverend Archibald Murray, resident missionary on Tutuila, assisted by two English helpers at the mission, Matthew Hunkin and George Lundie. Also on the vessel were four Samoan mission teachers who had been selected for service on Savage Island.

Reverend Murray had heard of a Savage Islander living on the Manu'a Islands, the easternmost islands of the Samoan group, and so this is where he headed first with the aim of engaging this man to assist in getting the mission teachers ashore. Liulauvi said he would accompany the expedition on condition he be returned to

Manu'a afterwards, and Murray agreed. The journey began with fair weather and Murray occupied himself with learning 'the names of several villages on Savage island and also a few other words which may be of some advantage when we arrive there. We also ascertained from him that the name of the island is Niue.'[9] Conversation soon became impossible as the *Samoa* encountered a storm and, as it was such a small vessel, was forced to haul in the sails and simply drift. Squally weather, strong winds and heavy seas continued until the ship arrived off the coast of Niue on 5 July 1840.

> *About 11 am [we] came near the shore, where we saw canoes coming off. They soon came alongside loaded with clubs and spears, and were paddled by extremely savage looking crews. The natives were very anxious about fish hooks, so much so that we could scarcely get them to listen to the object of our coming among them.*[10]

The vessel stood off the land; and when it came in again at another place, more vaka, loaded with clubs and spears and also some bananas, came out to trade. Murray noted that it did not seem to matter which part of the island people came from, the universal demand was for fish hooks. He described the natives as presenting a 'dreadfully wild and frightful appearance'; those on board felt intimated and threatened when surrounded by the canoes, and felt obliged to buy the clubs and spears in order to disarm them.

The *Samoa* continued around the coast to another village, which they thought was the home of Liulauvi: they decided to land him there and hope that he could persuade the villagers to take the four mission teachers.

> *... to this agreement he appeared very willing at first, but after a little further conversation with those from the shore, he became entirely opposed to it ... When we got opposite what appears the ruling village in the island, many more canoes came off to us, on board of which were exceedingly fierce looking men. We told some ... that we desired to put 4 teachers on shore with them. To this, their reply was as follows. No teachers must be put on shore with us for though we are the ruling people of the Island, our power is not sufficient to protect them, and ... the consequences would be that the whole island would ... kill both us and them.*[11]

That night a meeting was held on board and the Samoan teachers declared they were unwilling to go ashore after such a warning. Murray was forced to agree, especially given that Liulauvi was also unwilling to land. They already had one Niuean on board and they decided to lay off overnight, then try to persuade one or two more of the Islanders to return with them to Samoa. Three more men, possibly related to Liulauvi, came on board, then one was taken off by canoe.

We have three remaining and I think they would all go onshore were it possible for them to get there. But this seems to be impossible for we cannot go back to the places where they belong and they would not, on any consideration, land in any other part of the island. The reason for this appears to be on account of their continual wars.[12]

With the wind freshening and making it impossible to come in close to the island again, the *Samoa* headed back in stormy seas and reached Pago Pago harbour after five difficult days of sailing. A newspaper article written later by Reverend Murray noted their arrival in Samoa 'with three natives, and an immense quantity of war weapons ... One of the natives ... was afterwards of some service in the accomplishment of our object [to establish a mission]. Of the other two, one died shortly after their arrival, and the other left in a ship and was never heard of more.'[13]

The missionaries were beginning to see that the establishment of a church on Niue was not going to be an easy task. They could also see that the cooperation of Niueans who fetched up in Samoa, either on mission vessels or on whalers, could well be vital to their entry to the island. Of the two men taken by the Williams visit in 1830, one had avoided death back on Niue by escaping to sea again. This man, Niumaga, arrived in Samoa with another local, Nukai, on a whaler sometime during the 1830s. Nukai is better known on Niue as Peniamina (Benjamin), the name he was given at his baptism. It appears the two men arrived in Apia on board an American whaler under the command of Captain Simpson, who was said to have to have 'touched at Savage Island, and Peniamina had gone on board his vessel and refused to return to the shore'.[14] Another report described how Nukai was swept out to sea in a gale and picked up by the whaler.[15] When he reached Apia, Captain Simpson 'took an early opportunity of introducing his Savage Island friend to Mr Mills, the missionary at that place. Mr Mills took immediate steps towards turning Peniamina's visit to Samoa to account.'[16] Although the date of Peniamina's arrival in Apia is uncertain, Mills' tenure as missionary there dated from 1836. It seems that Peniamina worked at the mission station and was taught to read and write, given Christian instruction and baptised at the newly opened Malua Institute in Apia.

Peniamina was based in Apia, but when Reverend Aaron Buzacott left Rarotonga for Sydney, in March 1842, visiting the islands en route, Peniamina was on board the mission vessel. Also on board was a man named Ta'unga, a native of Avarua in the Cook Islands, who had been trained as a mission teacher and was being taken to the 'heathen islands' of Melanesia. Ta'unga is one the few indigenous mission teachers to have kept a journal that has survived to the present day; it is a rich source of information on the spread of the LMS missions throughout the

Pacific from the perspective of these indigenous teachers. Taʻunga noted the brief visit to Savage Island in the hope of landing four Cook Island mission teachers:

> *On Monday morning [18 April 1842] we got close to Niue and canoes came out to visit the ship … later on many more canoes came out and our ship was full of people. They came out naked. Buzacott took aside those who were only dressed in tikoru*[17] *and girded them with lengths of cotton cloth. But they did not take any notice, they just took the cloth off and some of them tied it round their heads. They are a wild crowd and of strange appearance. The teeth of the deep sea fishes are strung from their beards.*[18]

Taʻunga explained how Buzacott gave an axe to the people who had come on board and requested that they take it ashore to their chief: this was a method used in the Society Islands and the Cooks to win over a chief who could then influence his people. However, as mission visitors to Niue had already learned, such a system was ineffective on an island where there was little social stratification and chiefly influence was extremely localised. Every district was jealous of and hostile to every other district – as Buzacott learned when another group boarded the mission vessel and requested an axe and a fish hook for their chief. The vessel had drifted down the coast and these people asked to be taken back to their side of the island, lest they be killed.

The plan to land the four Cook Island mission teachers was met with rejection from the visitors to the ship, and when Peniamina's younger brother arrived on board with news of a plot to persuade the mission workers ashore and then seize them and take all their belongings, Taʻunga wrote:

> *when we heard the news we departed from that savage island and sailed on, praising God, for it was He who forewarned us of the intentions of those wicked people … we took Peniamina's younger brother with us … he was afraid to return ashore and told us that he would be killed because he had divulged their secret to us.*[19]

A breakthrough came four years later, when at last the LMS was able to land someone on Niue to spread the gospel. It was Peniamina, fresh from another spell at the Malua Institute in Apia, accompanied by Fakafitiniu, another Niuean who had arrived in Samoa on a whaling vessel the previous year and had been cared for by the mission at Apia. The visit in 1846 was part of a cruise on the mission vessel *John Williams* by the reverends William Gill and Henry Nisbet. On arrival off the coast at Mutalau, Fakafitiniu went ashore and asked if Peniamina and a Samoan or Rarotongan mission teacher could be landed. Peniamina was a mission helper but he did not have the status of teacher; Reverend Murray later wrote that he hoped

Peniamina 'really was a Christian'.[20] After discussion among the local people it was agreed that Peniamina, as a Niuean, would be permitted to come ashore but not the mission teacher.

Captain Morgan, in command of the *John Williams*, described the scene when Peniamina landed on 26 October 1846. About 200 people stood on the rocks around the landing area with spears and other weapons, but now they also displayed white flags as a sign of welcome. The landing at Mutalau is a difficult one. The surf is often heavy and the land drops steeply into the foaming water. Peniamina packed his personal effects into a cask and this was floated ashore by means of a long line. He then got into a canoe that was also attached to a line, and was hauled in through the breakers. 'When the vessel departed, Peniamina in civilized fashion ... took off his hat and waved his farewell to those on board.'[21] And thus, mused Reverend Murray in later years, 'we obtained a hold on this peculiarly intractable race'.[22]

The fate of Peniamina was unknown until two years later, in August 1848, when the *John Williams* arrived with the reverends George Turner and Henry Nisbet from the Samoa mission. Their trip to the New Hebrides and New Caledonia to check on mission teachers in that area was concluded with a stop at Savage Island.

> *Knowing the custom here of killing their countrymen who visit a foreign place, as soon as they return, with a view to prevent disease, we approached the island this afternoon with much concern for the safety of Peniamina ... a Savage Islander [who] was placed here, at his own request, last voyage. The first canoe relieved our minds. They echoed his name, pointed behind, and soon we had our old friend on board shaking hands with us.*[23]

Peniamina stayed on board the vessel overnight; he spoke of the time since he had been landed, the dangers he had faced and the progress he had made in spreading the gospel. He was now confident that the people of the Mutalau area were willing to receive a Samoan teacher to live among them. Furthermore, there was another area on the island where it appeared that teachers would be welcomed. The time and deliberation taken – in this case over the decision to accept a mission teacher – was to be a theme in Niuean contact history whenever major change was mooted by outside agencies. Niue may have already become inextricably linked with the outside world, but the pace of change was still at least partially in their control.

The effectiveness of Peniamina as a teacher was somewhat in doubt and the missionaries suspected that interest in the new religion by the Islanders was motivated more by the desire for material possessions than for salvation. Certainly most of Peniamina's personal property had quickly disappeared. Reverend Turner believed

Landing place at Mutalau, photographed by Graham Balfour in 1890. Balfour was a cousin of Robert Louis Stevenson and may have been on board the *Janet Nichol* when it called at Niue while making a Pacific cruise with Stevenson and his wife Fanny. Because of weather conditions the vessel called off Mutalau rather than Alofi. Balfour noted that it was 'a very bad landing at foot of 200ft cliff'. Wooden ladders allow people to reach different parts of the very steep cliffs

Pitt Rivers Museum, University of Oxford, PRM 1998.181.10.3

'a desire for hatchets and fish hooks is the principal motive at present',[24] and a recent Niuean writer has commented: 'the people's demand for teachers would probably have been influenced a great deal by seeing Peniamina's ability to read and write which seemed to go hand in hand with the possession of material goods'.[25] Nevertheless, the missionaries were confident that their true purpose would eventually be understood and, despite continued hostilities on the island, they were encouraged that progress was being made.

The following year, 1849 – 19 years after the visit of the Reverend John Williams and with the blessing of the local people – the mission vessel returned with a Samoan teacher, Paulo, and his wife to begin the task of establishing a mission station at Mutalau. At the same time, a Niuean chief, Laumahina, and his son Latoa expressed a desire to learn more about the mission work and were taken back to

Samoa. They would later be of much assistance to Paulo in his work. Peniamina meanwhile moved to another area along the coast. The LMS was becoming concerned that Peniamina's activities were 'inconsistent' – an allusion to the rumour that he had committed adultery. By the time of the next visit in 1852, Peniamina had left the island, and although he returned a decade later he was never again involved with the LMS.[26]

Throughout the1850s, the Samoan mission teachers worked tirelessly to establish the LMS on Niue, and the Niueans were now willing to embrace not only a new religion but a whole new social and economic structure. Brief histories of Niue focus on the 1860s and the arrival of the first European missionary, but the greatest changes arguably occurred in the 1850s. The Samoan teachers were spreading skills and beliefs learned in the training institute in Apia, and throughout this decade they were supported by frequent visits by the mission vessel *John Williams* with European missionaries on board. By the end of the decade the Samoan teachers numbered a mere five, each accompanied by a wife, yet the changes effected were fundamental and widespread throughout the island. Niuean cooperation was essential to this.

Beginning with Paulo alone in Mutalau, the LMS gradually established four more centres on Niue, each with its own Samoan teacher. By the late 1850s there was Paulo at Alofi, Samuela at Avatele, Sakaia at Makefu and Amosa at Hakupu – all coastal locations with access to the sea. Paulo began work in a very small enclave that was said to 'embrace a space of about 5 miles along the coast',[27] and he was frequently in danger from those in the 'heathen districts'. Yet five years later when Charles Hardie visited on the *John Williams*, he reported that 'the people now go from district to district without fear of each other … and the teachers are allowed to pursue their work everywhere without interruption and are very kindly treated'.[28]

In contrast to the slow progress in making initial inroads onto the island, this second phase seems to have occurred very quickly. Two possible factors account for this. Although there had been few outward signs of change in the previous 20 years, there had been a trickle of Niueans leaving the island and experiencing life on other Pacific islands and also on board whaling ships, mission vessels and the occasional trading vessel. The return of some of these men with stories to tell, possessions to show and new skills to demonstrate had gradually opened people's minds to the possibility that allowing outsiders onto the island could be beneficial. Second, the hostility that existed between districts of the island was converted from warfare into forms of rivalry and competition that could be exploited by the mission teachers. Districts became jealous of others where a teacher was based and pressed for their

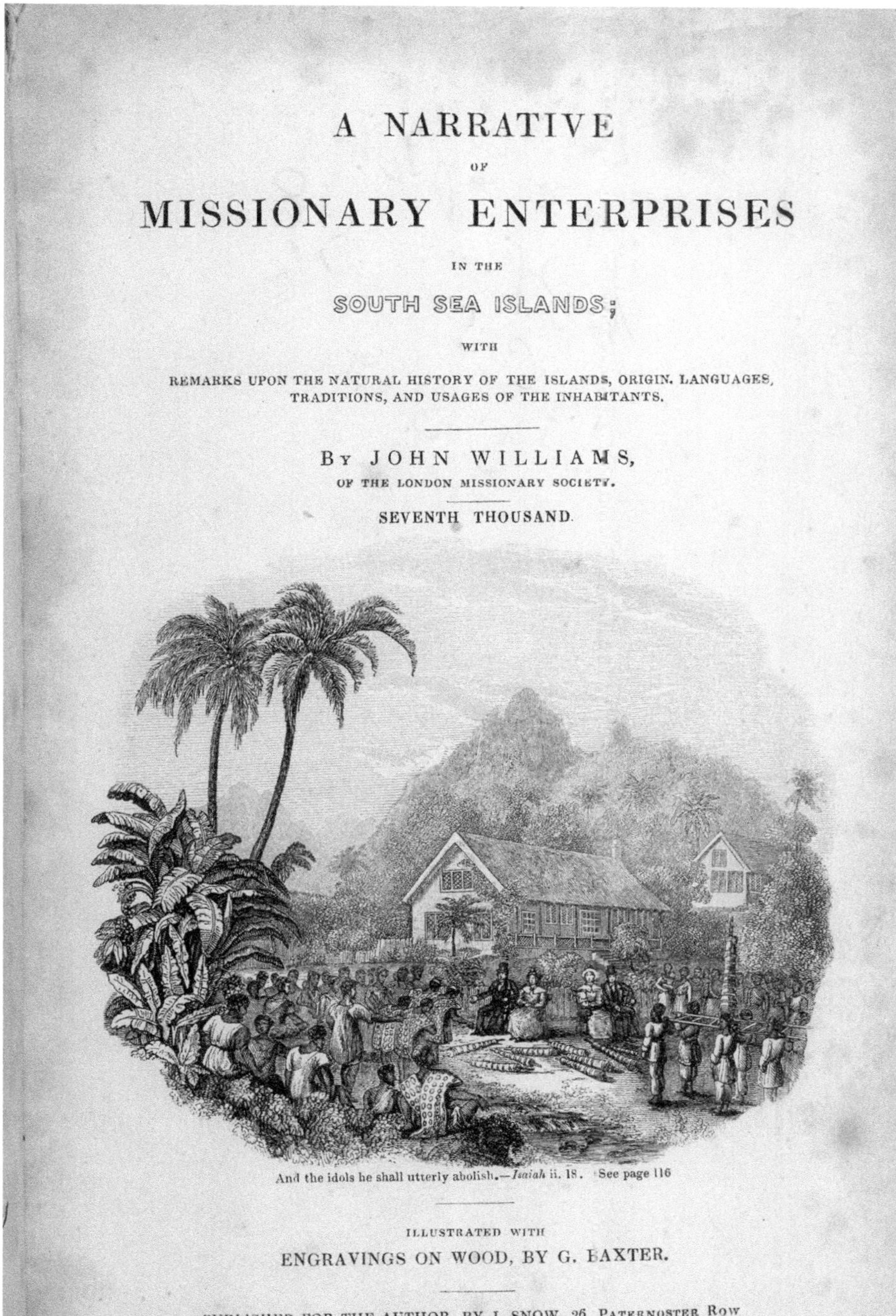

A NARRATIVE

OF

MISSIONARY ENTERPRISES

IN THE

SOUTH SEA ISLANDS;

WITH

REMARKS UPON THE NATURAL HISTORY OF THE ISLANDS, ORIGIN, LANGUAGES, TRADITIONS, AND USAGES OF THE INHABITANTS.

BY JOHN WILLIAMS,

OF THE LONDON MISSIONARY SOCIETY.

SEVENTH THOUSAND.

And the idols he shall utterly abolish.—*Isaiah* ii. 18. See page 116

ILLUSTRATED WITH

ENGRAVINGS ON WOOD, BY G. BAXTER.

PUBLISHED FOR THE AUTHOR, BY J. SNOW, 26, PATERNOSTER ROW

LONDON.—1838.

Reverand John Williams, *A Narrative of Missionary Enterprises in the South Sea Islands* (London: John Snow, 1838). Alexander Turnbull Library, Wellington, New Zealand, B-K-505-TITLE0

NINETEEN YEARS

IN

POLYNESIA:

MISSIONARY LIFE, TRAVELS, AND RESEARCHES

IN

THE ISLANDS OF THE PACIFIC.

BY

THE REV. GEORGE TURNER,

OF THE LONDON MISSIONARY SOCIETY.

LONDON:

JOHN SNOW, PATERNOSTER ROW.

MDCCCLXI.

[The Right of Translation is Reserved.]

Reverand George Turner, *Nineteen Years in Polynesia: Missionary life, travels, and researches in the islands of the Pacific* (London: John Snow, 1861). Alexander Turnbull Library Wellington, New Zealand, B-K-985-TITLE

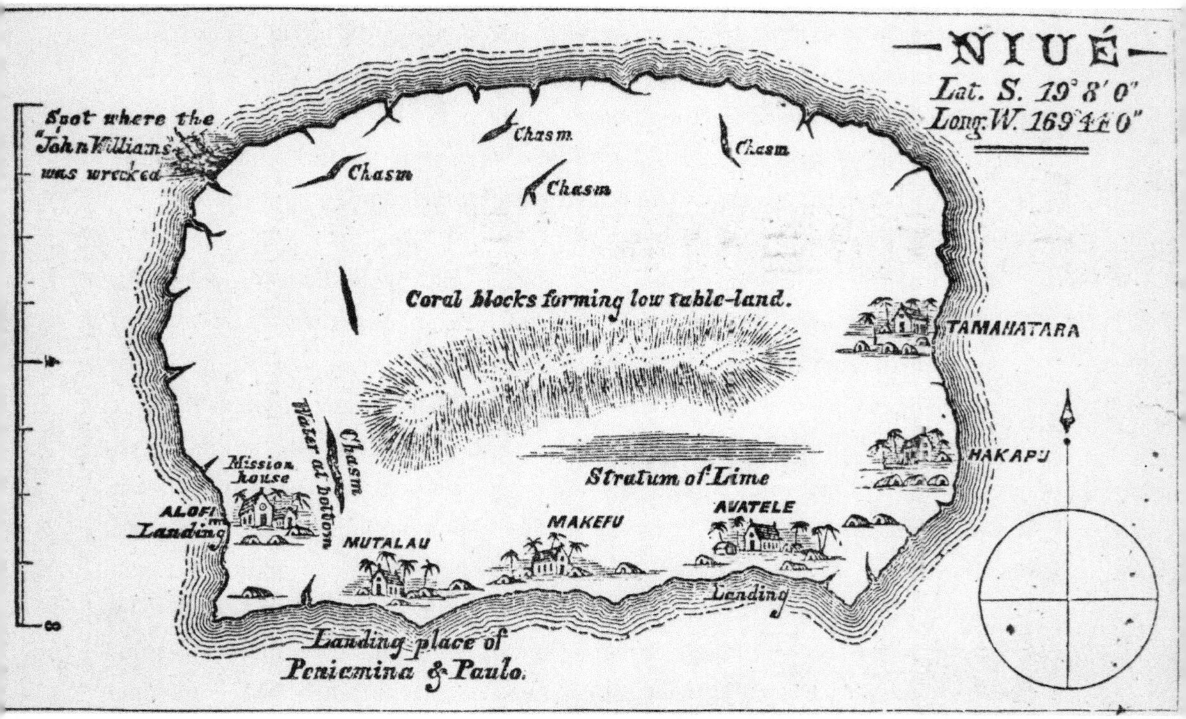

This highly inaccurate map appeared in a small volume written by Reverend Thomas Powell and published by John Snow in London in 1868. Powell had sent the manuscript to George Lawes on Niue for his comments and Lawes was very critical of the work, noting 'the map is all wrong'. It was nevertheless published as a further contribution to the work of the LMS in the Pacific.

Alexander Turnbull Library, Wellington, New Zealand, B-K-984-FRONTIS

Pages 63 and 64: The work of English mission societies in spreading Christianity around the globe was an expensive operation. Its continued success depended on donations from the English public and, in order to maintain and encourage generosity, a huge public relations programme was undertaken. Public lectures, journals, magazines, pamphlets, board games and books were used to promote mission work. There were also travelling artefact exhibitions and later, with the development of photography, lantern slides, postcards and illustrated writings. The LMS enjoyed the services of George Baxter, a skilled illustrator, who worked with the evangelical publishing house of John Snow in London to produce books such as these by Williams and Turner.

own teacher. Material progress such as the building of chapels and houses could be made competitive as each district sought to outshine the others. When money was needed for the support of the mission service, each mission station would vie with others to raise the largest quantities of produce for sale in the market in Apia. The various districts of Niue retained their own identity, and competition between them speeded the pace of change.

Much of the training of mission teachers in Apia involved practical skills, in keeping with the 'mechanic' origins of the LMS missionaries. These skills were put to good use in establishing a chapel and a house for the teacher. By 1852 the first of these had been built at Mutalau. 'The chapel … is 42 feet long by about 30 broad. It is enclosed with boards as is also the teacher's house. The procuring of these must have been a very laborious work as they have not a pit saw, and had them all to cut out with hatchets and axes.'[28] By 1854 a teacher's house and temporary chapel had been built in Alofi, and by 1858 'we found the chapel to be a new edifice and very well built, the best in fact that we have seen during the whole of our voyage'.[30] The following year when Reverend George Turner visited he found yet more construction had taken place at the third station in Avatele, and this outshone the previous efforts.

> *We found the teacher Samuela and his family … living in one of the best teacher's houses I have ever seen – quite a palace of a place, eighty feet by thirty, divided into seven apartments, well plastered, finished with doors and Venetians, and furnished with tables, chairs, sofas and bedsteads. We were delighted also with the size and unusually fine workmanship of the chapel. It is ninety feet by twenty-four, holds 500 people; but it is too small and they are about to build a larger one.*[31]

As chapels were built, they created a nucleus around which people began to cluster. Pre-contact settlement had often been inland, where food crops were cultivated.[32] Some coastal settlement had occurred near the sea tracks. The missions were all built in these coastal locations, and now Niueans were encouraged to move nearer the chapel to facilitate attendance at the frequent church services. A central meeting space, the malē, was marked out beside the church and new houses were constructed nearby. Loeb[33] suggests that the Samoans found the traditional Niuean structure built largely of coconut leaves was too cold; they showed the Niueans how to use new building techniques using coral, wood and plaster. The new homes had a lattice inner wall made of kafika wood, plastered on the outside with burnt limestone produced from a particular kind of lightweight coral rock known as puga. The construction of such houses helped create a clean and orderly village that pleased the sensibilities of the missionaries. Many of the Niueans, however, continued to live in traditional shelters behind the limestone houses, thus satisfying their own preferences and those of the church.

Clothing was also important to the mission teachers: they had been taught that the covering of the body was an outward sign of the acceptance of Christianity. All the early LMS visits off the coast of Niue recorded astonishment at the nudity of Niueans; and from the arrival of Peniamina and then Paulo in Mutalau, wearing at least some item of clothing marked out the adherents to the new faith from their naked 'heathen' neighbours on the island. Later in the nineteenth century, cotton cloth became readily and cheaply available and the ubiquitous Mother Hubbard garments for women and trousers and shirt for men became the norm, but to begin with some improvisation was necessary. Bark from the ovava – the huge Niuean banyan tree – was beaten to make cloth, and thin strips of this, used mainly as a belt to carry weapons, had been observed by early visitors. The origins of Niuean tapa cloth, known as hiapo, are uncertain but the art of decoration associated with hiapo is thought to have been brought from Samoa by the mission teachers.[34]

Certainly a common form of dress using hiapo appears to be associated with the arrival of the Samoans. A poncho-like garment known as a tīputa was originally Tahitian; it was introduced to Samoa by the Tahitian teachers who were instrumental in setting up the LMS mission there, and the Samoan teachers in turn brought the garment to Niue. At each stage the indigenous population adapted the style and decoration of the garment according to their own preferences, making the garment their own. By the early 1860s it was reported that Niueans had made over 500 pieces of hiapo cloth to send to the newly established mission station on Pukapuka in the northern Cooks.[35]

Outward appearances were one aspect of missionary change. The real purpose was, however, much more difficult to quantify for it involved changes to men's souls. The mission teachers devoted themselves to learning the Niuean language and then began preaching and teaching in the newly constructed chapels. They gathered around them a body of people interested in their teachings. These were known as 'inquirers' and there were hundreds of them at each mission station by the mid-1850s.

The Samoans worked hard on another task essential to the success of the mission: translating the Bible and instruction books into Niuean. Using texts already translated into Samoan, Paulo worked on Niuean versions, and the first copies, printed at the mission press in Apia, arrived with Reverend Hardie in 1854. He delivered

Tīputa, a poncho-like garment introduced to Niue by the Samoan mission teachers. Wearing clothing was part of the conversion to Christianity and tīputa were used until cheaper and more readily available cotton garments became common. Tīputa were made from hiapo and were decorated with distinctive Niuean patterns. Museum of New Zealand Te Papa Tongarewa, Augustus Hamilton Collection FE000289

1000 primers for use in the newly created schools and, five years later, a further 4000 arrived on the *John Williams*. The ability to read and write became a source of pride and prestige to Niueans, and by the time Reverend Turner visited in 1859 six schoolhouses had been built on the island.

Preaching by the mission teachers called for social changes and the abolition of such practices as war, theft, adultery, infanticide and suicide. Sunday was to be kept as the Sabbath, with no work done on that day. Punishments were introduced for breaking these new moral codes. They included a penalty that was to be used for the next 100 years on the island: building roads with makatea, a type of coral limestone. The number of days to be spent on this, or the length of roadway to be

Peniamina (centre) and other native mission workers. This photographic collage was tucked in the diary of S. Percy Smith and must have been given to him in 1901 by Reverend Frank Lawes. Lawes had prepared the collage to accompany an article he wrote for an LMS publication entitled *The Juvenile: A magazine for the young*, 1 January 1893. The article by Lawes was entitled 'Niue (Savage Island) Christians'. In it, Lawes explains that this group of Niue people were among the first to receive the gospel and all did good work in their island. Lawes wrote that Peniamina 'disappointed his friends but he prepared the way for Paulo, a Samoan teacher, who led very many Savage Islanders to the Saviour'. Sakaio, 'the quiet-looking man on the right hand of the picture, was a moderately brave soldier … and early became a Christian. As I knew him he was a deacon of the church, and a leader in all good work in his village. His son has been for more than twenty-two years teacher in Paulo's village.' Likoliko is below Sakaio. 'He was a great warrior; nine spear-heads were taken out of his body in fighting days. He was one of the chiefs who received and protected the first teacher. I knew him as a peace-loving citizen, noted for his industry and skill in fishing, and in making nets and canoes. In later years he was a judge of the island.' Patuki is at the top left of the picture. 'He made a name for himself by killing the teacher's pig. A teacher came from Samoa, bringing with him a pig, the first on Niue … Savage Islanders at that time were afraid of pigs. Patuki had the honour of ridding the country of this evil genius. After this he received the Gospel, and served the country as a judge.' Mose, in the lower left-hand corner, 'was the most remarkable man in the group. He was a shrewd, clever man, and one of the first to become a Christian. As deacon of the church, he served his generation, and took a full share in all public work in the land. He was always full and running over with old songs, legends and myths … and never tired of reciting them.'

Auckland War Memorial Museum Tāmaki Paenga Hira, New Zealand, MS 281 completed, was determined by the offence. It was obviously a punishment that was liberally administered as by 1859 there was reported to be a road six feet wide right around the island, fringed with coconut trees for shade. 'A missionary will find this road a great facility to his labours, as it will enable him to take a horse all round the island.'[36] Perhaps it was also a lesser evil than alternative penalties that involved flogging, or imprisonment in caves – a penalty that was particularly feared, given the association of such places with evil spirits.

The new teaching outlawing earlier practices such as war and infanticide resulted in an increase in population during the 1850s. The Samoan teachers kept a close tally of population figures for the purpose of determining the number of inquirers each station boasted and they reported these to the LMS with each visit of the mission vessel. In 1854 the total was 3000 people, rising to 4300 by 1859. Reverends Harbutt and Drummond noted in 1857 that 'there are now many instances of three generations living in the same family', and Reverend Turner commented in 1859 that women now appeared to be more numerous than men and 'we were all struck with the number of children to be seen compared with many other islands'. The population growth on such an isolated island was at odds with the common trend throughout the Pacific where the introduction of European diseases led to population decline.

The establishment of mission stations and the printing and distribution of books in the Niuean language led to economic changes. Books were paid for in kind; the main product offered in Niue was arrowroot. When the *John Williams* visited in 1857, 2000 pounds of arrowroot was loaded at Alofi and another 'large quantity' at Avatele in payment for the primer delivered in 1854. The arrowroot was sold on the open market in Apia and the proceeds were used by the LMS to defray costs.

The Samoan teachers also introduced pigs to Niue, and by the mid-1850s these animals were plentiful enough to be a regular trade item when whalers and trading vessels called. One observer noted in the early 1860s that there were many pigs on Niue but the Niueans did not often seem to eat them;[37] possibly this was because of their economic value as a trade item with Europeans and as a reciprocal exchange item with other Niueans.

In addition to the arrowroot payments made to the LMS, it became customary to give gifts of food items such as pigs, fowls, yams and coconuts to the visiting missionaries, and the ship's captain would also purchase food from the villagers. The mission teachers introduced the Samoan customs of fagai – extended family groupings which each contributed food for the pastor; and poa – an annual contribution to the pastor, at first in kind but later in money. Both systems tapped into existing notions of sharing and reciprocity that were common throughout Polynesia. All these economic developments, and the growing population, required increased production and harvesting of food crops. More and more people settled in villages near the coast, and their family land in the bush was kept for food growing. The daily journey from the villages to the bush and back with food became a feature of island life that persists today.

Twenty-seven years after the first tentative efforts by John Williams to introduce the gospel to Niue, two European missionaries stepped ashore at Alofi to hold the first communion service and carry out the first baptisms on the island. William Harbutt and George Drummond were on the return voyage to Samoa from a visit to the New Hebrides when they reached Niue on 1 August 1857. They recorded in their journal that they were 'probably the very first foreign visitors except the Samoan teachers, who ever set foot on this island [since] Captain Cook'.[38] With the exception of men from various whaling crews, they were correct.

Harbutt and Drummond came ashore on Sunday 2 August, confident now that the reception would be friendly. As they neared the shore they saw 'the beach and the neighbouring cliffs all crowded with natives' and noted with satisfaction that all were 'decently dressed'.

> *[W]e assembled under the shade of cocoa nut trees (the large chapel would not hold the vast assembly) and more than 2000 natives came to hear the words of encouragement and counsel ... after we had each addressed the assembly we baptised two children (a daughter of Paulo ... and a daughter of Peniamina). We then assembled round the table of the Lord. It was the first time these divinely appointed ordinances were ever celebrated on this island and truly it was a solemn yet delightful season to us all.*[39]

The following day the two missionaries again went ashore. They commented on the generous gifts given by the people, and the arrowroot loaded in payment for the schoolbooks previously delivered. When they left in the evening,

> *the whole population for miles around were gathered together and covered the beach and every available space in the face of the lofty cliffs on either side. Our arms were aching with the hearty shaking of hands all the way from the teacher's house to the boats; many rushed into the water to salute us again and bid us farewell.*[40]

A similar reception awaited the men at Avatele, where they called to take on more arrowroot. As they headed for Samoa, Harbutt's only regret was 'we have no missionary to carry on the work so well begun by the teachers'; but the way was now open for European missionaries based in Samoa to make regular visits and with each visit more people were baptised.[41]

When Reverend Turner visited in 1859, 11 years after his first visit, the reception was so friendly that he came ashore at Avatele and, after spending the night at the teacher's house, set out with the Samoan teachers Samuela and Amosa to walk the overland route to Alofi. 'It was heart-stirring at daylight, to hear the voice of prayer and praise proceeding from the cottages of the natives as we passed along the road.'[42] More inquirers were examined and again there were baptisms and communion. Turner concluded of the changes that had occurred on Niue: '*now* nothing would be more grateful to them than the arrival of white missionaries'. In England, the man who was to fill that position on Niue was already preparing for the voyage to the South Seas.

4. Her Britannic Majesty's Ships

To impress their minds with the dignity of our power

When Islanders on the west coast of Niue looked out towards the horizon at daylight on 6 July 1849 they saw for the first time an imposing symbol of the might of Queen Victoria's empire. There, with the southwesterly wind in its sails and under a clear blue sky, Her Britannic Majesty's ship *Havannah* came into view – a full-rigged 22-gun frigate of 950 tons with a crew of 250 men. As it came closer to the island the size of the vessel could be better appreciated, and some among the Niueans who had visited Samoa or worked on whaling vessels in the Pacific recognised the heavy guns on deck as belonging to a manuao – a man-o'-war of the Royal Navy.

With a mix of curiosity and apprehension the Niueans launched three vaka, and the four-man crews paddled to meet the imposing manuao nearly 5 miles off the coast. As they approached they noticed men standing on the decks holding long instruments up to their eyes. Fearing these might be firearms, the Niueans waved and indicated these instruments should be put away. Once the telescopes had been removed from view, they 'came boldly alongside', although they were reluctant to go on board. They did, however, hold up spears and other weapons which they had brought to barter. When they were joined by another 10 or so vaka their boldness increased, and before long the first successful encounter between Niueans and men of the Royal Navy had begun in earnest.

HMS *Havannah* was under the command of Captain John Erskine, and had recently left the Royal Naval Base in Sydney to begin a goodwill visit to the South Sea islands. This was the first such voyage to be undertaken since 'the pacification of New Zealand'[1] had freed up the navy to make regular inspections of all the islands considered to be within the British sphere of influence. The region was a large one. It extended beyond the official geographical frontiers of the British Empire to include those areas where there were trade and shipping interests.

Erskine commented in his report on the voyage that little had been done since the time of Cook to extend British acquaintance with the Pacific Islands. He felt that

This sketch of four Niueans in a vaka that appeared in John Erskine's work published in 1853 is the first known depiction of Niueans by a European. The visit took place in 1849. Typical of the time, the Niueans paddled out to the European vessel and the two parties met on the deck of the visiting ship. Alexander Turnbull Library, Wellington, New Zealand, B-K-948-23

'the illustrious Cook' had set an enlightened example in his interactions with Pacific peoples and he aimed to emulate it on this cruise. He was firm in his demand that 'no act of hostility towards any of the native inhabitants should originate with us during the cruise, but that a system of forebearance and conciliation towards them should be the rule to be observed on our part … as that best calculated to impress their minds with the dignity of our power'.[2]

Niue was the first encounter on Erskine's voyage, and hence the first opportunity for him to put his principles to the test. The encounter was brief and entirely offshore, but it appears to have been successful. Erskine noted that since the time of Reverend Williams' visit in 1830, 'these Islanders must have had a good deal of communication with passing ships … as they flocked alongside us without fear'. He gives a careful description of what he observed, looking down from the main deck of the sailing ship to the vaka below. The canoes were all of a similar construction,

> *from twenty to twenty-four feet long, made apparently of a single tree with raised washstreaks, the fore and aft parts covered over and handsomely carved. An outrigger, composed of one long spar, floating in the water parallel to the canoe, and supported by three transverse ones, forming a platform, on which lay their spears and*

> *other implements, projected on one side, making it necessary for them … to come on the weather side of the ship … Their paddles were short, concave in the blade, and beautifully shaped like a plantain-leaf. The men were in general perfectly naked, though a few wore a narrow waist-belt … they were not in any instance tattooed, and I remarked only one or two who had daubed their faces with streaks of black paint … several had their hair tied up into a large topknot … and some of the elder men … had long beards plaited and ornamented with pieces of oyster or clam shells, and a few wore moustaches.*[3]

Bartering soon began between the Niueans and the sailors, and Erskine described the items offered by each group:

> *Their articles of traffic were almost entirely weapons, viz. spears, single and double headed … all very nicely made and ornamented with a few feathers … They had also rounded staves … and what they seemed to put the highest value on, weapons … with a flat blade like that of a paddle which were, in fact, double-handed sabres: and these were carefully wrapped up in plantain-leaves, which they pulled off to display their goods in their full freshness. They had a few bananas and taro-roots, which they did not want to sell, and pieces of sugar-cane which they had apparently brought for their own refreshment.*
>
> *They refused tobacco, saying it was 'tabu' … they asked for covering for the head, and were much pleased with red worsted comforters and pieces of red cotton, which they tied on immediately as turbans. White and coloured handkerchiefs they would not look at … but the articles in most request were knives and fish-hooks, especially the latter, and black bottles were also much esteemed.*[4]

In addition to quantities of spears, Erksine bought from one canoe a 'pretty green parroquet, with a blue head and crimson breast, tied with a long string to a stick, which did not last many days'. This is the only occasion in accounts of bartering at Niue that a bird is mentioned. It was a hegakula or blue-crowned lory and it is not surprising that it lived only a short time on board HMS *Havannah,* for its habitat is the bush where it feeds on nectar, pollen and ripe fruit. The feathers were used to make girdles and headdresses, the red neck feathers being especially highly prized.[5] Possibly the Niueans recognised Erskine as a chief in his impressive naval uniform and therefore agreed to the barter.

Because of the swell running and the need to periodically fill the topsail to keep the ship off the dangerous coast, few Niueans actually came on board HMS *Havannah*. Those who did engaged in various antics with the crew – viewing a monkey kept on board, tasting wine and biscuits and dressing up in old uniform items. When the fife and drums were ordered up to play a lively air everyone joined in the dancing, while the men in the vaka around the ship beat time with their paddles.

Some Niueans watched the carpenter at work and, noting the usefulness of the chisel he had demonstrated, one snatched it up and jumped overboard. Erskine ordered a cutter to be lowered to retrieve the implement. The culprit was soon identified but paddled away quickly towards the shore, and Erskine ordered the cutter to return. Unlike earlier navigators, including Cook, he was not interested in retrieving stolen goods at any cost in order to uphold British authority.

During the course of the day the *Havannah* moved gradually northwards and as it did so groups departed and were succeeded by others. As the whalers and missionaries had found, there was no intermingling of vaka from different parts of the island, for considerable antagonism still existed. By evening it was calm and there was a full moon, so more vaka came out to barter. Erskine was anxious not to take them too far out to sea and tried various methods to persuade them to return to land. A blue light was burnt and a rocket fired in an attempt to frighten the men into returning to shore, the crew were all called inboard and the portholes closed, but the Niueans persisted in trying to exchange their last few items until the final possible moment.

In many ways the visit by HMS *Havannah* was a fleeting and superficial encounter, but it marked the start of contact between the imperial forces of Queen Victoria and the people of Niue. On this visit contact with Niueans was along a part of the coast not yet settled by mission teachers, yet it was obvious the Islanders were accustomed to bartering with Europeans. Erskine expressed confidence that if sea conditions had allowed them to land, 'I have no doubt … we might have done so without any apprehension of opposition.'[6] That supposition was not put to the test.

RIGHT: 'Indigenous people from Niue or Friendly Islands'. In 1853 the *Eugenie*, a Swedish vessel on a circumnavigation of the world to collect insect species, stopped off at Niue. The captain, Carl Skogman, did not go ashore but he allowed Niueans on board and trading took place, including pieces of hiapo. Of particular interest in the work subsequently published in Swedish and German were the lithographs of people encountered on the voyage. These sketches of four men are the first known portraits of Niueans. Their beards contain ornamental items. Other writers of the same period, including John Erskine and Frederick Mallard, also mention this: Mallard visited in 1853 and commented on 'gold sovereigns pierced by two holes and forming a pretty ornament dangling under the chin'. Alexander Turnbull Library, Wellington, New Zealand, B-K-949-304

C. S. del. Lith. Jnst. Arnz & Co Düsseldorf.

EINGEBORNE VON JNUI ODER FREUNDSCHAFTS-INSEL.

In his musings on the cruise in 1849, Erskine commented that earlier visits to Pacific islands by ships-of-war had often involved 'lamentable affrays with the natives'. He suggested that most of the atrocities that were said to have been perpetrated by the Islanders had in fact been 'provoked by acts of aggression or misconduct on the part of the white man'.[7] His comments seem prophetic, given the next encounter between a vessel of the Royal Navy and the people of Niue.

When HMS *Calliope* appeared off the west coast of the island in November 1852, the nature of the encounter was altogether different. This visit was a direct response to a report that European sailors were supposedly being held on Niue against their will. The *Calliope* arrived prepared to investigate a wrongdoing and, if necessary, mete out punishment.

The ship in distress was the sailing barque *Legerdemain*, which was reported to have been wrecked on a reef to the southeast of Niue in June 1852.[8] Working waist deep in water on the reef, the 23 crew and passengers had built a raft with timber from their wrecked vessel and, along with the three boats from the ship, had set out in search of land. They arrived off the coast of Niue after four difficult days. The men knew they had reached Savage Island, but with a heavy surf pounding the jagged coral reef they also knew a landing was impossible. The small convoy of boats and raft was being watched from the island, and vaka were soon launched. In their later accounts the sailors said that the Niueans took their raft and plundered all they could; items that were deemed useless were thrown overboard. The sailors were forced to take to the longboat; four men were in the pinnace, and contact with them was lost. The larger group of 17 men set sail in the longboat for the Navigator Islands 'in a miserable plight, having very little water, and scarcely any clothing or provisions'.[9] The whereabouts of the four men in the pinnace was uncertain, although by the time the *Calliope* arrived off the coast of Niue in November, these four were reportedly in the care of the missionary ship the *John Williams*.[10]

The captain of the *Calliope*, Sir Everard Home, heard the story of the *Legerdemain* while he was in the Fiji Islands. Hearing that 'some of the unfortunate crew had reached Savage Island, from whence it was not probable the natives (who are a very savage set) would allow them to go', the captain 'immediately … proceeded to Savage Island … for the purpose of rescuing the unfortunate seamen who had fallen into the hands of the savages'.[11] The *Calliope* arrived off the west coast of Niue, out from Alofi. It is most likely that the encounter between the shipwrecked group and Islanders had taken place off the southeast coast, near Hakupu. If Sir Everard had understood anything about Niue he would have known it was pointless trying to

Watercolour depicting the sailing frigate HMS *Calliope* in Sydney, c. 1850. The visit of HMS *Calliope* to Niue in November 1852 led to the worst encounter between Niue Islanders and the Royal Navy in the nineteenth century. Australian War Memorial, 302151

make one settlement responsible for what might have happened on another part of the island. He was, however, oblivious to island politics, and without any interpreter on board, he set about trying to ascertain the whereabouts of the missing sailors and to rescue them if, indeed, they were being held on Niue.

The account of events that was presented as part of the official record of the voyage of the *Calliope* explained how canoes came out to the ship, bartering took place, then – using some petty thieving as an excuse – the sailors seized several of the Islanders and held them below decks. Their canoes were lifted on board and the ship stood out to sea for the night. During the bartering the Islanders had presented some unusual items in exchange for fish hooks and beads – English shillings and American 20-dollar pieces – and these had 'decided the suspicions of the gallant Captain respecting the probable fate of the unfortunate shipwrecked crew'.[12] The sailors of the *Legerdemain* had removed coinage from their vessel when preparing the raft on Beveridge Reef, and they reported that this was something the Niueans had seized when they plundered the raft. In the five months that had elapsed there had obviously been some exchange on the island, for some of this coin was now in the possession of Alofi people.

The official account explained that the *Calliope* spent three days with a chief and 17 men held on board while they attempted to convey to others who came out to the vessel that there would be no further bartering and the prisoners would not be released until the white men were produced. At the end of three days no progress had been made and the decision was made to release the prisoners, 'which was done after explaining to them that if in fact they had killed the white men we would surely hear of it, and would most likely come back and punish them'.[13] The *Calliope* left the island and the episode was supposedly closed.

However, between the time of the shipwreck in June 1852 and the visit of the *Calliope* in November 1852, another vessel had called at Niue. The *John Williams*, carrying the reverends Murray and Sunderland, had checked on the mission station at Mutalau and then, on 2 July 1852, had laid off the coast at Alofi where it was planned to open a second station. Two teachers were landed and placed in the care of the chief, Togia. The missionaries were told of a shipwrecked party that had reached the island about a fortnight before their own arrival, but 'they made the heathen part of the island. The natives spared their lives but took from them the raft they had constructed and robbed them of almost everything they possessed.'[14] The missionaries recorded that 17 men had continued to Samoa by longboat and a smaller group had apparently headed for Tonga.

When Murray and Sunderland returned to Niue on 1 January 1854 they were told of the visit by the *Calliope* 14 months earlier. They were extremely concerned that the account they were given was to a large extent at variance with the official account already reported by newspapers in New Zealand and Australia. In their journal, they recorded the affair as reported to them by the Niueans in January 1854. Vaka had gone off to the man-of-war to barter with her and some of the Niueans had stolen hatchets and knives. When this was discovered, some of the Islanders were taken prisoner. Boats were lowered and the vaka were 'scattered and broken'. Shots were fired at the people in the water and two were injured; they were forced to swim for shore, but only one made it. The *Calliope* stood off the island with about a dozen prisoners. In Alofi there was great consternation. Believing the ship was in some way connected to the mission recently established, the villagers pleaded with the Samoan mission teachers to go out to the ship and secure the release of the prisoners. The Samoans were fearful for their own safety but finally agreed to go off in a vaka. However, they failed to reach the man-of-war. The Niueans told Murray and Sunderland that when the decision was made by Sir Everard to release the prisoners, 'they were put overboard when the vessel was some distance out to sea' and were forced to swim for shore. Three men came on shore early in the morning, very much exhausted, having been in the water all night. The other nine prisoners did not make it to Alofi. Murray and Sunderland recorded:

> *Two opinions are entertained by the natives as to the cause of death. The first is that they were exhausted and drowned at sea; the other is that they swam to shore at a place called Avatele, the people of which place are hostile to the Alofi people and that they killed them as they came on shore. Be that as it may, the Alofi people made war upon Avatele and killed three of their people and wounded others.*[15]

The man who was said to have started the stealing had made it safely to shore, but he too fell victim to the anger of the Alofi people. He was sent out to sea in a small vaka to perish there, a common punishment for serious misdemeanours. There was one further casualty. One of the Niueans who had perished was Togia, the chief of Alofi and the man who had enabled the mission to be set up in his village. When his wife learned that he had been either drowned or murdered, she committed suicide by throwing herself off a precipice into the sea. As Murray and Sunderland commented,

> *Thus by the conduct and mismanagement of those on board the man of war, 15 individuals have lost their lives, the people have been aroused to war and great difficulties have been thrown in the way of the [mission] teachers in the accomplishment of their benevolent work among the people.*[16]

Perhaps it was this last consequence – the threat to the successful establishment of an LMS mission station in Alofi – that prompted Murray and Sunderland to launch an attack on the Royal Navy and the damage it had done on Niue. Furthermore, it was now known that no sailors had been murdered: all those in the longboat made it safely to Samoa, and those in the pinnace to Sydney via Futuna and the Fiji Islands.[17] The two men began their correspondence in the *Samoan Reporter* and soon moved to the *Sydney Morning Herald*. By June 1854 there was considerable debate about the *Calliope* incident, made more emotional by the fact that in the meantime, Sir Everard Home had died and was therefore unable to answer the 'grossly exaggerated statements' made against his actions at Niue.

The arguments presented by Murray and Sunderland differed little from their journal report. They were answered by the new captain of the *Calliope*, J.C. Fitzgerald, who neither knew nor had served with Home; and the chaplain of the vessel, G.E. Carwithen, who had served with Home and had been present during the incident off Niue. These letters were responded to by Reverend William Mills, who had for many years been stationed at the LMS mission in Apia.

Carwithen spoke of the 30 or so canoes that came off to the ship as soon as they arrived, and how eager the people were to barter:

> *[T]he noise on deck was deafening, and in this clamorous fair there were also most amusing instances of theft being committed ... with a skill and cunning that would have equalled a London[er] adept in the art; but these petty thefts were taken no notice of until more valuable articles caught their attention ... the master's sextant was quickly pounced upon and thrown through one of the ports to some watchful friend who, in his canoe, seized the stolen property.*[18]

Mills responded by questioning the orderliness and control on board the man-of-war, and wondering why bartering had been allowed to proceed at all if the purpose of the visit was to investigate whether any English sailors were being held on the island. In the attempt to retrieve the stolen sextant, shots were fired and one man sank; another had his arm shattered. Surely, Mills reasoned, if there had been any Europeans on the island, the actions out at the *Calliope* would have placed them in grave danger and their fate would now have been decided by the desire for revenge.

Mills was also disappointed that Carwithen had omitted two important details. When the prisoners were put overboard, how far out to sea was the *Calliope*? 'I only wish the chaplain had stated [this] ... and also, *how many* canoes there were for conveying them ashore.'[19] There was mention of a native teacher who was on the *Calliope* and refused to go overboard like the rest but instead stayed on board and was offloaded at his own request when the ship reached Rotuma. Mills insisted this man, Ioane, was not a native teacher but was known to the missionaries, and he had described the ship as being so far out that he knew he would have drowned if he had gone overboard; being carried away to an unknown fate was the lesser of two evils.

Others also put their pens to work to debate the *Calliope* incident. One writer suggested the men of the *Legerdemain* were put at great risk when they approached the island, and concluded that 'the South Sea Island savages require at times chastisement as well as any other piratical wretches such as the Malays.'[20] The well-known Sydney-based Presbyterian minister, politician and activist John Dunmore

Lang referred to the incident as an 'outrage' committed by the *Calliope*; according to him, the only reason there were not more people speaking out against it in Sydney was the fear of causing offence to Government House and the Royal Navy. Lang warned that if the gentlemen of the *Calliope* could not give a satisfactory account of the facts recorded in Mr Murray's narrative, 'they may rest assured they will hear of it some of these days from the House of Commons'.[21]

Lively newspaper debate aside, nothing more was heard of the visit of the *Calliope* to Niue. Reverends Hardie and Sunderland, when they visited Niue in November 1854, found that 'the hostilities and bad feelings which took place after the visit of HMS *Calliope* had subsided';[22] and such was their joy at the progress made by the mission that the earlier dangers to their native teachers were now forgotten. Certainly the House of Commons at Westminster did not pursue investigations against such a worthy naval officer as Sir Everard Home, who was eulogised in Sydney and London. The incident was over; but it marked the first, though certainly not the last, clash that would occur between officials of the LMS and government officials as they vied for control on Niue.

It was 10 years before another of the ships of the Royal Navy included Niue in its cruise itinerary, and when HMS *Fawn* headed that way from Auckland in May 1862 Thomas Hood made no reference to the *Calliope*.[23]

HMS *Fawn* was a new style of frigate, powered not only by sails but also by motor. When it arrived 4 miles out from Avatele, the vaka that came out had trouble catching the ropes thrown to them, for the vessel was still doing 6 knots. Once the sails were shortened the vaka caught up, and soon there were up to 20 of them alongside. Hood commented that the men were 'quite sufficiently attired for the climate'. One came on board 'decently attired in a clean fringed mat … another [in a] kilt of green leaves of the Dracaena':[24] the influence of the mission teachers was evident. The Niueans set up 'little shops all along the deck' with pigs, plantains, bananas, malay apples, coconuts, spears and other articles of commerce. They were keen to trade and good at business, 'gained no doubt by their intercourse with whalers, sailing under the "Stars and Stripes", which we found were now constantly in the habit of coming here for supplies'.[25] The items most sought after by the Niueans were bright pieces of cotton, fish hooks, knives and trousers, and they also asked for Jew's harps,[26] but there were none on board.

When a Samoan teacher came on board the *Fawn* the officers were surprised to learn there was an English missionary residing in the next bay. There had been talk before their arrival of attempting a landing and becoming the first white men to

The screw sloop HMS *Fawn* somewhere in the United Kingdom, c. 1861. The visit to Niue by HMS *Fawn* in May 1862 was a friendly visit for all, although as the first steam-powered vessel ever seen in Niue waters it greatly alarmed the Niueans when it moved without unfurling the sails. Seeing the screw churning up the water and steam coming from the funnel, Niueans on board leapt into the sea.
Australian War Memorial, 302196

walk on the island. Now it seemed there was already a European on the island and the officers determined to head for Alofi Bay to meet him. The engines were started and, with steam coming from the funnel and the screw turning, the ship began moving forward with the sails still furled. This caused astonishment and alarm, and many of the visitors jumped overboard and swam to their vaka. Hood noted that this could also have been because they did not like going beyond the limits of their own village shore, but this man-of-war was obviously different from those that had previously visited Niue.

The *Fawn* rounded Halagigie Point and entered Alofi Bay, and as they approached the settlement they could see the white cottage and church of the mission. Thomas Hood was in the cutter, which was lowered and headed for shore. It was met by a vaka bringing out a letter to Captain Cator from Reverend Lawes, who 'had come out from England ten months ago with his young wife, to take charge of this isolated mission'.[27] The cutter reached the edge of the reef and the occupants were carried ashore on the shoulders of Niueans. Everyone shook hands and they were given the warmest welcome. They were not far from Opaahi, where James Cook had made his third and final attempt at landing nearly 90 years previously.

The visitors from the naval vessel had expected to find an island uninhabited by any European. Instead they were entertained in a well-built, well-furnished house by a well-educated Englishman who was obviously delighted to meet fellow countrymen.

> *Pleasant surprises are amongst the most agreeable things in life. I don't remember ever being better pleased than with our reception at Savage Island. It was scarcely possible to realise the fact of our actually being there, as we sat round Mr Lawes's comfortable tea-table, in a well furnished house ... There being no anchorage, Captain Cator was unable to gratify our entertainer's pressing wish that we should remain another day ... At sunset we reluctantly bade them farewell [and] left the shore ...*[28]

The visit of HMS *Fawn* was important for two reasons. The navy was made aware that there were English residents on Niue, and that there was a possible landing place. From now on visits by British ships were more regular and had less of a novelty factor, both for the Niueans and for the men of the Royal Navy. They became an established feature in the contact history of the island and, before long, would bring officials anxious to maintain and extend British authority in the region.

PART B.

EMPIRE

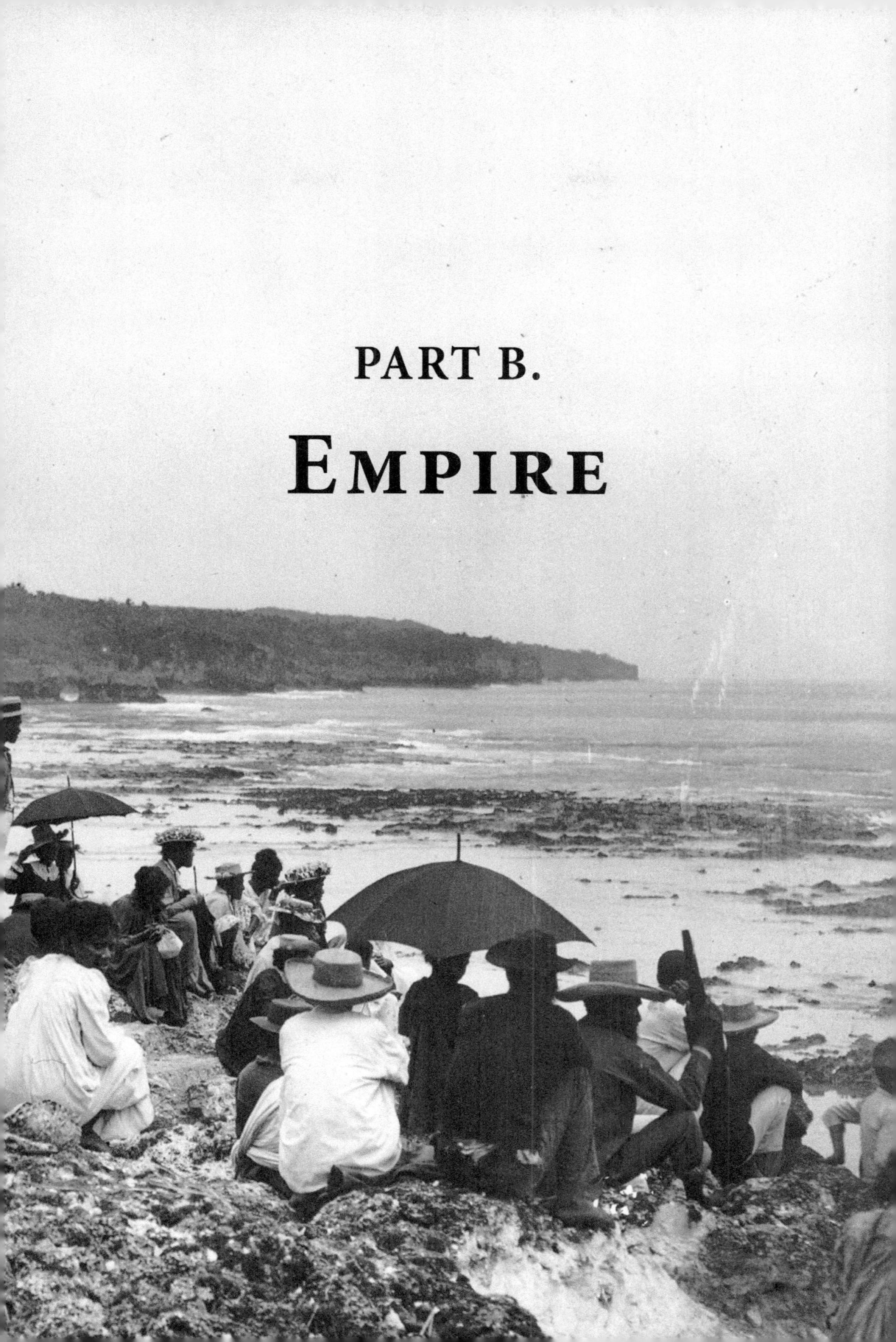

5. European settlement

One cannot but feel lonely on an island like this

The isolation of Niue and the difficulty in landing there made it unique in the Pacific in terms of European settlement. By 1860, when large European communities were established in all the main island groups of the Pacific, there was still not a single European resident on Niue. That was soon to change, but over the next 30 years only five European men, four of them with wives, ventured to Niue to settle: two English brothers as missionaries, and three men – an American and two Englishmen – as traders.

The first to arrive was William George Lawes, whom we met in the previous chapter. He was sent by the London Missionary Society in response to the call from the Samoan mission that Niue was now ready and in need of an English missionary to advance the work of the church on the island. Inexperienced but fired with conviction, Lawes was only 21 years old when he set out with his equally young wife, Fanny. Accompanied by the Reverend and Mrs Pratt, experienced missionaries from the Samoa station, Lawes and his wife came ashore at Avatele from the mission ship *John Williams* on 20 August 1861.

A portrait of William George Lawes in later life, published in 1909 in the LMS biography of him by Joseph King. Born in July 1839, Lawes was 21 years old when he sailed from England for Niue in November 1860 with Fanny, his wife of two weeks. The young couple were the first Europeans to settle on Niue and they remained until 1872.

Alexander Turnbull Library, Wellington, New Zealand, B-K-1093-352

After a stay of six or seven months to help the young missionaries settle in to their new life, the Pratts returned to Apia. George and Fanny Lawes, now with their first child, were at last alone on a South Sea island such as George had dreamed of when he made the decision to become a missionary. That had been three years earlier when, at a Sunday school gathering in Reading, England, Lawes had heard Reverend William Gill from the Rarotongan mission give an address. Gill had with him a Rarotongan named Isaiah, and Lawes was so moved by meeting him that he made up his mind there and then that he would serve as a missionary in the South Seas. George and Fanny Lawes were accepted onto the island with the blessing of the Niueans: they wanted an English missionary among them and they did all they could to help the young family.

After six years working alone to expand the LMS presence on Niue, George pleaded for another European missionary to assist him. The directors of the LMS in London finally agreed and sent reinforcements in the form of George's younger brother Francis (Frank) Edwin Lawes and his wife Sarah, both 24 years old when they arrived at the mission. The Lawes brothers worked together on Niue for four years, then in 1872 George and his family returned to England on furlough. While there, they were redirected to begin the first LMS mission in New Guinea. They never returned to Niue, although it remained dear to them: 'we have buried two [children] on Savage Island and the island is doubly dear to us on that account'.[1] Frank and Sarah continued their work on Niue for a staggering 42 years before retiring to London in 1910. During that time no other missionary lived on the island, apart from replacements during furloughs that the Lawes family took to England. The name Lawes became synonymous with the LMS on Niue.

At the outset, when George and Fanny Lawes arrived, Niue was something of an LMS 'laboratory'. Where else did an English missionary settle to spread the word and not have to contend with other Europeans behaving badly? No idle, blaspheming sailors waiting for the next vessel, no traders tempting the locals into debt, no merchants offering the demon drink, no beachcombers or other arrivals seeking the pleasures of the flesh. No other missionary society attempted to establish itself on Niue during the nineteenth century,[2] so there was no competition for converts as was common in other locations. The LMS truly had the ideal set of conditions in which to build on the work already carried out by the Samoan mission teachers over the previous decade.

It could have been the setting for an autocracy by the Lawes brothers, but they were both sympathetic men, passionate in their religious beliefs but very much aware that the cultural setting was not their own and that much of the time they were the students. They and their wives were all good listeners, wise teachers, willing students, hard workers, humane and humble people. The Lawes name came to be revered on the island.

When George and Fanny Lawes arrived on Niue a house had already been prepared for them in Alofi. Although it was described as 'a native built house', it impressed Thomas Hood when he visited 10 months after the Lawes' arrival.

> *[It is] a most excellent house, eighty feet long, with verandah and venetians … erected under directions of the Samoan teachers. The roof inside is quite an elaborate work of art; the thatch, neatly stitched down upon battens closely laid together, resting upon round rafters, most ingeniously fitted, has a very pleasing effect. Not a single nail is used in the building, everything being tied with cocoa-nut sinnet. The rooms are divided by thick walls six feet high, without ceilings, so the whole of the ornamental roof is visible. [They] had just finished and presented to Mr Lawes a sofa, nicely made and inlaid with … birds and fishes in tortoiseshell and mother-of-pearl.*[3]

By January 1863 the Lawes family was well settled. Glass windows had been shipped to Niue to add to the comfort of the house; and a second son had just arrived. Nevertheless, there were times of loneliness, especially during the cyclone season, as George described in his diary:

> ***12 Jan 1863*** *The wind increased during the night and this morning there was every indication of a gale of wind. This afternoon we had our house guarded with long poles to keep the thatch down and prepared for the worst. The sea is running mountain high, the wind increasing and the barometer falls. Poets may sing of the majestic beauty of a storm but there is not much poetry in living a few yards from the sea … one cannot but feel lonely on an island like this with the sea roaring and the wind howling and raging.*[4]

Within four years a larger and more elaborate house was built in Alofi. George 'had to do all the architectural superintending and measuring. The people cheerfully did the work.'[5] This was typical of the situation of most LMS missionaries by the 1860s. Their standard of living was high and, in many cases, far superior to what they could have expected in England. When Frank and Sarah arrived in March 1868, they lived in the 'native built house' in Alofi until they were acclimatised, then they went to live in Makefu. They moved back to Alofi to the large mission house after George left Niue.

The mission house was the largest home on the island but many comforts were of course lacking. Newspapers and specialty foods were especially missed, so it is not surprising that an unexpected gift from a passing vessel should warrant a mention in a diary or a letter. George recorded the receipt of three Sydney newspapers, a ham, preserved meats, fruit and bottled porter from a vessel in early 1863. A few months later 'two pairs of fine geese' were received from a 'very kind captain'. In another letter Lawes pleads for magazines, even a few months old, for 'we are in a chronic state of literary starvation here'.[6] When the HMS *Fawn* visited in 1862 Thomas Hood noted:

> *We were glad to be able to supply them with late English news, which one can well imagine must be most refreshing to people so isolated from the world. Now and then a whaler calls in and they get some American papers. A few weeks since they obtained a Boston journal, printed in 1834, something new, no doubt, in its way. It must be most tantalising to see, as has often happened more than once, ships sailing past without ever having any communication.*[7]

On several occasions when a ship passed by, a vaka or two were dispatched to try to intercept the vessel and pass on mail, for correspondence with the LMS and especially with family was the lifeline that kept the Lawes family going.

The role of the sole English missionary on the island encompassed a multitude of tasks:

> *[H]e must be nurse, when there is sickness within his own home; doctor, when there is illness in the homes of the natives; caterer in ordering his yearly supplies; accountant, in drawing up … the yearly expenditure; professor, in preparing … theological lectures for his students; architect and clerk of works, when buildings are to be erected; peacemaker, in domestic misunderstandings; host, when travellers call; governor-general, when chiefs want advice about the affairs of state; moderator, when Churches want pastors; correspondent for English Churches, Sunday schools, and personal subscribers; dentist and surgeon, school inspector and registrar-general of births, deaths and marriages.*[8]

The Lawes brothers were both fortunate in their choice of wives, and had long and successful marriages. Fanny and Sarah worked tirelessly to support their husbands. As well as bearing and raising their children (and both buried children on the island), they maintained a household where visitors were warmly received, they taught the wives of the trainee mission teachers and ran Sunday school, they ministered to the sick, they wrote material for LMS publications, they received and distributed bales of clothing from congregations in Britain and Australia; and later, they coped with the inevitable need for their children to leave them and travel back to school in England. And they did all this with equanimity and grace.

The Lawes brothers were based in Alofi, but as missionaries in charge of the LMS mission on Niue it was also important to visit the other villages around the island,

Francis (Frank) Edwin Lawes, missionary in charge of the LMS mission on Niue. Frank worked for the first four years, 1868–72, alongside his older brother George, and then took sole charge of the mission from 1872 until he retired to London in 1910. He died in 1918. He was greatly respected by the Niuean people. Courtesy of the Lawes family, London

Sarah Lawes, wife of Reverend Frank Lawes, was an important part of the Lawes team on Niue. She worked tirelessly for the LMS and came to be greatly loved by the people of Niue. Back in London after 1910 she had children and grandchildren around her and she was also very active visiting Niuean soldiers in hospitals during World War I. She died in 1917. Courtesy of the Lawes family, London

give support to the work of the mission teachers, check the work of the schools, prepare inquirers for admission to the church and perform any other tasks that were needed. The visit around the island took place once or twice a year, lasted for approximately five weeks and usually involved the whole family:

> *Our procession consisted of dear Fan in a fata – a thing not unlike a stretcher – lying down with her little chick, carried by 4 men, Harry in a box cushioned and with a pole tied on, carried by 2 men, myself on horseback and a hundred or two of men and boys to carry our boxes – relieving each other in carrying the fata.*[9]

After the arrival of Frank and Sarah the combined families made the circuit.

> *We are quite a large family and are making quite a Royal procession of it ... The order for our procession is as follows. Ally is carried in a fata, Frank on our old 3 mile an hour horse, Fan on our young 5 mile an hour horse and your humble servant on foot with gun. Harry on foot, Farani on a boy's back and Freddy on his nurse's back.*[10]

Every village made a great effort to welcome the missionaries and their families. They were accommodated in the homes of the mission teachers; as George explained,

> *we have not to sleep on the ground in wretched native huts. Our teachers vie with each other in making articles of European furniture for our accommodation. Every teacher's house has its beds, sofas, tables, wash handstand, chairs, bookshelves, rocking chairs etc. Many of these would not disgrace an English mechanic's home.*[11]

There would be a village gathering where a great deal of gift giving took place. On one occasion 300 bundles of taro, 145 branches of coconuts, 47 bunches of bananas, 201 ovens of cooked food, 13 pigs and 10 bundles of sugar cane were presented. This was then divided among the people, the missionaries and the mission teachers, and some was sent back to Alofi. Other gifts might include handcrafts.

> *This morning the little girls and young women brought their presents consisting of talo and new hiapo tiputas. They looked very, very interesting. The little tiny girls first and the young women behind each a new, pretty upper garment and carrying a talo or fowl – they deposited these at our feet, shook hands and then went.*[12]

Some visits were less festive, and the English missionary might be in demand as a doctor rather than preacher. On a visit to Avatele in August 1863, George Lawes noted: 'Dysentery and sickness of other kinds very prevalent. Medicine has been my chief work this week.'[13]

Island tours were the highlight of the year; most of the time the missionaries' work was centred on Alofi, in the church and the schoolhouse built on the compound that had been set aside by the locals for the use of the LMS. The Samoan teachers had set up a training institution in 1859, and taken in the first class of 15 young men for instruction. This was an important aspect of LMS strategy, and George Lawes picked up responsibility for the institution as soon as he arrived. The men were all church members and married, and they undertook training to become teachers in the villages on Niue or in outstations further afield in the Pacific.

While the English missionary directed their scripture studies, his wife instructed the teachers' wives in Bible studies, writing and arithmetic and dressmaking.

The coastal lugger *Niue*, presented to the New Guinea Mission by the people of Niue in 1891. The mountainous terrain of New Guinea made it very difficult to move from one mission station to another and it was decided a small coastal vessel, a lugger, would be best suited to moving staff and supplies around. In Niue enough money was collected to buy such a vessel and as a tribute to the 'way in which the people of Niue have shown their love for missionary work in New Guinea', the vessel was named the *Niue*. The image and description appeared in a book of missionary life and work by V.A. Barradale. Alexander Turnbull Library, Wellington, New Zealand, B-K 940-176

The five outstations on Niue gradually expanded to 11 – this made it easier for people to attend weekday services and for children to attend school.[14] As young men graduated from the institution in Alofi they gradually took over from the Samoan teachers until, in 1869, Samuela and Munamuna, the last remaining Samoan teachers, returned to Apia. The first of the Niuean teachers recorded in the LMS records – Nemaia, Tavita and Solomona – were out in villages by 1866.

In 1866 the first two men left for further training at the Malua Institute in Apia. 'We take a deep interest in these two young men, the first from Niue to carry the gospel into other lands,' wrote George Lawes to the LMS.[15] Fataaiki and his wife Loata were sent to the Union Islands (Tokelau), and Sionepaea and his wife Manapule went to Niutao in the Lagoon Islands (Tuvalu).[16] The Presbyterian mission in the New Hebrides requested Niuean mission teachers, and Solomona and Iona left in 1870 to take up positions on small islands to the east of Tanna.[17] The main contribution of Niuean mission teachers to other parts of the Pacific was to the mission set up by George Lawes in New Guinea. The link with Lawes meant a steady trickle of teachers and funds that continued well into the twentieth century. In addition, as growing numbers of Niueans began moving to other areas of the Pacific as indentured labour, institution graduates were sent to work among those communities in Apia, Malden Island and Flint Island.[18]

As well as the training institution there were numerous other classes run by the Lawes in Alofi, and in each village classes for children were run by the mission teachers. Although attendance at school was sporadic and only for an hour or two daily, the literacy levels on Niue rose steadily. Reading and writing were highly prized skills and there was competition for places in classes and a constant demand for writing and reading materials. The missionaries were indefatigable in their appeals to churches in Britain for support in fostering the schools. Sunday schools would often adopt a particular mission, and those that supported the mission in Niue received regular news from Reverend or Mrs Lawes, aimed at encouraging the contributions. The Redfern LMS in Birmingham and the Campbeltown Sunday school in Argyll, Scotland, were two groups that adopted the Niue mission as the target of their fundraising. When George Lawes set up a weekly writing instruction class in Alofi for 35 young men from around the island, he wrote to the young people of Redfern: 'some of them come ten miles – how would you like to walk twenty miles for a writing lesson!'[19] Frank Lawes continued this class, and in 1891 he set up a boarding school in Alofi to cater for these boys. Because of the shortage of paper and ink, the missionaries had to choose which children could use these materials; others had to work with slates: 'Those chosen hold their heads a little higher.'[20]

As literacy levels increased, so did the demand for the biblical works that were being translated into Niuean. The New Testament, *Maveheaga Foou*, was especially popular and when a new supply of copies arrived on the mission ship there was great excitement. 'The first who got them did not wait until they got home before they began to read them but sat down in our yard in groups to read and listen.'[21] Writing was popular too, and a flourishing letter service developed around the island. 'Heaps of letters are continually being sent from village to village, but … they are often … scratched on a cocoanut leaf, some of the better ones are written on paper with a pencil.'[22]

This engraving accompanied an article in *The Juvenile Missionary Magazine* of 1 June 1869. It was drawn by someone unfamiliar with Niue but imagining what it looked like from the description given by Mrs Lawes. The people came early to Alofi for the Mē, or annual gathering, bearing their contribution of over 13,000 lbs of cotton, wrapped in mats. Others carried great baskets of cooked food, sugarcane, bananas, coconuts and babies. Once they were in Alofi, people changed into their best clothes and the church services began. Mrs Lawes wrote: 'I wish you could have heard the singing. They sang a translation of "Beautiful Zion" and "Around the Throne of God in Heaven".' After the meeting was over came the feasting. 'It is a grand day on Savage Island.' British Library Board General Reference Collection, P.P.913.b.

The constant work by the Lawes to raise money for the Niue mission and teachers and for the worldwide work of the LMS culminated each year in the Mē – the annual gathering held to accept donations from all the villages. The first one was held in May 1863, though the timing gradually changed to August or September. The Mē was a most important gathering for the island. It was usually held in Alofi or Uhomotu (Tuapa), but sometimes also in Avatele. Every village brought their contribution in copra, fungus, arrowroot and cotton. This was accepted by the missionaries, who then arranged for the produce to be sold in Apia, Sydney or Auckland. The proceeds went to the LMS regional headquarters which had been established in Sydney to help maintain and expand its network of mission stations throughout the Pacific. The amount varied from year to year, depending on such factors as rainfall, hurricanes and market prices. The value of the Niue contribution ranged from £45 in 1863 to around £850 in 1873, with an average take of between £350 and £550.[23]

The economic burden on the Niue people was considerable, especially as the contribution was in addition to the food contribution for the Mē gathering and the burden of supporting their village teacher and family, purchasing their books and clothing, contributing to the costs of the vaka lotu, the mission vessel, and building and maintaining the church, schoolhouse and teacher's house in each village. Competition between villages was still very strong and this worked in the LMS's favour. In 1873 Frank Lawes wrote:

> *[T]he people of … Liku have for two years past been collecting fungus, they were most anxious to be first on the list of contributors. Hakupu was equally ambitious of the trophy but Liku gained the day, their contributions being £300 (population 420) and those of Hakupu £257 (population 700).*[24]

The competition also meant there was constant building work going on in the villages. When Frank and Sarah Lawes returned in 1882 from their first furlough in England, material progress was everywhere evident.

> *The first public work which Mr Lawes performed was to open a new school house in Alofi 97x24, a fine building of native material and construction. At Makefu – a new chapel finished and opened. Uhomotu – the chapel had been altered and renovated. Tamahatokula – a good house had been built for the teacher. Mutalau – the chapel had been enlarged.*[25]

Progress reports like this were regular features of the annual report to headquarters in Sydney, with mention of glass windows and French doors being purchased in Auckland and Sydney for the churches in Liku and Tamalagau, stone chapels being erected in Hakupu and Avatele, bells being bought in England for Alofi and Fatiau, and an extremely large mat being woven in Tamakautoga to match the size of the chapel.[26]

In each of the villages the LMS also appointed constables and judges, and representatives were chosen to meet in Alofi each month for a Fono, established by the LMS. It was 'half parliament and half law court. Nothing was too great or too small for its attention. Has a strong man encroached on a widow's yam patch … has a villager from Avatele been rude to a visitor from Tuapa.'[27] In these monthly deliberations the English missionary was adamant that his role was merely to give advice when requested.

By the 1880s the LMS network was very well established on Niue, but Frank Lawes had concerns. Each of the 11 villages now had its own ordained Niuean pastor as well as several native preachers, 28 in all, and they were beginning to show

This image of the church in Alofi appeared in the *Chronicle of the LMS* on 1 December 1892 to accompany an article entitled 'A short sketch of the Niue mission' written by Reverend Frank Lawes, who was home on furlough at the time. He had reopened the church in Alofi in early 1891 after repairs necessitated by extensive damage in the 1889 cyclone, and would have taken the photograph himself. The church in Alofi dated from the mid-1850s and although it was damaged on several occasions it survived until the 1959 cyclone. The original Alofi church was a landmark and featured in many photos, especially as most ceremonies took place on the green in front. The major change over the years was the replacement of the huge thatched roof with corrugated iron.

British Library Board General Reference Collection, P.P.950

independence from the English missionary in Alofi. Lawes doubted the ability of these pastors to undertake some of their duties, especially the admission of new members to the church. When the teacher Jeremia died in 1887, Lawes saw this as a notable break with the past, for 'he was the only survivor of those who met Mr Williams and Mr Barff when they called at Niue in 1830. He was received into the church by Mr Stallworthy in 1858.'[28] The younger teachers who were being ordained did not have these links, and perhaps Lawes felt there was less respect among them for the English missionaries. Certainly when he went on his second furlough from 1892 to 1894 he arranged for a replacement missionary to come to Niue,[29] something that had not been done during his first furlough from 1880 to 1882.

Mission teachers to New Guinea

THE CHURCHES IN NIUE developed strong links with the LMS mission in New Guinea, beginning in 1874 when the first Niuean mission teachers were sent from the training institution in Alofi to help their beloved George Lawes. Lawes was the first European to live at Port Moresby in New Guinea – just as he had been on Niue – and he started the LMS mission there in 1874. In keeping with LMS practice, teachers trained in places that were already Christianised were sent further afield to help spread the word on other islands.

New Guinea was the westernmost place in the Pacific where the LMS became established. The teachers sent from the Cook Islands, Niue and Samoa on board the vaka lotu the *John Williams* became known as South Sea island mission teachers. Once there, they faced many difficulties and dangers.

> *They go to a land 2000 miles or more away from home. They have hard and strange languages to learn. They run the risk of catching the terrible New Guinea fever [malaria]. They have to leave their little children behind in Samoa, because the climate is so bad. The people among whom they live are savages and cannibals. Many who have gone have died at their work, some have been cruelly murdered. But the supply has never failed.*[30]

In the first group from Niue there were five teachers – Isaako, Viliamu, Talima, Tufugalei and Siaosi – and their wives.[31] They travelled to Port Moresby along with six Rarotongan missionary couples. George Lawes reported that although the land was higher and swamp free around Port Moresby and the missionaries therefore believed they would escape malaria, it was in fact anything but healthy. When the Rarotongan and Niuean mission teachers arrived, they soon succumbed to malarial fever. Several of the Rarotongans died and all the Niueans were ill.

It was something of a lottery as to whether Niueans, and other South Sea island teachers, lived or died. Isaako served for 18 years, but died on the voyage back to Niue. Others lasted only days or weeks. Hatapu and his wife both died within a short time of their arrival in 1885. Tamatoa and his wife went in 1893 and he died of fever within 10 days of arrival.[32] At the LMS mission and training institution at Vatorata, on the coast southeast of Port Moresby, a memorial church was built; a tablet inside reads: 'This church is erected to the Glory of God in memory of the South Sea Islanders who came to New Guinea as missionaries and died in faithful service 1871–1899.' Ten stained-glass windows list the names of 82 South Sea Islanders who had died by this time.

On Niue all the village churches supported the mission in New Guinea. A village would be especially active if one of its own was going to serve, and food and other items would be prepared for the voyage. In 1876 the LMS recorded that over 10 tons of arrowroot was sent on the *John Williams* with the new teachers.

The rugged terrain of New Guinea meant that overland travel was extremely difficult or impossible, and the LMS realised that a small coastal vessel was needed to provide a link between the various mission stations on the main island and the outlying islands. The Niuean congregations contributed generously to this appeal, and a sailing vessel, the *Niue*, was purchased in 1891 (see photo, page 95).

Left: 'Hipa and Sifa, Niueans, Boku', Papua New Guinea, c.1908–10. Portrait by H.P. Schlencker.
Below left: 'Sifa (Niuean), two native girls and children'. Group portrait by H.P. Schlencker of members of mission, Kalaigolo, Papua New Guinea, c.1908–10.

Henry Schlencker, an Australian, served with the LMS in Papua New Guinea from 1890 until 1926. With his wife, Mary, he worked in the Boku and Kalaigolo areas, and had South Sea mission teachers assisting him. It is unusual to find a photo where the island of origin is given for a mission teacher and even more unusual to find the individuals named. Hipa and Sifa (Sifahemotu) from Hikutavake served in New Guinea from 1905 to 1907. They returned to Niue for health reasons. School of Oriental and African Studies, University of London, CWM/LMS/Papua/Photographs/Box 6, file 7

George and Fanny Lawes remained in New Guinea for over 30 years, despite personal losses. As well as losing several of their South Sea island staff, they suffered family tragedy too: their youngest son died of fever there, and their son Farani died in New Guinea in 1894 while he was working as a government officer. They left Port Moresby to settle in Sydney in 1906, and George died the following year.

Despite the difficulties, Niuean mission teachers continued to volunteer for service in New Guinea, with some gaps, until 1953, when the final two teachers, Sialetoa and Hunuki Motuvale, travelled west to serve the LMS.

Even more importantly, Frank Lawes was now working not in a 'laboratory' but in the real world. Traders had arrived on the island, and they provided competition with the church for the produce grown. More and more men were going offshore as indentured labourers and were returning with all manner of bad habits. The process had begun during the time of George Lawes but change was now speeding up and the LMS missionary was losing at least some of his hold over the Islanders.

Niue did not have products that were in demand in the European world, which meant the island did not attract any attention from traders – until the growth of the copra industry. In the wider Pacific, trade in coconut oil was slow until the early 1840s, when a technique was perfected for using the oil in the manufacture of soap and candles. The demand now increased but there were still difficulties. Producing oil from coconut flesh required heavy pressing equipment onshore, and ships collecting the oil had to carry barrels for storage. Some whaling vessels collected oil, but ships coming to the Pacific expressly for the purpose of purchasing coconut oil had to travel out with a cargo of empty barrels, which was not economical. The solution to this problem was to take not the pressed oil but the dried coconut flesh – copra – which could be loaded into the holds of vessels that had brought general cargo to the Pacific. At the port of destination the copra was then pressed, the oil extracted and the waste turned into oil cakes for cattle feed.

Most of the copra went to Europe and the trade proved lucrative, despite the loss of copra during the voyage due to the ravages of rats and beetles. The company that was most successful in this trade was the German firm of Godeffroy & Son, based in Hamburg. This company established Pacific headquarters in Apia around 1857 and developed a vast network throughout the Pacific. Traders were sent to islands and atolls, large and small, and at regular intervals the company vessel called to collect the copra that had been dried. The traders were of all nationalities; they were advised to take a wife with them, and they were given building materials for a storehouse and stock of trade to put in it. No salary was paid. The company would 'trust a man with so much goods and expect of him … so much produce at a fixed rate'. They were advised to 'give no assistance to missionaries by word or deed (beyond what is demanded by common humanity), but wheresoever you may find them, use your best influence with the natives to obstruct and exclude them'.[33] The reason for this advice was that the traders made the greatest profit when trading in glass beads, tomahawks and tobacco, but the missionaries encouraged Islanders to demand payment in piece goods to clothe themselves and in coin, in order to contribute to the church.

Frank and Sarah Lawes with four of their children and their Niuean helpers in the mission house garden. Closest to the children is a Niuean woman who may be the helper taken by the Lawes to England when they went on furlough in 1880–82. She appeared in the England census of 1881 as Linfala Hegafana, 46 years old, of Savage Island. The photo was possibly taken when the Lawes family returned from furlough as they brought with them a new baby, Louisa, born in England. This would mean the other girls in the photo are Winifred, Frances and Margaret. Frank and Sarah Lawes had 10 children, nine born on Niue. One died when very young and is buried on Niue.

Courtesy of the Lawes family, London

The association between Niue and Godeffroy & Son began in the early 1860s with a visit by a trading vessel up to three times a year; and in 1866 the company placed the first European trader on Niue[34] as its agent. His name was H.W. Patterson and he was described as 'American, with a Prussian bearing'.[35] Little is known of him except that he came with a wife, who died and was buried on the coast at Alofi, and two children whom he later dispatched to Apia and Sydney for their education. At some point he returned to Samoa and acquired a new wife. He seems to have held himself aloof from the local community and was seen by many as rather eccentric. There are stories of Patterson claiming to be the American consul in Niue and flying the Stars and Stripes in front of his store in Alofi. The Niueans reportedly tore down the flag and made items of clothing from it.[36] There is also a story of him challenging the trader E.O. Nicholas to a duel when Nicholas refused to let Patterson, who was already married, propose to his daughter Eunice.[37] Patterson's business on Niue eventually failed and, saddled with considerable debt, he committed suicide in 1899.

The significance of Patterson's arrival on Niue was the threat to the economic monopoly of the LMS. In his annual report for 1866 George Lawes noted that the contribution from the people to the Mē had been less than the previous year:

> *[A] fortnight before our meeting a schooner came from Samoa bringing an agent from the German firm there to reside on Niue to buy up cotton from the natives. They had long been without an opportunity to get clothing and could not resist the temptation of new pretty prints. They divided their cotton taking half for cloth and reserving half for the mission meeting. We cannot regret this but rather feel thankful for the spirit of liberality they have shown in bringing half they possessed to the cause of Christ.*[38]

It was a double-edged sword. The missionaries wanted the people suitably clothed and the trader provided the cotton fabric necessary for this. Trade might also stimulate 'industry' among the people – a desirable quality in Christians. However, it meant there was less to give to the mission; and Lawes also assumed the presence of a store meant 'we must expect that temptations will rise from it'.[39] When Frank Lawes sent in his report in 1870 he noted that there was the promise of a splendid crop of cotton 'as the people have been in every part of the island largely cultivating [it]', but he also noted that 'of late a mercenary spirit has begun more generally to manifest itself'.[40]

For the Niueans, the arrival of a trader taught them some important lessons in economics. When Patterson began buying cotton, prices were high on the international market because the American Civil War had severely interrupted the cotton industry in the southern states. The early 1860s were therefore boom years for Pacific cotton,[41] but by the late 1860s the price was falling. In order to buy from the stores and provide for the church, the Islanders turned increasingly to arrowroot, copra and fungus – a crop that was collected in the forests, dried and sold as a medicinal product in China.

Patterson's monopoly on Niue was short-lived. In January 1867 the mission ship *John Williams* was wrecked on the coast near Makefu, and among the crew stranded on the island for several months was a 35-year-old Englishman, Robert Henry Head. By the time a vessel arrived to transport people to Apia, Head had made up his mind to stay on Niue. He had struck up a friendship with Frank and Sarah

The wreck of the mission ship *John Williams II*, 1867

THE SECOND mission ship *John Williams* was on its maiden voyage in the Pacific in late 1866, early 1867 when it was wrecked on the reef off Niue. The account of its misfortune illustrates the difficulty for captains dependent solely on windpower. There were several missionaries on board the ship, and George Lawes was watching events unfold from the shore.

The letters these men wrote to their employer, the LMS, back in London, give a graphic account of events.[46] There were a large number of men, women and children on board, as the *John Williams* had already visited the Loyalty Islands off the main island of New Caledonia, and the French authorities had insisted the LMS remove the Samoan and Rarotongan mission teachers and their families who had previously been left there; there were 42 of them, making a total of 72 men, women and children on the vessel.

Excerpts from the letter tell the story:

> *For several days it was difficult or impossible to load or unload. The surf was heavy and the winds high. On the morning (of Tuesday 8 January) there was a light breeze off the land and the sea was much down though still rough in the boat opening. A boat came in with the remainder of our goods but they had to be landed by canoe. About 6pm it was dead calm ... we had very little fear for the safety of the ship she was so well out.* – Rev. Lawes on Niue[47]

> *When we returned to the ship in the evening no one suspected the slightest danger for a nice breeze was coming from the land which had it continued would quickly have taken us into safe waters.* – Rev. Davies, on board *JW*[48]

> *We were well out to sea then noticed the ship drifted astern. Before evening worship was over orders were given for all hands on deck and lower away the whaleboat ... to take the ship in tow ... the pinnace was next sent ahead, but with both boats having no effect upon her a third, the gig, was sent to assist, but with three boats well manned ... she continued to go astern faster than ever. All now felt very anxious.* – Rev. Chalmers on board *JW*[49]

> *It became painfully evident that we were making gradual and sure progress in the direction of the roaring surf.* – Rev. Davies

> *Soundings were taken but no bottom found, rockets were fired and blue lights burned to warn those ashore of our danger ...* – Rev. Chalmers

> *At 9.45 a rocket was seen to ascend from the ship and then another followed by a blue light. A canoe was launched immediately but was twice washed back by the strength of the current and the violence of the waves. As soon as the canoe had gone I started inland for the point towards which the ship was drifting ... the night was awfully calm and very, very dark ...* – Rev. Lawes

> *By 10 o'clock the reef seemed close under the stern, the white surf through the dense darkness could be distinctly seen and it became evident that the sooner means were taken to save lives the better. We had on board about 70 souls, men, women and children ... the gig came alongside and the ladies were handed down to it. Next the whaleboat and pinnace came and were soon filled ... the rope was cut away and the three boats lay off to watch what became of the ship.* – Rev. Chalmers

> *Many had to be almost thrown down into the boats. While this was being proceeded with the noise of the surf grew louder and louder making very evident the increasing nearness of the ship to*

the shore … soon we heard her strike upon the fatal reef and when she did so it seemed like the smashing of a thousand panes of glass. The crash I shall never forget. – Rev. Davies

Three miles from our house we came upon the ship just struck on the reef in a place where the sea is always rough … rain began to fall and never ceased the whole of that terrible night. I returned to our house in Alofi … fires had been kindled on the rocks … and torches were being prepared but the rain poured down in torrents and it was with great difficulty that the fires were kept up and any torches obtained. Our canoe soon returned with the tidings that no lives were lost and the boats were on the way to our station. – Rev. Lawes

The rain now came down in torrents as we made for the mission station a few miles off … when we got off the reef under Mr Lawes' house … a canoe came off into which we got two or three at a time, and were paddled in to the break of the surf when between the waves natives seized us and carried us with all speed to the shore. All inside the reef torches were kept burning … without these it would have been impossible to land until daylight. – Rev. Chalmers

A large double canoe was with difficulty launched to go off to the boats … it continued to go back and forward until all 72 were safely landed by which time it was 3.30am. The rain never ceased all night and the surf was very heavy so that landing even in a canoe was dangerous. – Rev. Lawes

About an hour after we landed daylight broke. I went to the scene of the wreck by land which is about 4 miles. We found the vessel thrown upon the reef with her back broken and the water as high inside as outside and the sea making a clean breach over her. – Captain Williams, master of the *JW*[50]

It was a providential thing that our large new house was ready … the Captain and missionaries are comfortable here and the officers and crew occupy our old house. The Rarotongan and Samoan teachers are distributed in the various villages … Every effort has been made to save what we could from the wreck … all has had to pass through the waves so that much is damaged and spoiled. The cliff is steep and the rocks at the top very rugged so that few large cases can be got up entire. We have given up our school room for a store house. – Rev. Lawes

It is a profound mystery to me that the ship should have come through so many gales and storms and thick weather, and amongst so many reefs, and then to drift onshore in the calm – Captain Williams

We are now alone again. All our shipwrecked friends have left us … the poor ship is still lying on the reef. A recent gale … has brought her as far as possible inland. The stern is now fast against the cliffs so that you can step from the rocks right onto the deck. A huge rock is right through the forepart of the ship. It is a most pitiable sight. – Rev. Lawes[51]

Opposite: These two engravings accompanied the news of the wreck of the mission vessel the *John Williams II* on the reef at Niue. They appeared in *The Missionary News*, 1 November 1867. In the prayer meeting are missionaries, native mission teachers and sailors. In the second image a lifeboat is being rowed out to the stricken vessel while a small tugboat can be seen on the right also heading out to help. The engravings were drawn from imagination, so often contain inaccuracies such as the lifeboat and tug. The people on the *John Williams II* were rescued by Niueans in vaka.

British Library Board General Reference Collection, P.P.952.e.

Lawes[42] and had made himself very useful helping around the mission, especially in the small store run from the mission house. More importantly, he had met Pelenise, a young Alofi woman employed by Mrs Lawes at the mission house. Robert Henry and Pelenise were married by Reverend Lawes on 18 September 1867, the first Pālagi–Niuean union on the island.

Head set up his own store just behind Patterson's at Makaheheke in Alofi North. He began as agent for the renowned Pacific buccaneer 'Bully' Hayes, but soon learned that this was a relationship destined for trouble.[43] He therefore cut his losses and began a new store in Tuapa, buying and selling in the Sydney market. He purchased cotton, copra and fungus from the Islanders. He later shifted his dealings to Auckland-based companies.[44] He established a home in Auckland as well as Tuapa and, with his wife and 15 children, he became a leading figure on Niue. He gave unstinting support to Frank Lawes and the LMS, acting as accountant and treasurer when the Lawes family were on furlough and giving substantial financial support to the church. As a fluent speaker of Niuean and a man of calm and even temperament, he was frequently in demand as a peacemaker and go-between. By the time of his death in 1921, several of his sons were in business on their own account on Niue and the first of the Pālagi–Niuean dynasties was well established.

One other Englishman established himself on the island before 1890. Edwin Owen Nicholas had operated a store in Windsor, outside Sydney, and in 1874 he met George Lawes as Lawes and his family were preparing for their deployment to New Guinea. There was an obvious spirit of adventure in a couple who, with seven children, decided to sell up in Australia and move to a little-known Pacific island. The Nicholas family arrived and set up their store in Avatele sometime around 1876–77, and Nicholas acted as agent for the Auckland firm of Henderson and Macfarlane. Like Robert Head, he developed a close relationship with Frank Lawes,[45] and several of his sons also went into business on Niue.

Like the Heads, the Nicholas family also had a home in Auckland so their children could be educated there; members of the two families often travelled back and forth together. Captain Ross recalled one voyage on his schooner, the *Olive*, in 1889 when he had on board Robert Head and Edwin Nicholas and their wives and some of their children. Arriving at Niue late in the evening, Ross was forced to lay off Avatele until the morning. 'The island looked strange to me, and our two passengers who had lived many years here informed me I had made some mistake, this was not Niue at all, it was some other island, but as there was no other island within 300 miles of it, it was puzzling.'[52] With daylight, they all saw what had happened. Niue

Born in southern England in 1832, Robert Henry Head left home at a young age and joined the Royal Navy. In his early thirties he moved to Australia to the mining towns, and he was in Sydney looking for work in late 1866 when the LMS ship *John Williams II* was taking on crew. Head was signed on and soon into the cruise the vessel was wrecked on the reef at Niue. This is where Head made his home; he married a Niuean woman, Pelenise, and became a trader and highly respected figure on the island. He had a home in the village of Tuapa and another in Auckland and his large family moved between the two. Head died in 1921 and was buried in Tuapa. His headstone reads: 'A friend of the people and a servant of God.' Archives New Zealand, Department of Internal Affairs Te Tari Taiwhenua, ABEP 7749 W4262/1336 34/7

From the village of Alofi, Pelenise was working for Mrs Lawes in the mission house when she met Robert Henry Head, shipwrecked from the *John Williams II* in January 1867. They were married by Reverend Lawes in September 1867 – the first Pālagi–Niuean marriage. The Heads raised 15 children, putting their eldest child, Ellen, in charge of their second household in Auckland. Pelenise always dressed in European clothing and was often seen alongside her husband as they greeted and entertained visitors to the island. She was awarded the King's Jubilee Medal in 1935. Pelenise is buried in her own village, Alofi. Archives New Zealand, Department of Internal Affairs Te Tari Taiwhenua, ABEP 7749 W4262/1336 34/7

The interior of the church in Alofi, taken by Thomas Andrew, a professional photographer from Auckland who accompanied Frederick Moss, a New Zealand MP, on a private cruise in 1886. Moss wrote that there were very fine churches at both Alofi and Avatele. The exteriors of both were built of coral stone, with the Avatele church 'larger and more elaborately finished'. However, the interior of the church at Alofi was 'particularly striking' with a 'long vista of simple, massive and sloping tree trunks' supporting a lofty roof. The altar in front of the pulpit is covered by a large hiapo cloth and the floor is covered in pandanus matting. Here the people would have gathered to listen to Reverend Lawes. Museum of New Zealand Te Papa Tongarewa, O.037791 had been struck by a fierce cyclone and everything had been swept bare. Churches and houses had been destroyed and at least 2000 coconut trees uprooted. The next few years were very difficult times on Niue, for the Islanders and for the traders too. Nicholas Senior died in Auckland in 1895, but his sons remained on Niue for another 20 years and more Pālagi–Niuean families resulted.[53]

By 1890 the geographic, economic and social landscape of Niue had changed markedly because of this small but influential group of Pālagi. All settlement was now based near the coast, in a circuit that could be accessed by the round-the-island road. The number of villages had increased to make access to the churches easier. Each village was based around the malē: the main buildings were the church, the schoolhouse and the pastor's house. Neatness and order were paramount and this was reflected in the whitewashed homes, even if the Niuean families were still living out the back in their traditional dwellings.

The need to support the work of the LMS and the arrival of traders seeking goods in demand on the international market had led to increased emphasis on the production of trade goods such as cotton, copra and fungus, and food items such as arrowroot, yams and pigs. Trading stores were opened in Alofi, Tuapa and Avatele, which strengthened the economic importance of these three villages; and new stores soon opened in other parts of the island.

The Lawes brothers and the Head and Nicholas families were especially influential on the island and through association with them, some Niueans rose in importance. The young men who were admitted to the LMS training institution in Alofi undertook several years of instruction and were then sent out to the villages, where they often became leading figures as native teachers and then ordained pastors. Other Niueans established links with the traders, and intermarriage between them, although infrequent at this stage, resulted in the growth of influential families on the island. While the Pālagi thought of the island as a single entity, Niue, the Niueans themselves continued to think in terms of their families and their villages. The Fono established by the LMS gave a voice to these village affiliations but difficulties in reaching consensus often resulted from continuing village rivalries.

There was only limited European settlement on Niue until 1890; however, another development brought Niueans increasingly into contact with Europeans. The trickle of young men leaving on a passing whaler or trading schooner became a steady flow as the need for indentured labour in copra plantations and guano fields throughout the Pacific grew, and the coming and going of these men was to have a significant impact on the island.

6. THE LABOUR TRADE

Our island is being mined

When George Lawes took up his pen to write a diary entry for 28 January 1863, he did so with a heavy heart. 'I have a sad, sad tale of European perfidy to record tonight.'[1] That day a group of Niueans from the village of Avatele had been seized by a Peruvian ship in search of labour to work the guano fields on the Chincha Islands off the coast of Peru. The villagers were inconsolable.

> *A sad night is this at Avatele, scarcely a family but has lost some one, many wives made widows, fathers sonless and children fatherless – the whole village is weeping and howling – nothing else can be heard. 'Rachel weeping for her children and refusing to be comforted.'*[2]

The next day Lawes discovered that the vessel had sailed up the western side of the island and round to Mutalau where an attempt was made to capture more men. In fact some of the Avatele men had escaped and when they finally reached Alofi overland they were able to recount the whole story to the distraught young reverend.

When a three-masted sailing ship had come into view off Avatele on the morning of 28 January 1863, the vaka had hurriedly been filled and paddled out to meet the visitors. The Islanders had become accustomed to the routine of a passing vessel looking for food items and they valued the opportunity for an exchange of goods. They were soon on deck with their piles of bananas, coconuts, pigs and handcrafts, but the visitors indicated that they wished the Niueans to go below deck with their goods and then everything would be purchased. A large number of Niueans obliged – at which point the hatches were slammed shut and the ship put out to sea.

All night the Niueans clung to each other in fear. They tried calling out and banging on the sides of the ship but crew members came below with pieces of wood and beat them. They heard the crew men speaking in a language they had heard once before, two months earlier when a Peruvian ship had visited Niue and taken 50 men away, supposedly on a voluntary basis. The men trapped in the hold now were definitely not volunteers. In the morning the vessel hove to off Mutalau. More vaka came out, but as soon as those in the hold heard a familiar language, they began screaming and yelling, trying to warn of the danger. They attacked the hatch from below and eventually broke through. Around seven of the Avatele men escaped overboard and the commotion frightened away most of the Mutalau men. There was gunfire and machete blows, and some of the escapees arrived on shore in a dire condition. When the vessel, now known to be the *Rosa Patricia*,[3] set sail towards the east it held approximately 40 Niueans who, with the exception of one man, Taole, were never to return to their homeland.

The men captured on the *Rosa Patricia* were right in guessing the language of the crew was the same as on a ship that had visited in November 1862. This was the *Trujillo*, also from Peru and in search of labour for the guano fields. Recruitment on that vessel was said to have been voluntary, with all men 'received aboard of their own desire'.[4] Lawes wrote, however, that 'these poor fellows were simply asked if they were willing to "ship". Upon saying "yes" they were immediately ordered below … in some instances it appears that they did not even wait for a reply, but hurried them below.'[5]

As a result of the visit by the *Trujillo* the Fono had met and discussed the issue of young men being shipped out from the island. Lawes noted in his January 1863 diary entry that if it had not been for a restriction placed on vaka going out to unidentified vessels, up to 100 would have been taken by the *Rosa Patricia*. The decision of the Fono was at least heeded in Alofi: vaka had not gone out from this village to attempt to trade with the *Rosa Patricia*. After the kidnappings in Avatele and Mutalau, the Fono met again and strengthened the ban:

> *A law was made appointing one canoe at each settlement to visit a ship when off and take to it a letter in Niue and English to let the Captain know that in consequence of the kidnapping no canoes would be off with goods for sale.*[6]

The prospect of trade and the lure of adventure were, however, more powerful than the prohibitions of the Fono. When the *Rosa y Carmen* hove to in March 1863, vaka made their way out before the nationality and purpose of the vessel had been established. Furthermore, George Lawes himself was tricked by the visitors. A crew member was seen coming ashore at Alofi and Lawes went to meet him. The man introduced himself as Michael Coney and explained the vessel was the *Sarah*, travelling from Tahiti to Sydney with a cargo of coconut oil. They would not have stopped at Niue but for the fact that their captain was ill and in need of medication.

After the event Lawes wrote: 'A deplorable specimen of humanity was this fellow – a loathsome, bloated sort of man, dirty and untidy, unshaven and unwashed, besotted and debauched. The sight of him was enough to give one the horrors.'[7]

Nevertheless, at the time he offered hospitality in the form of lunch at the mission house, and provided powders for the captain's condition. Coney then returned to the ship. Later in the day it became apparent that there was trouble at sea: of the eight vaka that had gone out, only three returned. Some men had been drowned, one had been shot and 19 were kidnapped. Lawes was distraught at the trickery that he had fallen for. 'Instead of having a cargo of oil they had a cargo of human souls,' he wrote. Reports from those who had gone out to the ship and returned, including Peniamina, revealed that the ship was crowded with men, women and children already taken from other islands, including Pukapuka and Tokelau. They were 'in a most deplorable state … dreadfully thin and almost starved to death'. There was evidence that dysentery had broken out. Lawes again wrote in his diary, 'Rachel weeping for her children and refusing to be comforted.'

> *The number taken does not at all represent our loss. Those taken were the pride and strength of our settlement here. No less than 83 women and children are left widows and orphans – many of the old men too have lost their sons to whom they look for strength and support in their old age. One old man has lost 3 fine sons and another lost 4 sons, one of them not long returned from a whale ship where he had been 3 years.*[8]

Once again the Fono met; this time it decided that in future no one would go out to any ship except the vaka lotu, and that anyone caught breaking this rule would be fined. Vaka stored around the coast were to be guarded, including on moonlit nights, to ensure the Fono was not disobeyed. When a fourth Peruvian vessel arrived on 25 April 1863, it tacked on and off the island, puzzled that no vaka were coming out. Finally a boat was sent ashore to explain that the vessel was the *Adelanta*,[9] and although it was from Peru and looking for labour, the Peruvian government had since become much stricter and only volunteers could be taken, and only then with a strict contract to be signed by each person going. This time men were wanted as farm labourers and shepherds and women for household help. Although Lawes and the Fono tried to prevent Niueans from joining the vessel, approximately 20 young men from Alofi and Avatele were so keen they swam out during the night.

When a whaling vessel, the *Rainbow*, visited Niue in June 1863 the captain gave Lawes further distressing news about the *Rosa y Carmen*. Captain Nicholls had his wife and two children on board and they were invited to stay ashore overnight.

The man who came home from Peru

ONE of the young men thrust down into the hold of the *Rosa Patricia* as it lay off Avatele in January 1863 was Taole, son of Hegatule. Taole and his brother were taken by force. He was the only Niuean taken by the Peruvian slave traders who ever returned to Niue.[10]

With the captives held against their will, the ship headed north from Niue, stopping at the Tokelau Islands, where many more people were kidnapped. They then sailed eastwards. 'The great heat and the stifling air of the hold, the close confinement and the scant and unaccustomed food killed many of the slaves. We had not been sailing many days eastward before a great sickness arose … Day after day dead men were hoisted up from the hold and cast overboard.'

Finally the slave ship reached 'a far-stretching land, with great mountains rising inland, a vast bare land, in no way like our islands of the ocean'. The captain of the *Rosa Patricia* sold the Islanders to people ashore. Most were taken to the offshore guano islands and were never seen again. Taole and his brother were hired to work at the main port of Callao, digging and carrying stones, carrying and wheeling loads of cargo to the ships. The work was hard, there was no pay and the men were constantly under guard. At some point Taole's brother was taken elsewhere and the two never met again.

Months became years and Taole had given up all hope of ever returning to his family in Avatele. Then an American whaling vessel dropped anchor in Callao, and Taole was very excited when he heard a Polynesian language – for many of the crew were Hawaiian. He made contact with some of the men. A plan was devised to get Taole onto the whaling ship, dressed as a sailor. The captain agreed, as he needed another crew member. The plan was successful, although when the whaler left port it was chased by another vessel, as the guards had discovered a man was missing and they would not give him up easily.

Taole now began his 'life as a whaling man and a sailor before the mast'. The ship sailed far to the north 'to a place where great islands of ice float upon the waters'. Taole became a harpoon man; he nearly perished in the cold, 'which numbed the hands and froze the very breath of man, and made the sails as hard and stiff as iron'. When the vessel reached Honolulu the captain was anxious to retain him but Taole had his sights set on returning home. He joined a barque heading south and when they called at Starbuck Island, he was overjoyed to find a gang of Niue men working the guano there for the Arundel Company. He joined them and nearly a year later, when the schooner arrived to return the gang to Niue, he went with them.

Taole had finally come home from Peru after many years. 'I saw the coco-nut palms of Niue rise out of the great waters, and I threw myself down and wept when I stepped ashore once more on the island of my birth.' His return to Avatele, to his old blind father, was filled with emotion as the people received him as a ghost, an aitu, risen from the dead. People came from all around the island to cry over him and embrace him and, as Taole explained, 'they wept also for those whom they would never see again … for I was the only one of the stolen men who ever returned to Niue'.

They brought news of the 'wretched slaver' that had called in March and had been crowded with sick people. When the *Rainbow* had called at Sunday Island in March 'the vile ship was there at anchor'. The natives were all encamped on the island, well guarded, 'the poor fellows dying with dysentery as fast as they could'. Nicholls had called again at Sunday Island three weeks before his arrival in Niue and found the slave ship had left. 'About 60 poor fellows had died of dysentery and were buried in holes in the sand on the beach.'[11]

Niue had seen the last of Peruvian slave ships; but the practice of contracting labour to work elsewhere was just beginning and was to become a common feature of life for young Niuean men. George and later Frank Lawes lamented the outflow of men – indeed it became a persistent theme in their official reports and letters.

> *Our great discouragement, and the great drawback to the success of God's word, is the fondness of our young men for going away in the ships and emigrating to other lands – Hundreds have gone to Samoa, Tahiti and now a number are going to Queensland. They go away from very good influence and are exposed to very little but evil …*
>
> *Our island is being mined. I have not time to write you all I could about the evils of this trade but you know quite well that it is an unmitigated evil. The only respect in which it is better than the Peruvian slave trade is that the natives go of their own free will. They do not go however with the consent of their friends or of the authorities.*[12]

Why were Niueans so keen to go on labour contracts to other parts of the Pacific? There was the usual desire of young people to see the outside world, to participate in adventure. Lawes commented that 'all our young men want to go and the little boys talk of nothing else but going to sea'.[13] It provided the opportunity to earn money and purchase trade goods to bring back to the island, which in turn elevated their status in their own community.

The desire to travel was accentuated by the isolation of Niue and the wish to escape the very church-dominated society that had developed after a decade of Samoan mission teachers, who were often harder taskmasters than the European missionaries. The onerous family, village and church obligations and the strictly enforced moral code could all be left behind in signing on for work on another island – although it was not altogether straightforward. The village patu usually arranged the labour contracts for their village and exacted a payment for this. In some cases money earned on contract was promised to the village church. In 1883 it was noted that young men from Liku had gone to Malden Island to dig guano for 10 months 'in order to obtain the funds to purchase doors, glass windows and a platform' for the new village chapel.[14] When a new chapel was opened in Fatiau in 1889 the LMS noted that 'young men who had been away working in other islands gave funds for painting the chapel and also for the purchase of a bell'.[15] Church, village and family made demands on returning labourers. Nevertheless, there was a freedom and independence associated with working offshore that appealed to many young men.

Both the Lawes brothers were very concerned about the labour trade, and worried that the men would not be treated well by unscrupulous Europeans. They were also deeply concerned that the men would be exposed to 'unmitigated evil' and would then cause social disruption on their return to Niue. In his 1866 report to the LMS George Lawes spoke of men returning home 'much worse morally. For the first time Niue soil has been polluted by a drunken native rolling in it.'[16] The monopoly the LMS had enjoyed was fast coming to an end, and naturally the missionaries lamented this state of affairs.

The irony of the situation was that it was the very presence of European missionaries on Niue that led to increasing contact with the outside world. Any remaining fear that 'Savage Island' might be a dangerous place to visit was dispelled by the knowledge that there was an English gentleman living on the island – and one, moreover, who was known for his hospitality. Even that one Peruvian vessel had made the most of George Lawes' eagerness to welcome other Europeans to his home. Landing at the island was still an obstacle, but Avatele and Alofi in particular became recognised as possible landing sites, weather permitting. From the 1860s on, the number of vessels calling at Niue increased rapidly and the departure and return of groups of young men became a regular feature of Niuean life.

The American-born William Henry 'Bully' Hayes, one of the most feared buccaneers of the Pacific in the mid-nineteenth century, tried his hand at taking contract labourers from Niue. His introduction to the island had come in 1867 when he brought his brig *Rona* from Auckland to rescue the crew and passengers from the *John Williams II* that had been wrecked on the Niue coast. He soon returned in search of labour for Tahiti and was successful, with the help of Peniamina, in obtaining upwards of 100 men who were taken as far as Manihiki in the Cooks and left there while Hayes returned to Niue, supposedly for more food supplies. He explained to Robert Head that the Niueans had refused to leave his ship so he had had no alternative but to take them. While arranging for food and water supplies his Aitutakian crew members came ashore and 'made plans to elope with a number of the girls.'[17] Despite Mr Head's warning to the village chiefs and the posting of guards on the coastline at night, a roll call later found that more than 30 girls were missing. The original group were collected from Manihiki and Hayes sailed on to Tahiti, where he sold them for $25–$35 a head. Although Hayes had promised to return them in two years, the majority never saw Niue again.[18] A protest was lodged about this shipment but when it was investigated in Tahiti it was decided the Niueans had been a willing party.

> *This is confirmed by a report written by Consul Miller of Tahiti on Dec 16, 1868 to Lord Stanley, which states: There has been introduced by the Brig "Rona", of Lyttleton, W.H. Hayes master, about 150 natives of Savage Island under contract for service, who have not, to my knowledge, complained of having been deceived in their engagement or ill-treated during the voyage hither.*[19]

This was Hayes' last visit to Niue, but the Auckland trading firm Henderson and Macfarlane was also calling at this time and taking labour for Queensland. In 1868 George Lawes noted, 'I do not know how many will go but I expect as many as the captain wants. This is the first shipment to Queensland – I wish I thought it would be the last.'[20] The trade was orderly and the Niueans keen; but the distance involved and the availability of Pacific or Kanaka labour closer to Australia meant it did not become a key destination for Niueans.

Much closer to Niue, in Samoa, Godeffroy & Son[21] were developing coconut plantations in response to the growth of the copra industry. In 1865 the first group of indentured labourers left Niue to work on the large estates outside Apia. The great majority of labourers for the German plantations came from the Gilbert Islands (Kiribati) and later from the New Hebrides and the Solomon Islands, but there was also a constant flow from Niue. This resulted in a distinct Niuean community in Apia and the creation of a settlement known as Aai o Niue.[22] Life on the German cotton and copra plantations was tough with a strict work regime enforced by harsh discipline,[23] but Apia was a popular destination for young Niueans as it offered the 'bright lights' unknown in Alofi. Apia was an important Pacific port, and some workers, when their contracts finished and they were due to be transported back to Niue, simply disappeared. Samoans were offered a reward for the return of any contract labourer who had absconded, but some were successful and found other opportunities on the island or escaped return to Niue by signing on to a passing vessel.

By the 1880s some Niueans were being contracted to work on British plantations in Samoa, principally those owned by William McArthur & Co. of London.

McArthur's plantations were on Savai'i, and evidence suggests the discipline there was just as strict as on the German plantations. One agreement to contract labourers from Niue in 1886 stated wages at $10 per month, but when three stowaways were found on the vessel they were contracted to work for two years at the rate of $1 per year.[24] When a group of Niuean workers on McArthur's plantation at Magia laid a complaint about housing, food and wages, the complaint was investigated, but the finding was perhaps not unexpected, namely that 'committing three of the ringleaders to jail for a fortnight will have a good effect on the others'.[25] Despite such treatment, Samoa was a popular destination for young Niueans seeking work opportunities into the twentieth century. And although there are fewer records of it, many also worked on plantations in the Tongan Islands.[26]

Englishman John T. Arundel provided the opportunity for other Niueans to work abroad. On a trip to the Pacific in 1860 Arundel called at the Chincha Islands and saw the guano being mined for refining into superphosphate. He also witnessed the growing copra industry on islands in the Pacific, and by the early 1870s he established John T. Arundel & Co. to operate in the Pacific, mining guano for the fertiliser trade and growing coconuts for the copra industry.

To begin with, the focus areas for Arundel's business were the Phoenix and Line Islands. Both island groups consist of widely scattered and extremely isolated atolls very close to the equator. They were uninhabited and apparently not claimed by any other nation, and Arundel was able to buy leases from the British government to operate his business. Typically one or two Europeans would be landed on an island with three or four Islanders hired for a one-year contract. They would be left with up to 30,000 coconuts for planting, a supply of rice and ship's biscuits and enough building material to erect a few 'tin shanties'.[27] On other islands, such as Baker and Howland, just north of the equator, guano deposits were mined, again with a European or two directing an Islander workforce.

By the mid-1880s the workforce for all these scattered islands seems to have come mainly from Niue. It is likely that the company preferred to take their workers from one island to prevent possible interisland disputes. Niueans had become known as good workers in both copra and guano production and were keen to sign on for contract work. In addition, Niue was en route from New Zealand to the Phoenix and Line Islands for the vessels servicing this region. Furthermore, John Arundel, a strong Congregationalist and grandson of an LMS official, knew Frank Lawes[28] and probably saw the Niueans as God-fearing and law-abiding people.

Over a 10-year period from the mid-1880s to the mid-1890s there was a steady stream of young Niuean men leaving as contract labourers to these remote atolls to the north. On some islands there were only three or four of them planting coconuts; on others there might be a group of up to 50 digging guano. There was no chance to decide that the work did not suit, no chance of shipping out on a passing vessel, and nothing to spend wages on. It was often a very long and difficult 12 months.

Occasionally there was excitement in the form of a passing vessel. When a British naval vessel appeared off Gardner Island in 1892, one Niuean swam out to the ship. 'After recovering from his by no means easy task, he explained that the island was inhabited by twenty natives, presumably Savage Island natives, two pigs and four fowls, and that some white man usually lived there, but at that time was absent.'[29] The British had in fact come to extend protectorate status over the island, not realising it had already been annexed to Britain and then leased to Arundel & Co. for £25 per annum. They proceeded to read the deed of protection to their Niuean visitor and presented him with a Union Jack, after which 'he swam ashore but not without difficulty'.

Getting close to any of these islands, loading the sacks of guano and negotiating the fringing reef was fraught with difficulty, and many a ship was wrecked. In 1891 the barque *Notero* from Auckland spent two weeks at Howland Island loading guano and then taking on Niuean labourers due to be returned home. Less than a mile out from the island the *Notero* hit a sunken, uncharted ridge of coral. All on board were forced to abandon ship. Through the night they clung to the boats while the barque gradually broke up around them. Next morning, after 'spending the night on the water in a rather perilous plight', the crew and the Niuean labourers landed back on Howland, where they had to wait 'for some time' before another vessel could be sent to transport them home. All their possessions and 600 tons of guano had been lost.[30]

The use of Niuean labour by the Arundel Company reached its height around 1890 and by the end of the 1890s had come to an end. Arundel's business operations in the Phoenix and Line Islands were never profitable and before long the company turned its attention to Northern Queensland. Eventually it became part of the Pacific Phosphate Company that was to have such devastating environmental and social consequences in mining the guano on Nauru and Banaba (Ocean Island).

But of all the islands associated with guano digging and Niuean labourers, the name that has lodged most firmly in the collective memory of the Niuean people is that of Malden Island. Lying only 4 degrees south of the equator in a lonely stretch of ocean, Malden is a solitary, barren outcrop of coral, 33 miles in circumference

WORKING FOR MR ARUNDEL

MOUGA was a young man when he left Niue in about 1873 to work as a contract labourer for J.T. Arundel in the Phoenix or Line Islands. Over a period of time he became very devoted to Mr Arundel, who was known as Aneru. It is not certain which islands Mouga worked on but by 1884 he was on Sydney Island in the Phoenix group. Arundel was there too with his wife Eleanor (Lillie) and daughter Lillian, and when a second daughter was born she was named Sydney after the island.

When the family left the island Mouga travelled with them to Samoa, Honolulu and on to San Francisco. On the journey Mouga looked after the children. Arundel and Mouga made a brief return to the Pacific before collecting the Arundel family from San Francisco and travelling to England, where they all stayed with Lillie Arundel's parents near London for at least a year around 1885–86. Lillie died after a long illness and the two young girls were left in the care of their grandparents while Arundel and Mouga returned to the Pacific.

Mouga now became separated from Arundel but continued to work for the company for a time. In 1887 he is listed as supercargo, in charge of all the trade goods, on one of the vessels charted to J.T. Arundel. From 1889 to 1891 he was working on Flint Island, but he was constantly unhappy not to be with Aneru.

By 1893 he had returned to Niue and married an Alofi woman. He now wrote constantly to the Arundel family; his letters were translated into English by Reverend Lawes. One gives the flavour of his writing:

Hiapo gifted to Auckland Museum by Mrs Sydney Aris, daughter of John Arundel, in 1948. She was born on Sydney Island (Manra) in the Phoenix group, where many Niueans worked as contract labourers. This hiapo, and the one shown in the frontispiece, may have been given to the Arundel family for their daughter, as one is dated July 1886, a year or two after she was born. Auckland War Memorial Museum Tāmaki Paenga Hira, AM30089

Mouga in London.
When Mouga accompanied the Arundel family to England in 1885 he was photographed dressed as a 'gentleman's gentleman', a valet, wearing a smoking jacket, dark trousers and shoes and holding a walking cane. Aris family archives, London

Dear Friends I have a great longing to see you all again but, alas, the remote distance of the land, the sea, the ocean. I shall not traverse it again, perhaps the goodness of God will permit us to meet again … I have not forgotten London and all the good things of that land.[31]

Mouga is one of only a very small group of Niueans who travelled to Europe in the nineteenth century. Four or five years before Mouga's visit a Niuean woman had made the journey with Frank and Sarah Lawes and their family when they went on furlough in 1880. She is not mentioned in any correspondence but she was in England for the 1881 census and so her name is recorded.[32] It is also likely that a few men working as seamen made the voyage to at least one European port in the nineteenth century.

When Mouga died on Niue in 1902, Lawes wrote to Arundel to relay the news. It was a testament to Arundel as an employer that he was so much loved by a worker. As Captain William Ross, a well-known sea captain of the time, noted in his memoirs, 'John Arundel's name was sort of sacred to [Niueans] for his many kindnesses to them; no other employer is ever spoken of as Mr Arundel is.'[33]

Large heaps of guano waiting to be sieved and bagged ready for transport to the western side of Malden Island. National Archives UK, CO1069-641(8) #5

'Native boys' at work digging guano on the eastern side of Malden Island. In the centre is the gang foreman in white jacket. National Archives UK, CO1069-641(8) #7

and 15 feet at its highest point. The climate remains fairly constant throughout the year, with a southeast trade wind and a temperature averaging 32° Celsius, and little variation between day and night. Vegetation is practically nonexistent and the only fresh water is from very unreliable rainfall.

In the 1860s Malden was visited by a passing British vessel. They discovered that although the island appeared very inhospitable, it was the site of immense guano deposits of a very high quality. Tests confirmed this, and Messrs Grice, Sumner & Co. of Melbourne acquired a lease from the British government and began assembling the necessary infrastructure on the island to support digging and shipping guano to agricultural markets in Europe, Australia and New Zealand. A workforce of around 100 to 150 was needed, and the company drew this labour from two locations: Aitutaki and Niue. The first contract labourers from Niue left for Malden in the early 1870s, and over the next 40 years somewhere between 2000 and 3000 Niueans experienced one year working on these guano fields.[34]

The Niueans and Aitutakians were kept in two separate gangs and each worked with a foreman. Their tasks included collecting, screening, bagging and trucking the guano from the deposit areas on the eastern side of the island, known as Frankston, to the wharf area on the other, known as West Side. The guano sacks were

Workers riding the trolley on the rail track across the barren landscape of Malden Island. They are using a large sail for power but when there was no wind, they had to push the trolley across the island. National Archives UK, CO1069-641(8) #3

transported on a tramline, using sails for power. The work was hard, it was a dry and desolate landscape, the wind often made it very dusty, and when it rained the guano became heavy and had to be dried and rebagged.

When a ship arrived to transport the guano, the 'native boys' were brought over to the wharf side to help. Conditions here were very difficult. Several ships went onto the reef and were wrecked; others put out to sea when the weather was bad and couldn't get back in for days. Loading often took several weeks. The bags of guano were heavy, and an average of 2500 a day would be loaded if weather conditions permitted. When the weather prevented work on the guano fields the men were kept busy repairing and maintaining equipment and buildings, mending guano sacks, collecting firewood or working on the tramline.

The company structure on the island was hierarchical: the 'native boys' were housed and fed separately from the six or so Europeans. There were different food rations for the Europeans, although they were sometimes all reduced to the same food if a ship was overdue with supplies. One diary entry noted, 'we are out of tobacco. The natives have had none for some time.'[35] Goats, pigs and chickens were kept, and the Niueans and Aitutakians sometimes supplemented their diet with

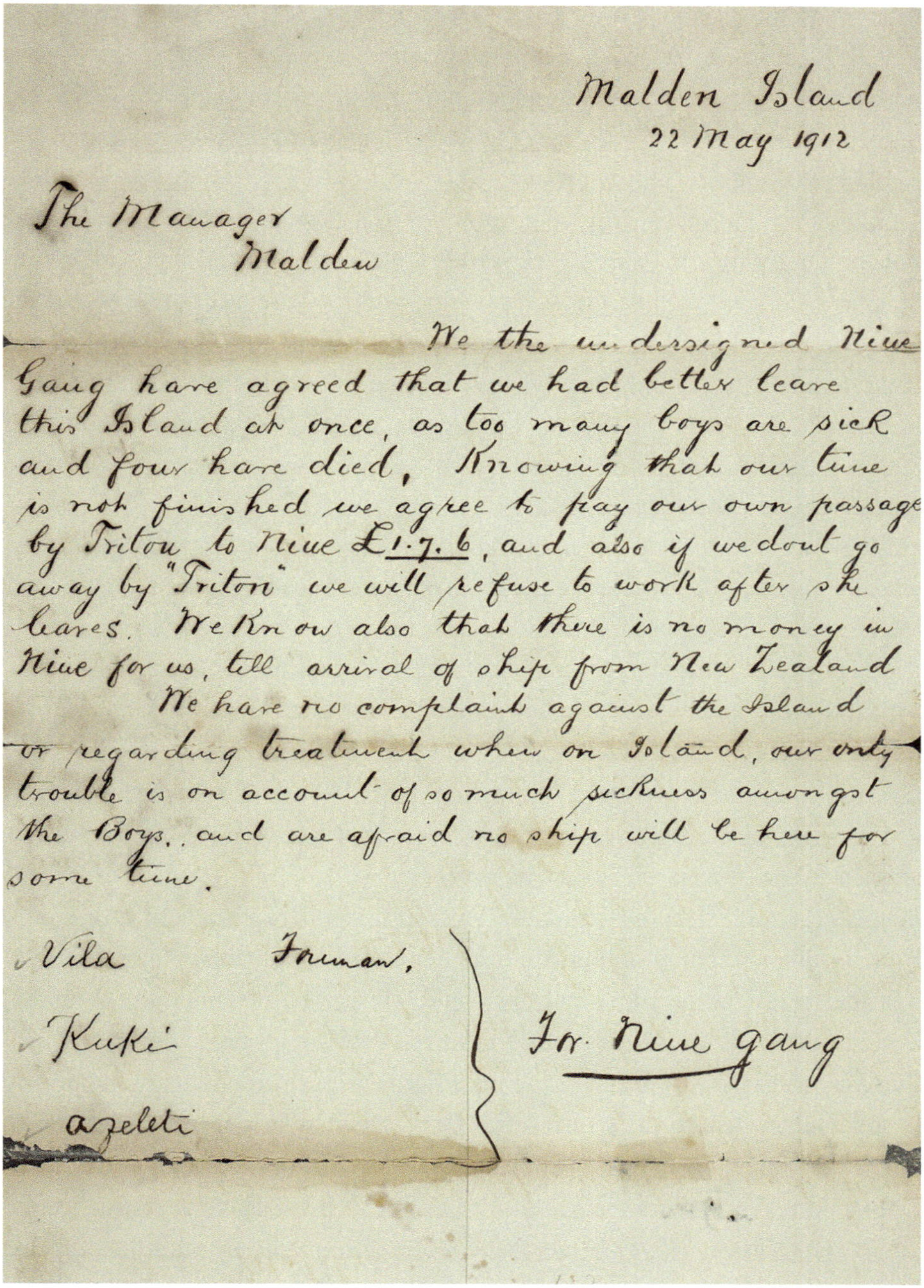

Malden Island
22 May 1912

The Manager
Malden

We the undersigned Niue Gang have agreed that we had better leave this Island at once, as too many boys are sick and four have died, Knowing that our time is not finished we agree to pay our own passage by Triton to Niue £1.7.6, and also if we dont go away by "Triton" we will refuse to work after she leaves. We Know also that there is no money in Niue for us, till arrival of ship from New Zealand

We have no complaint against the Island or regarding treatment when on Island, our only trouble is on account of so much sickness amongst the Boys, and are afraid no ship will be here for some time.

Vila Foreman,

Kuki

azeleti

For Niue gang

A letter from a gang on Malden Island asking to be released from their contract because so many of the 'boys are sick and four have died'. They ask to be allowed to leave on the next passage of the *Triton*; they agree to pay their own passage home and threaten to refuse to work if this request is not granted. Grice, Sumner & Co Papers, Alexander Turnbull Library, Wellington, NZ, MS-Papers-6524 fish, which they caught from canoes. A coconut plantation was developed, with nuts brought in on each schooner arriving with a new labour force. There was a native store where they could buy goods, often for the return home. On arrival and departure, the Islanders' boxes were checked to make sure they were not bringing in alcohol or taking out company property.

The ships that transported the guano away to Australia and New Zealand were not the same ships that carried the labour force to and from Aitutaki and Niue. Smaller schooners such as the *Alma* (which sank at Malden), the *Olive* and the *Countess of Ranfurly* were used to transport the men, as they were suited to reef conditions at Aitutaki and Niue. When one of the schooners arrived, it usually had on board 50 to 80 men and supplies for those on Malden. Pumpkins, sweet potatoes and up to 2000 coconuts would be unloaded; and water and food supplies were then loaded for the return journey.

The men worked long hours, including Saturday. Sunday was a holiday. Occasionally they were given a holiday for working hard loading a ship, for working extra time on loading or for dealing with a crisis such as a shipwreck. On occasion the 'native boys' refused to continue working through a weekend even when 'considerable inducements were offered'. Sometimes extra work was rewarded with an additional ration of meat, as the arrival of a ship always meant new food supplies. Overtime was sometimes paid. When they were involved in very heavy or dangerous work, such as securing the chains to a ship as bad weather approached, the workers might be rewarded with a ration of gin.

Sickness and injury were common. Accidents recorded included a broken arm from a shipboard fall, head injuries from being struck by a pick, severe foot injuries after being run over by a rail truck, and injuries from falling into the hold of a ship while loading. Sickness usually involved dysentery, which affected both the Europeans and the Islanders. The numbers sick were recorded regularly and peaked in June–July, when up to 20 men might be recorded as sick on any one day. One European woman died of dysentery, as did several Islanders. Another problem was that labourers sometimes arrived on Malden with a pre-existing problem: venereal disease. Occasionally these men were returned immediately with the outgoing gang, but others slipped through the medical check on arrival and some died on Malden. The company established a burial ground and it was regularly maintained. When a Niuean died the native mission teacher, whose position was paid for by Grice, Sumner & Co., conducted the burial service in Niuean.[36]

Frank Lawes continued to bemoan the loss of young men from Niue to other

Public Notices

MALDEN ISLAND GUANO.

AGAIN VICTORIOUS!

WINTON WINTER SHOW, 1902.

1st PRIZE for 10 Acres Turnips, sown with broadcast drill—Thomas Miller, Oreti Plains.

Manure Used – MALDEN ISLAND GUANO ONLY.

RESULT—50½ TONS TO THE ACRE.

SOLE AGENTS—

NEW ZEALAND LOAN AND MERCANTILE AGENCY COMPANY, LIMITED.

Advertisement for Malden Island guano, *Southland Times*, 11 June 1902. This product was particularly popular in Southland for swede and turnip crops. Malden Island guano was also sold to Australia and Britain. Papers Past, National Library of New Zealand, paperspast.natlib.govt.nz

islands; however, he now made a distinction between the various destinations. In his report to the LMS in 1875 he noted:

> *The effect produced on the character of those who had gone to work in other lands by residence there depended in a great measure on the moral tone and supervision to which they were subject. Some returned in 1875 from Malden Island. There they had been under a healthy discipline and thus they came back better and wiser than they went. Many had gone to work on Flint Island for Mr Arundel whose influence had been very salutary.*[37]

The main feature of life on Malden, or on any of the islands worked by the Arundel Company, was the isolation and the impossibility of leaving. The men had no way out except the schooner returning them to Niue at the end of their contract. The fact that John Arundel and Grice, Sumner were prepared to pay for the services of a Niuean mission teacher was of some satisfaction to Reverend Lawes. By contrast, those who went to Samoa, Tahiti, Queensland or Tonga had other opportunities, and were exposed to all manner of influences, and some did not return even though they may have left a wife and children on Niue. Attempts to tighten regulations and ensure that families had been catered for before men could go on contract, and the necessity for a bond, did not prevent this loss of population.

The church kept a close record of population numbers by village and by gender, and the pattern was worrying. By 1900, of a total population of 4015 on the island,

2250 were females and there were 561 people 'away from the island'.[38] From 1875, in fact, there were never fewer than 360 involved in contract work abroad, and visitors commented on the noticeable imbalance of population. That said, some of the Niueans who went on contract work were women. The guano islands used exclusively male labour and this sometimes included quite young boys who accompanied their fathers.[39] The copra plantations, on the other hand, took some couples as labourers, sometimes with children.[40] While the coconut trees were becoming established, cotton was also grown and it was found that women and children were better than men at the weeding and picking involved. Moreover, women and children were paid at a lower rate, so there were savings to be made.[41] It was felt, too, that the presence of married women and families among the workers helped to set a better moral tone and hopefully to curb some of the excesses of young single men – especially in relation to alcohol. Sometimes women left Niue for the same reasons as the men: a sense of adventure and desire to experience life beyond the strictures of the LMS.

By the beginning of the twentieth century the flow of labour from Niue was an established part of island life. One of the early resident commissioners reported to the New Zealand government on this trade. He noted that the Niueans were realising that their labour was valued by employers and were now more insistent on fair payment in cash rather than the trade goods that had previously been supplied, often at a considerably lower cost to the company involved.

> *There appears to be a false impression in the minds of these employers of native labour that they are conferring a benefit on the island by taking labourers away under contract; but the facts are that, unless the men are treated and paid in a reasonable manner, and return at the end of their term with a fair amount of money, instead of boxes full of shoddy goods, the island is a distinct loser by the system.*[42]

The movement of groups of contract labourers to isolated guano and copra islands and to the copra plantations of Samoa and Tonga continued until the outbreak of World War I. Contracts for groups of workers to be picked up from and delivered back to Niue became less frequent. This did not mean that the outflow of people from Niue ceased, but it began to take a different form as Niueans, with increasing confidence, made their own individual decisions about emigration – and they now looked to the country to which their island had been annexed: New Zealand.

7. The call for British protection

Stretch out towards us your mighty hand

Now that English missionaries and traders had settled on Niue, and with the growth of the labour trade involving especially English and Australasian companies, it was inevitable that sooner or later there would be talk of protection and assistance from Britain. The first recorded informal request was to Reverend Turner when he visited Niue in 1859. It was relayed to Turner by the Samoan mission teachers working on the island, who said the chiefs had asked how they could obtain a protectorate from Britain. Turner pointed out that such a request should not be made to the missionaries but must be put to one of Her Britannic Majesty's official representatives, either the British consul in Samoa or the commander of any of Her Britannic Majesty's ships that might call at the island.[1] There was no follow-up to this query.

Four years later, after the raids by the Peruvian slave ships, George Lawes noted in his diary that a great Fono had been held. The chiefs from all the settlements had met to make a law about visiting ships and how to keep their people safe.

> *The old men came to me again this afternoon and I had a long, long talk with them about the laws and customs of England and also about Niue laws and offenders. They signified officially to me the desire they expressed to Mr Turner 4 years ago to obtain a British Protectorate. This has been a day of talking.*[2]

After a visit by another Peruvian vessel, Lawes noted:

> *Old men have again asked for British protection. They are very earnest about it and do not see the force of my words that England cannot take care of such little children, such a long way off. However I will transmit their wish to HBM Consul in Samoa to be forwarded to the proper quarters.*[3]

The 'old men' referred to by Lawes were heads of magafaoa – extended families – the basic group in Niuean society. Each district had a number of magafaoa, and at times in the past there had been discussion and cooperation among them. The arrival of Europeans and increasing contact with the outside world necessitated

‘Tuapa landing, Niue’, photographed by Thomas Andrew, a professional photographer who accompanied the New Zealand parliamentarian Frederick Moss on his tour of the Pacific in 1886. Vaka can be seen stored on the cliffs and wooden ladders are in place to give access to the reef.

Museum of New Zealand Te Papa Tongarewa, C.001516

some form of cooperative government if Niue was to coordinate its approach to the new arrivals. Furthermore, the LMS was keen to have recognised leaders within the society through whom they could ‘influence the people’.[4] Every visiting mission vessel had tried unsuccessfully to identify a leading chief through whom they could work; and the absence of such a person was one of the reasons it took so long to establish a mission on Niue.

The extended family with an iki or chief was the usual form of social grouping in traditional politics, but there were times when a patuiki, or chief of chiefs, was recognised as the highest chief on the island.[5] It was perhaps the threat from an outside source, such as invasion by other Polynesians, that united the Niueans; but for much of the time, and certainly leading up to and during initial contact with Europeans, there was no single accepted political ruler of the island. On the contrary, there was frequently open hostility between different parts of the island.

Mission teachers' wives and children on verandah of mission house, photographed by Thomas Andrew in 1886. This group of proud women are dressed in their best and display their decorated hats. The training institution in Alofi was established in 1859 by the Samoan teachers and it became an important part of the work of the European missionaries. Men were trained as mission teachers and were then sent either to the other villages on Niue or to LMS outstations in other parts of the Pacific. The men had to be married and their wives were given training by Mrs Lawes in reading, arithmetic and sewing. Museum of New Zealand Te Papa Tongarewa, O.037940

With the arrival of Europeans the need for a united political response was vital, and this was encouraged by the Lawes brothers. The growth of villages centred on the mission stations provided a political unit, and from the early 1860s representatives from each of the villages came to Alofi each month to a Fono to discuss issues such as the visits by the Peruvians and the traffic in labour. When Commodore James Goodenough, senior officer on the Australian Royal Naval station, called at Niue in November 1873 on HMS *Pearl*, there was a Fono in progress in Alofi.

> *[We] found [the Fono] sitting under a grove of coconut trees, and occupying a circle at least thirty five yards in diameter; not sitting in a circle, but the men from one village in a group together, then those of another village a little apart, all squatting on the ground, and dressed generally in straw hats, and blue or red flannel shirts … After two or three had spoken, and we had sheltered from the rain, the natives asked me to speak to the Fono …*

> *'Mr Lawes says that some of you speak of having a king. Is not your Fono enough? If the men of the families of each village meet to discuss village affairs, and if the village heads speak together in the Fono, is this not enough to settle all your business without a king?'*[6]

The idea of a patuiki continued to be discussed despite Goodenough's assurance that a Fono was sufficient; and three years after his visit, in 1876, a patuiki was agreed on. It was an elected office, not a hereditary position, and within the context of interest in the British Empire and Queen Victoria, the position became cloaked in European terminology. The word 'king' was used; there was to be a 'coronation' during which Frank Lawes was asked to 'anoint' the elected leader. He declined to do this but he agreed to draw up a paper which the king would sign in lieu of a 'coronation oath'. Lawes noted that 'the change was to a great extent nominal as the chiefs still had large authority in their several districts'.[7] In other words, iki were still powerful within their magafaoa but now there was to be a recognised patuiki, a king at least in name. The man elected was Mataio Tuitoga of Alofi, 'a quiet, peaceable [man] and I believe a Christian,' wrote Lawes. 'All the villages took part in the ceremonies of the day.'[8]

The election of a patuiki was a response to political engagement with the European world. The concept of a Fono, iki and, at times, a patuiki was part of the structure of traditional Niuean politics but it was the arrival of the LMS and the introduction of Christianity that created the notion of a united island. The Fono was placed on a regular footing with monthly meetings and was based, as it always had been, on families and the land areas they controlled.

The position of patuiki existed for a 41-year period from 1876 until 1917. There was often protracted disagreement on who should fill the position; and there was always an understanding that the power of the patuiki was dependent on support from the other iki.

The 41 years during which a patuiki was recognised on Niue coincided with the period of engagement with the British government – and, rather unexpectedly, the New Zealand government. It covered the period of petitions for British protection, the declaration of a British Protectorate and the annexation of the island to Britain, followed rapidly by the handing over of responsibility for the newly annexed territory to New Zealand.

Little is written of Mataio Tuitoga, the first king; but the second, Fataaiki, is better known and is closely associated with the petitions for protection. The third and final king, Togia, was elected after bitter dispute in 1898, and was the figurehead

Fataaiki, patuiki of Niue, November 1888 to December 1896; he is in ceremonial dress and is holding a decorated katoua. Fataaiki trained as a mission teacher in Alofi and Apia and served in the Tokelaus before returning to Niue to serve in Hakupu. As patuiki, he is closely linked with the first two petitions asking for British protection. Rev. Frank Lawes wrote that Fataaiki was 'a clever man and a born ruler'. This image was probably taken by Lawes, and Percy Smith obtained a copy when he was on Niue in 1901. Author's collection

during the 1900–03 time of political change. He was an old man, rather ineffectual, and he was sometimes mildly ridiculed by European writers, especially because he appeared in 'regal clothing'. He was nevertheless accorded status by visiting officials, naval officers and politicians, for kingship was a concept they understood and respected, even if this Niuean version was somewhat unusual. When Togia died in early 1917 his position as titular head of the island was taken, not by another elected patuiki, but by the New Zealand resident commissioner now established on Niue – a position with considerably more power.

While the Fono in Niue was discussing changes in the 1870s and deciding on the election of a patuiki, the British were also reviewing their role in the wider Pacific. The growth of a large European community in Fiji based on the sugar industry, and considerable conflict there between settlers and the indigenous community, had forced Britain to declare Fiji a British colony in 1874. The British government had been reluctant: colonies, they had discovered, were expensive; and the real 'jewel in the crown', India, was the main object of their financial and political resources. But in the Pacific, there was increasing trade by British merchants, and growing pressure

The lime plaster wall surrounding the schoolhouse in Avatele, photographed by Graham Balfour. Lime was often used to decorate walls and sometimes graves. On a visit to Niue in 1886 Frederick Moss noted a grave where the plastered coral mound took the form of a ship, indicating that the man had been a sailor. Pitt Rivers Museum, University of Oxford, PRM 1998.181.10.2

from English missionary societies for direct British involvement to regulate trade and labour practices, and to protect but also discipline British subjects. The labour trade was a particular problem, as growing numbers of Islanders were taken to the plantations of Fiji and Queensland and also to the smaller islands leased from the British government for copra and guano production. Britain looked for a solution that did not involve the annexation of yet more island territories and the placement of an administration on each one.

The answer came with the idea of a High Commissioner for the Western Pacific – an official with a roving brief over that part of the Pacific where there were British interests. The area became defined as:

> *Samoa, Tonga, the Union, Phoenix, Gilbert, Ellice, Marshall, Caroline, Solomon, and Santa Cruz Islands, Rotuma, New Guinea eastward of 143°E., New Britain and New Ireland, the Louisiades, and all other islands in the Western Pacific Ocean not being within the limits of the colonies of Fiji, Queensland or New South Wales, and not being within the jurisdiction of any civilised Power, and the waters within three miles of every island or place thereof.*[9]

Niue and the islands known loosely as the Cooks were not specifically named, but they were considered to lie within the jurisdiction of the new Western Pacific High Commission.

The office of high commissioner would be held by the governor of the new Crown Colony of Fiji; and Fiji would be the centre from which law and order would radiate to cover all British activities in the region. The high commissioner had access to the court system of Fiji to regulate the labour trade. Regulations were spelt out in an Act for the Prevention and Punishment of Outrages upon Natives of the Islands of the Pacific Ocean, passed in the British Parliament in 1872 and later amended and known as the Pacific Islanders Protection Act. However, the high commissioner could only regulate the activities of British subjects; and the legislation dealt with the transport of contract labourers but said little about work conditions on the plantations. The high commissioner could appoint deputy commissioners to act on his behalf, but he had no treaty-making powers.

The first Governor of Fiji and High Commissioner for the Western Pacific was Sir Arthur Gordon, and it was in his role as high commissioner that he visited Niue in November 1879. Earlier that year Gordon had been back in London and, discovering that George Lawes was home from New Guinea on furlough, he had arranged to meet him to discuss the situation in Niue. Lawes wrote a lengthy letter to his brother Frank to make sure he understood the background to this visit, which Gordon proposed making as soon as he returned to Fiji.

Gordon, George Lawes explained, 'is one of the few men in his position who have an eye to native, as well as British interests. He has the best interests of the natives at heart.'[10] Lawes said that the object of Gordon's visit to Niue was to place a deputy commissioner on the island if the Niueans would accept one and pay at least part of his salary.

> *The only way I see of preserving the independency of Niue is by adopting some such plan as Sir Arthur Gordon's. He will be able to explain to you his ideas and wishes better than I can. But – with the patus he can do nothing without you. I should be inclined to advise them to accept the offer. If you think so remind the patus of the time when at a great Fono they all held up their hands to kaufakalataha mo Peritania. Sir Arthur's proposal, whatever it may be is Peritania's answer to the oft repeated request of Niue.*[11]

Lawes stressed that the plan would depend very much on who was put in the position of deputy commissioner; but he felt it was the best way to proceed and he urged his brother to 'render [Sir A] every possible assistance. You may think him a little *fakatokoluga* [boastful] but I have found him kind, wise and judicious.'[12]

When Sir Arthur visited Niue on 21 November 1879, he was well received by Frank Lawes and the assembled Fono and crowd. In the speech he made, which was recorded by Lawes, he gave some very sage advice, based on an earlier discussion with Reverend Lawes about laws passed by the Fono to prevent the sale of land and the introduction of alcohol:

> *no doubt men will come among you who will try to make you break [these laws]. There will be men who covet your land and will try to persuade or frighten you into selling it. If you do so you will lose all power over your own island and become strangers in it. There will be those who will try to make you permit the sale of spirits. If you allow this your race will dwindle away and die out of the land.*[13]

The high commissioner suggested the people of Niue should promise not to break or change these laws without the consent of Queen Victoria. 'She is very strong, and by this means you will share her strength.' He did not promise any closer form of political partnership and he did not establish a deputy commissioner on the island. He did, however, appoint Robert Henry Head as his acting deputy commissioner, an honorary and, as later transpired, meaningless title. When Head used this title in 1887 in a letter to the then High Commissioner for the Western Pacific, Sir George Mitchell, an indignant reply came back, asking by whose authority Head had assumed this title. Head replied that he had been appointed by Sir Arthur Gordon during his visit in 1879 but, as the title obviously had no significance, Head signed this letter simply 'Your Excellency's most obedient humble servant'.[14]

During Gordon's visit nothing is recorded about him meeting with the king Tuitoga. Tuitoga appears to have had a very low profile; and when he died in July 1887, a new and stronger candidate came forward. Fataaiki was well educated and well known. He had trained at the LMS Institution in Alofi and then spent time at the Malua Institute in Apia before heading to Tokelau as a mission teacher. George Lawes wrote to the LMS in Apia expressing regret that he had not been returned to Niue: 'I should be very glad of Fataaiki here, he would do more good among his own countrymen, with whom he has great influence, than on one of those small islands, but his heart seems to be set on foreign work.'[15] Fataaiki and his wife Loata did eventually return from their overseas mission work, and he became established as mission teacher in Hakupu. When Frank Lawes was on his first furlough, Fataaiki came over to Alofi twice a week to take classes on his behalf at the LMS Institution. On the death of Tuitoga, Fataaiki seemed an obvious candidate for election as king. Nevertheless, there was some opposition and the process took many months – perhaps also held up when, in February 1887, Fataaiki's wife died during a malarial fever-type epidemic on the island. Finally in November 1888 agreement was reached and Fataaiki was sworn in as king.

Fataaiki is best known for his association with the first two formal petitions asking for British protection. The first letter was written in November 1887, during the interregnum between Tuitoga and Fataaiki. It was clearly the work of the latter and concluded with the line, 'I, Fataaiki, wrote this letter.'

> *We desire to pray your Majesty and your Majesty's kingdom if it be your pleasure, to stretch out towards us your mighty hand, that Niue may hide herself in it and be safe. We are afraid lest some other powerful nation should come and trouble us ...*
>
> *Our king Tuitoga died on the 13th July last, but before his death he wished to write to the kingdom of Great Britain, to beg your Majesty to send the powerful flag of Great Britain to unfurl in this island of Niue in order that this small island of ours may be strong.*[16]

The request was forwarded by Reverend Lawes to the Western Pacific High Commission in Fiji; but the reply, delivered by a passing naval vessel a year later, revealed that Niue was now a small pawn in a much larger game of imperial politics, centred on Samoa but involving the much wider spheres of influence of Britain and Germany in the Pacific. By an agreement known as the Berlin Convention of April 1886, Niue was included in one of the areas that the two great powers designated 'neutral regions', meaning Britain was unable to extend any official protection as requested by the Niueans.

When a London newspaper reported, inaccurately, in October 1888 that a British naval vessel would be calling at 'Savage Island in order to establish a British protectorate there', there was a very rapid response from a German newspaper to the effect that 'the British Government is certainly not in a position to assume the protectorate over Savage Island since ... that island is declared neutral territory'.[17] The naval vessel, HMS *Calliope*, was in fact delivering the letter of refusal from the High Commissioner for the Western Pacific.

By the time a second formal petition was sent from Niue, Fataaiki was well established as patuiki. He believed that ongoing troubles in Samoa might have rendered the Berlin Convention null and void, and he wrote a petition in February 1895, addressed to the high commissioner in Fiji, 'begging for the protection of the British flag' and this time signed, 'I am Fataaiki, King of Niue Fekai'. [18] Again a short reply was delivered by naval vessel, to the effect that Niue was still neutral territory.

'Chief's wife', an image of a Niuean woman taken by Graham Balfour during a visit to Niue in 1890. It is possibly a woman from Mutalau as this is where Balfour landed.

Pitt Rivers Museum, University of Oxford, PRM 1998.181.10.1

Niuean men photographed by Ernest W. Henderson during a cruise through the Pacific in the yacht *Sybil* in 1888. Henderson was looking for scenes of island life and portraits of different types of Pacific people, which he could then take to England and sell to magazines. Some of his photos appeared in the *London Illustrated News* in 1890 but there was nothing of Niue. In collections of Henderson's work, the only images taken on Niue were a series of these men showing their features and their dress – 'slop' clothes, such as were worn by crew on ships of the time.

Trustees of the British Museum, Oc.B55.23AN502845

There was a sense on Niue that the need for British protection, and the presence of a British representative on the island, was becoming increasingly urgent as more and more men left the island on labour contracts and more trading companies set up stores in Niue.

Fordyce, Schultz and Company of Sydney and the Friendly Islands (Tonga) opened a store in Tuapa in the early 1890s; and in February 1896 Fataaiki wrote to the high commissioner in Fiji to protest that their trader, Mr McDonald, had broken the law by selling a bottle of spirituous liquor to a man from Makefu. Fataaiki requested that the high commissioner make it known to all traders that this was contrary to Niue law.[19] Other companies were also arriving on the island: the Cook Islands Trading Company to Tuapa in 1896; and the Pacific Islands Company, which bought out Henderson and Macfarlane and set up branches in Avatele, Alofi and Tuapa. Lever Brothers, after calling at Niue for several years to purchase copra, opened a branch in Avatele in the late 1890s.

This image of children on the beach at Avatele was taken by Charles Rudd, a professional photographer from Melbourne, sometime in the 1890s. Rudd travelled extensively in the Pacific and his images appeared in newspapers and magazines in Australia and New Zealand.

State Library of Victoria, Melbourne, Australia, H39363/18 Image no. a17269

When Fataaiki died on 15 December 1896, it was difficult to see who would replace this 'sane, clear-sighted and statesmanlike' man.[20] It took 18 months before Togia Puletoaki of Tuapa was finally elected, some say because no one else wanted the office. At 70 years of age, King Togia was an old man and lacked the education and political skill of Fataaiki. He was nevertheless destined to become the best known, and certainly the most photographed, of the three Niuean kings of this period.

The third formal petition was sent from Niue by King Togia in October 1899,[21] and the same curt reply was received from Fiji, referring the king and chiefs of Niue to earlier replies to the same request. But just as imperial politics had prevented a positive response to these petitions, now suddenly a new agreement in Samoa changed the ground plan. The Berlin Convention became void and, on 14 November 1899, the Samoa Convention resulted in the division of the Samoan Islands between Germany and the United States. Britain, in return for relinquishing claims to Samoa, was given other areas of the Pacific including the northern Tongan island of Vava'u, previously a German coaling station, and Niue. The Western Pacific High Commission in Fiji was now in a position to respond to the repeated requests from Niue to unfurl the British flag on the island.

When Basil Thomson was sent from the Western Pacific High Commission to negotiate a British Protectorate over the independent kingdom of Tonga in early 1900, he was invested, as Her Majesty's Envoy Plenipotentiary, with full treaty-making powers. As Niue was nearby and its requests for protection were well known, it seemed expedient 'to visit the island and announce a favourable answer to the petition forwarded 13 years before'.[22]

Basil Thomson reached Niue on board HMS *Porpoise* on 21 April 1900.

> *I lost no time in sending a boat ashore for Mr Frank Lawes, the representative of the LMS, who, from his long residence and his kindly influence over the natives, has long been regarded by them as their adviser in all matters at issue between the Europeans and themselves, and who has so modestly and tactfully discharged the duties of his unsought office that Europeans and natives alike have cheerfully accepted his arbitration. He came on board at once, and willingly tendered his services, nominally as interpreter, but actually as a great deal more than that. He is a man of middle age, of gentle, sympathetic, and rather melancholy mien, with a vein of quiet humour, and a manner that would inspire confidence and affection in the native races of any country.*[23]

Frank Lawes immediately explained that the key to Niuean politics was rivalry between villages. He suggested that the vessel move offshore from Tuapa, as this was the king's village. It would then be in order to invite the iki from the other villages to Tuapa; but to remain at Alofi and expect everyone, including the king, to come there would cause much resentment. However, Thomson had heard that at Tuapa:

> *the anchorage was vile, and the landing-place such that it would be necessary to wade ashore in full dress uniform, [thus] we decided to brave the royal displeasure, and to send a message explaining that a Queen's ship is not as other ships, and that, although, out of consideration for her safety, our bodies must be landed at Alofi, our hearts would certainly be in that capital of capitals, Tuapa.*[24]

Togia accepted the situation and, suitably attired as king, set out from Tuapa to Alofi, as did the iki and inhabitants of all the other villages. Awnings were erected, and when the royal party arrived on the village green at Alofi, Thomson spoke to them through Reverend Lawes and explained the reason for his visit. Queen

Togia and party arrive in Alofi for British Protectorate ceremony, 21 April 1900. Togia had agreed to come from Tuapa to Alofi for the ceremony. He dressed in a Western-style suit but was persuaded to change into a Samoan-style dress. He was accompanied by his young wife and many advisors and supporters, all wearing their best clothes, which for many included items of uniform.

Wide World Magazine, vol. VI, Jan. 1901, courtesy of the University of Chicago Library, Illinois

Togia, patuiki of Niue, posing with two of his elderly advisors. The helmet he had been wearing is now lying in front of him. *Wide World Magazine*, vol. VI, Jan. 1901, courtesy of the University of Chicago Library, Illinois

Victoria had answered the petition of the late king Fataaiki, by taking Niue under her protection. The people need never fear seizure of their country by another of the great powers, and their young men working on plantations in other countries would now be able to claim the protection of the British Consul. As a token of this protection, the Queen had sent them a portrait of herself to be the property of the Niuean people. Togia was then invited into the schoolhouse to sign the treaty with Britain. There was room on the document for three signatures to the agreement, but Lawes reasoned that, given village rivalry, this was insufficient and an extra one was added.[25]

The treaty signing was followed by a flag-raising ceremony and a dose of the pomp and ceremony that the British were so renowned for. Sailors erected a flagstaff brought from Sydney for the purpose, the fife and drum band and a naval guard of honour assembled, and Thomson, dressed in formal naval uniform, read the

'The flag went slowly aloft …', British Protectorate ceremony, 21 April 1900. Basil Thomson, Her Majesty's envoy plenipotentiary, arranged for a ceremony after the treaty signing. A naval guard of honour assembled, a flag was raised, the fife and drum played and Thomson read the proclamation declaring Niue was now a British Protectorate. *Wide World Magazine*, vol. VI, Jan. 1901, courtesy of the University of Chicago Library, Illinois

proclamation. The flag was run slowly up the pole while the band played the British national anthem, and a royal salute thundered from the guns of the ship lying at anchor in Alofi bay. Thomson observed those around him:

> *Here were some thousands of natives, clad for the most part in clothes made by the slop-tailors of Europe, gazing in open-mouthed wonder at a handful of officers in gold-laced uniform performing a ceremony intended in some way to change the tenor of their lives. And behind lay the island, unchanged and unchangeable through the centuries.*
>
> *The foreigner has been too strong for them, but the island will be too strong for the foreigner. The foreigner has landed and brought with him the disease they feared so much, but let him hoist flags and fire guns … he will never conquer the stern fact that the island lies remote from the great highways of the ocean, and turns a frowning cliff … upon those who would beguile her into commerce.*[26]

When the formal ceremony was over, Thomson spent some time learning about the island. He noted the welcome arrival of Robert Henry Head on the schooner *Isabel* that day from New Zealand. Head had been recommended as the most suitable person to act as registrar to the consul in Tonga, in whose province the new protectorate was to be placed. 'I was a little bashful in approaching him with the offer,' wrote Thomson – for 23 years before Sir Arthur Gordon had offered him a similar post – 'and the letter of appointment was still to come.'[27] He found, however, that despite his 70 years Head was willing to accept the unpaid office.

In his capacity as Her Majesty's Envoy, Thomson endorsed the two laws of Niue prohibiting the sale of land and the sale of liquor; and he dictated a short penal code to Frank Lawes with 'penalties ranging from a fine of a plaited straw hat to a maximum of six months' labour on the roads'.[28] He also saw to the appointment of quarantine officers at each of the four villages where there were landing facilities – Alofi, Avatele, Tuapa and Mutalau – for there were cases of bubonic plague in Australia and New Zealand. The quarantine officer was to board each and every ship arriving and inspect the Bill of Health before allowing any contact with the shore.[29] Both the penal code and the quarantine regulations were soon after put to the Fono for ratification.

When Thomson sailed again for Tonga he left Niue a British protectorate, with the Union Jack flying in Alofi and an unpaid official representing the Queen. But as he wrote in his account of events, 'a protectorate is probably a prologue to annexation more or less delayed'.[30] It was to be possibly the shortest delay ever between protectorate and annexation: King Togia was going to have to dress in royal regalia twice more before the year was out.

8. Annexation to New Zealand

I contend that the extension of our boundaries ...
will profit our colony for all time

The first visit to Niue by a New Zealand premier almost ended in disaster. Less than a month after Basil Thomson's visit to establish a British protectorate, Richard Seddon, Premier of New Zealand since 1893, embarked on a month-long voyage to the South Seas. It was ostensibly a health trip, a much-needed rest for the premier before the next parliamentary round. Niue was included in the circuit, and Seddon came ashore with his wife and five of his children, together with an entourage of private secretaries and personal assistants, on 31 May 1900. They discovered the landing at Alofi was extremely precarious; and after 24 hours on the island, the return to the government vessel *Tutanekai* was anything but easy. Mrs Seddon, a woman of imposing stature, was almost lost off the wharf into the sea, but fortunately for good relations it was only the sailors who ended up capsized.

Seddon's visit to Niue was without warning, for there was no means of communication except by visiting ship. Nevertheless, as the vessel came into sight, everyone prepared to welcome the visitors. As Thomson had arranged, a ship should first be visited by a designated health officer to establish there was no sickness on board. The man who came out to the *Tutanekai* was a trader, H.W. Pearse, who had established his own business in Alofi after some time as representative of the Cook Islands Trading Company in Tuapa.[1] The delegation from New Zealand was invited ashore and, as it was late in the afternoon, arrangements were made for everyone to stay overnight. Mrs Lawes, Mrs Head and Mrs Macquarie, the wife of another trader, opened their homes to the guests, as did Mr Pearse, 'whose Rarotongan wife and half-caste family were as hospitable and courteous as their European sisters'.[2]

Through the night there were feverish preparations for the next day: Islanders were busy cooking umu kai, organising dances, building shelters and bringing their horses to Alofi to transport the premier and party to Tuapa to meet King Togia. People from around the island gathered in Tuapa, bearing food and dressed in their best clothes. When the premier's procession reached Tuapa they faced a fierce challenge by warriors and were then welcomed by Head Senior, 'a very old trader'.

'The two kings, "Dick" and Togia'. Premier Richard Seddon made a tour in the Pacific in May 1900. His trip was extensively photographed by Frederick Sears and an account by Edward Tregear was published soon after their return to New Zealand. J.C. Beaglehole Room, Seddon 179-1-12, Victoria University of Wellington, New Zealand

Finally they were received by Togia, 'an old and venerable-looking man', and his young wife, who wore her white wedding dress 'for she was recently a bride'.[3]

Togia and Seddon both made speeches, and Seddon presented the king with a large Union Jack, 'an emblem of their being children of the great Queen and Empress'. When it was explained that the king was the owner of a fine portrait of Queen Victoria, delivered the previous month by the British envoy, Seddon promised an equally large portrait of himself 'to act as a companion portrait'.[4]

Dancing and singing followed, gifts were presented, and the visitors were entertained to 'a most delicious afternoon tea' at the home of Robert and Pelenise Head. Seddon made a concluding speech of thanks to the entire gathering in Tuapa, stressing that this day would be forever remembered and that in the future, as premier of New Zealand, he would be able to help the people of Niue – the only (oblique) reference to future New Zealand involvement with Niue.[5] The party then progressed back to Alofi, where they were entertained at a feast at the home of Mr Pearse before being ferried back out to the *Tutanekai* and sailing for Rarotonga.

Clothing fit for a king

NIUEANS showed an interest in European clothing from the earliest contacts and items of used clothing soon became desired objects of barter from passing vessels. The introduction of clothing that covered the whole body, especially the female body, is usually attributed to the missionaries, but it was often 'due more to the desire to wear the strange garments and gain a certain prestige thereby'.[6] This certainly seems to have been the case in Niue.

Men who worked as contract labourers in other parts of the Pacific would often bring back clothes for themselves and their families. One group of men, who were left by the Arundel Company at Enderby Island in 1887 to salvage all they could from a large German ship wrecked there, had a wonderful time. When Captain Ross returned to collect the group and the equipment they had salvaged, he found that they had also collected clothing to take back to Niue. 'When left, they had perhaps a spare garment amongst them, but nothing else. Now they had at least three sailors' chests each full of choice gear to take home to Niue.'[7] The company officials agreed that the men could keep much of this gear as a reward for their work.

The LMS on Niue also went about collecting clothing for the locals: Mrs Lawes was kept busy in the 1860s acknowledging contributions of 'bales of clothing' from different church groups in Britain. This clothing supplemented the use of tīputa and was valued for its novelty factor, although much of it was unnecessary, and even sometimes harmful, in the tropical climate.

Once trading stores opened on the island, the bright cottons used for making 'Mother Hubbard' dresses were in demand. One European woman

When Togia met the parliamentary party in 1903 he was 'dressed in a black frock coat, with three rows of gold braid round the cuffs, and a red stripe up the sides of his pants, and a belltopper on his head'.

Auckland War Memorial Museum Tāmaki Paenga Hira, Henry Winkelmann Album 264 item 82 who landed at Avatele in the 1890s with her trader husband was struck by the colourful array of cotton garments worn by the women who were waiting to welcome them: 'All the women were dressed in long gowns of the brightest colours – red, green, blue, scarlet, and indeed of every hue imaginable.' Village rivalry extended to clothing, too: the trader's wife witnessed a scene outside a trading store when people came in from other villages with their copra. The Avatele locals tried to be first when the trader began business. 'Perhaps the trader had just opened a case of something lovely in the way of prints – a green and yellow check upon a brilliant scarlet ground – and the Avatele women are determined that none of the print shall go to Hakupu.'[8]

Uniforms were the type of clothing perhaps most prized in Niue. Visits from the Royal Navy had shown what splendid uniform items were available, and Niueans obtained these wherever possible. When Frank and Sarah Lawes went home on furlough in 1881 they arranged to collect some uniform pieces for King Tuitoga from the father of Edwin Nicholas, a trader on the island. Nicholas wrote to Lawes in England to let him know that his father had a 'suit of clothes and a cocked hat for the king'.[9] By 1900 – the year when a protectorate was proclaimed, swiftly followed by annexation – there was a wide variety of uniforms in evidence and everyone donned their Sunday best each time another vessel carrying officials came into the bay.

Basil Thomson, the British envoy, described 'men in slop clothes' (cheaply made clothing especially for sailors) and with 'villanous, billycock hats set at a rakish angle' (felt hats much like bowlers). King Togia, Thomson explained, was 'an old man in a strange, ill-fitting uniform and a tall hat of ancient date ... his uniform was bespattered with yellow anchors and other nautical devices'.[10] As Thomson watched the entertainment on the Alofi green to mark his visit, he noted an elderly gentleman who appeared in a nautical uniform and who had discarded the hat he wore earlier in the day for a 'homemade cocked hat, hastily constructed in imitation of mine'.[11] It was a typical Niuean response and Thomson seemed to enjoy the joke.

Six months later Lord Ranfurly was on the Alofi green for the annexation ceremony, and once again Niueans gathered from all over the island, wearing their best clothes. Togia appeared in his royal regalia. He was accompanied by his guards, many of them in 'extraordinary uniforms', including one man 'in a wonderful cocked hat'. 'Another ... looked grand and solemn in a top hat of the days of Dickens, while two or three wore the uniforms of the guards of well-known English railway companies.'[12]

Perhaps the only item of European clothing that was not popular on the island was footwear. Trousers, jackets and headgear, yes; shoes or boots, definitely not. As always, Niueans took the fashions in clothing, for both men and women, and adapted them to suit their own situation and preferences.

Had this been simply a goodwill visit by a politician on a voyage to restore his health? Did the people of Niue have any inkling that, in a year, Niue would be included within the boundaries of New Zealand? It is difficult to know; but in New Zealand there was certainly a growing understanding that Premier Seddon had a Pacific agenda.

New Zealand politicians had maintained an intense interest in the South Pacific throughout the second half of the nineteenth century. They had frequently urged the imperial government to take control of islands in the Pacific and had often suggested they could be annexed or federated to New Zealand.

The motives behind these requests were mixed. Its geographical proximity meant New Zealand was more interested in the region than Britain. There were commercial motives, both in direct trade with the Pacific and in the control and protection of shipping routes. In an age of coal-fired ship engines, coaling stations were critical, and these had to be located where there were natural harbours suitable for vessels delivering coal supplies, and for the safe harbouring of steam ships while coal supplies were loaded. Towards the end of the nineteenth century the construction of the Panama Canal,[13] with the potential that this offered for trans-Pacific shipping, and the laying of the trans-Pacific cable from San Francisco, which necessitated relay points along the route to New Zealand and Australia, made strategic territory in the Pacific vital.

Earlier New Zealand premiers George Grey, Robert Stout and Julius Vogel were all keen for New Zealand to extend its influence to the South Pacific. Richard Seddon, however, was the most vociferous and imperialistic of New Zealand's politicians. The canal and cable constructions coincided with his term as premier; and another major development – the proposed federation of Australian colonies – helped crystallise his desire for a Pacific empire. There was an option for New Zealand to join the Australian federation; but Seddon preferred to think of a Pacific federation, including Fiji, Samoa and Tonga and centred on New Zealand, as a counterbalance to the influence of the Australian federation.[14]

When Samoa was divided between Germany and the United States in 1899, Seddon was bitterly disappointed that European power politics had overridden New Zealand aspirations. In early 1900, in spite of his constant harassment of the imperial government, a federation between Fiji and New Zealand was finally ruled out and, at the same time, a British protectorate was established over Tonga. There appeared to be only one remaining area where New Zealand could exercise influence: in the spread of ocean sprinkled with isolated islands and atolls known as the

'Fills the bill': Seddon as a Fijian chief. New Zealand Premier Richard Seddon was very keen to create a Pacific federation centred on New Zealand and including Fiji, Tonga and Samoa, as a counter to the federation of Australian colonies. He was particularly interested in Fiji with its large European population and its sugar industry. This cartoon appeared on the cover of the *New Zealand Graphic and Ladies' Journal* on 13 October 1900. National Library of New Zealand

The federation of six British colonies into the Commonwealth of Australia is shown here as an ogre threatening the small Pacific islands, but New Zealand, draped in a Māori cloak, is shown as the protector of the Pacific peoples. The cartoon appeared on the cover of the *New Zealand Graphic and Ladies' Journal* on 20 October 1900, the day after Lord Ranfurly had annexed Niue. National Library of New Zealand

Cook Islands. Some of these had already been annexed by Britain, and protectorate status had been given to the remainder, so they all came under the jurisdiction of the Western Pacific High Commission. Some argued that nothing further was needed. But Seddon pressed the case with London to allow annexation of the area to New Zealand; and London – worn down by this persistent colonial premier, and occupied with war in the Transvaal – agreed to the idea. In the swirl of imperialistic rhetoric that accompanied New Zealand's enthusiastic participation in the South African War, Seddon prepared at last for the creation of a New Zealand Pacific empire.

Months of communication between New Zealand and Britain, through the Governor of New Zealand, His Excellency the Earl of Ranfurly, to the Secretary of State for Colonies in London, paved the way for a voyage by the governor to the Cook

A scene in Alofi village photographed by Malcolm Ross, official correspondent on the voyage of the New Zealand governor, Lord Ranfurly, to annex the Cook Islands and Niue in October 1900.
Ranfurly Collection, Alexander Turnbull Library, Wellington, New Zealand, PA1-q-633_036

Islands and Niue in October 1900. If the governor was satisfied that the inhabitants wished to cede full sovereignty, he had the authority to annex the islands. Lord Ranfurly was to carry out the annexation as the representative of Her Majesty's government, not as the Governor of New Zealand, and he was to annex the islands to the British Empire and not to the Colony of New Zealand. Both Wellington and London knew that annexation to New Zealand was the ultimate goal, but there were legal and constitutional issues to settle before this could become a reality.

In Wellington, Seddon introduced legislation into parliament 24 hours before Ranfurly departed on his voyage. 'I contend', said Seddon, beginning a long debate, 'that the extension of our boundaries, the bringing in of people and communities with us whose interests are identical, is in truth the interests of our colony, and will profit our colony for all time.'[15] The legislation was to extend the boundaries of New Zealand to include the area of the Pacific encompassing all the Cook Islands, both the southern and northern groups, and Niue. The right to do this rested on the Colonial Boundaries Act passed by the British Parliament in 1895. It gave self-governing colonies the right to extend borders to include neighbouring

People gather on the wharf at Alofi in 1900 as the governor's party prepares to come ashore. The landing at Alofi was extremely precarious. When bad weather threatened, the decking was uplifted and stored; if this was not done in time, the planks were likely to be swept away and scattered along the coast. Ranfurly Collection, Alexander Turnbull Library, Wellington, New Zealand, PA1-q-633_035-bottom

territory not already claimed by another power, and it retrospectively gave legality to New Zealand's earlier extensions to the Chathams, Auckland Islands and the Kermadecs. The legislation was rushed, many members of Parliament were surprised by it and debate went on until 2.30 am, when the motion was finally carried.

Ranfurly sailed from Wellington on board HMS *Mildura* on 30 September 1900. He headed first for Rarotonga and then Mangaia, Aitutaki, Penrhyn and Manihiki, before arriving at Niue on 18 October. There he welcomed Frank Lawes on board to discuss the issue of annexation. Ranfurly was left with the impression that:

> *Niue ... was likely to prove a difficult task. It had only lately been proclaimed a Protectorate, and the people, we were told, were not likely to agree to annexation ... I felt the position was going to be by no means an easy one, my instructions being only to annex with the sanction of the inhabitants.*[16]

Ranfurly wrote to King Togia. The reply, addressed to 'the Great Chief of Britain who has come to Niue', informed him: 'I will concede to your request and come to

People gathered on the cliffs overlooking Alofi Bay, waiting for a decision on annexation. Governor Ranfurly was in discussion with Togia and other iki and when a decision was reached a signal was sent to the governor's vessel, the *Mildura*, and a ceremony began. Ranfurly Collection, Alexander Turnbull Library, Wellington, New Zealand, PA1-q-633_035-top

Alofi tomorrow morning.'[17] The governor's party went ashore first thing on Friday 19 October, accompanied by marines and sailors. A guard of honour was posted in front of the mission house and, as the governor stepped onto the island, a 17-gun royal salute was fired from the ship. Hundreds of Niueans gathered in the LMS compound. Togia arrived from Tuapa, accompanied by his bodyguard and once again suitably attired, this time 'in frock coat, a black belltopper, and uniform trousers with a band of red running down the side'.[18]

Discussion on the issue of annexation lasted several hours. Togia insisted that the decision be made not by him alone but in consultation with the iki from all the villages. Ranfurly stressed the advantages of becoming part of the British Empire, 'an Empire that was the greatest in the world'. Togia listened, then spoke with the other chiefs. Eventually, 'greatly to the surprise of the traders, one after another of the chiefs declared himself in favour of annexation'.[19] The deed of cession, signed by Togia, Patuiki of Niue Fekai, and by iki from the 11 villages, reads:

Governor Ranfurly read the Treaty of Annexation, the Union Jack was hoisted, the marines saluted and the guns from HMS *Mildura* fired a royal salute. Niue was officially part of the British Empire.

Ranfurly Collection, Alexander Turnbull Library, Wellington, New Zealand, PA1-q-633_037

> *We, the King and Chiefs of the Island of Niue, do hereby consent to her Majesty Queen Victoria taking possession of this island, and in proof thereof have hereto subscribed our names this 19th day of October 1900.*[20]

While this process had been going on, the marines and sailors had given up any hope of there being a ceremony and had drifted off to shady spots to await developments. A signalman now informed the *Mildura* to stand by for saluting; the men were hastily rounded up and paraded by the flagpole recently erected in front of the mission house and the ceremony of annexation took place. Lord Ranfurly read the Treaty of Annexation, Captain Baynes hoisted the Union Jack, the marines saluted and the guns from HMS *Mildura* fired a royal salute. The captain called for 'Three Cheers for the Queen' – and Niue was officially part of the British Empire.[21] After lunch at the mission house Lord Ranfurly was presented with gifts from each of the village groups: hats, fans, necklaces of shells or yellow pandanus berries or frangipani, spears, model canoes, fowl and tropical fruit. There was singing and dancing – and then, always pressed for time because of the need to conserve coal supplies, the governor and his entourage rejoined the *Mildura* and sailed for Tonga. Malcolm

Ross, official newspaper correspondent on the voyage, noted with satisfaction, 'thus ended our last and most successful annexation'.[22]

Lord Ranfurly was back in New Zealand by the end of October and cabled the High Commissioner for the Western Pacific:

> *I have the honour to inform you that, in accordance with instructions received from the Secretary of State for the Colonies, I annexed the whole of the islands in the Cook and Hervey Group, also Niue, or Savage Island.*
>
> *I understand from telegrams received, that these islands will be managed by New Zealand, also Penrhyn and Palmerston. The intention is that the boundaries of New Zealand shall be enlarged, with the view of extending over this area, and the Secretary of State has informed me that, as soon as the annexation has taken place, Her Majesty would be advised to issue an Order-in-Council to that effect.*[23]

The legislation to extend New Zealand's boundaries went to London for Royal Assent, and when this was granted through an Order in Council, the governor in New Zealand was given the authority to issue a Proclamation stating that the islands in question had been annexed to New Zealand. The Proclamation was announced on 11 June 1901; and responsibility for the administration of these islands now shifted from the Western Pacific High Commission to the New Zealand Parliament.

Not everyone was happy with this arrangement – and some were exceedingly surprised. At the Western Pacific headquarters in Fiji, the high commissioner had for several years expressed grave misgivings about New Zealand's ability to undertake such a responsibility. Sir John Thurston had advised that Her Majesty's government should retain direct control over the islands and not sanction 'any of the Australasian colonies satisfying themselves with petty annexations in the South Seas and assuming obligations they cannot discharge'. He was particularly critical of New Zealand interfering in Samoan affairs; and he concluded, 'certainly New Zealand should not be allowed to interfere further in the Pacific'.[24]

On Niue there was considerable disquiet. Niueans and Pālagi believed that Niue had been annexed to Britain, not New Zealand; and now, to rub salt in the wound, they learned that Niue was to be grouped with the Cook Islands for administrative purposes, and a resident agent on Niue would answer to the resident commissioner in Rarotonga. Frank Lawes expressed the general opinion when he wrote:

> *Seddon's hobby of Island federation is a case of trying to join together what God has separated by hundreds of miles of ocean. If New Zealand persist in their present policy of federating Niue with Cook and other islands, which is quite different from the agreement made between King and chiefs of Niue and Lord Ranfurly, annexation will be a constant source of irritation and will be anything but a blessing.*[25]

He made this opinion known in Wellington, too, when he wrote to the governor, Lord Ranfurly. Ranfurly replied that he would 'bear in mind the wishes of the chiefs that the Resident should be a married man and not from Rarotonga'.[26]

Robert Head put the issue more directly in a letter to Seddon:

> *The King and Chiefs accepted annexation on condition that the island should be governed by the British Government and not from the Colony of NZ or from Rarotonga. The King and Chiefs who signed the document of annexation were most emphatic in this matter.*[27]

Premier Seddon received a similar letter from the Auckland trading company Vines, Utting and Perston, who claimed to be in a unique position to advise on Niue as they were responsible for 'fully two thirds of the trade' to the island. In their view, the people of Niue 'strongly objected to annexation to New Zealand, in a great measure owing to their aversion to being governed from Rarotonga'.[28]

Despite these cautions, the New Zealand government pressed ahead with existing plans. It secured the services of Stephenson Percy Smith to head to Niue as acting resident agent; his brief was to set up the necessary administrative structures for the island and to draft the necessary legislation. Percy Smith had retired as government surveyor in late 1900; and, as a self-taught ethnologist and scholar of Polynesian societies and languages, and co-founder of the Polynesian Society, he was seen as the ideal man for the task. He sailed from Auckland in August 1901 on the maiden voyage of the *Countess of Ranfurly* – a vessel that was to become well known in Niue waters. In keeping with the proposed administrative arrangement, he went first to Rarotonga and collected the resident commissioner, Colonel Walter Gudgeon, before sailing to Niue.

The group arrived in early September 1901 and, after initial welcomes, Smith settled in to the tasks ahead. He had long discussions with Frank Lawes, and then began drafting laws and arranging a new system of administration. The most important aspect to tackle, he felt, was the Fono, which had been nominated by the patuiki 'from people who are likely to support his views solely'.[29] 'It is not popular and will have to be removed,' Smith noted in his diary. 'Also, the judges, so-called, who keep all the fines inflicted, and above all revenue has to be raised to meet the expenses of government.'[30] In another entry, Smith noted that the king would have to be told that he could no longer levy tributes for his own benefit. Just as the 23 village judges kept fines imposed for their own purposes, so too did village policemen – and there were 140 of them. Both positions would need to be regularised, the number of office holders greatly reduced and all payments made over to the government.[31]

Arrival of S. Percy Smith on Niue. Percy Smith was appointed acting resident agent on Niue by the New Zealand government. He arrived in September 1901 with the resident commissioner for the Cook Islands, Col. Gudgeon. This photo was taken by Josiah Martin, a professional photographer of Auckland. Percy Smith is sitting on the office chair at the right; Gudgeon, in white, is addressing the gathered crowd; and Rev. Lawes, holding an umbrella, is interpreting for him.

Auckland War Memorial Museum Tāmaki Paenga Hira, New Zealand, MS 281, 11

The labour trade was also in need of greater regulation. 'The whole system of recruiting men for labourers is rotten to the core,' wrote Frank Lawes to John Arundel in early 1901; and he added, 'the king has had [as] much to do with making it what it is as any living man.'[32] He was referring to the practice of the iki and the patuiki charging a commission to put names forward for selection as contract labourers; and also, in some cases, taking a percentage of moneys earned on contract. A recent incident had highlighted the involvement of the chiefs in the labour issue. Arundel and Company had returned a group from Baker Island in May 1900, and had reported that 13 men had died on the island. They now wanted to recruit another group, but the iki from Alofi South round to Liku decided that they would not allow any more men to go to Baker Island.

S. Percy Smith's takai, 1901

WHILE PERCY SMITH was acting government agent on Niue in late 1901, he made a takai, a journey round the island, and he recorded observations in his diary.

Thursday 3 October 1901

On this day I left Alofi with Rev Lawes for a journey round Niue. [We] were accompanied by Rev Lawes' son Frank, Ikihenga and Mokelagi, two of the chiefs of Alofi, and several bearers to carry our clothes and the stores put together by Mrs Lawes. The bearers walked all the way round the Island whilst we others rode.

I had been along the first mile of road before but after that it was all new to me. For three to four miles the road runs along the upper plateau ... there is mainly yellow guava (kautonga), it is thickly carpeted with ferns ... and here and there a clump of trees. One gets a more extended view over the Island now and then ... we now left the main road and descended the rocky hill to the lower terrace to the village of Taumakatonga, where we found all the inhabitants assembled to meet us, dressed in their best.

There is a neat church here built ... either of lathe and plaster or solid coral blocks, gleaming white under the coconut trees. The teacher residences are the centre of civilization and we always stayed in them on our journey. They are fair-sized houses with several rooms and with bedsteads, dining tables, washstands and the floors being covered with several thicknesses of mats ... as soon as we changed, the Patus and Ikis gathered in the teacher's house to present food to me ... There are always speeches made in which they apologise for the meagreness of the feast ... though ... generally there is several hundredweight of things.

This place is on the coast, about 100 feet above the sea, and being on the lower terrace the ground around is terribly rocky though the vegetation grows everywhere. Here is a taue or fort, but it is a mean affair after a Maori pa, it is merely a place surrounded with enough rocks in which a few people could remain and keep off their enemies.

After tea ... I explained, through Mr Lawes, the purpose of my visit. The people of the village must select from amongst themselves a good man to become a member of the Great Council of Niue.

Friday 4 Oct, 1901

S.E. trade wind and hot. We had breakfast early and after the horses were fed ... on the leaves of the ti, we left for Avatele, riding along the lower terrace which was as rocky as ever but with little cultivations of taro and banana here and there among the rocks ... In this part of the Island there are more breadfruit trees than I have observed elsewhere ...

We soon arrived at Avatele, which is supposed to be the seat of the small disaffected party who do not care for British rule. There was the usual feast spread out in the teacher's house, and outside another given by the people ...

We went across to the beach for there is a little sandy beach here in a corner of the coast ... all the young boys of Avatele were indulging in surf riding (fakatu-peau) on a board ... we then went up to the Councillor's house where we found a table spread with all the delicacies of the season, including some excellent fish, of which we generally get too little here, which is strange as the people are great fishermen ... We then met the people in the church and I explained to them about the election. This church is about 80 feet long and it is floored with one mat of that length.

We left Avatele and ascended to the upper plateau by the usual rocky road and then, turning off the main road to the south we visited Fatsiau, a small village with church and teacher's residence. Here another feast was spread out that we returned to the people.

Leaving Fatsiau after an hour's talk, we went on to Hakupu. Passed small cultivations of sugarcane and manioc and travelled through forest for some way. Hakupu – quite the nicest village I have seen in the island. There is a large church and a commodious teacher's residence where we put up. There were large numbers of people to welcome us and of course a feast … After a rest we walked with some of the people to the edge of the plateau and had a fine view of the eastern ocean, which, for a wonder, was somewhat calm. Along this coast, some years ago, was found large quantities of oregon timber, which is to be seen now in houses, church and … in furniture. It appears that a timber-laden ship bound for Australia met with a very severe gale off Niue … and became a wreck. Her crew took to the boats and reached Samoa but the vessel drifted on and broke up on this coast.

S. Percy Smith was the retired government surveyor in New Zealand and a co-founder of the Polynesian Society. He was sent to Niue as acting resident agent for three months in 1901 to make arrangements for the New Zealand administration of the island. Auckland War Memorial Museum Tāmaki Paenga Hira, New Zealand, C25897

Saturday 5 Oct. 1901

We left Hakupu about 8 and travelled northward along a good road … we passed through belts of native forest where the road is beautiful and the trees 100 to 120 feet high … the large trees are mostly kafika. We came to Liku about 11am … [had earlier visited Liku and commented on the village built under groves of coconuts, with smooth grass underneath and a white coral church. There was a beautiful tree here, very much like the rata, called feka-kai].[33] *After lunch we headed north again … to Lakepa. There was a fono going on to say goodbye to a young man and his wife, who are to leave for New Guinea by the mission ship* John Williams *which is expected here early next month. They go as missionaries.*[34] *The people of Lakepa were giving them a feast and presents, among which were 1400 fathoms of sinnet, made of coconut husk, and which is used for twine, cords and ropes. This is much valued in New Guinea … The feast [included] a taro pudding 9 feet long. But that is a mere baby. On one occasion at Liku the people gave Mr Lawes a taro pudding 220 yards long! It is baked in a long narrow trench by the usual method with hot stones.*

We then mounted and went on to Mutalau, another large village near the NE end of the island.

Sunday 6 Oct. 1901

Remained all day in Mutalau for church services … Very hot … towards dusk it became cooler and Mr Lawes and I walked down to … the landing place for this settlement … the reef is only 15–20 yards wide and being so near the NE end of the island the swell raised by the constant trade winds sweeps round and breaks heavy on the reef. There are two caves there about 25 feet above the sea in which the natives keep their canoes but in heavy westerly weather they are not safe there and have to be removed.

Monday 7 Oct. 1901

We left early, the day being hot … and rode towards Tuapa and then turned north along a bad, rocky track to the village of Hikutavake which is situated on the lower terrace … the church is new and has an iron roof and therefore is hot … then walked to a remarkable cleft in the rocks called Matapa … large and very picturesque. The sea comes in at the lower end making a beautiful, clear, deep pool … with perpendicular and even overhanging cliffs on either side. It is a very interesting place. We all went in and had a good swim, which was very refreshing in the heat.

After dinner we rode about 1½ miles along the lower terrace over a very rough, rocky track until we came out on the main road near Tuapa or Uhomotu. After a change we went over to the old man's house and found him in his naval uniform, cocked hat and feathers and with a great feast laid out … the queen was there also nicely dressed in white …

Then we rode 6 miles to Alofi and finished our takai of the island.[35]

Matapa chasm. On his takai around Niue, Percy Smith visited Matapa chasm where everyone 'went in and had a good swim'. This image was probably taken by Percy Smith on this visit in 1901.

Alexander Turnbull Library, Wellington, New Zealand, F-116318-1/2

> *The king was delighted at the prospect of sending the whole party from his end of the island ... [When] men were not forthcoming, boys were sent ... in large numbers. The king and chiefs are utterly indifferent so long as they get the bounty and also get some money from each man engaged.*[36]

This case was fresh in Lawes' mind when Smith arrived, and it no doubt featured in the long discussions the two held in relation to the new administration of Niue.

Smith began his work by organising for the election of a new Island Council, with representatives from all the villages. 'In the past the King chose the Council members but I am trying to have the principle of representation of the people carried out.'[37] On 3 October Smith and Lawes set out to travel round the island on horseback, visiting each village and explaining the importance of the upcoming election to the new Island Council. At each gathering, Smith explained that it was important to elect a good man, as they would have to enact the laws of the country and help the resident agent govern.

The news of the election was well received, according to Percy Smith – although he did wonder how the king would take it: 'It must be a bit of a blow to the king to know I am taking away his own council and getting another one elected and that I am taking away ... all his fees and tributes.'[38] These 'fees and tributes' included money demanded from ships that called, and an annual payment from traders. However, Smith planned to give Togia a salary as president of the Island Council, and he hoped this would placate him.

By mid-October elections had taken place and a messenger was sent out to all the villages calling the new Island Council to meet in Alofi. Over a three-day period they discussed the draft legislation that Percy Smith had drawn up. It was novel to have written material to consider, but they soon got into the rhythm: the council discussed, amended and passed five new laws.[39] The Niue Council Act, including a salary of £50 for the king, was passed first, followed by discussion on the Revenue of Niue Act, which was designed to raise revenue 'for the purpose of the proper government of Niue Island': all duties, fees and fines that had previously been paid to individuals would be now be paid into the 'Revenue of Niue Account', administered by the resident agent. The Native Magistrates and Police Act reduced the number of magistrates from 23 to five, and policemen from 140 to 11; they would henceforth be paid a salary of £6 and £3 respectively per annum, instead of collecting fines. The Marriage, Divorce and Registration Act made provisions for the resident missionary and the village pastors to conduct marriage ceremonies, and for all marriages, births and deaths to be officially registered. Applications for divorce were subject to

First Niue Island Council, 1901. One of Percy Smith's tasks was to set up a new Island Council which would meet quarterly in Alofi to discuss island issues with the New Zealand resident agent (after 1903, the resident commissioner). The first Council met in Alofi on 22 October 1901 and after two days drawing up laws, Smith 'photographed all the Councillors in a group'. In fact, Smith himself is in the photograph, on the left, so possibly it was taken by Rev. Lawes, who was at the meeting to interpret for Smith. Alexander Turnbull Library, Wellington, New Zealand, F-116257-1/2

a payment; and fines were imposed for failing to register births and deaths. Finally, the Emigration Act sought to regularise the labour trade, and to give protection to families left behind on the island. Young men hoping to go away to work had to be at least 16 years of age; they would have to sign the labour agreement in the presence of the resident agent after first providing proof that they had made provision for any family remaining on the island; and they would have to pay a fee of 4 shillings in order to obtain a pass to leave. When all the work was finished, Percy Smith took the councillors to see the site he had chosen in Alofi for the new Residency. He then took a group photo – and the first Island Council meeting under New Zealand administration ended.

All five Acts seemed perfectly reasonable and necessary for 'good governance', yet they reflected the prevailing Eurocentric attitudes of the time and consequently

On 31 October 1901 the Niuean pastors from all the outer villages came into Alofi for their monthly meeting. These men were often referred to as teachers, for the village pastor was responsible for running the village school. Smith recorded in his diary that he had taken their photograph but Rev. and Mrs Lawes were not with them as they were ill with influenza.

Alexander Turnbull Library, Wellington, New Zealand, F-115298-1/2

were carefully drafted to make a distinction between 'natives of Niue' and 'white people'. Native magistrates had no jurisdiction in any case where white people were involved; Smith advised the New Zealand government that the resident agent should be given judicial powers to deal with such situations. Native pastors in the villages could officiate only at marriages between natives; marriages between whites, or between whites and natives, must be conducted by the resident missionary or by the resident agent. Under the Revenue of Niue Act, it was illegal to import any spirituous liquor for sale, barter or gift to 'any native of Niue or native of other islands of the Pacific located in Niue'. Whites[40] were not included in the liquor ban. Similarly, they were exempt from the regulations embodied in the Emigration Act, which resulted in cases of whites leaving native wives and children on the island and not being seen again. This legislation, and the paternalism and racism embedded in it,

Sketch of the tomb of Fataaiki, from Percy Smith's diary. Percy Smith wrote extensive notes while living on Niue. Much of his writing was subsequently published in the *Journal of the Polynesian Society* but he also kept a personal diary while there. When describing where he was living in Alofi, he sketched the tomb of Fataaiki, the patuiki, who had died five years earlier.
Auckland War Memorial Museum Tāmaki Paenga Hira, New Zealand, MS 281, 20

At what is known as Tomb Point, in front of the Alofi church, two nineteenth-century patuiki, Tuitoga and Fataaiki, lie buried. Fataaiki's tomb is little changed today from the sketch by Percy Smith.
Author's collection

was to underpin New Zealand's administration of Niue for at least the next 50 years, reflecting attitudes similar to those embedded in Crown–Māori relations in New Zealand.

For Percy Smith the next two months were very frustrating. He felt his main work was done, and although there were clerical details to attend to, he found these boring. He spent more and more time taking photographs, collecting bird and plant specimens, recording items of Niue folklore and 'sitting on the grass … below the mission house looking out to sea and longing for a ship to come'.[41] After lavish farewells he finally left Niue on 26 December 1901 and headed back home to retirement.

Smith had hoped that the resident agent for Niue would arrive on the island while he was there so he could brief him before leaving, but because of the erratic nature of shipping to Niue, this did not happen. Christopher Maxwell arrived in early January 1902, and had to rely for help on the copious notes left by Smith and the wise counsel of Frank Lawes. All the villages contributed to building the

Mapourika lying off the reef at Alofi during the New Zealand parliamentary visit in May 1903.
Auckland War Memorial Museum Tāmaki Paenga Hira, New Zealand, Henry Winkelmann Album 264 item 15

Residency in Alofi. By 1903 it was completed and Maxwell was installed, in time to receive a New Zealand parliamentary tour on 16 May.

Headed by Hon. Charles H. Mills, Minister in Charge of the Cook and Other Islands, and comprising 33 members of the New Zealand Parliament, the group was on a familiarisation trip to Seddon's new Pacific empire. As usual, the vessel arrived at Niue unannounced, and when all these men landed – a little surprised that there was no immediate welcoming function – they spread out to visit the island, or at least that part of the island that could be easily reached on foot from Alofi. One visitor was more adventurous and went by horse to Avatele. He paid for his recklessness, however, as the horse refused to make the return trip; he was forced to return on foot, and when night fell the journey became a hazardous and terrifying one.

The following day the Niueans were ready to welcome the parliamentary party. King Togia made the journey to Alofi once again, and everyone gathered on the Alofi green. 'We had learned that the Niue people were the most dissatisfied with the annexation to New Zealand of all the Islanders, and that we were likely to hear

The resident agent, Christopher Maxwell, had made some improvements to the wharf at Alofi and the 'sea was as smooth as glass, and there was no ground swell', so the landing was without difficulty.
Museum of New Zealand Te Papa Tongarewa, Henry Winkelmann LS 005256

a good deal of grumbling. In this we were not disappointed,' noted one of the reporters travelling with the tour.[42]

Two meetings were held with Charles Mills. The first was with a delegation representing the white traders on the island. In 1900 the man who seemed to be at the forefront of the younger traders was Harry Pearse, but now a new name came to the fore: Leslie Rex, a trader from Tasmania who had settled in Avatele in 1899 to help run the business for Lever Brothers, major traders in copra. Rex put questions to Mills on a number of matters relevant to the traders. When the issue of spirituous liquors was raised, there was an obvious tension between Rex and Robert Henry Head, who was also present: Head was in favour of a move to have prohibition strictly enforced for all inhabitants on the island, whereas Rex, who had recently imported a supply for European consumption, was anxious to maintain the status quo. Import duties imposed on tobacco were another source of concern to the traders, as well as the cost of trading licences.

The next morning people arrived in Alofi from all over the island and gathered on the green in front of the Alofi church where 'the big korero' was to be held.

Museum of New Zealand Te Papa Tongarewa, Henry Winkelmann LS 005278

Togia, patuiki of Niue, arrived from Tuapa and asked to be presented to all the members of the New Zealand party, so 'they filed past the old chap and shook hands'. In this image Togia is meeting Mills, watched by the resident agent Maxwell (in nautical cap) and Robert Henry Head (with white beard).

Henry Winkelmann, Alexander Turnbull Library, Wellington, New Zealand, PAColl-6118-70

In the general discussion with those assembled before Togia and Mills, Pulekula, a native pastor from Liku, spoke of the general dissatisfaction with the constitutional arrangement that had seen Niue annexed not to Britain but to New Zealand, and then not to New Zealand directly but via Rarotonga. 'We wish, I say, to have direct communications from Niue to New Zealand, and from New Zealand to Niue, and not to have any connection with Rarotonga whatsoever.'[43] The other speakers – Togiafulu, Tatagata and Hegotule of the Island Council; and Uea, the native pastor of Alofi – strongly reiterated Pulekula's stance on annexation. They also called for total prohibition of alcohol; a reduction of the tax on tobacco and horses and on the personal luggage of Islanders returning from labour contracts; and an end to the fee for emigrating. The *Auckland Star* reporter noted that there was some friction between these speakers and the interpreter, Robert Head Junior. 'Whenever the natives said anything disagreeable to the interpreter he appeared to argue the point with them, and it was only after protests' that some of the complaints were put forward. This was particularly noted when one Islander complained that the traders

Many speakers put forward grievances to the visiting party. They were most dissatisfied with annexation to New Zealand and especially with administrative control through the Cook Islands, and they made this clear to the visiting parliamentarians. Largely as a result of this visit the Cook Islands Amendment Act removed the link to Rarotonga and gave Niue a direct link to Wellington.

Henry Winkelmann, Alexander Turnbull Library, Wellington, New Zealand, PAColl-6118-82

For the younger members of the island population, the parliamentary visit was a chance to gather on the mission house wall and watch all the excitement of a visit by so many people.
Museum of New Zealand Te Papa Tongarewa, Henry Winkelmann LS 005307

gave IOUs for goods, rather than cash; and Head, who had recently set up his own trading store in Alofi, did not seem keen to pass on this complaint.

When the discussions ended, the festivities began. In the evening there was a brilliant display of fireworks and the ship's guns were fired. 'It is to be hoped the entertainment thus afforded the natives will reconcile them to the payment of heavy customs duties and other drawbacks incidental to their New Zealand relationship,' concluded the *Auckland Star* article. The parliamentary tour – often referred to in the New Zealand press as the 'Parliamentary Picnic' – continued on its way, but its members had been given the message that the annexation of Niue was far from satisfactory. One Opposition member, interviewed on his return to Dunedin, summed up the situation in Niue as:

... in a chaotic condition. This island never was a Cook island, but had been taken over and put under the jurisdiction of the Cook group, and was in a seething condition now, the natives being very dissatisfied, and with good reason, owing to the stupid way in which they were dealt with.[44]

The link to Rarotonga was the biggest problem. Within the Cook Islands there were local island councils, but there was also a federal council consisting of representatives from each of the islands. Niue had its island council but was not represented at the federal council level; yet it was subject to federal council rulings and was under the administrative direction of the resident commissioner in Rarotonga. Customs regulations meant all shipping to the group had to report first to Rarotonga so that import duties could be levied, and this meant vessels headed for Niue had a long and expensive detour.

Robert Head Junior, representing the traders on Niue, had visited Mills in Wellington before the parliamentary tour to express their concerns. Mills had also received complaints about the situation from the Auckland Chamber of Commerce, which represented the companies trading with Niue, so he was well aware of the economic issues involved.[45]

The extreme dissatisfaction with these arrangements was the driving force behind the introduction of the Cook and Other Islands Government Act Amendment Bill, introduced by Mills in September 1903. This bill, when it was passed, gave Niue what it had wanted: its own resident commissioner answerable directly to Wellington, with no connection to Rarotonga. Alofi was declared a port of entry for customs purposes; now shipping headed for Niue could come directly, and any tariffs due would be paid in Niue to the Niue Government Revenue Account.

In the space of four years, from the arrival of the British envoy in April 1900 to the creation of a separate administration for the island in late 1903, so many changes had occurred in Niue. Queen Victoria had died and King Edward VII was on the throne. Niue may not have achieved its prime desire – to be directly linked to Britain – but the people had made their feelings known and had succeeded in achieving a second-best solution.

For the majority of the population, life continued as before. They moved between their village and their bush section growing and harvesting their food crops, they fished and hunted and tried to meet their commitments to family, village and church. Reverend Lawes was still on the island, and the church still dominated village life. There were good years, and years when drought or cyclone devastated their bush gardens and sometimes their villages. Young men still left for labour contracts in other parts of the Pacific, and some never returned. But in Alofi there was now a new building, the New Zealand Residency, just south of the LMS mission house; and in the next few decades authority and power on the island would shift from one to the other.

PROTECTED
Sears/00

PART C.

New Zealand Administration

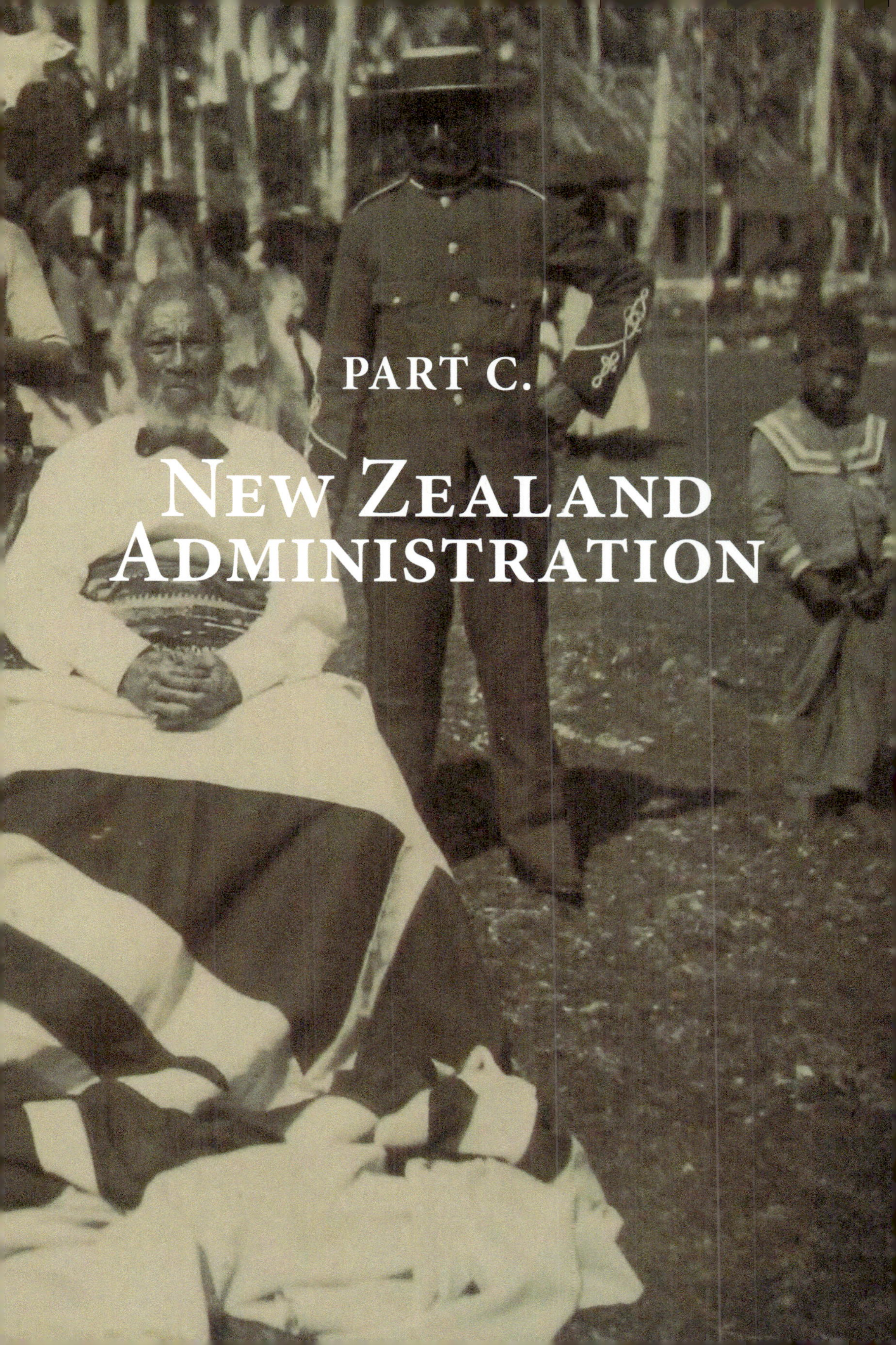

9. From rhetoric to reality

Let New Zealand and Niue be one kingdom

When Togia, Patuiki of Niue, learned that his island was to be administered directly from Wellington, he wrote to his friend, Premier Richard Seddon, 'It is very good my kingdom is not to be connected to Rarotonga. Let New Zealand and Niue be one kingdom.'[1] Seddon may have been the master of rhetoric when it came to empire building, but the reality of administering small, isolated islands at great distances from New Zealand, and of making New Zealand and Niue 'one kingdom', was to be the task of others.

The first sight of Niue from the deck of a ship arriving in Alofi Bay: the rugged coastline and fringing reef, vaka stored on the cliffs, the precarious jetty, the neat white houses in a row, the mission house with white limestone wall, and the imposing church (off to the right). This image was taken by Auckland photographer Josiah Martin when he arrived with Percy Smith in 1901.

Alexander Turnbull Library, Wellington, New Zealand, F-116279-1/2

Early in 1902, responsibility within Cabinet for the new island territories was placed within the portfolio of the minister for trade and customs. This reflected the belief that the development of trade in the islands and the customs duties levied on goods entering the islands would provide the main revenue sources to enable the islands to be self-supporting. Charles Mills therefore became the minister responsible for the Cook and Other Islands; and with the change of arrangements for Niue in late 1903, he now dealt directly with the resident commissioners in the Cook Islands and in Niue. With no dedicated government department to administer this new function, Mills was kept exceedingly busy trying to fulfil some of the promises made by Seddon, including a dedicated shipping service, improvements to landing areas, development of infrastructure on the islands and myriad other issues placed before him by the resident commissioners and the people of the Cooks and Niue.

On the ground in Niue was Christopher Maxwell, resident agent since January 1902, then resident commissioner from January 1904. He may have been recommended for the position by Percy Smith, for it is likely they had encountered each other professionally in the past: Maxwell had worked for several years as an officer of the Native Land Purchase Department in the far north of New Zealand, and Smith had carried out much of the surveying work for this department.

Maxwell was a hands-on, no-fuss sort of man. He threw himself into the practical projects that he felt were necessary for Niue: roadmaking 'to render the present

Christopher Maxwell. He typically appeared in white suit and naval cap. Here he is carrying out his role as health officer, coming out to the *Mapourika* in a vaka in 1903 with yellow health flag flying, to examine the ship's bill of health before the parliamentary tour could land. This system had been introduced by Basil Thomson in April 1900 in an attempt to prevent the introduction of disease.
Museum of New Zealand Te Papa Tongarewa, Henry Winkelmann, LS 005255

Blasting the reef at Avatele. This photo was sent from Resident Commissioner Maxwell to Percy Smith in 1906 to show the work that was being carried out on Niue to improve landing sites. Maxwell actively participated in dynamiting the coral reef at Avatele to widen the boat channel.
Alexander Turnbull Library, Wellington, New Zealand, F-115885-1/2

road around the island smooth and suitable for wheeled vehicles or bicycles' and 'a highway intersecting the island from Alofi to Liku [to] open up the country';[2] the construction of reservoirs in every village to conserve rainwater and ensure the villagers had a constant supply of pure drinking water; developing the jetty and approach at Alofi to facilitate the loading and unloading of vessels; and blasting shipping channels at Avatele and Tuapa to allow vessels to come closer in to shore. Maxwell was in his element supervising the road building, working in the forge, dynamiting the coral reef, pouring cement on the Alofi wharf or designing the plumbing for the reservoirs. He did not have a sense of self-importance, just an enthusiasm for practical progress.

Of course, Maxwell's approach did not always meet with approval, and there were some problems that he found more difficult to deal with. He met regularly with the Island Council, chaired by Togia, and some of the issues raised here he did not feel comfortable dealing with. There was another call for total prohibition on all alcohol, which he did not agree to. The village councillors organised a petition with 1267 signatures, and presented this to Maxwell to be forwarded to the minister. Maxwell felt 'the rights of any community of white British subjects, however small, must be respected', but the minister felt there was sufficient support behind the petition to warrant a compromise solution. He decided that all liquor required in Niue should be imported by the government and disposed of under a system of state control. Europeans only could purchase liquor, and only for their own use.

Similarly, when the Island Council urgently requested a 'suppression of immorality' ordinance to deal with what they saw as a rise in immorality after the suspension of the old laws of the island, Maxwell was reluctant to deal with the issue. 'I do not think it possible to render a people virtuous by Act of Parliament',[3] he wrote to Mills. Maxwell nevertheless listened to the Council's concerns and an ordinance was introduced to deal with matters of immorality, such as women going off to a vessel 'for immoral purposes'; men returning from other places as carriers of venereal disease; women cohabiting with European men; and adultery. Fines ranged from hard labour on the roads for men, to weeding roads or making hats or mats to a certain value for women.

There was much friction between the Administration and the people over payment for all the infrastructure work around the island. Maxwell, who was trying to keep within the annual revenue collected, found it impossible to pay for road work on a daily rate. For the most part he used a piecework method, where workers received food and tobacco for their labour on a section of road. Togia and members of the Island Council constantly complained about this; and they also sought increases in their own pay for attending meetings. In late 1904 there was talk of strike action, and Maxwell wrote to Mills explaining that some Niuean men who had recently returned from Sydney 'have become imbued with the glorious principles of labour unions and strikes, as enunciated by their white friends, the seamen and firemen on the steamers'.[4] However, no changes were made to either rates of pay for councillors or the payment system for road works.

In late 1906 two petitions were organised on Niue and forwarded to Wellington for consideration. There was a new minister for trade and customs, James McGowan, who responded to the petitions, which had one complaint in common: everyone objected strongly to the subsidy being paid from Niue funds for the government schooner, the *Countess of Ranfurly*. The schooner had been purchased in an attempt

In the early years of New Zealand administration of Niue there was a great deal of roadmaking activity and it was mentioned in every annual report. Roadmaking consisted of clearing the undergrowth, filling up the crevices in the jagged limestone with branch coral carried from the beach, and spreading a layer of sand over the top. Where the road had to go from the lower to the upper terrace of the island, much cutting and dynamiting of rock was required. This image, which is undated but was taken in approximately 1915, shows men cutting into the upper terrace.
National Archives UK, CO1069-641(5)

to provide a more reliable shipping service to the Cook Islands and Niue, but it had proved to be a failure and was losing money. In the Cooks there were now steamers calling regularly and they offered a much faster and more assured method of getting fruit to the Auckland markets. The schooner was better for the Niue run, but it was unreliable and often unable to carry all the goods prepared for export. Everyone felt that Niue was paying for a white elephant and called for the vessel to be sold.

In addition to the shipping problem, the Island Council highlighted the absence of two important officeholders on Niue: a school teacher ('what country where His Majesty King Edward VII rules is without a public school teacher?') and a doctor.[5] They also complained that they did not know the amount of revenue collected annually or the expenditure of the Administration; and they called for a Niuean to work alongside the treasurer.

The Europeans in Niue expressed a strong desire to be represented on the Island Council. An earlier response to this demand – that they were represented by the resident commissioner – did not satisfy them as they did not have 'sufficient confidence' in him and felt they had been 'completely ignored' by him.The traders were dissatisfied with the public works programme undertaken by Maxwell and requested that a committee be formed, made up of Europeans and Niueans, to consider all public works expenditure in advance.[6]

Wellington's response to both petitions would have given the petitioners little satisfaction, apart from the news that the government was planning to sell the *Countess of Ranfurly.* The minister explained to the council that the provision of a teacher and a doctor would be far too expensive. In relation to revenue and expenditure, he had instructed Mr Maxwell to henceforth have the annual accounts translated into Niuean and distributed. He told the Europeans their numbers were too few to warrant representation on the council; and he flatly rejected the idea of a public works committee: 'The Resident Commissioner and the [Island] Council are the recognised administration of the Government and the Minister cannot sanction the interference of any irresponsible advisory body.'[7]

Maxwell was no doubt relieved to go on furlough at the end of 1906. While he was in New Zealand he visited the Niuean group, led by Farani Fataaiki, who were performing at the Christchurch Exhibition; and he talked with McGowan in Wellington. He returned to Niue in February 1907; but suddenly in July he was gone. No explanation for his return to New Zealand was given in official papers or the press, but the following year a divorce case in the Auckland Supreme Court cited Christopher Maxwell, Resident Commissioner in Niue, as having 'committed adultery with a native woman there'.[8] He had broken the Suppression of Immorality Ordinance which he had signed into law, and when his wife found out in June 1907, he had no alternative but to depart.

Maxwell's replacement came in the form of Henry Cornwall, sectional clerk in the General Post Office in Wellington. His credentials for the position were that in 1903 he had undertaken an audit of the Administration accounts in both Rarotonga and Niue, and he had relieved on Niue during Maxwell's last furlough. Also, he came from a government department associated with Island affairs, albeit through the sale of postage stamps. This was to be the norm until the 1940s, as there was no dedicated Island Territories staff. People were 'loaned' from other departments, usually Customs or Post Office, and simply had to learn on the job. There was no planned rotation of staff; and in the case of Niue, the need to find a replacement was frequently rushed, for once staff were placed in a position on the Island, they were left there unless – or until – their behaviour forced a hurried change.

Henry Cornwall served as resident commissioner on Niue from 1907 until 1917. He had valuable financial and administrative skills but he also had a fierce temper and was feared by many. His demise came when, like Maxwell before him, he was accused of breaking the immorality laws and forced to leave the island hurriedly. Auckland War Memorial Museum Tāmaki Paenga Hira, New Zealand, C25895

Henry Cornwall, described by one newspaper in New Zealand as 'that rotund, comfortable, little man',[9] had a much greater sense of his own importance than Maxwell. There is no doubt he had useful financial and administrative skills, but he had two attributes which, over a 10-year tenure as resident commissioner, were to cause grief to many: a foul temper and an interfering wife. He began in a very businesslike way by assessing the situation on the island and, after three months, informing Wellington:

> *The position briefly is this: Niue urgently requires both a mail and cargo service and a school, but, owing to her limited resources, she could not bear the cost of both; therefore, if the New Zealand Government is unwilling to help Niue in one of the projects, one or the other will have to be abandoned – an event I should deeply deplore. As the matter is one looming large in the Native eye just now, I should be glad if you will inform me by return boat the Minister's views on the subject.*[10]

This elicited a speedy reply from Minister McGowan: if Niue could provide a school building and residence for a teacher, New Zealand would pay the salary.

Finally, a decision had been made on an issue that had been tossed back and forth over the previous five years. The initial idea had been to select three boys a year and send them to St Stephens School in Auckland.[11] There they would learn

English and also technical skills that would prove useful on their return to Niue. Debate stalled over whether this was the best way to use money or whether better value would be got by sending a European teacher to the island to run a school in Alofi for 50 to 60 students.

Cornwall obtained a decision in favour of a teacher being sent to Niue, and the Island Council was enthusiastic about the plan. They inspected several sites in Alofi, and chose a piece of land at Tufu, in Alofi South. The owners agreed to sell, subscriptions were collected by the council and £108 was paid over. The resident commissioner prepared the papers for the land to be transferred to the Crown, drew up the plans for the building and sent orders for the material needed from New Zealand. By mid-1909 the school was ready to open, with 64 boys, and a European teacher, Mr Malcolm, was appointed. He came with experience in teaching writing and arithmetic, and he was also 'a practical carpenter [with] experience in saw-working and some knowledge of blacksmithing'. His wife could contribute practical lessons in 'domestic economy'.[12]

Places in the new school were offered to each village, based on population. Children boarded at Tufukia[13] – a system that imposed a heavy burden on families as they had to bring food in each week to Alofi from the outlying villages. Village meetings were held and it was decided to erect a large native house in the school grounds for the pupils to have their meals in, and to appoint a Niuean couple to help out with this aspect of school life.

The opening of the school was marked by a large gathering from around the island, in what was one of the last big gatherings attended by Reverend Frank Lawes. Resident Commissioner Cornwall acknowledged the 'great assistance' of Lawes in bringing all the negotiations over the school to 'a successful issue'; and later in 1909 Cornwall wrote to the minister, alerting him to the fact that Lawes was preparing to leave Niue.

> *The Rev Lawes is no ordinary man – he has lived among the natives of Niue for 41 years, during which time he has translated the greater part of the Scriptures into the Niue tongue, and taught the majority of the Natives to read and write their own language. He has accomplished a great work amongst the people of Niue, and by his unselfish life and charming personality has won the esteem of all.*[14]

The retirement of Frank and Sarah Lawes and their departure for London marked a watershed on Niue. In the time they had served, a new breed of LMS missionary had emerged, and no one was ever to stay as long or win as much respect as they had done. The men now sent out around the world by the LMS were university educated and often academic in their approach to the work entrusted to them. Never again was a novice sent to Niue; it was always someone who already had experience in the Pacific or in Africa.

The replacement for Lawes was Reverend Gavin Smith, who had served previously in New Guinea. Smith had the huge task of trying to fill the shoes of Lawes, and he lamented that wherever he went around the Island he heard the words '*ai pihia a Misi Farani* [not like Mr Frank]'.[15] Relations between the Administration and the LMS immediately took a turn for the worse as resident commissioner and missionary-in-charge crossed swords – or rather pens – over where their control lay. The conflict is well illustrated by the situation in Alofi. A large parcel of land centred around the landing site had been gifted by the original owners in 1891 'for the work of God … and for other Government purposes, if this is necessary and with the approval of the Missionary and teacher and Deacons [of Alofi]'.[16] The Alofi church and mission house and the LMS school and training institution were on this compound, and in 1902 it was agreed that the new Residency would be built here. By the time Gavin Smith arrived, the Administration was actively carrying out works around the landing site, to improve both the jetty and the access road down to it. These developments were directly in front of the mission house, and the new missionary frequently objected to them. In addition, the main road, which had earlier skirted round behind Alofi village, now ran directly through it, slicing through the LMS and government compound.

When coconut trees were felled at the landing reserve without the LMS being consulted, Smith protested in writing to the resident commissioner: 'I do not think the church deserves such a lack of common courtesy on the part of the Administration.' Cornwall promptly replied: 'As the works in question cannot affect the Church of Niue … I fail to see that the Administration was under any obligation to specially make known to you its intentions in the matter.' From down the road the reply came back: 'The tone of your letter shows that nothing further need be said or written between you and me.'[17]

Developments at the wharf were part of the increasing presence of the Administration in Alofi. During Cornwall's term on the island, new housing was constructed first for the teacher in charge at Tufukia, then for his assistant, and then for a medical officer and a chief of police.[18] The resident commissioner was granted an assistant and, in time, a house was built for him. Land was acquired in Alofi South for a quarantine station and a sanatorium when cases of tuberculosis increased; Cornwall envisaged the site would be most suitable for a hospital in due course.

When a Resident Commissioner's Court was established in 1909, the prospect of jail sentences became a reality and another piece of land was acquired for a lock-up.

Throughout Niue, but particularly in Alofi, there was growing evidence of the machinery of government. While some Niuean families benefited in particular by association with Pālagi and by living in Alofi, life was changing for all Niueans in a number of ways. Economically, exports were becoming a bigger factor in island life. Copra and hats made up over 90 per cent of exports; and all around the island more land was being used for coconut plantations and large quantities of pandanus were being grown and processed for hat making. Much of the road development was aimed at making it easier to get the copra to Alofi for shipping. A good road across the island to Liku was especially needed, as over 60 per cent of the copra was produced on the eastern side of the island. Niueans now spent more time on export crops for which there was a cash return. There was now a cash value on most things, not only export and import products but also labour and island food. Women were producing a staggering quantity of hats, on average 40–50,000 a year; much of their day was spent gathering and processing pandanus and weaving the hats. In the warmer season, the women spent many hours weaving in the coastal caves where, because of the moist atmosphere, the pandanus remained more supple and pliable.

Production of export crops exposed Niue to a volatile global market, and at times Niueans attempted to counter this. In 1908, a fall in copra prices led to the declaration of a fono or ban on copra making. A number of island elders joined the call to refuse to offer copra for sale. Resident Commissioner Cornwall found out who the organisers were and those in official positions were removed from office.[19] The fono was crushed and a new ordinance introduced to prohibit 'general meetings of the people of the various villages', except with the prior permission of the resident commissioner.

In 1911 a native cooperative trading movement, Niue Kautaha, was set up. The idea apparently came from Tonga and was taken up by a 'few influential Natives', then by hundreds of members; soon it had 'taken root deeply … unsettling the ordinary course of trade considerably'.[20] By this, the resident commissioner meant that not so much trade was going the way of the European traders – although one of them, George Nicholas, agreed to work with Niue Kautaha. The immediate effect was to stimulate production, and although the traders were unhappy with this development, it seems the cooperative lasted for at least a decade.

Alongside the production of export crops, all Niuean families also had to meet the needs of their family, church and village. The LMS noted a growing reluctance

Hat making was an important industry on Niue. Large quantities of pandanus were grown, cut, dried and woven into hats for the New Zealand market. This image appeared in the annual report from the resident commissioner in 1906, and the 1908 report recorded annual hat production at almost 50,000 items. Within a few years the hat trade declined dramatically due to competition from much cheaper imported hats into the New Zealand market.
Alexander Turnbull Library, Wellington, New Zealand, S-L-1298-8_9_bw

to carry out work for the church without a monetary return. Gavin Smith lamented that he had to fight to get the mission house in Alofi rethatched: 'Get it done with iron and let the Society pay for it' was the response.[21] Similarly, work on improving the roads led to calls for daily wages rather than piecework or village responsibility for sections of roading.

The old ways were still important, especially when bad weather produced food shortages. In January 1915 a fierce hurricane hit Niue. The church at Mutalau was completely destroyed, other churches were damaged and hundreds of houses were damaged or destroyed. The coconut, banana and breadfruit crops were decimated.[22] When a severe drought followed the hurricane, the people were thrown back on traditional ways to feed the families. This meant keeping their children out of the local village school or withdrawing them from Tufukia, as all hands were needed for food

The Alofi reservoir. Providing a water supply was a priority for the New Zealand Administration and the solution was to use large areas of roofing as water catchment and to pipe the water into a reservoir. People could then come and fetch water with cans and buckets. Here in Alofi the catchment was the roof of the new Residency but in all the other villages rainwater was piped from the church roof. This image is undated but is in the early period of New Zealand administration. It was the first reservoir to be built and was operating by 1904. The large roof of the residency can be seen in the background. Courtesy Morris family, Wellington, New Zealand

collection in the bush and on the reef. At times like these the roots of the tī became an important food source and the entire village would be involved in collecting and preparing the roots for the long and laborious cooking process in the umutī.[23]

Most Niueans still travelled around the island on foot, and carried their crops back from the bush gardens in baskets on their backs or slung from poles carried by two people. As the roads improved, some families used bicycles – often purchased by men away on labour contracts – which they would load with baskets of food such as taro and then push rather than ride. Some Niuean families also had horses, again often brought back by men returning from labour contracts.[24] The number of horse-drawn vehicles was small and probably restricted to the European community, but the overall increase in horses and bicycles on the roads necessitated the first Niue Traffic Regulation Ordinance in 1916.

In the villages the construction of reservoirs had improved the water supply, but it still required considerable effort to collect and carry cans of water to the houses. In times of drought the supply was restricted to once or twice a week and the village constable had the sometimes unenviable task of keeping the tank locked and dealing with the protests. In the island interior, galvanised iron tanks, with iron roofing to collect water, were constructed for plant irrigation and also in an effort to provide drinking water for people working in bush gardens. This was an attempt to reduce the use of young coconuts for drinking and to keep them instead for copra production.

Thatched roofs were becoming less common as people stopped growing the sugar cane previously used for this purpose, and as corrugated-iron roofing – which was also useful for water collection – became more available. European traders opened small stores in the outer villages, and some Niueans set up their own small outlets. People could now buy imported foodstuffs such as corned beef, as well as bread from four local bakeries.

After the sale of the *Countess of Ranfurly*, the New Zealand government subsidised a schooner service to visit Niue five times a year. The *Kereru* called regularly at Niue, until it was destroyed by fire in Auckland harbour in early 1916; it was replaced by the *Awanui*. The LMS vessel called twice a year, and occasionally a vessel called from Samoa to collect copra.

Boat day was a major event on Niue, and people came to Alofi from all over the island, dressed in their best. It was a chance to socialise and exchange news, to purchase goods from the main trading stores and to sell handcrafts to the visitors. Occasionally there was someone or something special brought ashore from the schooner. In July 1914, the LMS missionary James Cullen reported to London: 'we have had an invasion of the moving picture people who came … with the intention of holding shows in the [LMS] school buildings in every village, and staying here to Christmas.'[25] Cullen was vehemently opposed to such a plan; he refused them access to the school buildings and hoped to prevent them 'getting a footing'. There is no indication of how many people saw a moving picture show, but by October the 'moving picture people' had departed again – on a vessel that delivered a man with a motor car. He offered rides and 'for the first week or two was much patronised. The Natives were delighted at being able to get around the island in one and a half hours and they had many joy rides.'[26] When the British naval vessel HMS *Torch* called in 1914, the boys from Tufukia school were ferried out, amid great excitement, to visit the ship.[27]

Perhaps the greatest change for the people of the island came with the creation of a New Zealand Administration. There was now a clear concept of an entity called Niue. This concept made geographical sense, but not historical or cultural sense.

People still identified as belonging to Mutalau or Liku, Hakupu or Tuapa, and the family and village entity was still most important to them. Yet Alofi was becoming dominant in island affairs: it was from here that all law emanated and decisions were made that affected the whole island. Reverend Lawes had considered the villages furthest from Alofi as 'purer' than those on the western side which had been corrupted by Europeans. Now, though, the Administration saw it the other way round: those on the eastern side, the 'outer' or 'back' villages, were often regarded as difficult and anti-government.

The Island Council, with representatives from all the villages, came to be seen as merely rubber-stamping the wishes of the resident commissioner. The Aid to Revenue Ordinance, passed in 1916, stated that 'every male Native who is over the age of eighteen years shall pay to the Government an annual contribution amounting to ten shillings' towards the cost of maintaining services on the island. For the first time there was a direct tax on Niue, going into the consolidated budget and being used for island-wide services. This concept was difficult for many people to accept. Some wondered why the councillors always seemed to be 'tau tagata gaki' or 'yes-men' who agreed with the resident commissioner.[28] Gavin Smith noted frequently, however, that Cornwall's temper was well known and not to be challenged. 'The Council was a mere tool ... the Councillors said if they were not willing to agree with the Resident he got angry and they got frightened.'[29] When Togia, the by now very elderly patuiki, died in 1917, his position as president of the Island Council was assumed by the resident commissioner. Many saw this as yet another example of Cornwall's desire to take personal control of island affairs; however, it was not in fact his decision. Maui Pomare, the minister responsible for Niue since 1912, had indicated that his intention was to place the resident commissioner at the head of the Island Council,[30] and this provision was included in the Cook Islands Amendment Act of 1916. Togia's death in 1917 brought this provision into effect.

Relations between Resident Commissioner Cornwall and the people of Niue, both Niuean and European, deteriorated over time. Frequently this was alluded to in official LMS correspondence: 'The [RC] has fallen out with nearly every European on the island over his wife's rows.'[31] When Rev. James Cullen arrived on the island in 1914 he tried to be charitable. 'I think the man really wants to make good, but he is cursed with an abominable temper, and is said to lose all control over himself at times. It is a pity that the New Zealand officials are so often men who have had no experience in governing others.'[32] On several occasions letters or petitions were sent to Wellington asking for Cornwall's removal, but nothing was done. When he

A full-page spread in the *Auckland Weekly News* on 14 August 1913 reflected the general lack of knowledge in New Zealand about Niue. The caption reads, ‘Land of bananas and cocoanuts: Scenes on Savage Island, lying between Tonga and Samoa.’ The top left photo shows the technical school at Tufukia; top right, the wharf at Alofi. The image on the middle right is of Matapa; it is captioned ‘Canyon, near Niue.’ Sir George Grey Special Collections, Auckland Libraries, New Zealand, AWNS-19130814-41 went on furlough in late 1915 the intention in Wellington was to return him to the Post Office and send someone new, but in the midst of war this was impossible and Cornwall returned.

Other officials sent from New Zealand to staff the growing Island Administration also found Cornwall difficult to work with. This was one reason for the high staff turnover – sometimes after only six months. Alexander McDonald, sent from Customs as assistant to the resident commissioner, departed rapidly in 1915 after a major row during which Cornwall threatened to shoot him. The press reported that McDonald's return to New Zealand was due to 'failing health', but he was immediately declared fit to enlist and sailed with the Niue Contingent the following year.[33]

In 1917 the situation on the island reached crisis point. The chief of police and the medical officer, with Cullen as witness, were forced to confront the resident commissioner with the fact that serious charges were to be laid against him for immoral behaviour and for 'trying cases in the court when he himself was a great offender'. The situation had become so serious that a demonstration was being planned for the next court day, and a number of women – including one with a baby that she asserted was Cornwall's – were to be paraded before him. 'The Niueans were not shocked by his offence but by the fact that he hauls others to court and fines them £5 while he [goes] free'[34] for the same offence. The medical officer, Dr Barraclough, gave Cornwall a lifeline: resign due to 'ill health', accept a medical certificate, and the matter would not be referred to Wellington. Cornwall reluctantly agreed and he and his wife left by the next vessel.

Two resident commissioners and two rapid departures from Niue should have rung warning bells back in Wellington, where there had been a dedicated Minister for the Cook and Other Islands since the Reform Party had come to power in 1912. The portfolio had been separated from Trade and Customs and Maui Pomare had been made minister. Before long he had established a government department to handle the affairs of the Cook Islands and Niue, so there was now a small group of officials in Wellington with oversight of Island Territories. However, when Cornwall made his hasty departure from Niue in late 1917, the New Zealand government had little time to reflect on the needs of the Island Administration. They had more pressing demands in the shape of war in Europe and the Middle East.

10. Involvement in World War I

I am the island of Niue, a small child that stands up to help

In March 1916 a group of 125 Niueans gathered on the deck of a New Zealand troopship and watched as the vessel came into the port of Suez at the northern end of Tahi Kula, the Red Sea. This very busy Egyptian port – filled with troopships and supply vessels, the wharf area crammed with men and equipment – was a world away from Alofi or Avatele with their sporadic ship visits. One Niuean had died on board that morning as a result of 'pneumonia supervening measles', and 15 others, also ill, were stretchered off and transferred to the hospital in Suez. The remainder of the group were sent by train to the New Zealand Base Camp at Ismailia. On that first train ride the men from Niue saw the great expanse of desert, mud villages, date palms, camels and donkeys. They had arrived on the other side of the world to fulfil the commitment made by their leaders to 'help King George'.[1]

They represented a tiny but important contribution to what was the greatest global clash of empires the world had known. For World War I, the Great War, was above all else, an imperial war. It marked a period of open and bloody hostility between empires that were competing, challenging, negotiating for hegemony over vast tracts of the earth's surface, and over its people and resources. It drew in people who lived in all corners of those empires so that the war was truly on a world scale, both in terms of the geographical spread of conflicts and the geographical spread of participants.

There were difficulties for the British government in this. To accept white colonials into the British Forces was one thing, but many of the colonies had black and coloured inhabitants and they also volunteered to serve. This did not sit comfortably with prevailing Eurocentric views. There was a belief that using black or coloured troops would 'undermine the dignity of the white man'[2] and this view applied whether such troops were ranged alongside or against white troops. However, the British army soon discovered that to mount a war on so many fronts, over so many parts of the globe, required a huge support structure and the offer of troops from many British colonies and territories provided the labour for the war effort. From

India and Ceylon, from Kenya and Uganda, from Swaziland and Bechuanaland, from Egypt and China, from the West Indies and Mauritius and from the Pacific came men by the hundreds of thousands to support the war machine. They carried supplies, loaded and unloaded vessels, stood guard, manned ammunition dumps, dug trenches and built duckboards, served food and cleaned latrines. And Niue, one of the most isolated and far-flung territories of the British Empire, was a small part of this colonial effort.

Niue's involvement in the war began with the arrival in September 1914 of a vessel bringing news that Britain was at war with Germany. As was typical in all parts of the empire, the rhetoric of imperial loyalty came from the Europeans on the island. Reverend Cullen wrote to a fellow missionary:

> *The last vessel brought us the terrible news of war, though our news is very meagre. How awful it is and how impossible for us to realise all that it must be for those at home. We are racked with anxiety as to what may happen to our dear ones, but our utter helplessness throws us more entirely upon God. Even in this distant island we are greatly affected.*[3]

The small group of Pālagi on the island had either been born in England, or their parents had been born there. They had a strong sense of belonging to the British Empire, and of loyalty to King George V. They responded, spontaneously and independently, in the same way that officials, missionaries and traders responded throughout the empire: they offered funds and troops. When the ship that had brought the news of war in Europe sailed from Niue two days later, £165 had been raised to contribute to the Red Cross Fund in New Zealand, and Resident Commissioner Cornwall had met with Togia and the Island Council and drafted an offer of troops from the island. The idea was Cornwall's, the wording was Togia's.

> *To King George V, all those in authority and the brave men who fight. I am the island of Niue, a small child that stands up to help the Kingdom of King George. There are two portions. We are offering– 1) money, 2) men.*[4]

The Pālagi could of course donate money; but as for troops, it was Niueans who were offered – to be accompanied by officials in the role of officers. Recruiting for a Niue Regiment got under way immediately, spearheaded by Resident Commissioner Cornwall and Chief of Police Sergeant Frederick Holmes, a veteran of the South African War where he had served in the British Imperial Army. Many young Niuean men saw this as yet another opportunity to embark on an overseas adventure, and were keen to join the regiment and participate in the drilling practices on the Alofi and Hakupu greens. Some of these men had already been away from the island on labour contracts so they had some experience of travelling abroad, although always within the tropics. They also had at least some knowledge of English. Others were younger and had never left Niue before but had grown up with a desire to get away from the island and experience life elsewhere.

Support for the regiment was not universal on the island, however. There were reports of some men taking their families and hiding in the bush when the recruitment party came round the villages. Sergeant Holmes reported a native preacher, Ikimatatoa, speaking out against participation in a war on the other side of the world and fumed, rather pretentiously, in a letter to the resident commissioner that 'it is hampering and interfering with me in my arduous and unthankful job of raising a native regiment'.[5] No further incidents were officially reported and the first flush of patriotic fervour subsided as the onset of the cyclone season left Niue in a news vacuum. The Pālagi felt they had taken action to support the imperial cause, and the Niueans who had signed up were happy to participate in marching and drumming. Nothing more could be done but consciences were salved.

The participation of Niue men in the war may well have ended here, with evidence of willingness to serve but no practical way of doing so; however, in New Zealand, events of 1915 changed the situation for the Niueans. There had been an offer to dispatch a Native Maori Contingent to the South African War of 1899–1902, but this had not been accepted by the imperial government in London. By 1914 there was a new breed of Māori leader in the New Zealand Parliament, who saw participation in the war as a way of proving loyalty and worth in order to achieve greater equality with Pākehā. These new leaders – Maui Pomare, Apirana Ngata, Peter Buck and Taare Parata representing the four Māori electorates, and James Carroll, the only Māori to hold a general electorate seat – pressed for Māori to be allowed to enlist and for a Maori Contingent to be formed. This time the request to London was successful when it was pointed out that Indian troops were already guarding the Suez Canal and France was bringing in African troops to serve in Europe. A contingent of 500 men was assembled and trained, and departed from New Zealand in February 1915, headed for the port of Suez.

The Maori Contingent arrived in Egypt and was quickly deployed to garrison duty on the Mediterranean island of Malta. These were, after all, 'coloured' troops and were to be used in support roles. Events on the Gallipoli peninsula from April 1915 soon changed the role for Māori. Reinforcements were needed for the New Zealand forces struggling against the Turks on Gallipoli and the Maori Contingent was called into action. In August 1915 they participated in the attack on Sari Bair and distinguished themselves with their fighting prowess. But over 20 per cent were killed or wounded, and when they were withdrawn from Gallipoli back to Egypt it seemed there were not enough men to continue with a distinct Maori Contingent. A decision was now made to spread them in platoons to other infantry battalions.

News of this development caused great protest back in New Zealand, where the Native Contingent Committee was finding it increasingly difficult to recruit replacements for those who had been killed or wounded; the loss of a separate identity for the contingent threatened to make this even more difficult. Maui Pomare was in a particularly difficult political situation. He had led the cry in Parliament for Māori to be allowed to participate and he chaired the Native Contingent Committee, whose task it was to recruit Māori men. But as Member of Parliament for Western Maori, that part of the North Island comprising principally Taranaki and Waikato, he represented the two areas that had suffered most during the land wars of the 1860s. The confiscation of hundreds of thousands of acres of their best land made these Māori reluctant to now send their young men to support a European war on the other side of the world. Pomare was unable to convince his own electorate to participate; and Waikato Māori, in particular, remained obdurate.[6]

The most difficult drafts of reinforcements to fill were those in September 1915 and February 1916, when the Māori troops were not grouped as one distinct unit. Fortunately for Pomare, he had one other political card to play. In his capacity as Minister for the Cook and Other Islands he had received offers of troops from New Zealand's newest territories, the Cook Islands and Niue. The offers had initially been politely ignored; but they were now seen as a way of filling reinforcement quotas. In accepting the offer of troops from the Pacific territories, Pomare, ever the politician, made good mileage from it. When 50 men arrived in Wellington from Rarotonga, he marched them in to the parliamentary debating chamber to sing for the assembled politicians; and he decided to sail to Niue on the troopship to personally accompany the Niue Regiment to Auckland.

A year after Niue offered troops, *Te Anau* arrived off Alofi to transport the men to New Zealand. Around 150 were passed as medically fit and were included in the contingent. Uea, the native pastor from Alofi who had questioned the members of the parliamentary tour in 1903, was accepted as chaplain. The group comprised 73 married men, 30 of them with families of one to four children. One family farewelled four sons and several families farewelled two sons each.[7] Pomare inspected the men in Alofi and they were rowed out in small groups to *Te Anau*. One man

Niue Contingent leaving Niue. The only known photo of the Niue Contingent lined up on the green in Alofi on 13 October 1915. They are being inspected by the New Zealand minister responsible for the Cook and Other Islands, Maui Pomare, prior to embarkation for Auckland. Out in front is Sergeant Holmes of the Niue Police who was to lead the contingent. The minister is in the white suit and directly behind him is the resident commissioner, Henry Cornwall. Author's collection

volunteered at the last moment and when his wife discovered her loss, she swam out towards the troopship, crying and calling for him. The people crowded around the cliffs at Alofi and watched their young men depart – not to labour for a year on Malden Island or Samoa, but to fight in unknown lands far away in a conflict they didn't understand and about which very little news would filter back.

The Niueans were taken into camp at Narrow Neck, (Nalo Neke), on Auckland's North Shore and for the next three months underwent basic training. Those with a little knowledge of English were put in charge of their fellow Islanders and were responsible for translating and explaining. The food was different and adjustments had to be made when it was found these men were not used to a diet of meat. Uniform items were uncomfortable and, in the case of boots, crippling for men who had always gone barefoot over the hard coral surface of the island. For some of the Niueans, boots had to be specially made to fit. For the first time, with the exception of a few who had travelled to Auckland or Sydney on trading vessels, the men were out of the tropics. Even the Auckland summer took its toll, and on Christmas Day 1915, the first Niuean death occurred when Vilipate of Liku died of pneumonia.[8] In

Niue soldiers during training at Narrow Neck camp in Auckland. The men from Niue faced many difficulties during training, including language, food, illness – and having to wear boots: most had never worn boots before and had to have them made especially to fit their feet, which were very broad due to walking barefoot on coral. *New Zealand Herald* Supplement, 30 October 1915, Sir George Grey Special Collections, Auckland Libraries, New Zealand, 7-A14272

total 13 men would be hospitalised in Auckland and prevented from going on to the Middle East because of illness.

The group in training at Narrow Neck was being prepared to serve as the Third Reinforcements to the Maori Contingent. The Niueans were the single biggest component of this reinforcement, with a slightly smaller number of Māori recruits and a group of around 50 Cook Islanders. Into the mix were added a small number of other Pacific Islanders – several from Tonga and one from the Ellice Islands – who had arrived independently in New Zealand seeking to enlist.[9] A group of four Niueans also arrived from Tonga in time to enlist with their fellow countrymen. Two of these men had worked as indentured labourers in Tonga but had not returned to Niue at the end of their contract; instead they got a passage to Auckland and enlisted. It seems likely the other two men were in a similar position.[10]

Once they had completed their training, those who were medically fit were embarked for the five-week voyage to Suez. The Third Reinforcements became part of the Pioneer Battalion, formed in February 1916 as the men were en route to Egypt. The formation of the Pioneer Battalion was the solution to the problem of the Māori demand for a separate identity for the Māori troops. The battalion consisted of Māori and Pākehā, but the Māori identity was stamped on the regimental badge with a Māori warrior's face above a crossed pick and axe – symbolising the work to be undertaken by the Pioneers; for this was a labour force to be employed digging trenches, building roads and laying light railways and 'the other hundred

Niue Platoon of the Third Maori Contingent. There would have been three platoons of Niueans but only two group photos have been found. Sergeant Uea, the only man in long trousers, is sitting in the front row next to two Pālagi officers. Uea was the oldest man in the Niuean Contingent and, as a pastor, he accompanied the men as an army chaplain. Photo taken at Narrow Neck camp on the North Shore by the Auckland photographer William Beattie. Author's collection

and one labouring jobs an army needs to do'.[11] In Egypt the Niueans trained for general fitness but also for fighting, as Pioneer units were often close to the action.

Although the Secretary of State for the Colonies had been informed of the inclusion of Niue Islanders in the Third Reinforcements, and had agreed to 'endeavour to use their services in a suitable climate', when the order came to transfer the New Zealand Division to France in April 1916, the 60 Niueans who were at that time still healthy were included with the rest of the Pioneer Battalion. They were railed to Port Saīd on the Mediterranean and embarked on a transport vessel with almost 2000 men on board, bound for Marseilles in the south of France. They arrived in France shivering to a cold spring. After a 58-hour train journey to the north of France, the Pioneers were marched to Armentières and into the combat zone. There, in a cold and wet landscape, with mud and rats their constant companions, the Niueans helped undertake the physically demanding work of trench digging in the water-sodden fields. As it was considered unsafe to move parties in and out of the trenches during daylight, the work was done at night. By late May, after a month at the Front, the rate of pneumonia among the Niuean men was so high that the

A Niuean at Gallipoli

WHEN WORLD WAR I began in August 1914 a young Niuean by the name of Hono Paufai was working in a barbershop in Queen Street, Auckland. In January 1915 he signed up to serve in the New Zealand Expeditionary Force and was attached to the Auckland Infantry Battalion.

Private Paufai (12/2078) departed from New Zealand with the 5th Reinforcements in April 1915 and arrived in Egypt at the end of May. Here the men undertook two months of training before they were called in to support their battalion on the slopes of Gallipoli in August 1915.

The second major offensive at Gallipoli took place in August, and when the transport ships carrying the 5th Reinforcements arrived off the coast, the men were rowed ashore and committed straight to battle. 'Theirs was a most unenviable situation. Some lasted no time at all. Others were wounded making their way up Rhododendron Spur … their Gallipoli service was reckoned in hours, not days.'[12] Hono Paufai reached the heights of Hill 971, Koja Chemin Tepe, before he was shot in the chest.

Hono Paufai served with the Auckland Infantry Battalion at Gallipoli. His photo appeared in the *Auckland Star* when he was listed as seriously wounded but his name is spelt incorrectly and he is incorrectly listed as being in the Maori Contingent.

Auckland Star, 30 September 1915, 8, Auckland Libraries, New Zealand

It needed six men to get a stretcher down from the high slopes and then there was a further long, difficult carry for two or four men, often under sniper fire, down to the casualty clearing station near the beach. Those who survived the evacuation were transported out to hospital ships and transferred to the British hospital at Malta in the Mediterranean.

Hono Paufai made it to Malta; he was classed as 'seriously ill with gunshot wound to chest' and shipped on to England, where he entered the King George Hospital in London in late August. He underwent surgery and was in hospital for the next six months until he was considered fit for invaliding back to New Zealand. On 15 March 1916, the day the main body of Niue men disembarked at Suez, Paufai sailed for Suez from southern England. Here he was once again hospitalised as he had contracted pleurisy. He was admitted to the New Zealand General Hospital at Pont de Koubbeh in Cairo, the very same hospital where increasing numbers of Niueans from the main body were being sent as they succumbed to pneumonia or dysentery; some must have been there at the same time as Paufai.

In mid-April, Paufai was invalided back to Auckland and entered Auckland Hospital. For the next two and a half years he was in and out of hospital, and he died at the hospital annex in November 1918, five days before war ended.

Hono Paufai does not seem to be well known on Niue and it is not clear which village he came from. He gave simply 'Niue Island' as his place of birth and listed his mother, Loine Paufai of Niue Island, as his next of kin. He was mentioned in a letter from Reverend Cullen on Niue in 1917, when he referred to the fact that 'one of our men … was at the landing at Gallipoli'. When the Alofi memorial was being prepared in the 1920s, the resident commissioner's office sent a list of names for inclusion on the Roll of Honour and Hono Paufai was the only name listed that was not part of the Niue Contingent. As Cullen wrote, 'even little Niue has her share in the glory of that gallant though unavailing enterprise'.[13]

decision was taken to withdraw them from France and assemble them at the New Zealand Convalescent Hospital in Essex, England, for treatment and recuperation before sending them home.

In June 1916 over 100 Niueans arrived in the small village of Hornchurch and captured the imagination of the inhabitants. The idea of men from a 'south sea island' had an exotic ring to it. The villagers embraced them and went out of their way to make the stay in Hornchurch pleasant. Daily fruit collections were held to give the men more of an island-style diet. There were church services, with the Niuean chaplain Uea providing readings. Most importantly, the men were visited by old and dear friends from Niue – Frank and Sarah Lawes – and when the reunion was reported in the LMS magazine, the writer noted, 'Great was the delight of people and missionaries to thus meet again.'[14] Sarah Lawes organised for groups of men to visit London, where she met them at Victoria Station and showed them around the main sights of the city. Some, however, were too ill for this; and there were another four deaths in Hornchurch.[15]

The main body of Niueans were returned to New Zealand in two groups in June and July 1916, but there were individuals scattered through Egypt, France and England who could not return with their comrades. It is one of the enduring themes of the story: from the time of arrival at Suez the Niuean group became splintered. Men were transferred to hospitals, became separated from their countrymen and

Left: Headstone Vasau and Moki. **Right**: Headstone Filitoua and Taleva.
These two Niuean headstones are in the churchyard of St Andrew's in Hornchurch, Essex, England. They are official headstones but, unusually, they are shared by the four men who died there of pneumonia. Hornchurch was the main New Zealand convalescent hospital in England and the people of the village showed great kindness towards these men from 'the South Sea Islands'.
Author's collection

were isolated by illness and by language. There were times when a Niuean was alone in a hospital, and conditions were particularly difficult if he didn't speak English. A medical orderly in the New Zealand General Hospital at Pont de Koubbeh in Cairo spoke of the problems for the Pacific Islanders: 'they were terribly poor and difficult patients to deal with cause half of them couldn't speak English and they were terrified of this dysentery'.[16] Caring for the men was especially difficult when staff were unable to convey to the Niueans why a special diet was required or why a certain medication needed to be given. In England, a hospital in London contacted the Lawes family and Sarah was able to visit Falaoa, who was 'very lonely as he could not speak English'.[17] For brothers Finiki and Lavaika from Alofi, transferred from Hornchurch to the London General Hospital, she was a welcome visitor.

> *Their greatest pleasure was a visit from Mrs Lawes, who kindly came very often to chat with them in their own language. Their faces would light up with joy when 'Misi Farani Fifine' […] was announced, and through her we were able to find out anything they wanted to have or to know.*[18]

These men faced a further hurdle when they were well enough to travel and were returned to New Zealand with only one or two other Niueans, or sometimes alone, on a large troopship. Of course, there were some who did not return. There are headstones for Niueans in Suez and Cairo, in the north of France and in Hornchurch, and five men died and were buried at sea off the west coast of Africa en route back to New Zealand.[19]

Once the men were back in New Zealand they had to wait for a ship to take them back to Niue. Army authorities decided not to issue Niueans with rail passes or leave, so they were kept in convalescent hospitals in Auckland. There was some embarrassment on the part of the New Zealand government that they had brought the Niueans back rather than deploying them in a better climate – as they did for the Cook Islanders serving in France: they too suffered greatly from pneumonia,

The majority of Niuean soldiers were returned to New Zealand in August or September 1916 and were kept in convalescent hospitals awaiting passage to Niue. The group here were being entertained at the Auckland Trained Nurses' Club in Epsom by Nurse Nobbs, who had worked in Rarotonga. The mayoress of Auckland, Mrs J.H. Gunson, was a guest at the gathering and is in the centre of the group. Sir George Grey Special Collections, Auckland Libraries, New Zealand, 31_WP8025 but after they were moved to the Sinai and Palestine they were able to continue serving until war ended. Never again was a large group of Pacific Islanders deployed to France but as the first main group, the Niueans suffered greatly and no solution except withdrawal could be seen. There was a suggestion that the Niueans could be sent to Samoa to support the New Zealand occupation of the former German colony, but the government realised that this could cause problems between Niueans and Samoans. There was nothing for it but to return the Niueans home, with thanks for their service.

The men arrived home in September and October 1916 to great excitement and joy. There had been no warning of the arrival of the schooner *Awanui*, but when news went out from Alofi that it was carrying soldiers, families came from around the island to search for their men. There was 'a massive feast of welcome in honour of the heroes that supported Great Britain's call for volunteers';[20] and another welcome feast a month later when the USSC vessel *Talune* arrived with more men. There were stories to tell, sad news to pass on to some families, new babies to meet and, for the families and for the men, there was the inevitable dislocation that comes with absence to be overcome. One small newspaper in New Zealand, the *Thames Star*, picked up the story of the Niue Islanders in a moving article entitled 'Vasau and Taleva':

> *Vasau and Taleva came from the farthest corner of the Pacific to fight for the King of England. They trained hard in New Zealand and Egypt … their hearts were quite sound and loyal. And today Vasau and Taleva are both sleeping peacefully in a quiet English churchyard while the tide of war still rages …*
>
> *Vasau and Taleva came from Niue … the people of Niue … are adventurous and hard-working, so they go to all the other islands to work for wages. But they always come home to Niue to die. In Niue there are gravestones all along the roadside, for every Savage Islander is buried on his own land.*
>
> *But Vasau and Taleva will not be buried on their own land. Instead they are sleeping peacefully at the far end of the earth.*[21]

Almost one year after the return of the main body of Niueans, the people of Alofi spotted a sail on the horizon and, as it got closer into the bay, a large crowd gathered at the wharf to observe. It was a lifeboat with mast and sails and, on board, six men brandishing rifles and machine guns. There were many returned servicemen in the crowd on the wharf and they were very surprised when they recognised the flag atop the mast: it was German. Someone called from the shore: 'You Germans? How you get here from way off?'[22] The boat came in as close as possible, although the men aboard were wary. It turned out they had been shipwrecked and were now

A war memorial was erected on the Alofi green in front of the mission house. It was concrete with a marble tablet listing the names of those who died while enlisted. The New Zealand minister of defence, Sir James Allen, arrived in February 1920 with a parliamentary delegation to officially thank the people of Niue for their contribution to the war effort. Sir James unveiled the memorial and presented a captured German gun that was mounted alongside the memorial.

Archives New Zealand, Department of Internal Affairs Te Tari Taiwhenua ACGA 8280 IT667 IT 122/3 1

Marble tablet with Roll of Honour. The war memorial on the Alofi green has been replaced several times because of the ravages of climate, but each time the marble tablet has been reused. It still stands on the Alofi green as part of what is now a National Memorial.

Author's collection

suffering from scurvy: they were in desperate need of fresh water and soft food such as bananas.

The captain of the vessel was the infamous German raider Count Felix von Luckner. His vessel, the *Seeadler*, had been wrecked somewhere in the Society Islands in August 1917, and he had made the decision to leave the main body of his men plus some American prisoners on an atoll and head off in search of another vessel that he could capture and use to pick up his men. He was heading for the Fiji Islands but came in to Niue in the hope of securing food and water. He was pleased to find the locals were friendly: the machine guns were put away and the

Germans gratefully took on board gourds of fresh water and bunches of bananas. They made no attempt to land and no mention was made of any Administration officials appearing on the wharf. With no radio link there would have been no way of passing on the news of the German visit to New Zealand.

Von Luckner learned that quite a number of the Niueans had been recruited and sent to the trenches in France. Many had contracted 'tuberculosis from the unaccustomed climate' and those who had been returned to the island were 'worn-out shells of men'. One of the island chiefs was on the wharf and von Luckner recorded speaking with him. The chief told him:

> *White man send missionary. Missionary say we must not fight. Because all men children of God. All men brothers. They say we can have war no more. Then they say we must go fight. They have war. We no fight for ourselves, they say, we fight for them. How, if men are brothers? Our men killed. Our men come back sick with cough. Cough never goes away.*[23]

With a full load of provisions to counteract the scurvy, the small vessel and its German crew left Alofi and headed westward. Von Luckner believed the Niueans had a strong impression of the fighting power of the Germans, and those who had been in the trenches in Flanders knew about it first-hand. The sudden appearance of armed Germans at their remote island could, he believed, only increase their admiration. For the people of Niue, it was a brief but real reminder that the world was still at war.

News of the end of war in November 1918 reached Niue just before Christmas that year. There was much celebrating, with speeches and festivities in the villages and a coconut planting programme – the trees would serve as a memorial of the war and its significance. When the new resident commissioner sent his annual report to Wellington in late 1918, he noted 'There is the sadness of lonely Niuean graves in countries the names of which were hitherto unknown to the Natives', but he also noted a wider knowledge of the world and 'a pride in the nation to which they belong'.[24] It remained to be seen whether New Zealand had fully recognised its small territory lying alone in the South Pacific – or had the men been returned and the island forgotten?

11. The interwar years

I see no reason to disturb him

When the Armistice came on 11 November 1918, New Zealand had more pressing business in the Pacific than affairs in Niue. Four days earlier the *Talune* had arrived in New Zealand-administered Samoa from Auckland. Despite evidence of influenza among the passengers and crew, all were permitted to disembark and by the time the bonfires were lit along the beachfront in Apia to celebrate the news of war ending in Europe, the first victims of the influenza pandemic were dying. The disease devastated Samoa: 22 per cent of the population died.[1] There had already been an outbreak of influenza in Rarotonga in September 1918, with 45 deaths. Quarantine restrictions imposed in the Cooks meant the outer islands were spared the disease. Niue was also spared:[2] for once the irregularity of shipping there worked in its favour.

The New Zealand government had sent a force to seize the German colony of Western Samoa in August 1914, and had remained as the occupying force throughout the war. In the postwar settlement in Europe, former German territories were handed to Allied governments to be administered as League of Nations mandated territories. New Zealand was given the mandate for Western Samoa. As the *Evening Post* commented: 'Although New Zealand has had a stake in the Pacific for twenty years ... she is only now beginning to wake up to the responsibility of being a Pacific Power.'[3]

The interwar years in the Pacific were dominated, from New Zealand's perspective, by issues in Samoa and, to a lesser extent, the Cook Islands. Niue was largely overlooked. As far as Wellington was concerned, as long as there were five or six officials on the ground in Niue they could be left to 'get on with it'. When Joseph McMahon-Box, the young assistant in the resident commissioner's office, applied in 1918 to extend his three-year term on the island by another two years, the secretary of the Cook Islands Department in Wellington wrote on the application, 'I see no reason to disturb him.'[4] The minister approved the extension of an appointment that eventually spanned 28 years, the whole interwar period. 'Do not disturb' was the sign hung on the Niue portfolio in Wellington, with the result that personnel decisions were always made reactively and were often piecemeal and ill-considered.

There was another feature of appointments to Niue that was unique to the island. Roles were often conferred on officials who had already been appointed to other positions, to avoid the difficult task of finding someone new who was prepared to move to the island. Cornwall, who was well qualified in matters of accounting and auditing, had pointed out to Wellington in 1916 that he was both treasurer and resident commissioner – which made a nonsense of the directive that all accounts signed by the one should be countersigned by the other. Cornwall suggested the obvious answer was to make McMahon-Box the treasurer, and this was duly done by December 1916.

This amalgamation of functions resulted in both the Tufukia headmaster and the medical officer also taking on the role of deputy or acting resident commissioner at various times. As assistant to the resident commissioner throughout this period, McMahon-Box performed almost every function except that of medical officer – a position that was very difficult to fill, as few doctors were prepared to tolerate the isolation and the poor salary. Doctors who were dispatched to Niue were frequently nearing the end of their careers: some were elderly and infirm. One seemed 'clearly not fit for work but struggled on'[5] – he died of heart failure six months after arrival; and another was too frail to visit the outer villages so the sick were forced to come to Alofi. Sometimes locums were sent for short periods – notably Dr Peter Buck, MP for Northern Maori, who stayed for three months from late 1912 and found much of interest for his anthropological research.

The position of chief of police also proved difficult to fill. When Sergeant Holmes left Niue in late 1915 to accompany the Niue Contingent into camp in Auckland, his replacement was soon causing havoc and scandal. His preferred entertainment was to take the doctor's horse and trap and ride out around the island, 'driving [furiously] and generally showing off. He has been in the habit of driving native girls about at night time, and his conduct has become the talk of the island.'[6] He was dismissed and, after two more unsuccessful appointments, in 1919 the position was offered to the ever-reliable Joseph McMahon-Box.

Although the medical and police personnel changed frequently, the administration personnel often had protracted lengths of service on Niue – not necessarily by choice. It is true that McMahon-Box married locally – to a young granddaughter of Robert Henry Head – which meant he had more substantial ties to the island, but even he applied for transfer and was rejected. Every resident commissioner in the interwar period applied for transfer or promotion and, with one exception, was rejected. Most wanted to remain in the Islands but were keen to move to a position either in the Cooks or in the Samoan administration. Niue was the most difficult post for Wellington to fill, and it did not acknowledge the need to rotate staff and avoid them becoming 'islandized',[7] especially in such an isolated location and with such a small community. Every job application from officers in Niue for a position elsewhere received the reply, 'already filled from New Zealand' or simply, 'application unsuccessful'. McMahon-Box tried several times for a transfer to Rarotonga. In 1929 he wrote to the minister:

> *[N]o opportunity has been afforded me to have even a sporting chance of applying for [other positions ...] As you must know there is but a limited amount of experience to be gained [here] and after too many years of it one's ideas are inclined to become cramped and confined to one little circle.*[8]

His requests were ignored and he remained on Niue.

Administration officials made considerable efforts to obtain salary increments, education allowances for children sent to school in New Zealand, and compensation for furlough not taken. The only person who had any success in these areas was Guy Morris, appointed resident commissioner in 1918. The Cook Islands Department was obviously delighted to receive his application for the position in Niue, as he was a well-qualified lawyer, recently returned wounded from France. He was successful in gaining transfer to Rarotonga after two and a half years on Niue, but was called back 15 months later following the Makefu murder. Two and a half years later he left for a position back in the Justice Department in New Zealand; and he secured a payment in lieu of furlough, despite a Crown Law ruling that this could not be done.

Niueans may not have been aware of the administrative battles between Alofi and Wellington, but they were certainly aware of the presence on the island of the New Zealand Administration, and of the strengths and weaknesses of the incumbent resident commissioner. The personal attributes of individual commissioners were frequently talked about and Island Council members often made their feelings known in writing to the minister in Wellington. Guy Morris was much liked – especially after 10 years of Henry Cornwall. The island councillors had written to Minister Pomare, 'we do not wish you to send us such another as Mr Cornwall who behaved like the devil.'[9] 'Misi Moleti' was seen as exercising strong but fair leadership, and he had expertise in dealing with court matters – a very necessary skill, given the plethora of laws and ordinances in place. When he left for Rarotonga

Murder at Makefu

ON 8 APRIL 1921 Hegotule, the village constable at Makefu, was murdered. Resident Commissioner Evison, who was at the time the headmaster of Tufukia school but was appointed resident commissioner on the departure of Guy Morris, needed to ensure law and order were maintained, and to catch those who were responsible. He found the inhabitants of Makefu had been sworn to silence; he was pressured by the European inhabitants of the island, who felt they may be in some sort of danger; and he believed the unrest on the island was sufficient to request the visit of a warship and the supply of rifles for protection.

Evison organised for the whole male population of Makefu to swear an oath on the Bible that they were innocent. The medical officer listened to the heart rate of each man before and after the oath was taken, and six suspects were chosen on this basis. Makefu was isolated so that people could not come or go or travel through the village without a pass, and fishing activities were also restricted. This was made possible by the creation of a guard of 40 men, many of them returned soldiers, under the military-style command of a trading company employee who had served on the North-West Frontier of India.[10]

The suspects were narrowed down to two: Matiu, a former island councillor, and his nephew Ulumotu. Matiu was charged with murder and Ulumotu with conspiring to murder. Matiu was known to the New Zealand Administration on Niue as an 'agitator', for he was one of few councillors who were prepared to speak out against the resident commissioner. In 1919 Morris had removed him from the council on the grounds that he was 'a constant source of annoyance … an obstructionist to every Government proposal, and … with a good deal of power among the natives'.[11]

John Evison, who came to Niue in 1915 as head teacher at Tufukia. He had previously taught in Southland and Taranaki. He became resident commissioner in 1921 when Guy Morris left for Rarotonga. Evison was a popular teacher but he had no expertise to deal with the murder in Makefu and he found the whole episode very stressful. He resigned in late 1921 and returned to New Zealand. The following year he was appointed supervisor of education in the Cook Islands. Auckland War Memorial Museum Tāmaki Paenga Hira, New Zealand, C25887

Evison tried to obtain the services of a solicitor from New Zealand but this request went unanswered and the trial proceeded, with Evison now in the position of judge. It was vital, he felt, to obtain an outcome, for 'non conviction means absolute lost prestige'.[12] An outcome was achieved: Matiu was found guilty of murder and sentenced to death. Ulumotu was found guilty of conspiring to murder and sentenced to 10 years' imprisonment. The death sentence was commuted to life imprisonment by the New Zealand governor-general and both men were transported on HMS *Chatham* to jail in Auckland. Within 10 days of arriving at Mt Eden Prison, Ulumotu died of pneumonia.

Two people in particular found the events surrounding this murder case very disturbing. One was Alan Hotham, commodore of HMS *Chatham*, who was responsible for bringing the two convicted men to New Zealand. When he read of the death of Ulumotu he wrote to the minister of defence that he was 'full of remorse' that the men had been removed from the tropics and that for 'humanitarian reasons' such prisoners should be held in either Samoa or Suva.[13]

The second voice raised loudly against the proceedings was the Auckland solicitor E.B. Vaile, who was a son-in-law of Robert Henry Head and had handled his affairs for many years. He claimed, through a series of letters to the *Auckland Star*, that Ulumotu had confessed to the crime on board HMS *Chatham* and had written a confession that had been handed to Vaile in Auckland, possibly by Commodore Hotham. Ulumotu confessed to the murder but said he was persuaded to blame his uncle, who was a man of 'high standing', and the belief was he would not receive the death sentence. If this was true, the murderer was now dead and an innocent man imprisoned.

Vaile visited Niue in late 1921 to arrange settlement of the affairs of Robert Head, who had died earlier in the year. It seems that while on the island he was told about the court case conducted by Evison and was horrified at what had occurred. As summarised by another writer to the *Auckland Star*:

> *the trial of the condemned man was a farce. The prisoner was not represented by a solicitor or anybody else, and if he attempted to defend himself, he was immediately silenced. The public was excluded from the Court, material witnesses [Matiu's wife] were refused a hearing, and the Judge was an ex-schoolmaster who lacked legal training.*[14]

There was pressure on the Cook Islands Department to launch a full magisterial enquiry, but the only indication that any notice was taken of the complaints was that Matiu was moved to a prison in Samoa to see out his sentence. Matiu was described in the press as 'a victim of a glaring miscarriage of justice' and the murder trial as a 'wretched affair',[15] but the case was not revisited and, more importantly, the functions of resident commissioner and High Court judge on Niue were not separated out and entrusted to different people.

Guy Morris, a lawyer and returned serviceman, became resident commissioner in 1918 after the hasty departure of Henry Cornwall. Morris served two terms on Niue between 1918 and 1925. Here he is photographed at the Residency in 1923 with his wife Maude, son Bill and a new daughter, Maile, born on Niue. Courtesy of Morris family, Wellington, New Zealand

there was no replacement on the horizon and John Evison, headmaster at Tufukia, stepped into the position of resident commissioner in addition to his education duties. He was a successful headmaster and was also liked – 'we find him a very suitable man';[16] but a murder in the village of Makefu in 1921 proved beyond his field of expertise and he soon resigned. Now the medical officer, Dr J.P. Ellison, found himself acting resident commissioner, although no one seemed to know if a warrant had been issued for his appointment.[17] The situation was becoming ridiculous and Wellington was confused. Councillors petitioned for the return of Morris: 'he was a fine man and we thank you for sending him and we would like him to return to us'.[18] Guy Morris was persuaded, with a 20 per cent salary increase and the shipment of his car from Rarotonga to Alofi,[19] to return to his former position in Niue. Morris was ambitious, however, and after another two and a half years on Niue he announced that he was leaving the post and moving back to New Zealand to further his legal career.

Morris's successor, Arthur Luckham, is a difficult personality to evaluate. He appears aloof from any real engagement with the people; and, mysteriously, he left in 1931 after six years to return to Aitutaki. It was mysterious in the sense that his files, both in Wellington and on Niue, have been purged and hence the reason for what was effectively a demotion is unknown. No doubt it was known on Niue, however; the LMS missionary at the time commented to London 'the outgoing

Island Council, late 1920s. This image was taken at the Residency in Alofi but the councillors are not named. The man in the centre with bow tie is the resident commissioner from 1925 to 1931, Arthur Luckham. Directly behind him is his assistant, Joseph McMahon-Box.

NZ Ministry of Foreign Affairs Collection, Alexander Turnbull Library, Wellington, New Zealand, PAColl-0797-1-3

Commissioner is a real black sheep, and has been reduced to a smaller job, although the Department say it is merely a readjustment of men and positions.'[20]

Luckham's replacement, a temporary appointment that eventually lasted 10 years, was Captain William Moody Bell. He brought to the position a military style perfected during service in the Samoa Administration of the 1920s: tropical suit, pith helmet and fly whisk, an upright comportment and an ability to bellow at the person who failed to salute, open a door on cue or jump to attention. Yet he was a likeable figure in many ways and was often forgiven his pomp and posturing. His association with Niue lasted for many years after his resignation in 1941, for he had continuing trading interests that frequently brought him back to the island.

As this procession of resident commissioners came and went, the one constant remained: 'Misi Puha', Joseph McMahon-Box. From 1915 to 1943 he ran the Administration office. The Islanders' opinion of him depended on their own relationship to the Head family, into which he had married. Factions for and against him were inevitable in such a small community and, with growing family demands

Island Council, March 1932. Seated are Resident Commissioner Moody Bell, with his fly whisk, and his assistant Joseph McMahon-Box. The councillors are named also. Standing, left to right: Pitevalu (Tamakautoga), Harry Nemaia (Alofi South), Lagatule (Liku), Misihepi (Makefu), Patali (Alofi North), Harry Lupo (interpreter, Avatele), Togiatu (Lakepa), Manetoa (Tuapa), Tagamaka (Hikutavake), Kalauta (Avatele), Makatogia (Mutalau), Hifoheulu (Fatiau) and Galiki (Hakupu).

NZ Ministry of Foreign Affairs Collection, Alexander Turnbull Library, Wellington, New Zealand, PAColl-0797-3-3

and pressures, he lost the impartiality required of an Administration official. He left Niue in 1943 a broken man, and died a few months later.

The administration of Niue in the interwar period was dictated by the clauses – all 675 of them – of the Cook Islands Amendment Act of 1916. The bill, introduced by Pomare in 1915, sought to consolidate all previous laws and ordinances that related to New Zealand's island territories. It aroused very little discussion in the House of Representatives but was considered at length by the Legislative Council in a debate that was to prove one of the most insightful ever conducted in the New Zealand Parliament on the subject of administration of island territories. Many of the issues that were to dog the Niue Administration – including the combination of functions in the hands of too few officials, and the length of service that should be expected in such an isolated community – were raised by Legislative Council members,[21] but the bill nevertheless passed into law with only minor changes.

Maui Pomare, Minister for the Cook and Other Islands since 1912, lost the portfolio briefly after the war when a new Department of External Affairs was created to deal with the Samoan mandate. The Cooks and Niue were added to the responsibilities of this new department, but Pomare successfully argued they should be dealt with separately. Prime Minister Massey agreed and reinstated Pomare's portfolio in late 1920. Resident Commissioner Morris heard the Cooks and Niue were to stay under Pomare's control and wrote to the minister: 'I am glad as I am afraid that otherwise we should have been overshadowed by Samoa for some time to come.'[22] Although the departments were separated, Samoa and the Cooks demanded more attention in Wellington and Niue remained the Cinderella.

Isolation was recognised as the main problem for Niue. With no wireless link, the only communication was via passing vessels and, especially during the summer cyclone season, these were few and far between. When the *Awanui*, chartered for the Niue run, went aground on the reef at Alofi in January 1919, it was nearly three months before its fate was known in Wellington. The loss of a replacement schooner, the *Jubilee*, in 1920 while en route to Niue was similarly not reported in

When the schooner *Awanui* went aground on the reef at Alofi in 1919 some of the crew wanted to go in a small boat to Samoa to raise the alarm but the resident commissioner would not allow this as it was the cyclone season. The replacement vessel for the *Awanui*, the *Jubilee*, went missing en route to Niue on its first run there. It left Auckland on 15 August 1920 and was finally reported missing in late October. In late November the NZGS *Tutanekai*, with relatives of the missing on board, set out to look for signs of the *Jubilee*. Those lost included Frank Head, Motu Haller and his Pālagi wife Edna, three Niuean passengers, including Fohetaha, who had served in the Niue Contingent, and six Niuean crew members. One of the unnamed Niueans was the oldest brother of Robert Rex. There were also four European officers, including the captain, W.H. Champion. The inquiry into the loss of the *Jubilee* decided it had been hit by a cyclone not far from Niue in early September 1920.

Courtesy of Morris family, Wellington, New Zealand

The *Tutanekai*, searching for the *Jubilee*, called at Alofi and the passengers came ashore. The woman on the right is from the ship. One Niuean woman on the left is taking home a can of water from the reservoir. Duncan Collection, Alexander Turnbull Library, Wellington, New Zealand, PA1-o-827-17-6

Some of the visitors from the *Tutanekai* were taken by dray to look around the Alofi area.
Duncan Collection, Alexander Turnbull Library, Wellington, New Zealand, PA1-o-827-18-2

The *Kaeo*, another schooner, went aground on the reef at Tuapa in 1923. Because it was not the cyclone season, the resident commissioner gave permission for three men to go by boat to Samoa to raise the alarm. The journey took nine days but they reached Apia successfully and were able to get news to New Zealand. Finally it was decided to provide Niue with a radio link to Apia.
David Alexander De Maus Collection, Alexander Turnbull Library, Wellington, G-14753-1/2

New Zealand until it was too late to search for survivors. Morris stressed the need for a wireless connection, and his appeals were further strengthened by the wreck of the *Kaeo* on the reef at Tuapa on its first run to Niue in 1923. The fate of the *Awanui* and the *Kaeo*, both schooners, reinforced the need for a steamer service to Niue, for without engine power, vessels were as vulnerable to disaster on the reef as the *John Williams* had been 50 years earlier. At last in 1924 a steam vessel, the *Rama*, was contracted to cover the Auckland to Niue run, and in the same year arrangements were made for the installation of radio-telephone equipment in Alofi to link the island, via Apia, to New Zealand.

These two developments caused considerable optimism on Niue that now the copra trade, which had been steadily decreasing in revenue internationally, could be replaced by a trade in bananas. This perishable fruit required careful picking, handling and packing and speedy transport to market in Auckland, and a steamer service appeared to be the answer. There was a further setback, however, when the *Rama* was wrecked in the Chatham Islands. The decision was now made to fit out the *Hinemoa* for the Niue run, and when it began operation in 1925 it seemed that finally a solution had been found to enable an alternative income source for Niue.

The steamer service brought with it another vexatious issue for Niue, however: the issue of Sunday labour. The LMS was totally opposed to Sunday work and had considerable support from the villagers in this. The Cook Islands Department recognised this as a problem and promised to try and avoid the vessel arriving in Niue at weekends. However, the *Hinemoa* also called at Apia, where there was a much bigger cargo of fruit waiting to be taken to Auckland, and on the return journey it could not be delayed by a stopover in Niue of more than a day. The Samoan crop could not be jeopardised by the much smaller Niuean crop.

Sense and reasonableness might have prevailed if the personalities had been different, but two new men on Niue were short on sense and reason. Arthur Luckham was the resident commissioner, and the LMS was now headed by Reverend Caleb Beharell, a fiery and litigious man who had been brought to Niue in 1920 after the death of Reverend Cullen. The two now went head to head.[23] Accusations flew between the mission house and the Residency; complaints and petitions were sent to the minister in Wellington – with new-found speed thanks to the wireless link; and everyone, from the minister to the captain of the *Hinemoa*, hoped fervently that weather conditions or mechanical problems did not necessitate a weekend stopover at Alofi.

It was not just the matter of loading of the vessel: the bananas had to be harvested and transported to Alofi. Reverend Beharell railed against Sunday work, stressing always 'the sanctity of the Sabbath'. Luckham saw him as a direct threat: 'The whole position is summed up in a very few words, that the Missionary wants to dominate this Administration, as he does the Natives, naturally I will not tolerate any interference from him therefore he does not like it, hence his noxious manner.'[24]

The argument extended further when Beharell accused Luckham of deliberately locking the village reservoirs to prevent villagers from washing their clothes for an upcoming church festival, and to deny drinking water to those who refused to work on a Sunday.[25] This led to a dispute over who owned the reservoirs – given that they were usually built on church land and the catchment was the church roof – but Luckham pointed out that the reservoirs and the piping from the roofs had been funded by the Administration. Arguments, claims and counterclaims flew between the two men whenever Sunday work was needed; and Wellington was asked to make a Crown law ruling on the question of who owned the water in the reservoirs.

The old *Hinemoa* was replaced by the brand new MV *Maui Pomare* in 1928 but the problem continued. The Minister was now running out of patience. Sunday work was an issue in other islands but it was generally accepted as necessary on occasions. After yet another letter from Beharell, Pomare responded: 'I am forced to the conclusion that a good deal too much is being made of the question of Sunday work at Niue and I think that a broader outlook should be advocated by you as the Head of the LMS in the Island.'[26]

When the LMS foreign secretary visited Pomare in Wellington, the minister spoke to him about Reverend Beharell and sought an assurance that 'a change [would] be made and that the new appointee would be acceptable to all concerned.'[27] Beharell left Niue on furlough in 1928 and was replaced by Harold Taylor. The issue of Sunday work did not disappear, for there was genuine opposition to it from many Niueans, but the heat went out of the dispute. Taylor continued to suggest to the resident commissioner that Sunday work was undesirable, but he accepted it was sometimes unavoidable.

During Taylor's time on Niue in the 1930s there was a change in focus away from confrontation towards cooperation with the Administration, especially once the 'black sheep', Luckham, had been dispatched back to Aitutaki. Captain Bell arrived as the new resident commissioner, and he and the LMS missionary established a friendly and productive relationship. Taylor's passion was education. The Administration had established one government school at Tufukia, but all the other villages relied on the LMS for schooling. The church provided a schoolhouse in each village, and the Niuean pastor in the village was the teacher. Taylor saw this teaching role as central to maintaining the influence of the church on the island. From an early age children came to know the village pastor as their teacher and learned to respect and obey him. Of course the pastors lacked teacher training, and Taylor acknowledged on his arrival that standards of education were variable and often very low. Teaching was in Niuean but more and more families were demanding that their children learn English, as this was already seen as a passport to work. Learning English was only possible in the government school, where there was a New Zealand-appointed teacher and Niuean assistants such as Fasene and Malama Head who spoke good English.

The Administration hoped to open more government schools around the island. The first of these, Tuatea school at Hakupu, was completed in 1920 and staffed with a teacher from New Zealand. Although land was promised in other villages, lack of finance limited any further developments, and in 1925 it was decided to give the LMS an annual subsidy to help with the schools in villages not yet catered for by the Administration. In this way 'the difficulty of financing further schools is thus disposed of for the present.'[28] Reverend Taylor worked hard to maximise the benefit

Albert Edmond arrived in 1938 as head teacher in charge of government schools. Coming ashore at Alofi, he gets his first view of his new island home. During his time on Niue with his wife and two children, the younger one, a nine-year-old girl, fell on the reef below Tufukia and was killed. She was buried near the Alofi church. Sir George Grey Special Collections, Auckland Libraries, New Zealand, 1029-Album-198-1

of this subsidy, but his arrival on Niue in 1930 coincided with budget restraints in New Zealand made necessary by the economic depression, and before long the subsidy was slashed.

Taylor now devised and wrote up a careful plan for the continuation of the LMS schools in the care of a second missionary, a European with teacher training. He felt confident that, if New Zealand would fund such a person, the schools would be greatly improved. He was bitterly disappointed in the late 1930s when he learned that the construction of a third government school was to begin at Mutalau and, when it opened, the LMS would no longer be required to provide schooling in that village.[29] The Administration was, in Taylor's view, playing on the goodwill of the LMS to provide education services until such time as they were replaced by government schools and then the church was expected to 'roll over' and accept a reduced role and influence on Niue. 'It is a dirty trick,' wrote Taylor, designed to 'extinguish LMS educational work'.[30] Relations between Taylor and Bell were no longer so cordial, and when Taylor was asked for advice about children from Lakepa attending the new school at Mutalau, he was unwilling to give it. Bell saw the need to build government schools – both to improve the level of teaching and instruction in

English, and also to avoid any future situation where other churches set up missions on Niue and claimed subsidies for their own schools.

A programme to send students to New Zealand for further schooling had been adopted in the Cook Islands soon after World War I but the scheme had been rejected by the Administration in Niue, who felt there was greater value in using the money to bring European teachers to the island. Nevertheless, during the interwar period some young Niueans, including a small number of girls, did receive part of their education at Māori church boarding schools in New Zealand. The *Auckland Star*, under the heading 'Wide-eyed Niueans dropped into Fairyland', reported the arrival of 'two rather scared-looking Niue boys' when the *Hinemoa* berthed in Auckland in July 1925.

> *[T]hey stood close together on the deck, somewhat dazed, as their big brown eyes tried to take in the meaning of the bustling city with its clangour, its streams of people, and its towering buildings which, compared with their own palm-thatched huts, are veritable skyscrapers ... They are bound for St Stephen's Native School in Parnell, and before they return to their coral-island home ... they will be quite men of the world and ... they will be set up with a string of experiences that will keep their native village open-eyed with astonishment for months.*[31]

There are other instances of Niuean children receiving some of their education in New Zealand, and it seems that some funding was available for this. A few attended Te Aute College in Hawke's Bay and St Cuthbert's College for girls in Auckland. Patricia Tuagatagaloa spent four or five years in New Zealand at Turakina Maori Girls' College in Marton in the late 1930s.[32] For the great majority of Niuean children, however, Tufukia or Tuatea was the most they could aim for.

The development of medical services on Niue was another focus of Administration work throughout the interwar period. The Islanders had donated to Red Cross appeals in New Zealand during the war years, and at the end of the war the Red Cross therefore decided to donate £1000 towards building a hospital in Alofi. The governor-general of New Zealand, Lord Liverpool, announced the gift, and the New Zealand government's decision to add to the fund, when he visited Niue in June 1919. Every village also contributed an umu of puga, or burnt lime, for the walls of the buildings. The new hospital, built on the land already set aside for this purpose in Alofi South, was delayed because a large quantity of materials was on board the ill-fated *Jubilee*; but it was eventually opened in 1922 and named the Lord Liverpool Hospital.

The existence of a hospital did not, however, lead to immediate acceptance of such a service by the Niuean people. Suspicion, fear and uncertainty had to be overcome, and this required an education campaign around the island. The medical officer often went around the villages giving talks on public health issues, sometimes illustrated with lantern slides showing various diseases in their most advanced and grotesque forms. A nurse was appointed from New Zealand in 1920 whose job was to work with the women – especially new mothers, to try and reduce the alarming infant mortality rate. With the support of the Island Council and the village constables, hygiene campaigns were instigated to improve sanitation and cleanliness; and these became regular village inspections. In the 1930s Bell turned habitual village rivalry to good use by holding the 'Cleanest Village' competition: villages were to be judged on a whole host of categories including cleanest houses and village green, least number of breeding places for mosquitoes and flies, cleanest banana plantations and packing sheds, best flower gardens and stone walls, and most aid-to-revenue and dog tax paid. The winning village would receive a new reservoir with the words 'Winners of the Cleanest Competition 1933' emblazoned on the side. In the small print it was pointed out that the village was to supply all the materials and the labour for such a reservoir – a condition which some may have seen as a rather hollow victory.[33]

Throughout this period there was a gradual acceptance of Western medicine by Niueans, and the prevalence of tropical diseases such as yaws and hookworm was greatly reduced. Tuberculosis was tackled with an education programme about the dangers of spitting, and of overcrowding in poorly ventilated housing. Epidemics of pneumonia, conjunctivitis, infant paralysis and typhoid occurred frequently and put heavy demands on the hospital and staff. The medical officer was provided with a car, which made it easier to visit villages. Gradually the hospital became more accepted as somewhere people could go to be healed; but it was onerous for the families, who had to supply the patients' meals.

Visits to the hospital to treat yaws were particularly difficult. Yaws was a tropical disease that affected the skin, bone and cartilage. It often caused swelling on the soles of the feet, which then became ulcerated and made walking extremely painful. Many patients had a weekly journey of 5–10 miles to the hospital in Alofi, either on foot or, if they were lucky, sitting on the seat of a bicycle while someone walked alongside pushing it.[34] In 1930 a lorry was purchased for hospital use, which made it much easier for people to get to the hospital in Alofi. The lorry transported patients; and it also collected food parcels as it passed through the villages, to be sent to patients in hospital.

L.A. Hawkes was matron at the Lord Liverpool Hospital in the late 1930s. Part of her work involved visiting the outer villages to check on outpatients and children and to give health talks. In the 1930s the health programme was aided by the purchase of a truck and a car for these village visits. This one is to Mutalau. L.A. Hawkes Collection, Alexander Turnbull Library, Wellington, New Zealand, PA1-o-1270-9-3

The Island Council passed a number of ordinances that reinforced the health programme. These included the enforcement of various public health measures such as village cleanliness and animal control, and the introduction of compulsory notification of sexually transmitted diseases in an effort to control their spread. A health column was started in the LMS newspaper, *Taiahau*, and a health programme was included in the school syllabus. By now girls were also being taken in to Tufukia school, and those who went the furthest with their education were often employed in the neighbouring Lord Liverpool Hospital as trainee nurses. Although it was accepted that these girls would soon marry and move back to their villages, any health training they received was valuable to the family and the village.

Throughout the interwar period the Island Council continued to meet four times a year. The change of council leadership from patuiki to resident commissioner had already been made. As Reverend Cullen had noted in 1914, Togia 'is now an old and helpless man over 90. He has been retired from the Island Council but will be paid his salary until his death.'[35] When Togia died in 1917 the Cook Islands Amendment Act had already come into effect, with important changes for the Island Council. Henceforth members were to be appointed by the governor-general of New Zealand on the advice of the resident commissioner, who was himself to be president of the council. On Niue the council was less than happy when it was informed of the changes, and deputy resident commissioner John Evison was asked to send a letter to Wellington explaining that the councillors 'fail to see how the Governor General, without actually knowing them personally, can gauge their ability to be members of a Council'.[36] The council subsequently put forward a proposal to the minister that they be allowed to select their own president, and suggested Uea would be the ideal person. The minister replied simply: 'This is not in accordance with the law.'[37] When Guy Morris became resident commissioner he used a system of asking each village to nominate two men as councillors; he chose one of them and forwarded the name to Wellington for approval. When Morris removed the Makefu councillor Matiu from office in 1919, he was reprimanded by the Cook Islands Department for taking the law into his own hands: 'Members of the Island Council are appointed during the pleasure of the Governor General, the Resident Commissioner has no power to remove them.'[38] The 1916 Amendment Act had, as was pointed out in the Legislative Council debate, 'deprived the islanders of all right to have a say in making their own laws'.[39]

Life was changing for Niueans, even in the villages furthest from Alofi. More reliable shipping, and the abolition of the £1 departure tax, meant the flow of people to and from the island increased. The growth of the banana industry meant greater cash inflows when times were good, but also more pressure to prepare for boat day, as bananas had to be picked, sorted, crated and trucked to Alofi; then everyone gathered around the wharf to share the excitement of the day. In addition to the regular steamer there were now other visitors to Niue. Passing yachts, especially American ones, called during the winter sailing months; and by the early 1930s there was a demand for Pacific cruises away from the main hubs of Suva and Honolulu.[40] The MV *Maui Pomare* began carrying tourists on its island run, and Niue was included. Now, on boat day at Alofi, small stalls were set up around the wharf area with locals selling handcrafts and fruit.

Not just people, but ideas, commodities, fashions and music came in on the boats – and over the airwaves. Niueans working around Alofi, within earshot of imported radios, were captivated by the sounds of such greats as Glenn Miller, Benny Goodman, Duke Ellington and Louis Armstrong. Dances were organised in the cargo sheds on the Alofi wharf. Electric lighting, designed to aid ship loading, also made the area a magnet for night-time revellers – much to the consternation of the LMS, who complained of 'the dangers arising from these imported customs … the Niueans not yet [being] ready for experiments in promiscuous dancing'.[41]

This image is from a family album belonging to Eric Alexander Maunsell from Dunedin, who went on a winter excursion on the *Maui Pomare* in 1935. Maunsell photographed men unloading the ship and carrying goods up from the wharf. Robert Rex recalled working on the wharf in the 1930s: 'In those days everything had to be shoulder carried up from the jetty to the cargo shed and it takes some strength to carry copra sacks down and throw them in the lighters.' Maunsell Collection Album 424, Hocken Collections Uare Taoka o Hākena, University of Otago, Dunedin, New Zealand

Passengers on the cruise could purchase handcrafts from Niuean men who came alongside the ship in their vaka: these ones have spears, basketware and bananas for sale. Maunsell Collection Album 424, Hocken Collections Uare Taoka o Hākena, University of Otago, Dunedin, New Zealand

Above and opposite: Advertising brochure for tours by NZGS *Maui Pomare*.
By the 1930s Pacific cruises were becoming popular and there was a market for tours away from the tourist hubs of Honolulu and Suva. The New Zealand Department of External Affairs, responsible for the *Maui Pomare*, saw an opportunity to combine trade with tourism and instigated a winter excursion scheme. The first 11 passengers made the round trip from Auckland to Niue and then

SAMOA–NIUE ISLAND TRIP.

AUCKLAND to NIUE, £10, thence to APIA, £13, thence to DUNEDIN or LYTTELTON, £26, thence to WELLINGTON, £27 10s. thence to AUCKLAND, £31.

ROUND TRIP *(from any port)* ... **£30.**

The above trip occupies approximately 23 days, with one day ashore at Niue and two days at Apia (Samoa).

M.s. "MAUI POMARE" leaves New Zealand ports every five weeks on this trip. Schedule of dates may be obtained from agents (*see over*).

NIUE ISLAND.

NORFOLK ISLAND TRIP.

		£	s.	d.
AUCKLAND to NORFOLK, £7	*Round Trip,*	12	0	0.
WELLINGTON - AUCKLAND - NORFOLK - AUCKLAND	*Round Trip,*	15	10	0.
LYTTELTON - WELLINGTON - AUCKLAND - NORFOLK - AUCKLAND	*Round Trip,*	17	0	0.
DUNEDIN - LYTTELTON - WELLINGTON - AUCKLAND - NORFOLK - AUCKLAND	*Round Trip,*	18	0	0.

KINGSTON (NORFOLK ISLAND).

Arriving from the Islands direct at Dunedin or Lyttelton, the vessel proceeds to Wellington, thence to Auckland, thence to Norfolk Island, returning to Auckland before proceeding on the Niue-Samoa trip, returning direct to Dunedin or Lyttelton.

Round Trip, from New Zealand port back to New Zealand port, including Niue Island, Samoa, and Norfolk Island, occupying 30 days: £40.

W. A. G. SKINNER, GOVERNMENT PRINTER, WELLINGTON, N.Z.

Apia in June 1934. At Niue the passengers came ashore by surfboat and were shown around the island by Resident Commissioner Bell while the vessel was being unloaded and loaded. When they returned to New Zealand, the tourists 'expressed themselves well pleased with the trip'.

Alexander Turnbull Library, Wellington, New Zealand, Eph-B-SHIP-1930-01

Around the island a new activity became popular and caused great excitement and village rivalry. In his annual report for 1922, Dr Ellison expressed his pleasure at 'the way people are taking up the systematic playing of cricket under the Marylebone rules and the support they are giving to the newly-formed Island Cricket Association'.[42] The Europeans on Niue may have thought cricket was going to follow English rules and etiquette, but it soon developed its own island style. William Bolton, the teacher established at Hakupu by this time, devoted pages in his writings to descriptions of inter-village games.[43] In one glorious match 44 men recently returned from working in Samoa were challenged by Hakupu, who fielded an equal number of players. The entire malē and roadway became the cricket field. The glass was removed from the church as a precaution; scoring was kept by means of slits on banana leaves; fielders ran into and behind houses and into the bush to retrieve the ball, which was made from the rubber of the banyan tree and likely to shoot in any direction once it hit the rough coral ground or a coconut tree; and the game lasted eight hours without a break before Hakupu was declared the winner. On other occasions games lasted for several days, and when Liku came to play, Bolton noted that such was the feasting that 'Hakupu won but Hakupu was eaten out'. English cricket had been adapted to suit Niuean ideas of hospitality and reciprocity and to give vent to village rivalry, and Marylebone rules were not going to stand in the way of a great day's entertainment and hilarity.

In the 1928 New Zealand election, Pomare's Reform Party was voted out of office.[44] The Cook Island portfolio was placed in the hands of Sir Apirana Ngata, and in 1932 the government decided to take Niue into the External Affairs portfolio, alongside Samoa. The rationale for this was that the *Maui Pomare* was under the control of External Affairs and as it serviced both Niue and Samoa it seemed sensible, at least to officials, to deal with the two territories together. Furthermore, there was still a considerable Niuean workforce in and around Apia, including men and women now contracted to work on the New Zealand Reparation Estates. These were coconut and rubber plantations taken from German owners at the end of World War I and now operated by New Zealand officials. Workers were hired in Niue for one or two years' work on the estates with the express agreement that they would be returned to Niue at the end of the contract. Some payment was held back until they arrived home, as a means of ensuring the labourers did not disappear in Samoa. The Niue Administration was not in favour of the scheme as it was felt the labour could be better used at home. Resident Commissioner Bell, with his previous experience in Samoa, was particularly opposed, as he was 'afraid of the Mau influence on these people':[45] 'Owing to the very disastrous effects of the Mau on peace, order and good Government I am very anxious to keep the Niueans away from that Territory.'[46] Nevertheless, small numbers of Niuean men, often with their wives and children, were accepted as contract labourers to Samoa throughout the 1930s.

Despite a change in government department, Niue was still being overlooked in Wellington. In 1935 the first Labour government came to power under Michael Joseph Savage, but Niue was not on his radar. The new medical officer to Niue was Dr Harold Lange,[47] who tried on numerous occasions to make the new Labour government aware of Niuean issues, 'but nothing has come of my suggestions'. He lobbied parliamentarians to send someone 'to investigate thoroughly local conditions ... It is some years since Niue was favoured by a visit from Parliamentary leaders and then only for part of a day, which is hopelessly inadequate to meet the people and learn their wants.'[48] Dr Lange was ignored as the Department of External Affairs continued with the well-tried policy of 'do not disturb', until the actions of the resident commissioner forced them to act. This time it was not sexual impropriety or moral outrage that forced action but the purchase and sale of Niuean hats.

Captain Bell, sent to Niue to replace Luckham in 1931 ('the position is a temporary one only and no definite period of appointment can be given'),[49] had already retired from government service and was in receipt of a pension. Forced by government policy during the Depression to make financial cuts, External Affairs topped up Bell's pension rather than giving him the full £500 resident commissioner's salary, and in so doing made a significant saving. The temporary appointment eventually stretched to 10 years. A murder in Liku in 1932 placed Bell in the same position as Evison had been in 11 years previously, and he applied for a transfer on the grounds that 'having condemned to death a Native inhabitant of the small island [I have] to administer',[50] he was now working at a severe disadvantage. But External Affairs informed Bell they had no intention of considering a change for him.

Bell remained on Niue but his salary was a constant worry to him as, although he was a bachelor, he supported his widowed sister and her family in New Zealand. While one of his nieces was staying with him on Niue, Bell had come up with an idea: he would purchase hats and other handcrafts from Niuean women and his niece would act as agent in New Zealand in selling to retailers in the Canterbury region. The Niuean women were enthusiastic, especially because the resident commissioner was offering cash for their products while the traders were still trying to deal in IOU notes, whereby the recipient was tied to redeeming the voucher in that trader's store. The Island Council supported the sale of goods for cash.

> *Before Miss Smith [Bell's niece] bought baskets we received small prices and often only trade or a piece of paper showing how much we could buy from the store in the future. We want a fair price for our goods and we want cash, we did not get this in the past.*[51]

The women may have been happy with the arrangement, but the traders were not. They felt the resident commissioner had an unfair advantage and they were incensed to see the commissioner's car returning from the outer villages, piled to the roof with hats and baskets. E. Jennings, manager of the Burns Philp (South Seas) trading company that had begun business on Niue in 1931, and Harry Collins, who had begun his own business in 1917 and now had 10 retail outlets around the island, led the charge in complaining to Wellington. 'Government officials should be entirely disassociated with any aspects of trading' was the sentence underlined in the reply from External Affairs.[52] Bell persisted with his scheme, claiming it was not him but his niece who was buying handcrafts. The protests to Wellington continued until External Affairs was forced to act. In December 1941 the department sent a cable informing Bell that a judge would be appointed to investigate his trading activities. He was shown the cable, wrote on it, 'I tender my resignation' and left by the next vessel.[53]

Once again Niue was without a resident commissioner, and Wellington was scrambling to arrange a successor. Once again, the situation had arisen during wartime and, faced with a shortage of government employees because of war service, External Affairs appointed that reliable official on Niue, Joseph McMahon-Box, after 27 years' continuous service, finally as resident commissioner.

Niue and World War II

IN SEPTEMBER 1939 the news that the world was at war came to Niue by radio. Reverend Taylor wrote to his colleague in Samoa:

> *Isn't the news horrifying. We feel too shocked yet to think about it. Our folks are full of queries – but they are not passive sympathisers. Getting on for 300 of them have volunteered for service. Whether their offer will be accepted or not I do not know. But that number out of a total population of little over 4000 makes a high percentage.*[54]

Taylor reported that Niue had already been instructed to get in supplies of food in case shipping services were disrupted, but when they tried to order goods from New Zealand they were told many of the items were unobtainable as imports had already been restricted or forbidden.

In New Zealand the military authorities and the government were seeking to establish clear guidelines for the mobilisation of manpower. One particular area of concern was the large number of requests coming for voluntary enlistment from men in the Pacific territories. In July 1940 External Affairs reported to Defence that it had been informed by the resident commissioner in Niue that 'he is besieged with appeals for permission to join in the war'.[55] The reply from the army secretary a week later said no further voluntary enlistments were being accepted. 'Men will be obtained by ballot pursuant to National Service Regulations, 1940, which apply to people resident in New Zealand only.'[56] July 1940 marked the introduction of conscription, compulsory military service, for all men aged 19 to 45 in New Zealand. It was to be done by ballot but certain categories of people were exempted; eventually, in 1943, this included Pacific Islanders resident in New Zealand.

The final official attempt by Niue to get men from the island accepted for service was in January 1942, when McMahon-Box passed on a request for Niueans to be accepted. If the policy already established could not be altered, he asked that New Zealand recruit parties from Niue work on unskilled jobs in New Zealand so Europeans could be released to serve overseas.[57] The offer struck a chord with Foss Shanahan in the Prime Minister's Department, and he put the idea to the Joint Chiefs of Staff: 'This offer evidences a commendable spirit and, if accepted not only in respect of Niue but also in respect of other Pacific Islands under the control of New Zealand, would cement the relationship between New Zealand and these territories and identify the residents even more closely with the war effort.'[58] The offer was declined on the basis of 'shipping and other difficulties'.

With no chance of sending men from Niue to serve in the 2nd New Zealand Expeditionary Force, all that could be done was to prepare to defend the island itself, in case the enemy arrived on its shores. This possibility became more likely following the Japanese attack on Pearl Harbor in December 1941. Resident Commissioner Bell issued 'instructions should an enemy raider appear': if raiders landed, people in the nearby villages should hide in the bush. 'If caught, do everything you can not to help the enemy.' Perhaps the most useful advice in a list of instructions was to speak only in Niuean.[59] Niueans remember taking items such as bikes, sewing machines and beds and hiding them in the bush gardens in case of enemy occupation.[60] The aged field gun, gifted to Niue in recognition of service during World War I, was buried up at Fonuakula in case its presence in Alofi should be seen as a sign that the island was fortified.[61]

In early 1942 a Home Guard was established, although there was virtually no military equipment on the island. The new resident commissioner, McMahon-Box, requested a machine gun and ammunition from New Zealand, and although it had been determined that the Japanese threat lay further to the west in the Pacific, and therefore 'Niue [was] of little importance strategically', it was agreed to meet McMahon-Box's request 'for the effect on morale'.[62] Robert Rex recalled the arrival of the machine gun and the lack of know-how about operating it. He had served earlier in a territorial force in Fiji and agreed to test the gun off Tomb Point in Alofi. Once the technique was understood, all members of the Home Guard enthusiastically practised, firing out into Alofi Bay and quickly exhausting the supply of ammunition.[63] Further machine guns, rifles and rounds of ammunition were gradually supplied throughout the war; they were collected and returned to Trentham military camp in May 1945.

A coastwatching service was also set up, with stations at Avatele, Liku and Hikutavake and with headquarters at Alofi. As there was no radio communication on the island, a runner had to be dispatched if a ship was sighted; on many occasions the ship had disappeared before word reached Alofi. Nevertheless, radio communication with Apia enabled news of any sightings to be fed into a wider network of coastwatching stations, including the one on Raoul Island where Niueans were working.

The location of Niue relative to Tonga, Fiji, Samoa and the Cooks prompted McMahon-Box to suggest to Wellington that the island held a 'central and important position … as a base operating either for or against these other groups' and offered 'good landing grounds for planes'.[64] Enquiries to the military authorities quickly received the reply, 'many surveys of Pacific by aerodrome constructors have never produced any suggestion that an aerodrome at Niue was necessary'.[65] That idea was shelved for another 30 years.

Niue's experience of World War II was very different from that of World War I. Niueans resident in New Zealand were accepted for service in the 2nd NZEF, but they were scattered through the various battalions and no count of their numbers was ever attempted.[66] In World War II there was much fighting in the Pacific but it was further to the west and never reached Niue's shores. The names of some individuals who served during World War II are included on village war memorials around Niue, but the main focus of commemoration is firmly fixed on World War I.

Opposite: Map of Niue Island, 1942. The 1903 map of Niue prepared by Lands and Survey, New Zealand, shortly after annexation, was used by the War Office during World War II when possible sites for landing strips were being considered throughout the Pacific. Two possible sites are drawn over the older map.

Archives New Zealand, The Department of Internal Affairs Te Tari Taiwhenua, AECO 18642 W2057 PMW2057/2

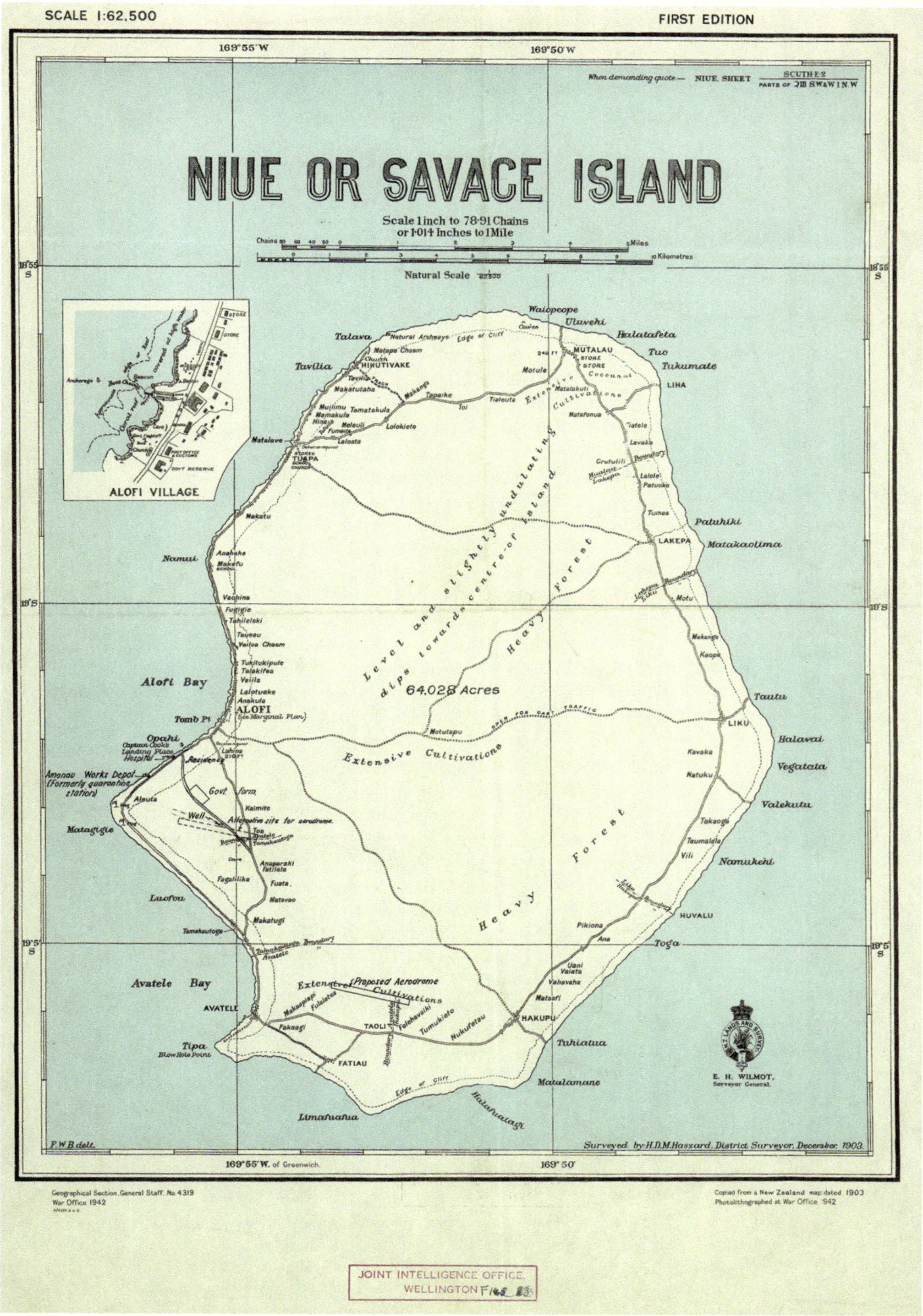
SCALE 1:62,500
FIRST EDITION
169°55'W
169°50'W
NIUE OR SAVAGE ISLAND
Scale 1 inch to 78·91 Chains
or 1·014 Inches to 1 Mile
Chains
Miles
Kilometres
Natural Scale
18°55' S
19°S
19°5' S
ALOFI VILLAGE
Waiopeope
Uluvehi
Halatafeta
Tuo
Tukumate
LIHA
Talava
Natural Archways
Edge of Cliff
Matapa Chasm
HIKUTIVAKE
Tavilia
MUTALAU
STORE
Motule
Makefu
Extensive Cultivations
Tuapa
Matalave
Makatutaha
Tamatakula
Lolokieto
Laloata
Level and slightly undulating dips towards centre of Island
Heavy Forest
64.028 Acres
Patuhiki
LAKEPA
Matakaolima
Namui
Alofi Bay
ALOFI
(See Marginal Plan)
Tomb Pt
Opahi
Captain Cook's Landing Place
Hospital
Residency
Amanau Works Depot (Formerly quarantine station)
Govt. farm
Well
Alternative site for aerodrome
Matagigie
Luofou
Motu
Tautu
LIKU
Halavai
Vegatala
Valekutu
Namukehi
HUVALU
Toga
Pikiona
Avatele Bay
AVATELE
Tipa
Blow Hole Point
Proposed Aerodrome
Extensive Cultivations
TAOLI
FATIAU
HAKUPU
Tuhiatua
Matalamane
Limahuhua
Halahuatagi
E. H. WILMOT,
Surveyor General.
F. W. B. delt.
Surveyed by H. D. M. Haszard, District Surveyor, December 1903.
169°55'W. of Greenwich.
169°50'
Geographical Section, General Staff, No. 4319
War Office 1942
Copied from a New Zealand map dated 1903
Photolithographed at War Office 1942
JOINT INTELLIGENCE OFFICE,
WELLINGTON

12. Accelerating Change

We ... have earned the right to play a leading role in the future of this part of the world

Peter Fraser was the first New Zealand prime minister since Richard Seddon to speak with confidence about the role of his country in the South Pacific. At the Canberra conference in January 1944, he articulated a policy based on 'vital concern in the peace, welfare and good government of Pacific territories'. Through 'their whole-hearted and sustained war effort', he said, both Australia and New Zealand 'have earned the right to play a leading role in the future of this part of the world'.[1]

A new international focus, and a new international confidence, meant administrative changes in Wellington. The Department of External Affairs, previously responsible for Western Samoa, Tokelau[2] and Niue, was reconstituted as the department responsible for New Zealand relations with Commonwealth and foreign powers. The necessary corollary to this was the creation of a separate Department of Island Territories to take over responsibility for Western Samoa, Tokelau and Niue plus the Cook Islands, which up to this point had had its own department.[3] While it might be tempting to believe New Zealand was now focusing on its Island Territories, the truth was that Commonwealth and foreign relations had become more important. In creating a Department of Island Territories a sleight of hand occurred at the bureaucratic level and Niue was quietly slipped back within the Cook Islands for administrative purposes. That is not to say there was any noticeable change in Niue, which still had its own resident commissioner and still reported directly to Wellington, but the separate acknowledgement of Niue was now often dropped and the bureaucratic mind reverted to the 1901 notion that Niue was part of the Cooks. There was no longer a separate annual report tabled in Parliament from Niue; it was included in the annual report for the Cook Islands, which now talked about the 'Cook Islands (including Niue)' or the 'Cook Islands (excluding Niue)'.[4] When Prime Minister Fraser sent a New Year message to the Pacific on 1 January 1945 he wished 'a happy and prosperous year to the Polynesian peoples of the Cook Islands, the Tokelaus and Western Samoa'.[5]

Fraser was interested in international affairs and took a prominent role in the setting up of the United Nations, in particular as chair of the committee charged with creating the Trusteeship Council. His government now embraced the ideals of self-determination for all peoples. Trusteeship meant working towards self-government for all countries and this involved a focus on education, health, economic and political development. More expenditure was required in New Zealand's Island Territories and a larger and more professional public service was needed to carry out the new ideals and policies. When interviewed by the *Evening Post*, Fraser declared:

> *I want to say quite frankly that to do justice to the Island Territories will cost a good deal more money than we have been spending for that work because the people are in the developmental stage and they are entitled to every assistance. It is our responsibility.*[6]

In a similar way to Seddon, Fraser painted his vision for the South Pacific with large brushstrokes. He spoke of ideals and principles, of priorities and responsibilities, but he left the finer detail to others. He undertook a Pacific tour over Christmas 1944 – the first such tour undertaken by air. Even the tiny island of Penrhyn in the northern Cook group had an airstrip by now, but there was nothing on Niue. The solution proposed was to fly low over the island en route from Rarotonga to Apia as an acknowledgement that Niue had not been forgotten; however, the USSC vessel *Matua* was due in Apia at that time and arrangements were made to transport the prime minister's party to Niue and back to Apia. So Peter Fraser did set foot on the wharf at Alofi, but the visit barely rated a mention in press coverage back in New Zealand. When Fraser spoke after his Pacific trip he made no separate reference to Niue; but, of course, when he spoke of the Cooks he meant the 'Cooks (including Niue)'.

On the ground in Niue, charged with translating the new ideals into practicalities, was Hector Larsen, resident commissioner since December 1943, when 28 years of service by Joseph McMahon-Box had come to an ignominious end. McMahon-Box had been in deep financial strife, and because of the impact of this on his health, the doctor had advised that he must be returned to New Zealand. He suffered a heart attack soon after his arrival in Auckland, and died four months later. His personnel file notes that at the time of his retirement he was still 'on loan from the Customs Department'.[7]

No one in Wellington had stopped to think about the ramifications of placing an officer from the New Zealand public service on an isolated island, in the midst of a very small community, and leaving him there for 28 years. No one had thought through his position when, as a man married into an influential Pālagi–Niuean family, he became vulnerable to family pressures, which could frequently place his personal and professional life in conflict. McMahon-Box was pressured to find work for family members in the Administration, and he was constantly requesting pay increases from Wellington to meet his family commitments. In late 1941 his duties were listed as: 'Assistant to Resident Commissioner, Treasurer, Registrar of the High Court, Registrar of the Native Land Court, Officer-in-charge of Police and Prisoners, Registrar of Births, Deaths and Marriages, Clerk of the Island Council'; and in addition 'he [had] discharged the duties of Collector of Customs and Postmaster', although technically the resident commissioner held these two positions. He had, a short time earlier, been relieved of his duties as meteorological officer.[8]

Larsen was one of a new breed of island administrators. He was not on loan from Customs or the Post Office; he was not a retired army officer already on a pension. He had begun as a cadet in the Cook Islands Department working in the accounting section, had worked for seven years in the Administration in Rarotonga, and had been moved to Niue when Captain Bell, along with his hat trade, had been forced off the island. He was promised the position of resident commissioner after a year as treasurer and deputy to McMahon-Box. For reasons attributed to 'the exigencies of war', however, the changeover from McMahon-Box to Larsen did not happen at the end of 1942. Larsen was sent to the Treasury in Apia with a promise that he would eventually be returned to Niue. This happened in late 1943, and he took up his new position as resident commissioner.

Larsen, who had a strong background in financial management, proceeded to study the Administration books – and he was appalled by what he found. There was evidence of serious financial mismanagement and even embezzlement. Dr Hunt, who had advised Wellington that McMahon-Box's health was precarious, also cabled to inform Island Territories that for the previous five years he had entrusted the bulk of his salary as a retirement fund into the safekeeping of McMahon-Box and that money had now disappeared. Harry Collins, an island trader, reported to Wellington that McMahon-Box had twice borrowed large sums from him to make up deficits in his cash reserves when the auditors were due.[9] Larsen called for an urgent audit of the Niue Administration accounts and began a new era of careful and open financial management.

Reverend Taylor, on Niue since 1929, observed the changing of the guard in the Administration once more.

Yes, Larsen looks like being an improvement on our ex-Resident Commissioner. He will not have to be much to be an improvement on our last three. One 'promoted' to Aitutaki, the next told 'retire or … ' and our most recent one leaving under a cloud so dense the detectives met him. He lifted practically every penny the old Doc had so we have been told, running near £1500, and there was another sum of nearly £1000 from a trader. The latter fact is not public knowledge yet so keep it under your hat.[10]

In a reference to the antics of previous resident commissioners, Taylor reported that Larsen had attended an Island Council meeting and had been 'brutally blunt'. He had told the councillors, 'we are not here to pick the best things from your feasts, or to sleep with your women'.[11] Larsen was out to make a clean start and to distance himself from the way affairs had previously been conducted.

Hec Larsen was an energetic man, 35 years old when he became resident commissioner. He was large in stature, in voice and in personality; a friend later described him as 'boisterous'. He threw himself into his new work, but at times, in letters back to Island Territories, he spoke of the worry and responsibility involved in the position. He requested salary increases and he applied for other positions but the reply from Wellington was always negative.

With the end of war in 1945 came a great burst of activity from the Department of Island Territories in Wellington. The minister was in fact the prime minister, and under his direction numerous surveys were launched to assess where things were at in the various islands. Education, health, agriculture, air services, trade – all were under the spotlight. When Taylor noted to a colleague in Apia that Niue had been visited by Dr Beeby, Director of Education in New Zealand, the reply from Apia was cynical.

So you have had your educationalists … You may be having the health deputation too, and the survey party and the – well each department in turn seems to be turning out to have a trip by air and to let off some overheated air! … there is a superfluity of deputations just now, methinks, with an eye on world opinion and to make it appear that 'we' are doing much for the poor benighted islander. My![12]

Larsen had already instituted changes on Niue before the arrival of the various review groups. Alarmed by the frequency of epidemics on the island, and realising that the medical officer, Dr Hunt, at 77 years was too aged and infirm to be effective, the resident commissioner had begun visiting and inspecting villages himself. Influenza and other infectious diseases were causing an alarming increase in deaths, especially among children. 'My printer … lost 4 children in 3 days during this last bout of sickness,' wrote Reverend Taylor in June 1944, when commenting on the

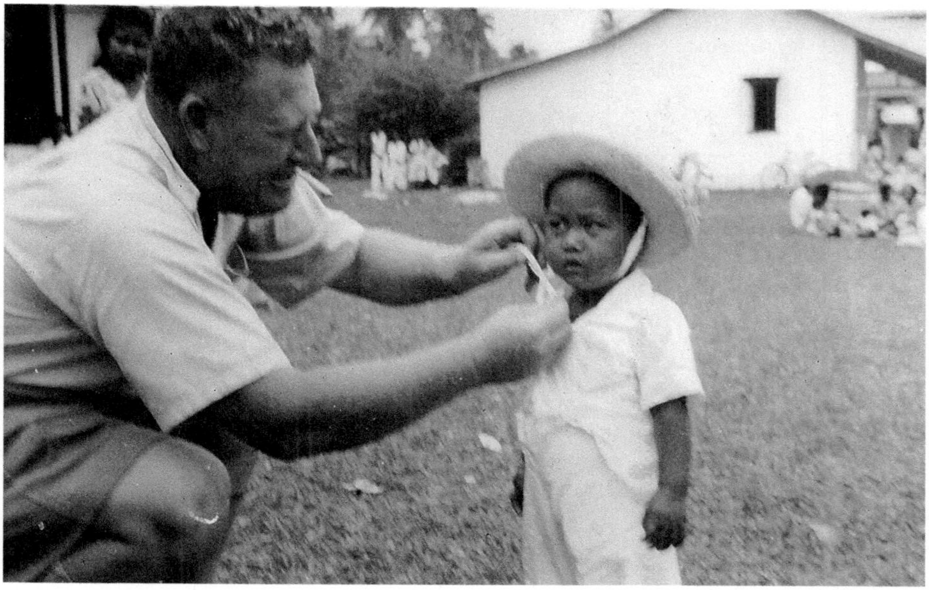

Hector Larsen was resident commissioner from December 1943 until his murder in August 1953. In this undated photo taken on a village green, Larsen stoops to tie a hat on a child.

Courtesy Alison Sandom (née Larsen) and Bill Larsen

epidemics of the previous 18 months. Larsen called for the strict application of public health ordinances in an effort to contain the spread of disease; and he was not averse to bawling out instructions for a clean-up in the village under inspection, or to prosecuting those who broke the ordinances. Each week he visited the hospital in Alofi and asked staff what he could do to help.[13]

Larsen had also turned his thoughts to improving health through the education programme. Two Niuean students had been sent to Fiji in the early 1940s to be trained as native medical practitioners. The boys had struggled: their schooling in Niue, and especially their level of English, had not been sufficient to prepare them for such training, and by 1944 they had been returned home. Larsen now pressed the Department of Island Territories to accept two students for further schooling in New Zealand for at least two years, to bring their English up to a level where they could cope in Fiji. He got approval for this. He approached the Tufukia headmaster to select the most suitable boys, and he brought Reverend Taylor into the scheme in order to get church support for the boys in New Zealand. Through the LMS network, board was arranged for school holidays with a church minister and also on a farm run by an LMS family. It was also arranged that the boys would attend summer Boys' Brigade camp each year. Larsen organised to have the students monitored and

The banana trade became very contentious as it was linked to the issue of Sunday work. There was several days' work involved in picking the bananas, crating them and transporting them to Alofi to prepare for shipping, but because the LMS was totally opposed to any work on a Sunday the bananas sometimes got left behind. Here crates have been delivered ready for packing in either Lakepa or Liku, the two biggest banana-producing villages. Courtesy Alison Sandom (née Larsen) and Bill Larsen

helped at all times, for he saw that without this support the scheme would end in failure. Ione Viliua from Tamakautoga and Dick Tafatu from Alofi North left Niue in June 1944 and entered Wanganui Technical College as boarders. For the next two and a half years they were closely monitored by Larsen, who wrote personally to them, encouraging them in their studies, and visited them when he was home on furlough.[14] At the start of 1947 they entered the Central Medical School in Suva, and they became the first successful graduates of this school from Niue.

Economic growth was a key strategy of the New Zealand policy to encourage the self-sufficiency of the Island Territories. With the end of war there was an increase in shipping availability and a push was made to increase exports from the islands. Agreements with the UK Ministry of Food to supply copra at guaranteed prices boosted Niuean exports, and the planting of bananas was encouraged to meet the demand on the New Zealand market. Once again Sunday labour became an issue. A compromise was needed to take advantage of the new market demand while respecting the sensibilities of a society that was still very much church dominated.

Workers to Sunday (Raoul) Island

LIKE MALDEN ISLAND, Sunday Island occupies a special place in the Niuean collective memory.[15] There are countless stories of the men who sailed 1000 kilometres south to work on this island in the Kermadec group, of the experiences they had and the possessions they brought back to Niue.

There was an early link between Niue and Sunday Island when a small group of labourers were contracted in the 1880s to help clear land and plant crops. Niueans were chosen because of their reputation as good workers and also because the Auckland firm of Henderson and Macfarlane was trading with the Nicholas store in Avatele by this time and could call at Sunday Island on either leg of the journey. Much of the planting on Sunday Island was of crops such as coconuts brought from Niue.

Sunday Island again became important in the Niue story in the 1940s. The New Zealand Public Works Department built a meteorological station and also set up a coastwatching station on the island during World War II, and these projects created a need for labourers for construction and for food production. In 1942 the resident commissioner on Niue was asked to supply a small labour force of six to eight men to work for one year.

Competition for the work was fierce and the Administration office in Alofi was flooded with requests: 'Please your kindly heart sign my name on that gang', 'I like to go and earn some money to build a new house', 'God bless you and let me go by this gang'[16] were some of the many letters received. Each village was therefore invited to send in one name; these were put in a hat and six were drawn out. The men had to be single and physically strong. They were to bring their own bedding and some were to take their own vaka and fishing tackle. Their task would be to plant crops taken from Niue anc generally to help the Europeans on Sunday Island. For this they would be paid one shilling per day and would receive their food – which made Niuean labour a very cheap option compared to bringing in workers from New Zealand.

When the MV *Tagua* called at Niue in November 1942, the six men had been selected and crops for planting had been prepared. In addition to supplies for the men themselves, the plants supplied for Sunday Island consisted of 500 bundles of maniota (manioc), 2480 taro shoots, 20 baskets of kūmara tops, 645 lbs of yams, and ready-made thatch to construct living quarters for the Niueans.[17] Written instructions explained that the taro and kūmara should be planted first for they would not last long. Yams could be cut up like potatoes and kept in a dark, warm place to sprout before planting. Maniota could just be stuck in the ground; it was the hardiest of them all.

The government continued to send men and crops for planting into the early 1950s. Most of the men seem to have enjoyed the experience and some returned for a second contract period. Pay rates gradually increased to 5/- per day and because of the colder weather in the Kermadecs, warm clothing items were supplied. Medical problems such as septic cuts, yaws or dental disease sometimes necessitated evacuation to Auckland for treatment. The men worked as general labourers and farmhands, assisting with the citrus planting scheme at the time. They were also valued for their assistance in unloading and loading vessels, often in very difficult sea conditions. A few of the Niueans became involved in the work associated with the meteorological station, such as putting up the weather balloon, taking daily readings and looking after equipment.

In the 1940s New Zealand maintained a coastwatching and meteorological station on Raoul (Sunday) Island in the Kermadecs. A small gang of Niuean workers was employed to work on the island. Here several proud young Niueans stand with their catch, a large kingfish. John Sorensen Collection, Alexander Turnbull Library, Wellington, New Zealand, F-113582-1/4

For the Niueans, one of the main incentives to work on Sunday Island was the access this gave them to ordering goods from New Zealand. The New Zealand authorities had envisaged an ordering service to meet the needs of the men while on Sunday Island but the Niueans were much more interested in what they could order to take home. A pricelist of goods shows what was in demand: musical instruments, especially guitars and ukuleles, household furnishings, clothing including cowboy shirts and silk underwear, boots and shoes, watches, safety razors, axes, chewing gum, chocolate and tobacco were all desirable items.[18] In addition, nearly every Niuean took home a hospital bed and mattress and a bicycle.

By the late 1940s, when men were being transported on the *New Golden Hind*,[19] it was noted that cargo space on the return journey to Niue, especially for beds and bicycles, was becoming a problem, but resident commissioner Larsen on Niue supported the men's right to purchase such goods: 'It is realised that the personal supplies of the Niueans at Raoul have reached somewhat large proportions, but I have always taken the view the single men employed should be able to spend their money how they wished.'[20] For the men, it was very important to arrive back in Niue with something to show for their absence. How much better to be able to come ashore at Alofi in cowboy shirt and boots and distribute chocolate and chewing gum, than to have money saved.

By late 1952 the operations on Sunday Island were being reviewed. A cutback in total numbers – leaving a basic staff from New Zealand to maintain the radio and weather station only – meant an end to the Sunday Island experience for young men from Niue.

Larsen began his term on Niue trying to walk a fine line between these competing demands. A meeting of church deacons in 1942 had 'decided that in view of the war situation, opposition to Sunday work should cease until such time as the seas become safe from the menace of enemy vessels'.[21] When war ended, the issue of Sunday labour arose once again; and a change in LMS leadership on the island brought it to boiling point. Reverend Taylor had resigned his position on Niue in 1945 because his wife was not well, and the LMS struggled to find a replacement. Eventually a minister was identified in Queensland who was prepared to serve in Niue, but this appointment caused bitter conflict and eventually the LMS acknowledged that they had made a mistake.

Reverend Caleb Beharell was 64 years old when he returned for his second term as missionary-in-charge on Niue in August 1945. While he was there in the 1920s he had been confrontational and litigious; age had not mellowed him and his uncompromising, fundamentalist approach to gospel work was as strong as ever. He met with the resident commissioner in October 1945 and set out his belief that now that the war had ended, there should be no need to load the boat on a Sunday. Larsen agreed with this: 'I strongly urge that [the] people's wish which is not an unreasonable one [should] be met', he advised Island Territories.[22] In January 1946, just before leaving on furlough, Larsen wrote to Beharell explaining the rulings made by the minister, Peter Fraser, in relation to the working of the *Maui Pomare*. In planning the ship's itinerary, needing to work the vessel in Niue on a Sunday would be avoided if at all possible. However, if it could not be avoided and there was already perishable cargo on board, the vessel would not wait over and any cargo left behind would not be paid for. Fraser asked for the issue to be fully discussed with the Island Council 'to ensure that they still wish to avoid Sunday work after thoroughly understanding what consequences may be involved'.[23] There was a note of determination in the directives of Prime Minister Fraser, but Sunday labour was an issue everywhere – in Rarotonga, Western Samoa, Tonga and New Zealand – and compromises had to be found.

Larsen went on furlough and Joe Empen, treasurer in the Administration, became acting resident commissioner. Debate over Sunday labour continued between Empen and Beharell. Empen went into all the possible scenarios in a series of letters to Beharell that were described in Wellington as 'masterpieces of thoroughness'.[24] In examining all the scenarios, Empen concluded that 'the only days of the week on which the ship could arrive and not in some way or another involve Sunday work are Wednesday, Thursday and Friday'.[25]

Larsen returned to Niue still hopeful of a compromise solution. He felt 'fairly confident' that the main banana-producing villages, Lakepa and Liku, would find a way to ensure their fruit was shipped. 'I see no indication that the people intend to give up banana growing,'[26] he wrote, and he noted that Lakepa had recently undertaken roadmaking at their own expense in order to open up additional areas for planting. Hope of a compromise faded when Beharell reported to Larsen in September that a meeting of Tiakono, all church elders, 'had come to a unanimous decision that no work was to be done on Sunday under any conditions whatsoever'.[27] Beharell considered the Tiakono was able to speak for the entire island but Larsen, who disagreed with this, now decided to call village meetings at which he would outline the shipping situation. Reverend Beharell would be invited to speak and a vote would be taken in each village.

The meetings took place over the course of a week in early October. Each side accused the other of manipulating, threatening and misleading the people, but the final result was a majority against Sunday work of any kind under any circumstances. Although Larsen saw that this meant the end of the banana industry for Niue and the accompanying loss of shipping carrying general cargo, mail and passengers, he advised Wellington to 'accept majority decision and treat as binding on all'.[28] In a confidential note to Wellington, Larsen blamed Beharell for the position they were now in. 'It is his well known, and almost fanatical, attitude in the matter which has caused the people to decide as they have.'[29]

Beharell meanwhile returned to the other matter that was occupying so much of his time in 1946: the centenary of the LMS on Niue. A building had been under construction on church land near the Alofi wharf and the opening was planned for late October, to commemorate the famous landing by Peniamina at Mutalau on 26 October 1846. The Centennial Hall, as it became known, would house the LMS Training Institution for young men studying to become pastors. For the opening, LMS officials were invited from far and near. Mr C.R. Lankshear, honorary secretary of the LMS in New Zealand, was to travel by the *Maui Pomare* from Auckland to represent the Congregational Union, and the mission ship *John Williams* was to come from Apia with a large party of LMS officials. A variety of factors meant that both vessels arrived in Alofi Bay on a Sunday morning.

The *Maui Pomare* called first and was forced to ride the tide, for the resident commissioner had enforced the Sunday ban fully and it was not possible to get a health or customs clearance for the vessel until Monday. Lankshear sat on board and wrote a note to Reverend Beharell on the shore.

> *[So] here we are, all dressed up and nowhere to go ... The Sunday labour call is again before us and is a problem, how to maintain Christian standards of living and routine and at the same time meet the needs of the workaday world. Tides, ocean currents and the weather take no thought for the Christian Sunday, and we must take thought to adjust ourselves to meet modern conditions. Just how to do this ... is a matter for the missionary statesman.*[30]

But Beharell was no 'missionary statesman' and he did not foresee that the same thing would happen the following Sunday with the *John Williams*. The mission vessel was carrying leading churchmen from the LMS in Samoa and descendants of Paulo, the first Samoan mission teacher on Niue, and it arrived early Sunday. Beharell requested a health and customs clearance so the passengers could land in time for the morning church service but the resident commissioner replied: 'Unfortunately gentleman it is your wish [to allow no Sunday work] and the government must respect your wish.' The incident was later recalled: '[T]he poor people out in the hot blazing sun [on the deck] were singing hymns. Members of the [Niue] church, especially women, were singing hymns on the jetty in Alofi but the others couldn't come ashore.'[31]

Within a year there were signs that not everyone was happy with the decision to ban all Sunday work, for the banana trade had ended and ships were calling less frequently. Larsen tried to engage Beharell in discussion about the situation but he would not consider any compromise. In May 1947 the village of Lakepa sent a petition to Peter Fraser, Prime Minister and Minister of Island Territories. Signed by 150 villagers, it explained that the village produced nearly a third of the total Niue production of bananas and wished to be allowed to ship the crop, even if Sunday work was necessary. The secretary of Island Territories, R.T.G. Patrick, advised the minister that approval of the petitioners' request would only 'precipitate a serious situation',[32] and so he suggested that Fraser should sympathise with the villagers but respect the wishes of the majority on the island.

In July a meeting was held in the village of Hakupu and the resident commissioner was invited to attend. There were two messages to be given. Hakupu was still opposed to Sunday work but would not stand in the way of others working on Sunday to get the bananas away. Second, the village pastor, Ikiua, apologised to Larsen. There had been a feeling that the resident commissioner and other Administration officials would not continue friendly relations with those who had spoken out strongly the previous year. 'They had all come to see how wrong they had been in this idea', and they thanked Larsen for his even-handed treatment.[33]

Hector Larsen and his son Bill in front of Arumaki Strickland's delivery truck in the late 1940s. Strickland arrived in Niue from the Cook Islands in 1946 and settled in Alofi North. He set up a number of bakeries and also a picture theatre.
Courtesy Alison Sandom (née Larsen) and Bill Larsen

Larsen passed on a report to Wellington and was instructed by Patrick in Island Territories 'not to take any active part in the efforts of sections of the community to resume Sunday work'.[34] He was therefore advised to keep his distance when a group called the Fruit Committee of Niue was created, with Leslie Rex, schoolteacher, as secretary. There was a representative from each village and the idea was to find a compromise that could include, for example, working through the early hours of Sunday, or working late Sunday after church activities were completed. Arumaki Strickland, visiting Niue from Rarotonga to set up a chain of bakeries and investigate the possibility of opening a cinema, was asked to speak about the fruit trade in the Cooks: he had been a member of the Cook Islands Fruit Advisory Committee for many years and knew the fruit industry well. The committee produced a petition for Minister Fraser in Wellington, but once again the reply was the same as it had been to Lakepa.

Increasing pressure from Fiji to have a guaranteed and substantial share of the New Zealand banana market forced Island Territories to relax their stance in relation to the Sunday work issue in Niue, and they began instructing Larsen to once again attempt talks with Beharell in the hope of reaching a compromise. Larsen tried several times but Beharell was adamant that compromise was out of the question. Numerous sections of Niuean society were, however, looking for a way through the impasse, and in late 1948, as Beharell was preparing to leave Niue at the end of a three-year term that the LMS was not willing to extend, a tentative start was made to shipping bananas once more. The Administration brought in new trucks so the transport of the banana crop to Alofi could be completed more efficiently, and gradually and cautiously the export industry was resumed.

Reverend Caleb Beharell bears considerable responsibility for the near collapse of the Niue banana trade. It was not the only issue he took exception to. He tried to prevent the introduction of cinema to Niue, calling on the New Zealand prime minister to issue an Order in Council to prevent it. He also objected to showing a copy of his proposed speech to be given during the governor-general's visit in 1948; Prime Minister Fraser was eventually forced to order Beharell to produce a copy of the speech beforehand or lose his right to speak. Beharell had begun work in the mission field before World War I. The LMS was now trying to reshape itself into an organisation in tune with the modern, post-World War II world and Beharell did not fit easily into this. LMS officials in Australia and New Zealand admitted privately to each other that the appointment of Beharell had been a mistake,[35] but there had been no other option available and they were still not ready to let Niuean pastors assume leadership of the church on Niue.

Relations between the LMS and the Administration improved with the arrival in May 1949 of the Reverend Maru George Check, the first missionary-in-charge to come from New Zealand rather than from England. He reported three months after arrival that 'the relationships between the Administration and the Mission have greatly improved'. He was prepared to compromise on the Sunday labour issue; he felt that the attitude of his predecessor had been 'entirely unreasonable and unrealistic'.[36] Check was concerned about the level of education offered in the LMS schools; he was prepared to work with the Administration in gradually giving them complete responsibility for primary education; and he set up a new post-primary class at the LMS centre in Alofi with a view to producing students for future training as pastors.

Within six months of arrival, however, the Checks experienced an unpleasant incident: an intruder crept into the mission house one night, entered the bedroom and placed a hand on Mrs Check. Her screams frightened the intruder off, but Check said she was 'traumatised' by the incident and took a long time to regain confidence.[37] Larsen placed a curfew on the village of Alofi and sent for a new chief of police from New Zealand. The incident was symptomatic of a growing social problem associated with young men who were aimless and unemployed. There had been signs of disenchantment during the war years: Taylor had reported 'a wave of lawlessness' in early 1942 involving arson and burglaries. The Burns Philp store was totally destroyed in an arson attack carried out by three men, who had escaped from the prison for the purpose and then returned to their cells.[38] Taylor reported to the LMS in London: 'The guilty parties are quite open that they want to get away to Samoa and the only way is to go as prisoners.'[39] Some young men managed to get passage to Auckland, where the new Pacific Islands church set up at Beresford Street tried to keep them safe, but it frequently reported on their court appearances. Back on Niue there was a split forming between those sections of society that were benefiting from association with the Administration through education and employment, and those who were not.

From 1945, as a result of the emphasis on development of infrastructure and services for the island, a new phenomenon appeared: a small but very visible and expanding expatriate community. More teachers, tradesmen, radio operators and administration staff arrived, and while the number had reached only 35 by 1950, it was nevertheless an influential group. Expatriate communities are strange beasts – they move away from the strictures of their own society but live outside the strictures of their adopted society. The postwar expatriate group on Niue was outside the orbit of church and village: they had no allegiances to either. They were highly visible and very vocal. They frequently made no attempt to learn the language, understand and respect the culture or mix socially with Niueans. They were a self-contained group and they made their own social life – and it frequently involved alcohol.

In a society where prohibition was still enforced, the introduction of cocktail parties and regular drinking sessions by the Europeans was a destabilising factor in society. Taylor commented in his 1945 report to the LMS that 'Europeans were drinking without considering the effect on the local population'. No doubt there were some among the Niueans who felt disillusioned and embittered by these double standards; and among the young men who had not continued with their education and who had not found employment with the only employer on the island, the Administration, there was an increasing lawlessness in the form of petty crime. There was also an upsurge in the production of bush beer, and the imprecise science involved in the manufacture of this product sometimes had disastrous consequences. In his final report to the LMS for 1948, Reverend Beharell reported on a shocking case of murder and suicide that had occurred under the influence of bush beer.

Dealing with such social issues was even more difficult than dealing with Sunday labour, and from the start of his time as resident commissioner Larsen continually requested that a chief of police be appointed from New Zealand. Joe Empen, appointed to carry out Land Court work, doubled in the police role for over two years despite a complete lack of experience in this field. In June 1946 the Police

Village cricket match: a typical scene in the 1950s.
Des Little, Auckland War Memorial and Museum Tāmaki Paenga Hira, New Zealand, C26745

Department in New Zealand reported that they could not 'find anyone interested in a three year appointment'.[40] A system of six-month appointments was trialled and when this failed, Larsen took responsibility for the police himself, although he noted to Wellington that 'this, of course, not only raises a number of difficulties, but I cannot devote sufficient time to the work required'.[41] When the Burns Philp store was broken into in September 1949 and the intruder entered the mission house in November that same year, Niue finally got a new chief of police, Constable John Flynn. Flynn arrived and immediately took charge of the police and the prison, but Reverend Check was soon complaining about another 'young bloke' coming to the island and letting his position 'go to his head'.[42] When Flynn drove his police vehicle through a crowd assembled outside the Centennial Hall to commemorate the arrival of Paulo from Samoa 100 years previously, Check was highly indignant and complained to the resident commissioner, but Larsen replied that it had been a mistake and had not been intended as an affront to the LMS.[43] When Flynn was accused of beating a young Niuean in an effort to extract a confession, the boy's father, accompanied by Check, approached the resident commissioner. Larsen said he was unable to give advice as he would have to hear any assault charge that might be laid against Flynn; the father should take whatever action he wanted.[44] Check later claimed that Larsen had actively talked him out of pressing charges against the police chief.[45] However, Flynn was removed from Niue and the short-term appointment system was reinstated until 1952, when a house was built that enabled the appointment of a married officer, Harry Williams, who accepted a three-year term. By this time, Larsen was so used to taking responsibility himself that he continued to visit the prison and oversee much of the work.

Relations between Larsen and Check – and hence between the Administration and the LMS – steadily deteriorated; and just as rifts were forming between groups at different social and economic levels, so people were becoming polarised in their view of the resident commissioner. For his part, Larsen made several attempts to move from Niue to positions in Auckland, Wellington and Rarotonga, but his applications were unsuccessful. As it had been in the interwar period, the effort of getting someone new to serve in Niue was difficult and Wellington took the easier step of leaving the incumbent in situ. There was a new focus on a professional public service, and annual assessment forms had been introduced. The secretary of Island Territories repeatedly noted on Larsen's assessment: 'It would be to Mr Larsen's advantage if he could have a period of duty in Head Office to enable him to obtain an overall view of general problems of administration of colonial and dependent territories.'[46] But there was no obvious replacement, so the recommendation was ignored.

Working alongside Larsen during his tenure as resident commissioner was a Niuean who was to assume an increasingly important role in Niue's postwar development. Robert Richmond Rex, youngest son of the trader Leslie Lucas Richmond Rex, had begun working for the Administration in the early 1930s under the tutelage of Captain Bell. Robert had had limited schooling: he had not begun at Tufukia until he was 11 years old and sufficiently robust to walk each day from Avatele to Alofi and home again. He was bright, though, and talk at Tufukia was that he would be recommended for further schooling, possibly at Te Aute College in Hawke's Bay. But this never happened – and Robert later attributed this to family rivalries on the island. He left Niue as a young man, worked on ships, lived with his father in Fiji, worked in a sawmill, experienced life. He recalled his father buying him an English dictionary and every day he learned a few new words. In the Depression of the 1930s, out of work, Rex returned to his mother in Avatele, worked the bush garden and went fishing; but he also found piecemeal work with the Administration: sawmilling, acting dispenser at the hospital, interpreter, managing the banana boxes on the wharf. When Larsen arrived, Rex was a trusted worker within the

Administration and was being called on especially for his translation skills and his ability as a go-between, a 'link between the two races', as he described himself.[47]

Larsen and Rex were almost the same age, and they established a good working relationship. Rex accompanied the resident commissioner on his frequent trips out and around the island, inspecting sanitation standards, visiting the hospital and the schools, listening to village meetings, looking at the state of the plantations. He also assisted with police duties and at one point was acting chief of police. He played an essential role at the Island Council meetings, for most of the councillors were unable to speak English and Rex had the task of translating often difficult ideas into Niuean. He worked hard to accurately interpret both sides of the discussion. As a young man he had often sat through long village meetings, and he had great respect for Niuean custom. He also had respect for the men on the Island Council, who were referred to as the 'biscuit and meat team' because they received bully beef and hard biscuits as rations when they attended council meetings. These men were, in Rex's opinion, 'good men, they were good examples to their own people, they were good workers … they had to work hard to lead their people'.[48]

Land disputes were becoming more common in the postwar period and in this area Larsen was entirely dependent on Rex. The resident commissioner was, by appointment, judge of the Native Land Court, but Rex could never remember Larsen sitting in a Land Court case. Instead he lobbied Wellington for a proper Land Court judge – and was successful in securing the services, for several weeks at a time, of the judge from Rarotonga.[49] In addition, he sent Robert Rex out to the villages to listen to the parties in a dispute, take notes and act as peacemaker. The notes were recorded for the future use of the Native Land Court when a judge was available.

Rex's translating skills were also needed in the High Court. When a case of manslaughter occurred in Liku in 1945, Larsen 'made no bones about saying that he considered it wrong for any man to hold the position of resident commissioner and judge of the High Court at the same time',[50] and he asked Wellington for a judge to be sent up. Judge Young asked about translation services and, when advised that Robert Rex would interpret at the trial, the judge arrived with a warrant of appointment signed by the New Zealand prime minister making Rex an official interpreter. It was a proud moment for Robert Rex when he took his place in the temporary courtroom set up in the banana shed on the wharf – the only place large enough to hold the gathering. There were a number of other instances during this period when a judge or retired magistrate was sent from New Zealand to preside in serious cases and it was agreed that a defence counsel should also be supplied from New Zealand to represent the accused.[51]

This did not mean that the resident commissioner was not involved in court proceedings: he constantly heard less serious cases and imposed sentences. Several hundred infringements of sanitation ordinances were heard each year, as Larsen battled to lessen the spread of infectious disease and to contain epidemics. It was especially bad in 1947–48, when a whooping cough epidemic caused the deaths of 57 children under the age of two years. Larsen closed schools, prohibited gatherings – including church services – and enforced quarantine of villages. He became exasperated at times that seemingly straightforward hygiene instructions were not being followed, and he was likewise intolerant of young men who did not seem to be making good use of their time. Rex recalled how Larsen would come out of the Administration offices in Alofi and, if he saw young men hanging around the stores, he would immediately walk over and quiz them. Why weren't they out in the bush doing planting or some other useful activity? If those same men later appeared before Judge Larsen on charges of petty crime, he was less than tolerant with them. His loud voice and forthright manner did not always win him friends, and over the course of nearly a decade the Niuean people came to have strong views of their resident commissioner, depending on their own first-hand experience of him or that of their family, friends or village.

One visitor to the island who was left with a very positive view of the resident commissioner was Frank Ponder, an architect with the New Zealand Ministry of Works (MOW). On his first visit to Niue in 1951 Ponder accompanied Ron Davies, officer for Islands Education in the Department of Education. Their task was to look carefully at the plan to build four new Administration schools round the island. The plan had been discussed since Dr Beeby's visit in 1945 and it had been agreed that schools would be built in Avatele, Tuapa, Lakepa and Liku which, alongside the three existing Administration schools, would provide primary education for all Niuean children. Each year in the annual report the plan was outlined, but there was no funding to make it a reality until 1951.

When Ponder and Davies arrived, Larsen was keen to get the building programme under way. Education was, he considered, the number one priority for the island. The men met with Hugh Hickling, headmaster of Administration schools, and Reverend Check, and they reached an agreement. Ponder recalled later how he planned to return to New Zealand and instruct his draughtsman to draw up plans for school buildings, but Larsen was having none of that. He wanted the plans

Accelerate class 1953. In 1950 it was decided to set up an accelerate class in Alofi for children from around the island who would possibly go on to New Zealand as scholarship students. For some families, it was too difficult to maintain their children in Alofi and they were taken back to their village school; others went on to study in New Zealand. The teacher was brought in from New Zealand to run the class and focus on English language skills. This class was taught by Peter Church. Back row, left to right: Vilau Kaleopa (Tamakautoga), Pitasoni Tanaki (Hakupu), Evonerofa Magatoa (Hakupu), Newstrong Makaefu (Mutalau), Dorothy Kauie (Tamakautoga), Kesimina Pasione (Hakupu), Sofina Magaoa (Hakupu), Kiliheke Tulilo (Hakupu), Ofania Makaea (Alofi North), Fanela Tavelitoga (Hakupu), Simoe Ikiua (Hakupu), Tunaga Tamatoa (Tuapa), Kulimani Mitiniu (Hakupu), Fenogaua Mokalei (Tuapa), Maihetoe Matagi (Alofi North). Front row, left to right: Atuua Tatui (Hakupu), Robert Matua Rex (Alofi South), Macmillian Etuata (Hakupu), Mitiniutama Mitiniu (Hakupu). Peter Church Collection, Tāoga Niue

drawn up there and then; and he provided Ponder with drawing equipment from the school and an electric light on the verandah of the Residency so he could work in the evening.[52] Dripping with sweat and constantly fighting mosquitoes, Ponder worked on the plans, which, wherever possible, would use local materials such as lime and adzed timber. Within weeks, sites had been chosen and work soon commenced. By October 1952 Larsen was able to report to Wellington that all four schools had been opened. It was a crucial achievement, alongside the establishment of the scholarships scheme. In order to prepare students for this, an accelerate class had opened at Tufukia school in 1950 and students were selected from around the

The mother of Niue Education

MALAMA VAILOA KERISOME was born in Niue in 1882. The daughter of a pastor, she grew up in Niue, then went to further her education in Samoa. Here she was trained by the LMS; and she was befriended by an American couple working in Samoa as evangelists for the Seventh-day Adventist (SDA) Church. Malama went on to study in Australia and also spent time in New Zealand before returning to Niue in 1915, a trained teacher and a committed member of the SDA Church.

Maui Pomare, New Zealand minister responsible for the Cook and other Islands, had also studied medicine at an SDA college in the United States, and he had met Malama in New Zealand. When he visited Niue in October 1915 he directed the resident commissioner to allow girls to enter Tufukia School and he recommended Malama be appointed to teach them. She had recently married Allen Head, a trader and son of Robert Henry Head. She began teaching at Tufukia in late 1915 and went on to serve Niue education for over 40 years.

When Malama Head set up a small Sunday school on Niue, it became the nucleus of an alternative church on the island. The Seventh-day Adventists had entered the Pacific in the late nineteenth century. On their mission vessel, the *Pitcairn*, they visited the widespread islands of the Pacific, setting up small missions from Pitcairn Island in the east to New Guinea in the west. The *Pitcairn* had visited Niue for a week in 1897, and although Rev. Lawes had been courteous, he had also made it clear there was no room for another mission on the island. Now that Malama Head was on Niue, the SDA sent Septimus and Edith Carr from Fiji in 1916 to help establish a church. They were replaced after two years by Ephraim E. Giblett, who departed in 1924,[54] leaving the small church on Niue in the care of Malama Head.

Malama Head (née Kerisome) was awarded an MBE for her work in education in Niue. She was also a key figure in setting up the Seventh-day Adventist church. Archives New Zealand, Department of Internal Affairs Te Tari Taiwhenua ABEP 7749 W4262/1336 34/7

It was a testament to the character and personal influence of Malama Head that her small church was accepted in Niue and became integrated into the LMS-dominated society, participating in LMS activities. When dissension was caused by the arrival of Mormon missionaries in 1952, no mention was made of the fact that there was already an alternative American-based church established on Niue.

Malama Head was instrumental in establishing the SDA on Niue, but she is best remembered for her tireless work in education. She and her husband Allen were leading citizens on the island. When Queen Elizabeth II visited New Zealand in late 1953, Malama Head and Sergeant Tohovaka were chosen to represent Niue, and she was personally presented to the Queen.[55] Four years later she was awarded the MBE for her services to education. She died in June 1963 and has since been dubbed 'the mother of Niue Education'.[56]

island. From this class many went on to further schooling in New Zealand; and from 1953 this included girls.[53]

While Larsen was in New Zealand on furlough in early 1952, a new issue was introduced into the mix of changes occurring on Niue. With the creation of the United Nations and the emphasis on self-determination and human rights, New Zealand had been a signatory to the Universal Declaration of Human Rights. In early 1952 Island Territories asked the deputy resident commissioner, Hugh Hickling, to make arrangements for the declaration to be translated into Niuean; he requested the help of the LMS with the translation and also with printing 500 copies.[57] In a public notice he then issued, Hickling explained that the full document would be distributed throughout the island but that, in the meantime, he was including an extract 'because of its particular interest at this time'.

> *Article 18 Everyone has the right to freedom of thought, conscience and religion; this right includes freedom to change his religion or belief, and freedom, either alone or in community with others and in public or private, to manifest his religion or belief in teaching, practice, worship and observance.*[58]

The 'particular interest' referred to the opening of a small Sunday school by a new trader on the island from Samoa. F.B. Krueger and family had arrived in 1951 and had opened a picture theatre. Krueger was Mormon and had started a Sunday school in his own home in April 1952. Meanwhile in Auckland the president of the Mormon Church had applied for permission to visit Niue and for two Mormon missionaries, known as elders, to be settled there. The American Church of Jesus Christ of Latter-day Saints (Mormons) had been established in New Zealand for over 70 years, working mainly among Māori communities. In accordance with Department of Island Territories regulations, the Mormons were granted permission to enter Niue. President Ottley would spend a day there in the course of visiting the Mormon missions in the Cook Islands and Western Samoa, and the two elders would remain on Niue to establish a branch of the church.

Reverend Check was in Auckland and learned of the Mormon plans to begin their work on Niue. Check was not well and had made the decision to resign his position in Niue for health reasons. He had agreed to return on the *Tofua* and tie up various loose ends before leaving permanently. When he heard the Mormon group was also travelling on the *Tofua*, Check changed his travel arrangements, flew part of the way and then took an earlier boat so as to arrive in Niue before the *Tofua* and warn the LMS of these new developments.[59] He wrote to the LMS in Sydney:

> *An additional trouble has come upon us in Niue in that the Mormons have arrived, sneaked in on the boat and have already started visiting each home in Alofi. They sent in a forerunner in the guise of a picture theatre operator who has been doing the spade work for a couple of months. The Administration appears to be giving them every assistance.*[60]

When Larsen returned from furlough on the same ship as President Ottley and his elders, he headed straight into a furore over the arrival of the Mormons. The two elders, Messrs Goodman and Berrett, had met Captain Bell on the *Tofua* and he had rented them a room in his premises in Alofi North. From here the men had begun visiting the villages. There was opposition, often in the form of threats and stone throwing, but the first baptisms were carried out in the Amanau caves, under cover of dark, in August 1952.

Opposition from the LMS to the arrival of the Mormons was spearheaded by Check, and Ottley accused him of 'issuing several vile tracts concerning us and our people'.[61] In August the LMS deacons on Niue wrote to Larsen and then drafted a petition to go to the minister of Island Territories, T. Clifton Webb. In it they referred to the Mormon Church as a 'false religion' and asked for it to be expelled from Niue.[62] When the minister's response came it was brief and unsatisfactory as far as the deacons were concerned, and they threatened to take their plea to 'our Queen, Her Majesty Elizabeth II, because you have not heard our voice'.[63] To counteract claims that Administration staff might lose their jobs if they joined the new church, Larsen issued a statement confirming that 'employees of the Administration are free to belong to any religious denomination they choose'.[64] Check now tried to distance himself from the controversy because of his health, and when he left Niue in late 1952 the heat went out of opposition to the new church. In all this controversy no mention was made of the fact that another American-based church, the Seventh-day Adventists, had been operating on a small scale in Niue since 1916. The Mormons quietly continued moving among the people. They found most support in those villages and among those people who felt marginalised by the changes taking place on Niue. When the deputy secretary of Island Territories, C.E.H. Quin, paid an official visit to Niue in July–August 1953, one of his instructions was to make an assessment of the situation now that there was another church operating on the island. After a meeting with the Mormon elders and village representatives, Quin assured them their position on the island was safe:[65] the duty of the Administration was to see that law and order were maintained, not to determine which religious denominations should be allowed to operate on the island.

In the decade to 1953 much had changed. War had ended and a period of optimism and hope for world peace had been followed by the onset of the Cold War. In New Zealand, there was a new, conservative National government in power and New Zealanders were fighting on the Korean peninsula. On Niue, the expatriate population had grown as more infrastructure work was undertaken. New schools had been built, electricity and telephone lines installed, and a new six-cell jail had been constructed at Fonuakula. Trucks and heavy machinery had been brought in; and a mobile clinic enabled the hospital to offer services in the outer villages. The government-operated *Maui Pomare* had been withdrawn from regular service and the USSC's vessels *Matua* and *Tofua* now provided the service. Niueans bound for New Zealand left the island on one of these two vessels; but often they now boarded a Pan Am or TEAL flight in Samoa or Fiji and completed their journey by air. New accommodation for officials had been completed, including a new Residency on the hill at Tapeu. Robert Rex had left his Administration work and had begun trading in Alofi. After Reverend Check's departure, the LMS had been placed in the temporary care of the Alofi pastor Neri Lupo. A Mormon church had been set up which, although small, offered an alternative to the long-established LMS. The annual report to Island Territories from the Niue Administration now included a section on human rights and the rights of women.

It seemed that everything had changed except for one thing: Hector Larsen was still the resident commissioner of Niue. The Department of Island Territories had paid lip service to the notion that rotation of officers was a vital aspect of a robust overseas service, but had ignored its own annual recommendations that Larsen should be moved to a new position, and it had rejected his most recent application for promotion.[66] However, when Ted Quin, deputy secretary of Island Territories, left Niue on 12 August 1953 after a month-long stay, he sounded no alarm bells that anything might be wrong.

13. An end to complacency

Deeply grieved and shocked at terrible news

The first top-priority radio message went out from Niue to Island Territories, Wellington, at 2.30 am on 16 August 1953.

> LARSEN MURDERED BY ESCAPED PRISONERS 1AM MRS LARSEN BADLY INJURED CHILDREN UNHURT STOP POLICE PRECAUTIONS TAKEN FOR REST OF COMMUNITY STOP AM ACTING MEANTIME PLEASE CONFIRM AND ADVISE URGENTLY STOP ISLAND AROUSED AND SEARCH ORGANISED FOR CRIMINALS STOP WILL ADVISE FURTHER SLAVEN.[1]

It was Saturday evening on Niue and the Larsen family – Hec and Jessie, 18-year-old Telma and nine-year-old Billy, along with their house girl, Margaret Jackson – had been to the evening performance at the picture theatre. They returned home at 9.30 pm. They were now settled in the new Residency at Tapeu, a little way south of the main centre of Alofi, up on the second terrace of the island – a commanding position but surrounded by bush and somewhat isolated from other houses. Hec parked the Plymouth in the garage attached to the house. As usual, the garage door was left unlocked. Jessie organised supper for everyone and then they all headed for bed. As usual, at midnight the power switched off and the house lay in darkness.

Up at Fonuakula, further inland but not far from Tapeu, the men in the prison had settled for the night. There were several men in each of the six cells and there was a fair amount of singing and shouting. Latoatama had been working at the Residency during the day, clearing and burning coconut fronds and doing general odd jobs. Folitolu and Tamaeli had stayed at the prison throughout the day and had gone searching in the surrounding bush for hens' eggs. Some of the other men had worked in the prison garden or gone searching for golfballs at the adjoining European recreation centre.[2] Solouota was the police constable who had been on duty at Fonuakula for the past week. He let the prisoners out at 10 pm to use the bathroom and then did a final lock-up for the night. He could hear a certain amount of revelry when he crossed to the warder's house but, guessing it would eventually subside, he retired to bed.

One group of men were not, however, planning to sleep. After breaking the ceiling of one cell, Latoatama, Folitolu, Tamaeli, Peleo, Loleni and Taofitau climbed up out of the building, exited the prison grounds and headed towards Tapeu. They took a bushknife from the prison kitchen and stopped to cut the telephone cables along the road. When they reached the grounds of the Residency one man climbed a pole and cut more cables. Loleni and Taofitau were nervous: they had thought they were going out drinking and now they were afraid to enter the grounds at Tapeu; they disappeared into the night. The other four entered Tapeu and Latoatama led them to the pump house, where he knew there were two more bushknives stored. He was, in fact, the only man who knew the layout of the grounds and the house, and he led the way to the unlocked garage.

Latoatama, Folitolu and Tamaeli had agreed that they were going to kill Mr Larsen and possibly Mrs Larsen. From the garage they entered the kitchen, passed through the dining area and crept quietly down the long hallway past the bedrooms until they reached the room at the end. No one spoke. Peleo was not holding a bushknife, and he stopped at the door of the end bedroom. The others, each with a bushknife, entered and took up positions around the nearest bed. They began their attack on the sleeping body and, when noises came from the other bed, they turned and struck several times at the second person. Then they turned and left the house the same way they had entered. Back up at the prison a frightened Peleo left the others and returned to his cell. The three who had carried out the attack each collected up the bundle of clothes they had prepared beforehand and headed for the bush.

At the Residency things were dire. Hec and Jessie Larsen were badly wounded, especially Hec. Jessie's yelling had woken Billy and he had run to his parents' room to see his mother lying on the floor. 'Get the doctor,' she told him and Billy had taken off as fast as he could. At this point the attackers were still in the house and Billy knew they had seen him go out the front door and across the lawn, for he heard them saying in Niuean 'there he goes' and 'get him'. Born and brought up on the island, Billy could run barefoot over the hard coral surface as well as any young Niuean, and he wasted no time in heading down the long driveway to the houses at Tufukia on the lower terrace. He ran to the house of the medical officer, Dr Johnston, and woke one of the Johnston girls, who woke her father. When he asked what the problem was, Billy suddenly realised he did not know: only that his mother was on the floor and was calling for the doctor.[3] Johnston hurried to the Residency and as word spread that something was wrong other officials joined him at Tapeu.

The funeral of Hector Larsen was held at the LMS church in Alofi on Sunday 16 August 1953. The burial took place in front of the church, close to the graves of Tuitoga and Fataaiki. In the centre of the photo is Charlie Slaven, now acting resident commissioner (in white suit with glasses and wreath). The two men in front wearing white trousers and dark jackets are Captain Bolton (white hair) from the *Maui Pomare* and his chief steward. On the left is a group of children. The second boy from the left is Bill Larsen with his head bowed. He is standing with the Shepheard boys and the Johnston girls. Behind them is Robert Rex. Courtesy Alison Sandom (née Larsen) and Bill Larsen

In his statement at the trial, Johnston described a scene of mayhem and horror. He had sat with Larsen, knowing he could not save him: Larsen died around 1.30 am, while Jessie was being transported to the hospital.[4]

Charles Slaven, treasurer in the Niue Administration and assistant to the resident commissioner, took control. Robert Rex was woken around 3 am and was asked to help, along with Chief of Police Harry Williams and Graham Shepheard, the headmaster at Tufukia. All police constables were brought into Alofi for briefing, and at 6 am Administration officials were sent to every village. The church bells rang around the island and the news was announced. Everyone was asked to cooperate in finding the three prisoners. The Residency grounds and the prison farm were searched at daylight and an evening curfew was placed on all villages. At a meeting on the village green in Alofi there was strong support for a proposal to sweep-search the island with 1000 men from daylight the next day, Monday.

Meanwhile, on Sunday, a funeral was held for Hector Larsen.[5] The flower-decked casket was carried one mile from Tufukia to the Alofi church on a Bedford truck draped in black crepe. Slaven, now acting resident commissioner, and his wife accompanied Billy and Telma Larsen; their mother was out of immediate danger but was too badly injured to attend. Hundreds of people came into Alofi from every village and lined the roadside. Eight Niuean pallbearers carried the coffin into the LMS church and a service was conducted in Niuean by Pastor Neri Lupo. European pallbearers then carried the coffin outside to the burial area in front of the church, where there were eulogies in English before Hector Larsen was laid to rest near the tombs of Tuitoga and Fataaiki.

Rumour and speculation were rife: there were stories of the prisoners, armed and dangerous, wanting to kill all Europeans on the island. All the expatriates were gathered together in two houses in Alofi South and, for those closer in to Alofi, in the building known as the 'bach' – the bachelor quarters used by unmarried expatriate officers. Robert Rex, who had had a lot to do with Larsen, was also asked to bring his wife and young family into the 'bach', and a guard was mounted on these houses during the night.[6]

Over the next three days searches were conducted on the island, and numerous reports of sightings of the prisoners were followed up. On Wednesday afternoon, the first definite sighting was made by a woman in Hakupu: she had gone out to feed her pigs and one of the prisoners had appeared and asked her what had happened to the resident commissioner. She said he was dead and his wife was in hospital, and the prisoner disappeared.[7] Robert Rex was sent over to Hakupu to speak with the woman and he ascertained it was a genuine sighting. A huge search was organised on the coastal side of the road between Hakupu and the old village of Fatiau. At nightfall, the searchers returned to their villages; the prisoners later said the searchers had passed within yards of them in the area where they had been hiding for three days, drinking coconut and eating ufilei, wild yam, and telie, a coastal tree whose bark and leaves have medicinal uses.

Before the search was resumed on Thursday morning, the three prisoners walked into the police constable's house in Vaiea[8] and gave themselves up. They had made kahoa, or lei, to wear around their necks 'as if they were going to a *fiafia*' [celebration],[9] but their manner was contrite and they agreed to Constable Mokoua placing handcuffs on them. The news was phoned through to Alofi, and Slaven, accompanied by Williams and other constables and Robert Rex, set out for Vaiea. Feelings were running high and there was a considerable crowd around the constable's house

Four days after the murder of Hector Larsen the three men involved surrendered to the constable in Vaiea and were brought into Alofi. They were paraded on the green in front of the Administration building for everyone to see – an action that was later criticised for inciting anger and shame.

Peter Church Collection, Tāoga Niue

when the party arrived from Alofi. The prisoners were put on the back of an open truck and the driver was instructed to stop at Avatele on the way through so people could see that the men really had been captured. Harry Williams pleaded for there to be no rough treatment, but in Avatele tension was high. Some villagers had come out with bushknives, there were calls for the people to deal with the men directly and, in a scuffle to pull the men off the back of the truck, their shirts and kahoa were ripped from them. There was a similar reception as the truck passed through Tamakautoga, and when the party reached the green in front of the Administration buildings in Alofi, a large crowd was gathered. Many 'demanded that [the prisoners] should be dealt with by the Niueans themselves, they were so upset at the shame these people brought on the island'.[10] The fear of local retribution for the crime had been a concern throughout the days of the search and officials had been instructed to reiterate constantly that no one should take the law into their own hands. Several officials later admitted that parading the men through the villages and on the green in Alofi was a mistake, as it not only incited anger but also increased the feeling of shame for the families of the accused.

The men were now locked in a small concrete cell behind the police chief's house. In the afternoon a launch arrived from Apia with two police officers who were to take charge of the situation. The Department of Island Territories in Wellington had requested assistance from Apia immediately after the murder but had asked that 'the party be limited to two as we are anxious to avoid too big a display of Samoan force in view of the cooperation being given by the Niuean people'.[11] One of the police officers from Apia was placed in charge: he took statements and gathered evidence for the trial. The three accused were to be kept in the cell behind the police house, as it was apparent there was little security at Fonuakula. Slaven reported in code to Wellington: 'Security conditions at jail appalling and actions native constables temporarily in charge appear criminally lax. Whole question jail security and police establishment require thorough investigation and reorganisation.'[12] J.B. Wright, secretary of Island Territories, softened this message when he reported on to the minister, T. Clifton Webb, that they had 'always been aware that conditions at the gaol are not perfect'.[13]

Recriminations were for later, however; the pressing concern now was to prepare for a trial while Jessie Larsen was still on the island and able to provide an eyewitness account of the attack. She needed to go to Auckland urgently for specialist treatment, and the medical officer wanted to be able to send her out on the *Tofua* on 9 September. Time was tight. In New Zealand, L.G.H. Sinclair SM of Auckland was appointed trial judge, E.T. Pleasants, Auckland, defence counsel and H.R.C. Wild, Wellington, prosecuting counsel. Warrants had to be prepared for these men to act as officials of the Cook Islands High Court, and travel arrangements had to be made to get them to Niue in time to conduct the trial and then leave with Mrs Larsen and family on the *Tofua*. They travelled by air to Rarotonga and on to Aitutaki, where they took the old *Maui Pomare* to Niue. Ted Quin accompanied them and took over as acting resident commissioner in Niue.

The trial was held at Tufukia School on 7 September before Justice Sinclair and six assessors – four Niuean and two European. The prosecution called Jessie Larsen and then others who had witnessed events that Saturday night. Counsel for defence said no evidence would be called but each of the three accused would make a statement. In their statements the three accused talked of the treatment they had received from Larsen while at the prison: they spoke of growling, hitting, swearing and being made to work long hours. After they had delivered their statements, the six assessors retired and within an hour had returned a unanimous verdict of guilty. The judge imposed the mandatory sentence of death by hanging and the men were taken back to the cell.

Robert and Patricia Rex with Jessie and Telma Larsen. This photo was taken at the Lord Liverpool Hospital, Alofi, shortly before the trial and the subsequent departure of the Larsen family from Niue on 9 September. Auckland War Memorial Museum Tāmaki Paenga Hira, New Zealand, C26734

There was a general feeling that the sentence would be carried out quickly. Gallows, referred to in official communications as the 'gear', were already being prepared to be sent from Apia. It would also be necessary to send a sheriff and hangman to oversee the execution, and also more police. For an island with no air-strip, this was a logistical problem. Many officials were uncomfortable with the idea of a hanging being carried out in such a small community, but Quin reported to Wellington that 'the population fully expect prisoners to be executed and while task unpleasant and personally most distasteful I consider it should be carried out here and the sooner the better'.[14] Arrangements were soon put on hold, however, for the prisoners indicated on the advice of their counsel that they would seek an appeal; accordingly, a stay of execution was issued.

The 'gear' was diverted to Auckland, the sheriff and hangman were put on hold, and the prisoners were transferred by the *Maui Pomare* to Auckland: they had the right to appear in person at the appeal, to be heard in the Supreme Court. A small piece in the *New Zealand Herald* on 12 October 1953, under the heading 'Convicted Niueans arrive' noted that the three men were transferred to the police launch at 9 am as the *Maui Pomare* lay in the stream before berthing. 'Few people saw their arrival at the Admiralty steps, where they stepped handcuffed into a waiting police van' which took them to Mt Eden Prison to await the appeal hearing. The appeal was heard at the end of October, and in November the decision was announced: the appeal had been rejected by the three judges; the sentence of 9 September was to stand, and the men were to be returned to Niue in order for it to be carried out. They were sent to Tonga, transferred to the *Tofua*, and arrived in Niue on 2 December.

There was one further process to go through. The governor-general in Executive Council – i.e. Cabinet when presided over by the governor-general – could exercise clemency and commute the death sentence to life imprisonment. While it waited for this ruling, Island Territories prepared for the eventuality that the hanging would go ahead. Arrangements were made to send the necessary personnel to the island and decisions finalised as to where exactly on Niue the hangings would take place and where the men would be buried. Officials doubted whether any hanging should be carried out on Niue; and the Crown Law Office in Wellington was asked for an opinion on whether the Cook Islands Act allowed for a sentence passed in one Island Territory to be carried out in another. When official word came on 8 December that the governor-general in Executive Council had decided not to grant clemency, the New Zealand Broadcasting Service, transmitting to the Pacific since 1948, reported the decision before Resident Commissioner Quin could announce it himself on Niue.

It seemed that all legal channels had been exhausted; but two days after the ruling against clemency, the defence counsel in Auckland notified Island Territories that an appeal was to be made to the Queen in Council[15] in London and a stay of execution was once again requested. Quin was notified in Niue and replied: 'Your emergency message received and arrangements postponed accordingly.'[16] The problem now was where to keep the three men while the appeal was being considered. An urgent request was made to Apia by the prime minister to allow the three men to be transferred there, and this request was acceded to – although reluctantly – by the New Zealand high commissioner in Western Samoa, who stressed that 'no question of them serving any sentence here or being executed here will be considered'.[17] The three prisoners left Niue for a second time in late December 1953 and were transferred to jail in Apia. Now the wait began for a ruling from the Privy Council in London.

When the appeal was rejected by the Privy Council in early May 1954, the minister for Island Territories, who was also the justice minister, was on a visit to

England. He was strongly of the opinion that the death sentence should now be carried out; but in his absence from Wellington the Executive Council agreed, on 18 May 1954, to grant clemency to the men. The sentence was commuted to life imprisonment and the men were almost immediately transferred by the RNZAF from Apia to Auckland to begin serving their sentences in Mt Eden Prison.

A number of factors had influenced the Executive Council to change its ruling on this case. The eight months that had elapsed since the initial trial had led to a weakening of support for hanging. The new resident commissioner to Niue, Jock McEwen, felt that an execution on the island at this late stage would do more harm than good. There were practical difficulties in carrying out such a sentence on Niue, and enquiries and legal opinions had made it plain that the hangings could not be carried out in the Cooks or in Western Samoa. And, perhaps most vividly in the minds of the New Zealand politicians, there had been a huge number of representations made to them to reconsider their original decision not to grant clemency.

The death sentence was a contentious issue, and since its reintroduction in 1950 by Prime Minister Sidney Holland's National government, it had been the object of much debate and dissension. During the 1950s, when the death sentence existed for the last time in New Zealand, there were 18 convictions for murder, 10 of which were commuted to life sentences. The case of the murder in Niue resulted in this issue being in the spotlight once more and liberal groups throughout New Zealand rallied to the cause of securing life sentences for the three young Niueans. Trade union organisations around the country, branches of the Labour Party, the Communist Party, women's guilds, churches, the New Zealand Peace Council and the Howard League for Penal Reform[18] all mounted campaigns in support of the Niueans. They did not deny that the murder had been brutal, but they believed the death sentence was barbaric and had no place in a civilised society. The publication of the statements by the three convicted men also raised questions about New Zealand's administration of its Island Territories and there were calls for an enquiry. The department and the minister of Island Territories were inundated with letters, petitions and pleas for clemency. The press entered the debate: the *Auckland Star* took the lead with an editorial that questioned how the Executive Council had come to its decision, especially as the day it refused clemency to the Niueans it granted clemency to a woman in Napier who was convicted of the murder of two elderly women. The three people the council had so far refused clemency were the only ones not 'of pure Anglo-Saxon descent'; and now the Niuean case added weight to the argument that the murderers not reprieved were either 'foreigners' or 'natives'.[19]

The Communist Party's newspaper, the *People's Voice*, ran a series of articles in which it called for an enquiry into the Holland government's administration of New Zealand's Island Territories. It accused the government of issuing platitudes at the United Nations in relation to island administration while, on the ground, the people were suffering real hardships. The paper gave full coverage to the prisoners' statements in relation to their treatment by the late resident commissioner who, as both judge and jailor, was 'acting contrary to elementary British justice'.[20] It also gave coverage to Reverend Check's view of the whole affair. Having become increasingly antagonistic to Larsen while on Niue, in part because of the arrival of the Mormon Church, Check now became the champion in New Zealand of the three accused: he made claims that over 90 per cent of the population was opposed to Larsen, who had 'grossly neglected the people'.[21] Check's support for the men, however, did not ring true when compared with an earlier testimony he had given in which he referred to the Niuean people as 'the most backward of Polynesian people', behaving like children and having 'no control over their emotions ... things that we take for granted are all important to them – food and water for example'.[22] Check had perhaps not realised the difficulties involved in obtaining food and water on Niue; as European missionary-in-charge he had enjoyed a special status there and had always been provided with the best the villages had to offer – even if that meant others went without.

While the Department of Island Territories dismissed without comment representations from the Communist Party for an enquiry, it took more notice when a group of university teachers and church leaders formed a committee in Wellington and sought a meeting with the attorney-general and the minister of justice. The Cook scholar, J.C. Beaglehole and other members of Victoria University's History Department, the educationalist W.J. Scott, Reverend Lloyd Geering and numerous other church ministers, including Ormond Burton, the prominent pacifist, could not be snubbed as the Communist Party had been. The Wellington Citizens' Niue Islanders Committee, as they were named, met with the minister and presented a series of thoughtful and reasoned arguments in favour of commuting the death sentence for the Niueans and setting up an enquiry into the administration of New Zealand's Island Territories.

> *We New Zealanders cannot, logically, shrug off all responsibility for such an event happening at least fifty years after we set up an effective administration on the island, when in other ways we show how little responsibility we consider the Islanders capable of exercising in the management of their own affairs.*[23]

They stressed that in no way did they concur with the 'unwarranted attacks on the character of Mr Larsen. [Our] case does not stand or fall on his character, and it deeply deplores his murder.'[24] Their grounds for clemency were founded rather on liberal colonial administration policies.

This idea struck at the real core of the issue. Some of the more thoughtful criticism of events in Niue came from groups who were considering the long-term relationship between New Zealand and its Island Territories. There was a need to review the situation where one man was responsible for a number of often conflicting functions; where the people themselves had little real control of their own affairs; and where the rhetoric of New Zealand as an island administrator was often at odds with the reality.

The murder of Hector Larsen on Niue was, and remains, a subject of shame, speculation and disagreement: shame that such a horrific crime was committed on an island that was strongly Christian and peaceful; speculation as to the motives behind the crime; and disagreement as to where blame should be apportioned. The details of the murder were shocking. The question needed to be asked as to how these three young men could have committed such an offence in cold blood. Their statements relating to verbal and physical abuse became the basis for the defence of provocation. In his confidential report to Island Territories after the trial, Judge Sinclair noted:

> *The only evidence of ill-treatment of the accused by Mr Larsen is the unsworn statements of the accused and I had no opportunity of ascertaining to what extent these statements are true. They are probably exaggerated to some extent but even if they are discounted substantially I cannot help feeling there is an element of truth in them. They have the simplicity of truth ... I do not think there was any real ill-treatment of the prisoners by Mr Larsen but rather a little bullying and interference with the privileges ... resulting in an accumulation of resentment against Mr Larsen personally.*[25]

Counsel for the defence, E.T. Pleasants, also forwarded a confidential report in which he referred to the three accused as 'misguided and foolish youths, of poor character as shown by their criminal records, [who] in some way nerved themselves up to commit this crime, but I cannot regard them as really dangerous characters'.[26]

The idea that the young men had 'nerved themselves up' was a reference to the subject of alcohol, specifically bush brew. Were these men in an alcohol-crazed state that enabled them to commit such a crime? It was certainly never raised in court but there was speculation that this was the only possible explanation for such a crime. The accused in their statements said they had not been drinking. Some of the other prison inmates said they had. One of the accused had been charged twice before with consuming a concoction of coconut milk and methylated spirits. Others have spoken since of the prevalence of bush brew at the prison and on the island in general – evidence of a growing social problem involving young men in particular. There had been other examples of crimes committed under the influence of bush brew, and it certainly provides a possible explanation as to how these men, who afterwards were so contrite and inoffensive and who served out their sentences as model prisoners, could have brought themselves to hack a sleeping person to death.

There was also speculation that the murder was politically motivated, part of a deep-seated plot to rid the island of New Zealand rule. The judge and counsels, in their reports on the trial, dismissed this theory; but there was a suggestion that the young men had been influenced by an older prisoner who had had a series of convictions and may have been the 'brains behind the murder'.[27] When the possibility of transferring the three prisoners to Apia was discussed with the New Zealand high commissioner, Guy Powles, he commented that the Samoan Administration had already accepted, two months earlier, 'one long term recalcitrant … at request of Quin. It has been said that this prisoner was behind the action of the three prisoners under discussion.'[28] There were undoubtedly people with a grudge against the resident commissioner, but it seems highly doubtful that there was a 'political plot'.

The man himself, Cecil Hector Watson Larsen, became the object of sincere and heartfelt sympathy, but also of bitter and personal character assassination. Aged 45 years when he was murdered, he was the sort of person who attracted comment, good and bad. There is no doubt that Larsen threw himself wholeheartedly into the position of resident commissioner on Niue. He spoke fluent Niuean; and he left his office daily to oversee developments around the island. His greatest enthusiasm was for education and in this he was active before the postwar reviews and recommendations. He was also tireless in his quest to improve village sanitation and hygiene conditions in an effort to avoid the introduction and spread of often fatal epidemics. He championed the idea of a new village for the people of Fatiau. He handled very public confrontations with the European missionaries, especially Beharell over Sunday labour, and Check over the arrival of the Mormons, with considerable forbearance.

Yet Larsen also attracted criticism and even hatred. In his handling of village sanitation issues and in his attitude to idle young men, he said what he thought and he said it forcefully. He made enemies in this way. No doubt, over a period of 10 years, he at times displayed an arrogance that comes from being the 'kingpin' for too

The Larsen family in happier times. This photo was taken over Christmas 1947–48 when the Larsens had their whole family on the island. They were preparing to head out for a picnic in the Chevrolet. Left to right: Hec, Alison, Bill (behind), Jessie and Telma. Alison and Telma, twins, were born in Rarotonga. They spent some of their time living on Niue but Alison was living in Auckland when the murder occurred. Courtesy Alison Sandom (née Larsen) and Bill Larsen

long. While he was much admired by the expatriate community who were pleased to count him as a personal friend, he had a larger-than-life personality that was sometimes hard for Niueans to handle.

Island Territories, as the department tasked with carrying out government policy in this area, had a significant and, in many ways, a culpable role in the events that unfolded in Niue. It accepted the need for regular change in Administration personnel – but only in principle, never in practice; it ignored its own recommendations to move Larsen to another position. It failed to provide effective support, especially in the field of policing: it is almost impossible to keep track of the different people who held the position of chief of police on Niue, so quickly did the personnel change. The department continued to accept the combining of functions in the hands of too few officials, even when those very officials pointed out the difficulties and conflicts. It neglected the need to bring about change to the way the Island Council was appointed and operated, although this was a necessary precursor to any move towards greater autonomy, such as was being discussed at the United Nations.

It might be more satisfying to find a single reason for a murder and place the blame fairly and squarely there. The three young Niueans were wicked men. The resident commissioner abused his powers. But the reason for the murder of Hector Larsen cannot be blamed on one person, or on three. It has to be blamed on a systemic failure going back 50 years. It has to be seen within the context of successive New Zealand governments' administration of Niue – their neglect, lack of understanding, oversight. It has to be seen within the context of colonial administration generally, and the administration of a small and isolated island in particular. The system of administration that had been allowed to evolve in Niue meant that Hector Larsen was let down by the New Zealand government. There were warning bells, some sounding back decades. As far back as the parliamentary debate on the Cook Islands Amendment Act of 1916, some very astute warnings had been sounded, especially in the Legislative Council.

> *You give them [the resident commissioners] absolute powers in many and varied capacities, you give them a few officials ... and then you say, 'We have provided constitutional laws for you. Go and do the best you can.' You give them power over life and property, and say, 'We have made every provision for you.' You leave it to these few men to carry out the laws, and make it impossible for them to do otherwise than fail to do so.*[29]

This lengthy debate in the Upper House of the New Zealand Parliament focused on virtually every difficulty that was to bedevil the Administration of Niue over the next four decades. Yet while the warnings were prophetic, there was no political will to make effective changes – until it was too late.

The impact of the murder was immediate and far-reaching. There was a grieving family involved: Jessie Larsen with Telma and Billy on Niue, and Alison in Auckland. The family was sent off the island on the *Tofua* after the trial, but when they reached Apia it was decided for medical reasons to fly Jessie on to Auckland, leaving the two children to continue by ship. In the circumstances that was a strange and callous decision. The New Zealand government felt a responsibility for the fact that a New Zealand representative had been killed in the course of official duty and made a one-off payment to Mrs Larsen later in 1953; and the Department of Island Territories paid her an annuity until her death in 1987. No payment could compensate, however, for the physical, psychological and emotional impact on the family.

There was a shocked community on Niue, too. The families of the three men in particular suffered a shame that has not completely dissipated even today. The wider community also felt great shame and apprehension as they waited to see how New Zealand would treat them in the aftermath of the murder.

In New Zealand the general public had now heard of Niue. The murder had fixed the island in the national consciousness, at least for the time being – especially in the context of debate over the death sentence, and in calls for an enquiry into the administration of Island Territories. The Holland government could no longer ignore Niue. It could no longer maintain the policy of 'do not disturb' adopted by successive New Zealand governments since annexation in 1901. What was needed now was a proactive policy that matched the reality on the ground in Alofi with the principles being espoused at the United Nations in New York.

FINLAND
N
EPUBLIC
ZANIA
UNIT
NICARAGUA
NEW ZEA

PART D.

THE ROAD TO SELF-GOVERNMENT

14. Political will for change

The Island Councillors were simply staggered at the amount of work the Administration was doing

Events in Niue had focused the political mind in Wellington. The assistant secretary of Island Territories, Ted Quin, had been sent in to Alofi as acting resident commissioner until a replacement for Hector Larsen could be identified. The situation called for careful consideration. The solution was a stroke of genius.

Jock McEwen, currently serving in the Department of Maori Affairs, was identified as the person to take up the position of resident commissioner in Niue. Of Scottish descent and the son of a primary school teacher, McEwen had been brought up in Feilding and had learned to speak Māori as a child playing with his friends on the local marae. A quietly spoken, sensitive man with a deep respect for language and culture, McEwen began learning Niuean as soon as the appointment was mooted with him. He was, in fact, a 1950s version of the first New Zealand government agent to Niue, Percy Smith. The two were of similar personality, both members of the Polynesian Society, both passionate about language and its central place in culture. Both compiled a Niuean dictionary during their time on Niue; and both earned the respect of the Niue people.

McEwen's deep cultural interests were in te reo and Māori culture: he could recite whakapapa and sing waiata; he could perform haka; and he became a skilled carver. When he arrived on Niue in late December 1953, the people waited to see how they would be treated by the new man, how the shame associated with the murder would be handled. McEwen, 'Makawini' as he came to be known, left no doubt that his aim was to understand the Niuean people, the Niuean way, and to work with them to improve the situation. He was respectful of the memory of Hector Larsen, he praised the work he had accomplished during his time in Niue – and now it was time to move on.

The village welcomes to Jock McEwen, his wife Ruth and their three young sons were joyous occasions after what had been harrowing times. Villages erected decorated arches along the road, and the family walked the last few hundred metres into each village. There was always a huge feast; songs were composed for the

Jock McEwen and family returning home after a fiafia, 1954. When the McEwens returned from a village welcome, their car was almost hidden under flowers and laden with handcrafts, food and live chooks. Left to right: Leslie Rex, Ruth and Jock McEwen, Mervyn Missen, Jim Little, James and David McEwen. Courtesy of McEwen family, Wellington, New Zealand

occasion; dancing and speechmaking took place. McEwen was often asked to speak to the people in Māori and when he did so and ended with a haka, the people were delighted, clapping and cheering and laughing. The McEwens were sent home with mountains of food, the car almost hidden under garlands of flowers.[1] It was as if the island was marking the start of a new era after the horrors of the murder.

From their first Sunday in Niue, another feature of this man was revealed to the Niueans: McEwen appeared with his wife and family in the church at Alofi and actively participated in the service. This was no official visit: they were practising Christians and attended church regularly, taking care to move around the island and avoid any rivalries between villages. McEwen was soon asked to read the lesson in Niuean and this became a regular feature of his attendance at church. Later, when his Niuean was more fluent, he was sometimes asked to give the sermon. There could be no better combination for a resident commissioner than to be deeply interested in the language and culture of the island and to be a committed Christian.

Furthermore, McEwen had clout back in Wellington. Almost 40 years old when he went to Niue, he was seen as a rising star in the public service and he had connections that enabled him to turn promises into reality. He had the ear of the secretary of Island Territories, Jack Wright. Besides, Cabinet was fully aware that change was needed in Niue. The political will existed to make things happen. The period of McEwen's term on Niue, from December 1953 until August 1956, was a period of great material change on the island, but it was in many ways a continuation of developments begun by Larsen. Some changes had been suggested by Larsen but turned down by the department or Cabinet. Now everything seemed possible. A will to make change happen, coupled with improving economic conditions in New Zealand, resulted in a threefold increase in expenditure for Niue.[2]

There was also infrastructure on the island that was finally ready to be used. The Ministry of Works had sent in a team from New Zealand in 1948 to begin preliminary work for the construction of an aerodrome. That project was shelved, but the men were kept in Niue to work on building new schools and the Administration housing project. Progress had been painfully slow, partly because of the New Zealand waterfront dispute of 1951, but gradually tools and equipment were assembled, local labour was trained, and plumbing and electrical workshops were built. By the end of 1952 the schools were operating and the houses were ready for married men to take up positions in the Administration. A significant cost overrun resulted in an official enquiry by the auditor-general, who concluded that 'the system of remote control from New Zealand [by MOW] had proved unsatisfactory'.[3] He suggested that future works programmes should be directly controlled by those on the spot, specifically the resident commissioner. McEwen thus had greater decision-making control over public works than Larsen had been granted.

By 1955, showing the members of the Island Council what was being done around the island was a regular part of council meetings. It helped to give the councillors an overall perspective on developments, rather than just a village perspective. One such tour was described by McEwen in a letter home.

> *At Amanau saw concrete blocks being made, sawmill working, rock crushing plant and new generators. New concrete building going up for PWD store and foundations of new transport building and new sawmill.*
>
> *Then to hospital – saw new 24 bed isolation block – well under way, new building for Matron and Sisters, new ablution block and dressing room. Then to a huge new rock quarry in Alofi and to wharf to see progress on extension of concrete jetty.*
>
> *After lunch round island to see new main road to Tuapa, new village tank being made at Makefu. Work on tank at Tuapa using the compressor and rock drills. New wing recently added to Matalave school. New tank underway at Namukulu. Mutalau the old school house now to be used as a community centre. At Lakepa men were*

> *altering the school and building a new milk room. At Liku another gang working on the school and nearby [the] new banana plantation with 600 trees. Biggest ever seen in Niue. At Hakupu the community copra drier … and a new milk room at the school. At Fatiau a taro trial plantation. At Avatele newly tarred road up the hill and new milk room at school and on way home another taro trial round the deep well. The Island Councillors were simply staggered by the amount of work the Administration was doing.*[4]

Change was all around. The erratic electricity supply was improved by the Cabinet decision to spend money on much larger generators: it would now be possible for Public Works to use their power tools at the same time as an operation was being performed along at the hospital. The telephone network was extended so that every village was in communication with Alofi. A new launch and lighters were ordered and a large winch was installed on the wharf, all of which contributed to a faster turnaround on boat day. Around the island a new mobile crane and a large bulldozer were in action improving road access to bush gardens, dragging large trees from the bush and speeding up construction work.

In the seven primary schools now established around the island the decision made in 1950 to commence teaching in the Niuean language and then introduce English from the third year was starting to pay off. In his first annual report to the minister of Island Territories in 1954, McEwen, who was very enthusiastic about this policy, noted there was little doubt 'that the children learn to read and express themselves in English much more readily as the result of their early instruction in Niuean'.[5] Teaching the Niuean language was assisted by the publication of a Niuean school journal, begun in 1950. An accelerate class at Tufukia, also begun in 1950, for children from around the island, was advancing the best students to a standard where they could take up scholarships to New Zealand schools or go into employment in the Island Administration.

McEwen took the next step in improving education in 1955 when he arranged for post-primary classes to be started at Tufukia 'without anyone in Wellington knowing anything about it'.[6] The buildings at Tufukia were becoming very dilapidated and plans were now drawn up for the development of a new school in Alofi, at Halamahaga. This site was closer to the centre of Alofi village, and the plan was that the Tufukia site would eventually be occupied by the expanding hospital. Such was the goodwill generated by Administration activity around the island that the villages all took turns to help clear and level the site at Halamahaga, and the first classrooms opened in 1957.

A Sunderland flying boat arrives from Laucala Bay in Suva to carry a patient out for urgent medical attention. In 1955 McEwen wrote home about the first such evacuation. People came from all over the island and lined the clifftop at Alofi, vaka had to be cleared from the bay and when the Sunderland roared in overhead the noise was astounding. Men, women and children wept as the young Niuean was taken out by lighter to the flying boat, which had come to rest out from Tufukia school. He was taken to Suva and then transferred to Auckland, where his sight was saved. Harry Coleman Collection, Auckland War Memorial Museum Tāmaki Paenga Hira, New Zealand, M1644-5

The hospital expanded and new equipment arrived. When a worksite explosion in 1955 threatened the sight of a 20-year-old Niuean, McEwen organised the first ever medical evacuation from the island by flying boat. Slowly, opportunities were opening up for girls on the island and by 1955 the Administration was employing young women for the first time as typists. The concentration of work opportunities for women as typists, teachers and nurses reflected a similar situation in New Zealand. By 1961 there was a small group of influential Niuean women who were successful in setting up an organisation for the women of Niue, with committees in each of the villages.[7]

McEwen worked hard to get the type of expatriate to the island who he believed would be most successful; it seems he personally tapped some of them on the shoulder. Larsen had been requesting an agricultural officer for some time, but to no avail. McEwen was given the green light to interview and appoint such an officer in Auckland en route to taking up his position in Niue.[8] Others were possibly attracted by the developments on Niue, and the fact that McEwen was in charge. The number of expatriates grew and most of them fitted in well to island life. Several of the single men who arrived married locally and became long-term, valued residents on Niue.[9] By early 1956 McEwen felt he had a really good team there. A few who were unsuited to island life had left; there was more social interaction between Europeans and Niueans; staff morale was high; and as staff arrived McEwen felt 'he could start the new men off with the same attitudes as his own'.[10]

Boat day 1954. Boat day was always an occasion to gather in Alofi. People came from all the outer villages, and some would set up stalls along the road to sell handcrafts. Some of the imported frozen goods would start thawing on the wharf and so would be eaten straight away. Tosisi kula, red sausages (saveloys), were a favourite with the children and some also remember mussels, pork bones and corned beef in barrels of brine as delicacies to be enjoyed after a boat visit.

Trustees of the British Museum Oc, B126.99

The weather didn't always allow for loading at Alofi. When the *Tofua* arrived in March 1955 it was too rough, so the ship went around the coast to Hakupu and everyone turned out to help. The men of Hakupu cut a wider track to the coast, three large vaka were brought from Alofi and Avatele, and in the hour and a half available before the tide turned and the weather worsened, passengers and mail were transferred over the reef. Food was short on the island until the next visit of the *Tofua* in April.

Des Little Collection, Auckland War Memorial Museum Tāmaki Paenga Hira, New Zealand, C27222

It was not all plain sailing for McEwen, however. Two issues in particular exercised him, just as they had earlier resident commissioners. One was the production of bush brew. In August 1954 McEwen reported to Wellington that 'there has been a noticeable increase in bush beer brewing and drunkenness recently. The imposition of heavier fines has had some effect.' The worst aspect of the situation, he felt, was 'the inclusion of quite young boys in bush-beer parties'.[11] A month later he noted that 'better work by the police has meant several of the more notorious bush beer brewers have been convicted'. McEwen recognised that the problem would not go away and he thought that the best way to prevent the younger ones from becoming involved was to provide some form of recreation and organised entertainment for them. He began a programme of community activities to address this.

The first community centre was opened in Mutalau, in a house formerly occupied by the village headmaster. Activities included 'evening classes … in music, English and arithmetic and various social functions'.[12] The centre was also used for talks by the agricultural officer or the child welfare sister; and a village library was created. Administration officials helped set up and train sports teams, and the Boy Scout movement was introduced. McEwen remarked to Wellington that in 'endeavouring to get some form of recreation in the villages to occupy the time of the youths more fully' the LMS pastors had promised their support 'and the Mormon elders have organised evening entertainment'.[13] He encouraged the creation of village committees, and by 1955 community halls were being built in Alofi South and Alofi North. Island and village activities and agricultural and health topics were reported on and discussed in the weekly bilingual newsletter *Tohi Tala Niue* that was now being produced by the Administration.

Both the LMS and the Mormon Church cooperated with McEwen; but there were still interdenominational arguments. Ted Quin, acting resident commissioner in the second half of 1953, and McEwen for much of 1954, found the absence of a European missionary-in-charge of the LMS an advantage in establishing good relations with the villages. The interim pastor, Neri Lupo, was a respected Niuean, and both Quin and McEwen found that he facilitated their contact with the people. When Reverend Kightley was appointed in late 1954, McEwen felt he was likely to be a much more agreeable man than earlier missionaries had been. 'I am hopeful that Mr Kightley's arrival will help to smooth over some of [the] interdenominational arguments as he appears to be a reasonable man and is used to a community which has several churches.'[14]

McEwen reported early in his time on Niue that 'troubles between LMS and Mormon adherents [were] still fairly frequent'.[15] They sometimes involved physical fighting, and there was also a 'flare up of tension' between the two groups when the Mormons in Makefu started building a thatched church right next to the LMS church on the village green. McEwen requested that Elder Slade go to Makefu and persuade the people to stop building. Elder Slade had 'a friendly discussion with the LMS pastor who assured him he would raise no objection to a Mormon Church being built in some other position in Makefu'.[16] Gradually the dust settled.

The trouble at Makefu was foremost in McEwen's mind when he received word in September 1954 that the Catholic Bishop of Tonga would be calling on the next *Tofua* visit to discuss the possibility of establishing a mission on Niue. 'I had hoped that we could have had a longer breathing space before any other missions were set up in Niue as the people are slowly getting used to more than one denomination. If a new Church is established now I am afraid there will be a good deal of trouble.'[17] When the bishop arrived, McEwen met with him and agreed there would be 'no official objection to the establishment of a mission', with the qualification that no mission schools could be set up as the Administration had already taken over the LMS schools. The Mormon Church was also informed that it could not establish schools.[18] The Island Council petitioned Island Territories to prevent another religion being permitted to come to the island, but the minister replied in early 1955 that he was 'unable to agree to the petition because of the right of all people to religious freedom'.[19] Father Therriault, an American who had been serving in Tonga for four years, applied for permission to land in Niue in August 1955. 'It looked as if there might be an ugly reaction,' reported McEwen, but Reverend Kightley was helping to calm fears. A month later, McEwen was able to report that Father Therriault, 'a tactful and pleasant man, has arrived and settled without problem'.[20]

The real difficulty created by the arrival of other denominations in Niue lay in the entrenched nature of the LMS, which had enjoyed a religious monopoly over the previous century. McEwen explained the situation to the department in Wellington.

> *In a society such as has existed here for several generations, the Church and the village social structure are practically one and the same. The introduction of a new sect not only threatens the existing church, but cuts right across the social pattern. For instance, in the past the whole village was responsible for cleaning the road frontage to the Pastor's house and for providing the Pastor's food; the village authorities were also church authorities and so on. A new sect not only threatens the position of the two-fold authorities, but provides an opposition which attracts those with a grudge against those authorities. It is inevitable that trouble will continue for some time.*[21]

Discussing the question of other denominations with the Island Council from time to time, McEwen felt, would 'gradually explode the myth about one church for ever in Niue'.[22] In these discussions, reference to the United Nations and the Declaration of Human Rights was always a useful way to justify the position New Zealand had taken. For while events on Niue itself had put pressure on the New Zealand government to pay closer attention to the island, a larger pressure had also come into play: the call within the United Nations for self-determination for non-self-governing countries.

New Zealand was in something of a dilemma. Prime Minister Peter Fraser had been instrumental in helping create the machinery of the United Nations, and New Zealand saw itself as a small nation with a big influence in this world forum. It supported calls to end colonialism and to allow self-determination for all peoples. But in respect to Niue and the Cook Islands, New Zealand did not regard itself as a colonial power. These territories were an integral part of New Zealand territory, into which they had been incorporated in 1901 by the application of the Extension of Boundaries Act of 1895. They were considered the same as the Chathams or the Kermadecs. The government decided to commission an economic survey in the Cook Islands in an attempt to get some direction on Island Territories policy. H. Belshaw, professor of economics at Victoria University, and V.D. Stace of New Zealand Treasury were sent to the Cooks in 1955. They spent most of their time in Rarotonga, but did make a tour of the other islands, and Stace spent a few hours ashore on Niue in October 1955. No mention whatsoever is made of Niue in the 204-page report,[23] but some of the recommendations were to have repercussions for the entire Cook Islands (including Niue).

Belshaw and Stace stressed that the Island Territories could not be an integral part of New Zealand: they lay at too great a distance from New Zealand, and had a completely different economic and social structure and different needs. They had to be thought of as non-self-governing territories which must be assisted towards greater independence. Economic development was vital; and in order to give the Islanders greater control over this development, political changes were required. In response to this, Colin Aikman, a constitutional lawyer at Victoria University, was sent to the Cooks in 1956 to draw up a plan for constitutional development. The result of Aikman's report was the Cook Islands Amendment Act of 1957. The Island Council was to be replaced by an Island Assembly, with greater powers to spend money raised in the islands and, in time, aid money provided by New Zealand.

On Niue, people could be forgiven for not realising that change was afoot: they were scarcely included in the surveys of 1955 or 1956. They could now listen in to the New Zealand Parliament via radio, and it 'caused them some bewilderment' that there was no mention of Niue during discussions on Island Territories. When McEwen commented on this, the secretary of Island Territories, Jack Wright, replied that he himself had felt sure that 'following the publicity gained by Niue over the last twelve months, there would be some mention of the island in the House. The fact that there was nothing said about Niue could, of course, be regarded as a good omen.'[24] The real reason was that, since the creation of the Department of Island Territories in 1943, Niue had been regarded as part of the Cook Islands. The annual report was still embedded within the Cook Islands Annual Report and documents still referred to Cook Islands (including Niue) and Cook Islands (excluding Niue).

The Cook Islands Amendment Act of 1957 did, however, contain a small section relating to Niue. While it acknowledged that Niue was more isolated and less developed than the Cooks, or at least than Rarotonga, the Act did make provisions for change to the way the Island Council was appointed and the authority it would have to make real decisions. McEwen had begun the change by calling the Island Council to Alofi on a monthly rather than quarterly basis. The new provisions, to be introduced in late 1959, would replace the council with an Island Assembly, elected by all Islanders 18 years and older, men and women, in a secret ballot. Assembly members would be elected in 13 village constituencies – increased to 14 shortly after, with the inclusion of the small village of Toi in the north. The resident commissioner would still preside as president of the Assembly but the Assembly would gradually be given more responsibility for raising and spending revenue.

In the meantime, the Department of Island Territories pursued what it termed 'a vigorous economic development policy' on Niue. Jock McEwen was hopeful of obtaining a second term as resident commissioner, but there were other plans for him: he was taken back to Wellington in August 1956 to become assistant secretary of Island Territories – a position that enabled him to keep a close and protective eye on Niue. He was replaced in Alofi by A.O. Dare, who was transferred from his position as official secretary to the Cook Islands Administration directly to Niue. Olly Dare was an enthusiastic and relatively young official who was well liked on the island, but his term there was short. Officially he served until late 1958, but he was absent for a large chunk of that time, working at the South Pacific Commission in Noumea and taking a long furlough to New Zealand. When Jack Wright retired to live in Apia in May 1958,[25] his former position as secretary of Island Territories was filled by the rapidly rising McEwen, and Dare was brought back to Wellington as assistant secretary. At least there were now senior departmental officials who understood first-hand the problems on the ground in Niue. It meant a voice for Niue within the department[26] – although it sometimes led to conflict with the man on the spot in Alofi.

That man was now D.W.R. Heatley. He came from the position of chief clerk in Island Territories. He had served in the Cooks in the 1920s and in Western Samoa in the 1940s and was said to be the most knowledgeable man on Island affairs in the whole department. But his appointment was something of a surprise as he was nearing retirement and in many ways was not the sort of official McEwen was keen on appointing. Reg Heatley was one of the old-school colonial administrators, set in his ways and insistent on protocols and routines. His appointment was referred to by Robert Rex as 'Jock's mistake',[27] and may have been the result of the need for a reshuffle in Wellington. Nevertheless he was intensely interested in his work and had a detailed knowledge of how government functioned in Wellington. When he arrived on Niue in December 1958, Heatley was prepared for what he imagined would be 'the quiet life'.[28] Within two months the quiet life was shattered.

On 26 February 1959 Niue was hit by a severe and prolonged cyclone. It was a miracle there was no loss of life as buildings, large and small, were shredded by the fierce winds. The Fiji meteorological station established straight after the war alerted Niue to the fact that a cyclone was forming, and warnings were sent out to the villages. The sea was huge: Selwyn Wilson, a young assistant in the Administration office, was standing at the radio station by the wharf, trying to get a message out to New Zealand, when he saw a wave come in that was above the height of the tall derrick. 'It rolled right up the hill, unbroken, to the lighter shed, bent all the steel [framing] and carried on unbroken onto the road through Alofi.'[29] Throughout the island, but especially on the northwestern side, there was total devastation. Alofi was badly hit. Most of the old Administration building was wrecked and the LMS church, which had weathered many storms in its almost 100-year life, was destroyed.

Reg Heatley, who was slow to realise the enormity of the cyclone, insisted on going up to Tapeu as usual for his afternoon tea. He was wet through but he sat in a small dry part of the lounge, surrounded by three inches of water, and had the afternoon tea his wife had prepared. When he returned to Alofi he soon saw what was really happening. The ride down to the village was 'a hair raising experience', for the winds were at their fiercest. The church in Alofi had gone. The Administration

The LMS church in Alofi, having weathered many storms in its 100-year history, was destroyed in the February 1959 cyclone; only the oval ends remained. The whole structure had to be removed and a new church built. Courtesy Selwyn Wilson, Waikanae, New Zealand

buildings were being evacuated; men were transferring files and young women were running with their typewriters to the concrete shell of the new Post Office, which served as a type of bunker. Sheets of corrugated iron were blowing around like pieces of paper, and sea spray and foam were everywhere.[30]

The cyclone was slow-moving; it hovered over Niue for nearly 24 hours. 'The next morning we awoke and it was calm and beautiful, a sunny day. But all around was devastation.'[31] Heatley and Jack Roughan, director of Public Works, were driven right around the island after gangs had gone ahead to clear a path. At each village the two men got out and walked through the village, talking to and reassuring people, assessing damage and generally showing that the Administration was there for them. When Heatley arrived back in Alofi he dictated a 700-word message to Wellington that took three hours to send out in Morse code.

The immediate needs were sanitation and housing. Village committees were organised to ensure cesspits were covered and begin clearing debris. Heatley requested between 200 and 300 tents as temporary accommodation and reported that relief food supplies were also needed. On Saturday 7 March, the RNZAF appeared overhead at Fonuakula and made an airdrop: bundles of clothing and tents fell from the sky, in the first such exercise ever carried out over Niue. Food supplies were prepared in Auckland for shipment by the *Tofua*, which was to proceed to Niue as soon as possible after it returned from an island circuit. There was considerable negotiation in Wellington to find a way to get the MOW architect Frank Ponder

Damage was particularly severe on the northwestern side of the island. In Makefu more than half the homes were destroyed and the rest were damaged. *Auckland Weekly News*, 25 March 1959, 29, Auckland Libraries, New Zealand

For the first time since the murder of Mr Larsen in 1953, Niue was on the front pages of New Zealand newspapers. Photos taken from the RNZAF flight showed how badly the island had been damaged, and organisations such as Corso and Red Cross began collecting supplies to be sent in on a special sailing of the *Tofua*. On the left in this picture is Mrs Malia Puletaha, who had recently settled in Auckland from Niue. *New Zealand Herald*, 12 March 1959, 15, Auckland Libraries, New Zealand

Pupils sit in the remains of Tufukia school with their teacher. Tufukia, which was very close to the coast, was not rebuilt after the cyclone. All classes were moved to Halamahaga, closer to the centre of Alofi and back from the coast. Archives New Zealand, Department of Internal Affairs Te Tari Taiwhenua, ABKK W4478/63

onto the island as quickly as possible to assess housing needs. A rather novel means was found: the icebreaker USS *Staten Island* had stopped over in Wellington on a voyage back from the Antarctic, en route to San Diego. Through the American Embassy in Wellington it was arranged to divert the ship to Niue to deliver food supplies gifted by the US government, and to deposit Ponder on the island.

The arrival of the vakatāvilivili – the whirling vaka – on the Alofi green on 24 March caused great excitement. People came from around the island, school children were marched into the village and babies were named after the event.[32] The helicopter had lifted off from the icebreaker when it was still a little way off the island, but during the morning the vessel came into sight in Alofi Bay and food supplies were offloaded. Apart from the novelty factor, the helicopter was invaluable in enabling Ponder, Heatley and Roughan to view damage from the air and to make an assessment of the needs of the whole island.

Ponder stayed on for two weeks. He began designing houses that could be built to a hurricane-resistant standard, and 'produced a series of house designs incorporating various local materials and easy-to-follow plans with perspective sketches and detailed models'.[33] The idea was to get the structural core of a house built to an appropriate standard and leave the owner to finish it off to their own requirements.

Finance would be provided for a minimal deposit to cover the cost of some of the imported materials. These would be imported in bulk by the Administration and subsidised by generous relief donations from New Zealand and elsewhere. A number of tradesmen would also be brought into Niue to assist with the building programme. The Island Council placed a ban on emigration for six months: everyone was needed for the task ahead.

Heatley was anxious to get started right away. He identified that the first priority was to build accommodation for the tradesmen who were due to arrive from New Zealand. When he was instructed by Island Territories to delay work on this until issues of land ownership were sorted, Heatley was furious – and he knew exactly which button to press to get action in Wellington. He resigned; and he tendered his resignation not to the Department of Island Territories, but directly to the minister. Within a week placatory messages had been sent and Heatley had agreed that he would stay on in Niue 'to handle the present difficult problems'.[34]

Wellington was acutely aware of the difficulties in Niue and gave considerable assistance. However, the whole process of applying for a new house, gaining finance, checking out siting and village layout, and getting approval from the Island Council was very time-consuming. By December 1959 Heatley reported to Wellington, 'slow progress on housing scheme. Nearly all on paper to date. The floor of one house was poured last week.'[35] This one house was the sum total of visible progress when, on 18 January 1960, Niue was struck by a second cyclone, stronger than the last but of shorter duration.

> *It appears that most of the houses still standing after the last cyclone have been weakened considerably and there were many that had been repaired and had new roofs, which just collapsed ... there are only 134 houses left standing on Niue, apart from Government houses ... the housing damage is fantastic, and it is amazing that there were no serious casualties.*[36]

This time, the island was ready to respond. Village committees swung into action; all the planning and paperwork existed to approve housing loans; and equipment, tools and expert labour were on the island. The task was nevertheless daunting. Heatley suggested to Wellington that they send a New Zealand Army construction unit for 12 months, and at least 300 precut timber houses. He got the precut housing but not the Army.

In late February Heatley was himself taken out to Suva by flying boat because of a medical emergency. After surgery and a brief period of convalescence, he boarded the *Tofua* and returned to Niue in time to leave once more at the end of March, this

A snapshot in Avatele in 1960 shows village life back to normal after two disastrous cyclones. Mrs Jackson, wife of the Avatele pastor, is weaving with pandanus in front of the pastor's house, watched by a woman and children returning from the village reservoir with their water buckets.

Courtesy Selwyn Wilson, Waikanae, New Zealand

time with two Niuean representatives, for the first ever face-to-face talks in Wellington between New Zealand government officials and Niueans.

Robert Rex was accustomed to the new surroundings in Wellington; but for Talaiti, the oldest member of the Island Council and representative of the small village of Vaiea, it was an entirely new experience. Because of his lack of English, the McEwens offered to have Talaiti stay in their home and, in meetings at Island Territories, Rex and McEwen were able to translate for him. Talaiti, a venerable and respected man, was later able to laugh with his friends on Niue when he recounted his first visit to the New Zealand Parliament. He became confused by the turnstile entrance, lost his footing and arrived in the lobby of Parliament sprawled over the floor.[37]

The visit by these men marked a new awareness in Wellington that it was vital to consult with the Niueans themselves. As John Springford, acting resident commissioner in Heatley's absence, had just pointed out forcefully to Wellington before the visit by the Niuean delegation:

> *It should be realised that Niue is in badly reduced circumstances and at a critical point in its history. Persons on the spot are in as good a position as any to evaluate the work ahead and what is required to remedy the situation. You naturally have many views on the situation but what about arguing each point that is made from here rather than arrive at solutions which to date are generally not practicable.*[38]

Niue Island Assembly, 1961. The Cook Islands Amendment Act of 1957 made provisions for the old Island Council to be replaced by a Niue Island Assembly, elected by universal suffrage in a secret ballot. The first Assembly was elected in early 1960. There were 14 village assemblymen, a president (the resident commissioner), an interpreter and a clerk. Back row, left to right: L.R. Rex (interpreter), Talipule, Farani Nogotau, Limatau Poepata, Feleti, Kaliatama, Arumaki Strickland, Liumaihetau, S.D. Wilson (clerk). Front row, left to right: Togia Pahiva, Tamatoa Tom, Robert R. Rex, D.W.R. Heatley (president), Talaiti, Tauehetagaloa, Peika, Ahetoa Aue.

Courtesy Selwyn Wilson, Waikanae, New Zealand

There was possibly a downside to having too many Niue experts in head office!

The building programme gained momentum as the year progressed, and it changed the landscape on Niue in ways that had not been seen since the Samoan mission teachers had introduced new settlement patterns and construction methods in the 1850s. The old houses, or their remains, were swept away and 'hurricane houses' started appearing around the green in each village. There was some tension between those members of the Island Council who wanted to take this opportunity to consider the layout and spacing of houses within an entire village before allowing work to proceed, and those who were anxious to just get on and provide new housing,[39] but inevitably compromises were found. As villages took shape again, some appeared more organised than others – but all were dramatically different in appearance.

It was not just the physical landscape of Niue that changed so much in 1960: the political landscape was also dramatically altered. The Cook Islands Amendment Act of 1957 came into effect the same year, and the Island Council was replaced by a new body, the Niue Island Assembly. And as Niue approached the centenary of European settlement on the island, further political change was being planned in Wellington.

15. A TIMETABLE FOR CHANGE

Give us time to think about this more carefully

Niue was moving towards self-government without realising it. The term 'internal self-government' was not used until 1962, when the Holyoake government in New Zealand – having determined for itself what the future policy for the Island Territories would be – introduced Niue to the expression. The whole process played out as a repeat of 1900 when political and constitutional arrangements for the annexation of Niue to New Zealand were made before the idea was mooted on the island.

Leon Götz, Minister of Island Territories, introduced the New Zealand policy in a series of careful steps. In March 1962 he went to Rarotonga on the government vessel *Moana Roa*. He then went on to the northern Cooks and visited some of those islands before arriving in Niue on 31 March for a three-day visit. In both Rarotonga and Alofi, Götz announced that from 1 April the Island Assembly would have financial responsibility not only for locally raised revenue, but also for all money provided by New Zealand, subject to certain ministerial controls. In addition to the annual subsidies, New Zealand would provide a further sum to serve as a development fund. No mention was made of the term 'self-government'.

Götz returned to Wellington, where the final touches were being put to the 'Future policy in the New Zealand Island Territories' paper that was being prepared for Cabinet by the Department of Island Territories. The paper was placed before Cabinet by minister Götz on 18 June 1962. A prime consideration was that in 1960 the General Assembly of the United Nations had adopted a resolution on colonialism. This contained an all-important paragraph.

> *Immediate steps shall be taken, in Trust and Non-Self-Governing Territories or all other territories which have not yet obtained independence, to transfer all powers to the people in those territories, without any conditions or reservations, in accordance with their freely expressed will and desire, without any distinction of race, creed or colour, in order to enable them to enjoy complete independence and freedom.*[1]

Minister of Island Territories Leon Götz visited Niue in March 1962 to explain to the Island Assembly that from now on it would have much fuller financial responsibilities. At the meeting with assemblymen are, at the head of the table, from left to right: Resident Commissioner Lyle Shanks, Olly Dare (resident commissioner, Rarotonga), Götz and Jock McEwen (secretary of Island Territories). National Publicity Studios Collection, Archives New Zealand, from a print held by Alexander Turnbull Library, Wellington, New Zealand, F-39912-1/2

New Zealand had some reservations about the resolution but finally decided to vote in favour of it in order to maintain its international reputation. The UN General Assembly was changing in composition and character as the first of the newly independent countries took their seats on the international organisation. In some cases their struggle for independence had been prolonged and bloody and they were adamant that other non-self-governing territories should be granted full independence immediately. New Zealand was feeling the pressure to formulate policy that was in step with the resolution on colonialism. The paper submitted to the Holyoake Cabinet outlined four alternatives for future policy and explained why only one was viable and realistic.

The UN resolution envisaged complete independence for all countries. 'Apparently it was beyond the comprehension of the UN that there could be any people who did not want complete independence.'[2] However, the minister considered the proposal 'farcical' in the case of the New Zealand territories, given their size and geographical circumstances. With a combined population of about 25,000 people

Three members of the Island Assembly examining the proposals put before them by Götz in March 1962. From left to right: Peika (Tamakautoga), Falani Nogotau (Liku) and Talaiti (Vaiea).
National Publicity Studios Collection, Archives New Zealand, from a print held by Alexander Turnbull Library, Wellington, New Zealand, F-39907-1/2

and with 19 islands spread over a million square miles of the Pacific, this was not a realistic option. Besides which, the Minister explained, they were confident that the people of the Cooks, Niue and Tokelau would not wish to sever their ties to New Zealand.

Complete integration with New Zealand was considered unworkable principally in financial terms. All New Zealand social security benefits would be payable in the islands and this would make 'an atoll dweller with three or four children on family benefit equivalent to a millionaire'.[3] Furthermore there would be vast increases in salaries and wages, which would mean all incentives to increase export production would disappear and the subsidies needed to keep the territories functioning would treble almost immediately.

A federation of Polynesia was a third alternative outlined, but this was also rejected: 'Even if it were confined to Western Samoa, Tonga, the Cooks, Niue, Tokelau and Ellice Islands, it would have no chance whatsoever of success.' Geographical, linguistic, cultural, social and economic reasons would all work against such a grouping.

The final alternative presented to Cabinet was for full internal self-government – an arrangement the Cook Islands and Niue were considered already very close to achieving. Having set up an Island Assembly and handed over financial power, all that was needed for now was 'to withdraw the Resident Commissioner from the Assembly, to constitute an executive body responsible to the Assembly, and to widen the power of legislation to cover all subjects other than constitutional enactments, external affairs and defence'.[4] In asking Cabinet to endorse the internal self-government alternative, Götz stressed:

> *There is little doubt that [this] alternative is the best from the point of view of the island people and also of New Zealand. There is little doubt too, that this alternative would be the one which the islanders would prefer. It is probably not the one which would appeal to the UN, but it may be acceptable if presented in the right way at the right time.*[5]

Cabinet agreed that a plan for internal self-government in the New Zealand Island Territories should be submitted to the UN that year. It also decided to invite the UN to send a visiting mission to the territories in 1963; and to hold a plebiscite, if required, to ascertain the wishes of the people. The aim was to be proactive, to initiate change rather than wait for it to be forced on them. A clear timetable could then be reported and signed off as each stage was reached. The only thing left for the minister to do was to inform the people of the Island Territories. He told Cabinet, 'self-government would be the option that the islanders would prefer'. He now had to convert this statement into 'self-government *is* the option that the islanders prefer'.

Götz decided to launch the policy in the Cook Islands. He was due in Fiji for a New Zealand trade fair in early July, so he would fly on to Rarotonga and speak in the Cook Islands Assembly. A trip by air ruled out a visit to Niue. Before he left New Zealand details of the policy were sent to the resident commissioners in both Rarotonga and Niue, with a strict embargo on the release of the information. They did, however, have the authority to speak with their Assembly members in committee and to give a brief outline of the four alternatives.

When Götz spoke in the Cook Islands Legislative Assembly on 12 July 1962, assemblymen and officials in Niue were listening in to a broadcast from Rarotonga. Reception was poor, static interference meant much of the detail was missed, but Robert Rex recalled later how 'for the first time the people of Niue heard the word self-government'.[6] The detail of the proposals had to wait for the September arrival of the *Tofua*, which brought a printed copy of the minister's speech to Niue for consideration.

Götz first outlined the three alternatives that New Zealand had already rejected. Particularly in the option of integration with New Zealand, Götz slanted the reasons against such a move to appeal to an island audience, and avoided any mention of the financial implications for New Zealand. He painted a scenario of the Pacific Islands being represented by a lone voice in the New Zealand Parliament, one voice for all three territories, and of policies once more being decided by people in Wellington. He then suggested the best move would be to keep the present link with New Zealand but to have full internal self-government.

While the Niue Island Assembly was waiting for a copy of the minister's speech to arrive, they tried to come to grips with the new financial arrangements as announced by Götz during his visit at the beginning of April. It represented a huge increase in work and responsibility for the members of the Assembly: the amount of revenue handled by them would increase from approximately £15,000 per annum of locally raised revenue, to around £280,000 per annum of local revenue plus New Zealand subsidies. Included was a sum of £25,000 spread over three years, which was for the newly announced development fund. This was also a huge undertaking for the Assembly, to oversee investment in projects that would give a profitable return and thus increase the prosperity of Niue. In announcing these changes, the minister had 'informed the Assembly that he considered it is the greatest step forward ever taken for the island. There is no doubt that such is the case.'[7] The Niue Assembly was henceforth to be responsible for preparing an annual budget for spending the appropriation ordinance, and this would be submitted through the Department of Island Territories in Wellington to the minister and on to the governor-general for assent. The minister, 'in his wisdom', could disallow any part of the ordinance but he would only do this if he considered a proposal to be 'deeply unwise'. The Assembly must consider its budget very carefully to ensure it was sound and sensible, and assemblymen must be prepared to say 'no' where it was unwise to say 'yes'.[8]

Within the Assembly there had already been discussion about electing some form of executive committee to oversee financial arrangements. There had also been a proposal to give groups of assemblymen the chance to become more familiar with selected activities of the Administration and to take a leading part in discussions when matters relating to those activities came under consideration in meetings. An executive committee was now essential, and in early July 1962 Lyle Shanks, the new resident commissioner, withdrew from the Assembly while discussion took place. 'Within a quarter of an hour I was recalled and informed that they had decided in favour of such a committee and had elected Messrs Rex, Strickland and

Tamatoa to comprise its members.'[9] The fact that the resident commissioner was to head this committee meant that discussion would be conducted in English, and as the meetings would be closed and confidential, there would be no interpretation service provided. The Assembly had accordingly elected members who were confident in speaking English, including Arumaki Strickland, a Cook Islander who had settled in Alofi North in 1946 and now represented the village. Niue now had its first embryonic Cabinet, working alongside the resident commissioner to prepare proposals for the full Assembly meeting. It was fortunate that Lyle Shanks served two terms as resident commissioner, from 1962 to 1968, and was able to provide continuity and sound advice to both the Assembly and the Executive Committee as they learned to handle their new roles.

The 1963 Cook Islands Amendment Act gave legal status to the new Executive Committee. But the members of the Niue Assembly were concerned at the pace of constitutional change that was being proposed and the timetable that would give them self-governance by 1965. They called for advice from New Zealand, but had to wait until January 1965 for that advice to arrive in the form of Jock McEwen and Professor Colin Aikman of Victoria University. 'The general feeling was that you had abandoned us,' said one speaker at the welcome, but 'through God's grace, you have finally arrived'.[10] McEwen and Aikman compensated for the delay by devoting 10 days on the island to intense consultation. They held meetings with the Executive Committee and the Niue Assembly. They also held public meetings in Alofi and Hakupu, and interest was so great that both these meetings went far into the night. Many of the discussions, including Aikman's talks on constitutional history, were taped and then broadcast.

There was a lot to absorb, but people were prepared to speak out and to question. 'There is one point that is not clear to me yet,' said Fakamautama, member for Hakupu, 'and this is it; I do not as yet know who wanted to give Niue self-government, is it Niue's wish or New Zealand's or whose?'[11] Aikman responded that New Zealand 'and all the other countries of the world' believed that self-government was important for the people of Niue. However, during the course of the visit Aikman heard many people requesting 'time to think about this more carefully'.[12] He concluded that much of the concern that was being expressed about self-government was because of the hasty timetable outlined. He felt that, in the case of Niue, this should be rejected to reduce the pressure for change. Instead, there should be a focus on one step at a time, and then, when the Niue people agreed and asked for it, another step. Tom Tamatoa, member for Tuapa, compared this approach to the

The Niue Development Board, set up in the 1960s to oversee the spending of development money from New Zealand, looked for new crops to replace bananas and coconuts. Passionfruit were planted on family land and hand-pollinated, often by women. By the late 1960s a factory had been built to juice the fruit. This photo was used as a postcard to promote the crop.

External Aid Division, Ministry of Foreign Affairs, Archives New Zealand, Department of Internal Affairs Te Tari Taiwhenua, AAEG 7398 W4835/3 introduction of the gospel to Niue over 100 years previously: 'It took many efforts to convince the people and it will be the same now.'[13] There were also similarities to the annexation of Niue to New Zealand: the overall outcome may have been decided by forces outside Niue, but the Niueans were determined they would play an active part in both the pace of change and the finer details of any arrangements.

Niue was thus cut loose from the Cook Islands timetable and allowed to progress at a slower, more acceptable rate. The Cooks achieved self-government in 1965. A new Niue Act in 1966 incorporated the legislation previously in the Cook Islands Act and its amendments, thus maintaining the status quo in respect of Niue. New Zealand was criticised at the United Nations for allowing the process to be slowed for Niue, but it stood firm, insisting that in the Declaration on Colonialism 'we find no suggestion that all the known views of a people should be disregarded in the interest of pursuing some supposed doctrinal imperative'.[14] There were special circumstances in many of the remaining tiny non-self-governing territories, which required quite different treatment from larger territories that had already become self-governing. Niue was such a case and must be handled accordingly.

Meanwhile, in Niue, the Executive Committee got on with learning the tasks involved in governing. To begin with, members would accept responsibility only for a single portfolio, while Resident Commissioner Shanks handled all other business and presided over the Committee and the Assembly. After the 1966 elections the Executive Committee was increased to four members, and Messrs Rex, Talipule, Siakisoni and Strickland were elected. Hon. Robert Rex, 57 years old and member for Alofi South, was elected leader of Government Business.

Rex was the man for the time. He brought to his new role a wealth of experience and wisdom that was now proving vital. Having worked for the New Zealand Administration in Niue for 20 years from the early 1930s, he had made the decision in 1952 to leave the security of government employment and set up his own trading store in Alofi. Robert and his wife Patricia invested everything they had, and more, in this venture and in so doing, they also invested their future in Niue. Rex was comfortable attending either a village meeting on the green or a committee meeting in the Assembly Room: he was a skilled orator in both settings. He had considerable expertise in achieving agreement among disputing parties. He had been attending regional Pacific meetings since 1950,[15] and had come to know personally many of the leading political figures of the region. And he was equally comfortable fishing alone in his vaka off the Niue coast at sunset.

When Ralph Hanan, minister of Island Territories, visited Niue in March 1968 he was again given the message that the pace of change would be determined by Niue. Hanan was happy with this, especially as he saw that village councils had been elected the previous year to take responsibility for local issues, thus giving more people experience in governing. There was also discussion that after the elections in 1969, the Executive Committee would move to a full member system – in other words the Executive Committee members would assume responsibility for all government portfolios. So there was progress.

Change was not limited to the political sphere, however. There was a clear understanding in the UN that social and economic development must accompany political change. A country, to be self-governing, needed its people to be educated, well housed, have access to a good health system and have employment in projects that would create personal and collective economic wealth. Niueans could be forgiven for not really noticing or fully comprehending some of the political developments occurring on the island throughout the 1960s, but they would certainly have been aware of many social and economic changes during this time.

The new hurricane houses were now a prominent feature in the villages. Some had been completed, but many were still only at 'shelter' stage: adding doors and windows, interior linings and decoration was the responsibility of the owners, and some were unable to afford the extra cost. One of the aims of the newly elected village councils was to generate community pride and encourage people to complete their homes. A well-drilling expert was brought to Niue, and the first deep-water bores were drilled around the island; this lessened the dependence on rainwater and made water supplies much more secure. In another big step, two United Nations agencies agreed to fund a water reticulation scheme to take the water supply into villages and plantation areas:[16] the scheme was commenced in Lakepa and gradually progressed clockwise around the island.

More and more Niueans were registering motor vehicles, especially motorbikes. Some individuals also imported buses, which meant that children could now be transported from the back villages to the high school established at the new site at Paliati, just out of Alofi. Here an increasing number of young Niueans had the opportunity to stay on at least to form four; and in 1966 the first eight candidates sat the New Zealand School Certificate exam: one was successful.[17] More than 30 students were now away on scholarships in New Zealand, and several more were doing agricultural training in the Pacific. Nurses and teachers were trained locally but many were sent on extra training courses to New Zealand and other Pacific countries.

Movies were now being shown in most villages. Two newspapers were available: *Tohi Tala Niue*, the Administration paper, which became a daily; and *Ko e Talahau Niue*, published more erratically by the LMS. A library also opened in Alofi, and regular supplies of books arrived from the New Zealand National Library Service. There were now women's committees in all villages and a central hall in Alofi where women could gather to weave and talk about matters of interest.

Most importantly, in 1967 Niue got its own radio station. The station went on air in a series of test runs leading up to the change to decimal currency in July 1967, and it soon became the voice of Niue. The studio was set up in the new Community Development Office, and a supply of portable transistor radios from Japan rapidly sold out. Expatriate officers, especially Harry Coleman, handled the technical side, and three Niueans – Tahafa Talagi, Terry Chapman and Hima Douglas – set about learning to be announcers. They rode out to villages on their motorbikes to record Niueans singing, and for the first time, 'ne fakafano ai e leo ha Niue', Niue's voice, was heard over the air.[18] This was a major step in fostering a sense of Niuean identity.

The LMS Church, that precious and deeply rooted element of Niuean life, was also undergoing change as the LMS in London sought to withdraw from direct administration of its worldwide organisation of churches. In a process that mirrored the political changes occurring in Niue, a new Island Church Council was set up in the early 1960s. There was wider representation from all the village churches, but the council was still chaired by the European missionary. Discussions took place on a constitution for the Niue church, and when the last of the overseas missionaries, Donald Reekie, arrived in 1965, final steps were taken to make the Niue LMS an independent and self-governing body. The name was changed to Ekalesia Niue and a constitution was adopted.[19]

Niue sent its first representatives to the Pacific Conference of Churches in Lifou in 1966, and Ekalesia Niue was accepted into this grouping. Discussion at the conference centred very much on the indigenisation of Christian worship, and the Niuean delegates got some idea of the changes that were taking place throughout the Pacific and the increasing independence of the churches in the region. Reekie stayed on in Niue as an advisor, but in 1967 he withdrew from the position of president of the Church Council, now known as Fono Ekalesia Motu, and for the first time this position was filled by a Niuean, Ikiua Lupo. In 1970, when Ekalesia Niue officially became independent, Reverend Tom Tamatoa became its new president. When Reverend Reekie left Niue in 1973, it marked the end of 112 years of service by English missionaries: this central facet of island life was now truly Niuean.

Limes were another crop that was found to grow well on Niue, and the Niue Development Board offered loans to buy lime trees. By the late 1960s fruit was being exported and experiments were being carried out into pressing limes for oil and juice. External Aid Division, Ministry of Foreign Affairs, Archives New Zealand, Department of Internal Affairs Te Tari Taiwhenua, AAEG 7398 W4835/3

The Niue Development Board encouraged the creation of a honey industry on the island. Hives were brought in and set up in a number of locations around the island. At Fonuakula, Foster Ikimau tends the hives. External Aid Division, Ministry of Foreign Affairs, Archives New Zealand, Department of Internal Affairs Te Tari Taiwhenua, AAEG 7398W4835 7398 Box 3

When the Niue Amateur Sports Association was set up and the first Niuean team went to the South Pacific Games in Fiji in 1963, this further boosted a sense of pride in Niue as a country. Niueans, from sportspeople to assemblymen and church representatives and government employees, were being sent out into the wider Pacific to represent the whole island. Whether it was the South Pacific Conference or the Pacific Conference of Churches or the South Pacific Games, Niueans were learning that, while they had affinities with other Pacific peoples and issues in common, they were unique as Niueans with their own language and cultural identity. This realisation brought with it a sense of confidence that was important if the political changes already well under way were to be embraced by the island.

Economic development also continued through the 1960s. Five-year development plans were drawn up and the Niue Development Board was set up to oversee expenditure of money designated for development by the New Zealand government. Traditional export crops were faltering. Bananas had always been problematic. Copra was a popular cash crop, but a fall in international prices affected output. Kūmara had also become an important export crop, but fungal infection and weevils often led to the rejection of the crop when it reached New Zealand ports. Agricultural experts conducted trials in a number of possible crops for export and by the late 1960s limes and passionfruit were flourishing and a honey industry was also under way. Limes and passionfruit were crops that Niueans could grow on their own land, and the new Development Board gave loans to enable people to prepare land and buy plants. Experts arrived from UN specialist agencies and from the South Pacific Commission to give assistance. A factory was built to juice passionfruit and to experiment in pressing limes for juice and oil: it employed Niuean staff under expatriate management.

In another agricultural development that had the potential to improve income for the local producers, cattle were introduced to the island. The idea was to adopt the well-established tropical form of agriculture in which cattle were grazed in coconut plantations. The 1967 annual report from the Resident Commissioner's Office noted that 'with the success experienced by the drilling of bores to provide water, the complementary economics of coconuts and cattle will become a principal factor in the development of the island'.[20] The first imports of stock arrived on the *Tofua* in late 1967. Five head of cattle came from Fiji, as well as a small flock of Perendale sheep, introduced for experimental purposes. Cattle imports increased steadily until there were nearly 500 on the island: two dairy herds, and the remainder beef cattle. The sheep flock had increased to 50 and was still thriving.[21] The sheep were confined to the experimental farm at Vaipapahi but the cattle were scattered around the island on government and private land and provided yet another new element in the Niue landscape. It was now possible to buy fresh milk in the trading stores in Alofi. The milk supply extended to a government-funded school milk scheme, and around the island milk stations were built at each school for daily deliveries. Fresh meat was also available from the government slaughterhouse outside Alofi, and such were the changes in dietary preferences, supply could never match demand.

By far the greatest financial undertaking in the 1960s was the construction of an airport. The idea had been suggested as early as 1945 when Prime Minister Fraser had called briefly at Niue, having travelled by sea from Apia; and it was repeatedly raised over the next two decades but with no actual commitment of funds. By the mid-1960s, the lack of air access to the island was seen as a major barrier to

Official opening of airport, 1971. The children from Tuatea school in Hakupu were brought to witness the official opening of the airport on 23 November 1971. An RNZAF Orion and two Ministry of Transport Friendships arrived with an official party from New Zealand and the Pacific. The first plane had touched down in October 1970, but at that stage much of the support work was still to be completed. Courtesy Young Vivian, Tāoga Niue

economic development, and the idea of an airport was again seriously considered. The RNZAF flying-boat base at Laucala Bay near Suva had been closed in 1967, and this added to the urgency for an airstrip on Niue.[22] When the aged Sunderland flying boats were replaced by new land-based Orions operating out of Whenuapai in Auckland, emergency medical evacuations were no longer possible from Niue.

The minister, Ralph Hanan, was anxious to provide an airport for Niue, and at a March 1967 Cabinet meeting he pushed through a proclamation for the governor-general's signature taking land at Niue for an aerodrome, before the concept had been discussed in Cabinet. In so doing, Hanan flouted standard Cabinet procedure. The concept of an aerodrome at Niue involved the possible 'future commitment of substantial funds of money' and should have been discussed first before a proclamation signed that 'would no doubt raise expectations as to the construction of an airport'.[23] Hanan received a written reprimand for his actions; he reportedly was rather proud of this and had the letter framed.[24] Hanan died suddenly in 1969 before the airport at Niue was completed but it was opened by his wife and named Hanan International Airport in his honour.

When construction on the airfield commenced in 1968 there was a further injection of equipment, personnel and supplies to Niue, which meant not only the airport but many other projects were also assisted. Wharf facilities were improved so that heavy machinery could be imported; and that machinery was used to seal not only the 5000-foot runway but also many of the roads around the island. Radio communications improved as a result of the need for aeronautical navigation facilities. Skilled workers were brought in from New Zealand, and they trained local labour. Some of the new arrivals became permanent inhabitants of Niue.[25] Locals were also trained in skills associated with running an airport, including flight control, weather forecasting, fire service and refuelling.

Anyone driving over the top road from Tamakautoga to Alofi could not help but be impressed with developments in the Fonuakula area. Passionfruit vines were flourishing; one of the dairy farms was operating here; the government settlement at Fualahi had been built to house expatriate workers; and the airport runway was taking shape. Down on the lower terrace at Amanau, construction had begun on the 40-bed Niue Hotel. The airport was completed by October 1970 in time for the first arrival, a calibration flight. Commercial flights began in mid-1971 with the commencement of services by the new Polynesian Airlines of Western Samoa and the official opening took place in November 1971.

Had Niue entered a 'golden era' of development and prosperity? Communications were about to take a huge leap forward. New crops and livestock held the promise of export growth. Water, electricity and phones were increasingly accessible. Schools and hospital services were improving. The Niue Island Assembly was taking more and more responsibility for decision-making.

But beneath this veneer of prosperity a disturbing and potentially destabilising trend was emerging: Niueans were migrating to New Zealand. Some have suggested that the reason was the opening of the airport, but the movement to New Zealand was well established by the time the airport opened; the airport provided a faster and more direct means of transport to New Zealand but it was not the reason for the move. Life in Niue was still difficult for most people. They had to spend many hours a week working in the bush to produce food for the family. The Administration, as the chief employer on the island, recognised the importance of the bush garden and set hours of work accordingly to allow men time to get to the bush after a day of paid employment.[26] There was still a strong commitment to village and church,

The Minister of Island Affairs, Duncan MacIntyre, paid an official visit to Niue in November 1970 to view development projects on the island. He was taken on a full-day tour starting at the Lord Liverpool hospital where he was shown round by Dr H.T. Nemaia, acting Director of Health. Out behind the hospital the Minister looks down on the cliffs and the reef with Dr Nemaia and Selwyn Wilson. This location meant the hospital was often hit by cyclones and finally, after the 2004 cyclone, a new hospital was built on the upper terrace, away from the coast.

Courtesy Selwyn Wilson, Waikanae, New Zealand

which took time, effort and resources. There had been a regular trickle of migration to New Zealand since World War II, and a number of factors increased this movement in the 1960s. Members of the UN may have been excited by the prospect of self-determination for all peoples, but on Niue it also created uncertainty and even fear. Niueans were New Zealand citizens and had free access to the country: would this still be the case when self-government was granted? Would it be better to leave now and get established in New Zealand before any political changes took place?

Assurances that New Zealand citizenship was not in jeopardy failed to reassure some people: they moved – usually to Auckland – and joined an ever-growing Niuean and wider Pacific Island community there. In a period of full employment they found work in the factories, and when the day ended they did not need to go to the bush to work. Life seemed easier. They were not immediately eligible for all social security benefits, as these carried a residential clause that did not count time living in Island Territories; however, the family benefit was available to any child who was likely to live permanently in New Zealand, and this was certainly a help to the family budget. Those who settled successfully encouraged other family members to join them, and often sent the money to Niue to pay for the journey.

On Niue the impact of migration was visible in the villages, where some of the hurricane homes were now boarded up; they stood throughout the village like markers to each family who had left. The demographic on the island altered, so that in the middle of the age spectrum there was an obvious dip. And, as one university researcher noted:

> *[W]ith the departure of up to half of the population of some of the back villages a great psychological pressure builds up on those who stay behind, as they watch the church empty, the social ceremonies become less frequent, the neighbours depart and the garden plots fall into disrepair.*[27]

It was the young men and the young families who were leaving – those who were vital for economic progress. Some left after they had acquired skills such as carpentry. Work on the Niue Hotel, for example, was seriously compromised by the loss of Niuean semi-skilled workers; in order to complete the hotel, workers had to be brought in from Tonga. More disturbingly, some of those working in the public sector on Niue and who were sent to New Zealand for training simply did not return. When a study of Niuean migration was commissioned in 1972, the author of the report emphasised that Niueans had no special need to leave Niue as, compared with other Pacific Islands, they had a relatively high standard of living. He concluded: 'The migrant is clearly not driven or expelled from Niue by sheer necessity. He is propelled by his New Zealand citizenship, his rising expectations, his kin in New Zealand, and by the rather disturbing belief that he is participating in the inevitable.'[28] This last line was a reference to the sense of fatalism on Niue, the sense that everyone else was moving so eventually they must too.

Migration created a particular problem on the island because of land ownership rights. Niueans might leave the island, settle in New Zealand and bring up their families there, but they retained their rights to family land on Niue, and some of this land was now becoming neglected and overgrown. Plans to develop areas for economic return often came up against the problem of absentee landowners, and attempts to contact owners in New Zealand were time-consuming and often

Niue appeared to be entering a 'golden era' of development in the 1960s but a disturbing and potentially destabilising trend was emerging: Niueans were emigrating to New Zealand and hurricane houses were being boarded up as families left. External Aid Division, Ministry of Foreign Affairs, Archives New Zealand, Department of Internal Affairs Te Tari Taiwhenua, AAEG 7398 W4835/3

unsuccessful. The issue had been discussed frequently in the Island Assembly, and in 1964 an idea was mooted that would have seen absentee owners lose their land rights after 20 years' absence. It was a discussion point only, but it was sent to Wellington for comment. McEwen was ill at the time and, in his absence, someone circulated the idea to Niuean groups in Wellington and Auckland for comment.

The response was swift. A Niue New Zealand Society was set up in Auckland to lobby for continued land rights, and when McEwen fronted before the group in January 1965, en route to Niue, he met with fierce and unexpected criticism – unexpected because he had been unaware that the Assembly's idea had been circulated. It was an idea that he personally was unhappy with. 'It is a very hard thing to take away a man's land rights,' he told the Niue Assembly when he arrived.[29] It was one of the discussion points during the McEwen/Aikman visit and three members of the Niue New Zealand Society had been included in the visiting group so their views could be expressed directly to the Assembly.[30] Both sides presented their arguments cogently and respectfully, but land ownership remained a complex problem for the island. Members of the Niue New Zealand Society returned to Niue in 1969 to talk in meetings around the island, ostensibly about land issues; but some on the island felt their aims were now more overtly political and were an attempt to criticise the leader of government and the Executive Committee.[31] In a radio broadcast, Robert Rex countered various allegations made by the visitors, and once again the tensions between Niueans living in New Zealand and those on the island were highlighted.

Resident Commissioner Lyle Shanks, who had overseen the initial political developments of the 1960s, had been replaced in 1968 by Selwyn Wilson, who had served in Niue as a young Administration assistant during the 1959–60 cyclones. Now, as resident commissioner, he was keen to encourage the devolution of power to the Niue Assembly. He was an astute listener and observer, and his monthly reports to McEwen in Wellington clearly show his efforts to step back and let Niueans take control, and his shrewd interpretation of political developments.

As the New Zealand officials gradually assumed a backroom role on Niue, local political personalities took on more prominent roles. Rex still provided leadership, with a steady but cautious approach to political change, but new men emerged at the 1969 Assembly elections – arguably the most crucial of the pre-self-government elections. Only one seat, Liku, was uncontested; and in five villages new men were elected. For the first time Talaiti, the longest-sitting member and member of the former Island Council, was challenged for his seat. Also for the first time a European, R.L. (Bob) Strickland, proprietor of Niue Motors, challenged Rex for the Alofi South seat. In two villages, Alofi North and Tuapa, there were women standing for the first time in Assembly elections. These challenges were all unsuccessful, but they showed an increasing interest in island politics. In another first, two former scholarship students who had returned to Niue to serve in the Administration decided to leave their permanent positions in health and education and stand for public office. Dr Enetama and Young Vivian were both successful, and were immediately elected by the Assembly to the Executive Committee. Another young man, Frank Lui, was also elected to the Assembly at this time. Lui had served one term earlier in the 1960s as the member for Alofi North. He had defeated and then been defeated by Arumaki Strickland. Lui now firmly secured the village seat. He entered the Assembly and became the unofficial voice of opposition to Robert Rex's previously unchallenged position.

In order to make progress, the Niue Assembly once again requested advice from New Zealand, and Professor R.Q. Quentin-Baxter from Victoria University was appointed constitutional advisor to the New Zealand and Niue governments. In

When the Minister of Island Affairs paid an official visit to Niue in November 1970 he was accompanied by Professor Quentin-Baxter and his wife, who had come to advise on constitutional issues. The whole party travelled around the island and are photographed in Liku. From left to right: Mrs MacIntyre, Assemblyman Sipeli, Jock McEwen (Secretary for Maori and Island Affairs), Mrs Sipeli, Mr Ngata (private secretary to minister), Mr MacIntyre (Minister of Island Affairs), Mrs Quentin-Baxter, Professor Quentin-Baxter, Robert Rex and Selwyn Wilson (resident commissioner). Courtesy Selwyn Wilson, Waikanae, New Zealand

late 1970 he travelled to Niue to ascertain Niuean views of their future and to make recommendations to both governments. His 1971 report was adopted in full by the Niue Assembly and became the blueprint for further development. Quentin-Baxter was a very experienced international lawyer and diplomat. He spent three weeks on the island listening patiently to Niueans as they expressed their wishes and especially their fears, and he won the hearts of these people. Naturally there were babies named after him. His report contains a strong sense of the Niueans' fear that self-government was going to involve the loss of New Zealand citizenship and financial assistance. This made everyone extremely cautious about further constitutional change. Quentin-Baxter described the Niuean community as extremely fragile, 'partly because of small numbers and limited resources, and partly because its people have another place to go'.[32] For Niue to survive and prosper, he felt, there must be a commitment by people to stay on the island, to put the interests of their community first. They had made considerable progress towards managing their own affairs and simply needed reassurance of this.

The main recommendations by Quentin-Baxter for amendments to the Niue Act of 1966 related to the Executive Committee. This body exercised its powers by delegation from the resident commissioner; but Quentin-Baxter suggested these powers should be legally conferred on it. The Assembly should in future select the leader of government business and then allow him to choose three other assemblymen as his colleagues in the Executive Committee, thus establishing the principle of collective responsibility. The changes were approved by the New Zealand Parliament and incorporated in the Niue Amendment Act 1971.

In the 1969–72 Assembly there was intense political lobbying and friction as the conservative elements faced the 'avant-garde led by Vivian, Enetama and Lui'.[33] Vivian introduced a motion in January 1970 that further constitutional steps should be taken, and this resulted in keen debate but was met with silence from Robert Rex. Wilson commented, 'In times past Mr Rex's opinion was accepted implicitly in the Assembly, but that is no longer the case. In the awareness of this he is being extremely cautious in declaring his hand.'[34] Rex may not have expressed a view but he was certainly listening and weighing up the options.

A debate in the Assembly in late 1971 showed up the need for collective responsibility by the Executive Committee, as explained by Quentin-Baxter and incorporated in the 1971 Amendment Act. Frank Lui, Member for Alofi North, introduced a motion that the 'ng' spelling, adopted by McEwen in his dictionary,[35] should not be used in schools; instead the 'g' spelling should be retained. There was loud and furious debate. The Executive Committee had already discussed the issue and decided in favour of the 'ng' spelling, but now, in the Assembly debate, a member of the Executive Committee, Togakilo, sided with Lui and the motion was passed.

Rex realised that he would need to actively campaign right around the island before the next election, and that he needed to lobby behind the scenes for support from assemblymen. In a shrewd move to bring the 'avant-garde' into the fold, Rex lobbied for their support of his candidature as the next leader of government, in return for seats on the Executive Committee. In the March 1972 elections only five seats were contested. Rex, Vivian, Enetama and Lui were all unopposed, and at the first Assembly meeting Rex's was the only nomination for leader of government, proposed by Lui and seconded by Vivian. The behind-the-scenes lobbying had been successful. Rex chose Lui, Vivian and Enetama for his Executive Committee, and now allocated the various portfolios carefully. Lui was the only new member. As Wilson reported to the secretary of Island Affairs:

> *In a move to get Lui entirely on his side, Rex has given him the relatively large portfolio of Public Works and Electricity. This was a shrewd move, because Lui had often been critical of various Public Works activities, and now the acid is on him to find solutions.*[36]

Vivian and Enetama retained portfolios in a number of areas, including those in which they had most expertise: education and health.

There was now a collective responsibility in the Executive Committee and Rex had a firm rein on its members. He accepted Vivian's desire to move ahead with constitutional debate, but insisted it wait until June when the UN visiting mission to Niue was due. Their report would give guidance in deciding the next steps to be taken in the process, and Robert Rex for one still wanted guidance and advice in his cautious approach to constitutional and political change.

The new Executive Committee after the March 1972 election lines up to meet the visiting UN mission to Niue in June 1972. From left to right: Frank Lui, Young Vivian, Robert Rex (Leader of Government), and Dr Enetama. Courtesy Selwyn Wilson, Waikanae, New Zealand

16. The final steps

We want to decide for ourselves what our future is going to be

The UN visiting mission to Niue arrived on the island on 21 June 1972 and was immediately confronted by a people who were clear about what they wanted. Jock McEwen, accompanying the UN team, reported back to Wellington that 'within 24 hours of their visit they had abandoned any ideas they had that Niue was just another oppressed colony struggling for immediate independence'.[1] Robert Rex made what McEwen described as 'an outstanding speech which set out with absolute clarity the attitude of the Niuean people'.

> *If after your visit you find things still unclear, one thing that will be clear to you is that we don't want independence. We regard New Zealand as our own country and as you know half of our people already live there. If you don't learn anything else, you will at least learn that we want to decide for ourselves what our future is going to be, and when that decision is going to be taken, and we want to do both of these things at our own pace. If it is self-government we want we will decide when that will be – not when mother New Zealand says and certainly not when the UN says.*[2]

The mission members spent five days listening to the views of all Assembly members, and attended very large public meetings in Alofi and Hakupu. The prevailing view expressed was a desire for self-government, tempered by an obvious concern about continued New Zealand citizenship and financial assistance. There was also a strong call for the continued independence of the Niue Public Service. In such a small community where personal contacts and relationships were so close, an independent body was necessary to monitor public service employment, and this was best done by the New Zealand State Services Commission.

In their report on the visit to Niue, the mission made special mention of the call by Hon. Young Vivian for a timetable for political and constitutional change. It noted that the Executive Committee agreed in principle with this idea but wanted the timing left to the discretion of the Select Committee, which had already been established late the previous year.

After the visit to Niue in June 1972, the UN visiting mission arrived in Wellington to talk with Prime Minister Jack Marshall. They also met with a group of Wellington Niueans at the Newtown church to hear their views on the proposals for self-government. Members of the UN team, seated left to right: Ambassador Salim Ahmed Salim (leader, Tanzania), Britta Scotsberg-Ahman (Sweden), Frank O. Abdullah (Trinidad and Tobago). Members of Niuean community, standing left to right: Hima Douglas, Rev. Lagi Sipeli, Jock McEwen (secretary of Island Affairs), Kelemu Moko, Atuhega Mokalei, Nasalita Dawson, Fisa Pihigia, Julia Uka, Tom Etuata. National Publicity Studios Collection, Archives New Zealand, Department of Internal Affairs Te Tari Taiwhenua, AAEG W2972/1

Three recommendations by the visiting mission concerned the position of the resident commissioner. He should no longer preside in the Executive Committee: this was the role of the leader of government and the constitution should state this. Neither should the resident commissioner be president of the Assembly: this role should be assumed by a Niuean, and this would give the people a greater sense of responsibility for their own affairs.[3] Third, the mission considered it both 'unsatisfactory and anachronistic for the Resident Commissioner to act as Judge'.[4] A solution to this situation was urgently required.

The mission acknowledged that emigration to New Zealand was a serious issue for which there were no obvious solutions: 'The future needs of the territory can be realised only if there is a sufficient number of Niueans who are committed to serving their own community in the island.'[5] Looking to the future prospects for Niue, the mission stated 'the possibilities of preserving Niue as a self-governing entity with a national identity of its own, which is the goal the islanders have set for themselves' would be seriously harmed by continuing emigration.

The visit by the UN mission gave encouragement and impetus to the move toward constitutional change. The Select Committee of the Niue Assembly considered the mission's recommendations, sought and received a further visit by Professor Quentin-Baxter in October to give advice, and by November 1972 submitted their report to the Assembly. On 21 November a resolution calling for a 'constitution providing for a self-governing Niue in free association with New Zealand'[6] was passed overwhelmingly by the Assembly.

Niue had made its decision in its own time and was now ready to speak to the other major stakeholders: New Zealand and the UN. Robert Rex prepared for a delegation to head to Wellington in early 1973 and present the Assembly's decision to the newly elected Labour government of Norman Kirk and his Minister of Island Affairs, Phil Amos. Prime Minister Kirk and Niue Leader of Government Rex issued a joint communiqué in Wellington on 2 March 1973, which stated that the delegation headed by Rex had informed the New Zealand government of the wish of the government and people of Niue to achieve the status of full self-government in free association with New Zealand in 1974.

A date had finally been put to the process. Agreement had been reached on a timetable. New Zealand citizenship was to be guaranteed. Economic and financial aid was to be maintained and, in contrast to the Cook Islands situation, this guarantee was to be written into the constitution. New Zealand would remain responsible for foreign affairs and defence, and a New Zealand representative would be appointed to be resident in Niue. A constitution would be drawn up and placed before the people of Niue in a referendum in 1974. Meanwhile arrangements had been made for twice-yearly visits to Niue by the chief justice of Western Samoa. The prime minister of Samoa considered they 'would be honoured to have their judge serve Niue',[7] and the new air link between Apia and Niue made the arrangement feasible. Finally, a problem plaguing the New Zealand Administration of Niue since its outset was to be solved.

The next step for Rex and his fellow politicians, now that they had told New Zealand of their plans, was to inform the United Nations in New York. In November

1973 Robert Rex, accompanied by Young Vivian and Terry Chapman, clerk of the Executive Committee,[8] flew to Los Angeles and on over the North American continent to a cold, wintry New York. There the Niue delegation prepared for Rex to address the Special Committee on Decolonisation, the body charged with overseeing the move to self-determination by all non-self-governing countries. Robert Rex later recalled the concrete jungle of New York, not seeing the sun, and how cold it was. On the day of his address he felt very cold, and could not decide if it was the weather or his nerves. A whisky helped, plus encouragement from his colleagues and the New Zealand delegation at the UN.[9] When he took the microphone, Robert Rex had Young Vivian and Terry Chapman sitting behind him. If he sounded alright, they would tap him on the back as a signal that all was well. Rex began rather nervously, the tap on the back came and, gaining his confidence, he once again gave one of his memorable speeches.[10]

Rex thanked the UN and, in particular, the Special Committee for the degree of attention they 'had focused on so few a people, and so small a country'. He explained the background to Niue's relationship with New Zealand, referring back to 1900 when the people of Niue 'had voluntarily given up their independence to become part of New Zealand'. Under New Zealand rule, foreigners had been prohibited from settling in Niue and indigenous land rights had been safeguarded. Following the Declaration on Colonialism in 1960, New Zealand had sought a new solution to the relationship, and many Niueans had been surprised, even mystified. They were quite happy with the way things were. Rex explained a key reason for this. 'For centuries, Niue existed as several hostile moieties, so they had no tradition of nationalism.' Many modern-day Niueans greatly disliked the idea of some of their own people presiding over them, preferring what they believed to be the impartial rule of New Zealand administration.

When Niue rejected the timetable for self-government by 1965 because it was prepared to accept the concept in principle only, with no attached timeline, 'it was, no more and no less, an act of self-determination'. Now, Niue was prepared to accept self-government in free association with New Zealand by late 1974. Such a solution, guaranteeing New Zealand citizenship while at the same time giving Niue unrestricted constitutional freedom to control and direct their own government, was what Rex described as 'an unusual solution', but a tiny country such as Niue had 'peculiar circumstances which require special solutions'. Rex concluded his address by thanking the United Nations, and he was loudly and warmly applauded. It was, he said, 'one of the greatest moments of my life'.[11]

Robert Rex, behind the first row of officials, with Young Vivian on the left and Alison Stokes along to the right, prepares to address the Special Committee on Decolonisation at the United Nations in November 1973. Behind Vivian is Ambassador Salim, who had led the UN mission to Niue the year before. In front, the New Zealand permanent representative at the UN, Malcolm Templeton, speaks on the issue of self-government for Niue; he was followed by Robert Rex, who gave one of his memorable speeches and afterwards said it was 'one of the greatest moments' of his life.

Courtesy Tony Johns, Wellington, New Zealand

Rex may have been warmly received at the UN, but his reception at Niuean meetings in New Zealand was not always such smooth sailing. There was a body of opinion, especially in Auckland, that felt self-government would lead to changes in the Niue–New Zealand relationship, if not immediately then certainly in the future. On occasions when Rex addressed meetings he was met with loud opposition, and he received threatening letters from Niueans in Auckland.[12] An article in the *Auckland Star* by the journalist Noel Holmes, placed prominently on the editorial page, suggested that self-government amounted, for all practical purposes, to independence, which would be 'plain idiotic' for an island the size of Niue that was losing population at such an alarming rate. Holmes believed that integration with New Zealand was the only viable option. At the end of the article he attached a footnote, printed in bold type:

Footnote addressed to Niueans in Auckland: Clip this article and send it to your relations in Niue. Tell them they can have integration if they want it. Tell them they will not lose their land. Tell them to demand a vote before anything is done. Tell them the truth.[13]

The article was indeed sent to Niue and, according to the resident commissioner's monthly report, it 'led to a lot of talk on the island'. Later in the year the article was again mentioned in the monthly report as 'it had led to increasing discussion about integration'. In the light of this the resident commissioner felt that the referendum should 'be held sooner than mid-1974'.[14]

There were others who felt that integration, which had been ruled out by Minister Götz in 1962, might have some merits, given the outflow in population over the succeeding decade. Even Jock McEwen considered the idea in a confidential letter to Selwyn Wilson in 1972. Stressing the importance of safeguarding the secrecy of this letter as it presented a view 'which may not be acceptable to either the UN or the Niueans', McEwen mused:

A type of integration with New Zealand should not be entirely ruled out, particularly in view of your falling population. This does not preclude the possibility of a large measure of local government being retained by the Niueans. Integration and a fair degree of autonomy are by no means incompatible.[15]

At all public meetings on the island, integration was the other option discussed. But the official New Zealand view – and the view adopted by the Niue Assembly – was that self-government was the desired goal; and by the beginning of 1974 there was increasing activity as Niue moved toward self-governing status later in the year.

In March Robert Rex was invited to attend the South Pacific Forum meeting in Rarotonga as an observer – a precursor to Niue becoming a Forum member following self-government. He once again met many of his friends from around the Pacific, and at the conclusion of the meeting he accompanied Prime Minister Kirk back to Niue for an official visit, the first by a New Zealand prime minister since Fraser's brief visit in 1945. Rex officially handed Kirk a resolution that the Assembly had passed earlier in the month. It asked the government of New Zealand to draft for Niue a constitution for self-government, and it suggested August as the date for the draft constitution to be put to the people of Niue in a referendum.

In addressing the New Zealand prime minister at a special meeting of the Niue Assembly, Rex spoke of 'the sorrows, the hardships, the achievements, and triumphs during the long years of association between Niue and New Zealand'.[16] He took the

After the Pacific Forum in Rarotonga in March 1974, Prime Minister Norman Kirk made a visit to Niue. It was only the second time since Premier Seddon's visit in 1900 that a New Zealand prime minister had set foot on Niue soil. He is walking through the main street of Alofi with Resident Commissioner Roberts. 'Death of a Prime Minister, Norman Kirk', Special newspaper supplement issued by INL Print Ltd, 9 September 1974, Author's collection

opportunity to stress that the final decision on the future of Niue must be decided by those 'who have chosen to stay on Niue. It is the prerogative of my people who have decided not to forsake their most precious heritage … *Nukututaha*.'[17] Kirk was warm in his praise for the way the Niue people had gone about the process of political change, and he promised ongoing support. If the island chose self-government, he joked, there would need to be a big party and he would be at it.

In New Zealand the new Niue Constitution was drawn up and submitted to Parliament. The Parliamentary Select Committee on Island Affairs, chaired by Koro Wetere, accepted written and oral submissions on the proposed changes for Niue. Individual Niueans and Niuean groups in New Zealand prepared submissions and a petition, all opposed to self-government. When they appeared before the select committee, their views were reported in the press under headings such as 'Islander advocates full integration', 'Niue should be part of New Zealand' and 'Integrated Niue more favoured'.[18] A delegation from Niue consisting of Rex, Vivian and Lui also appeared before the select committee and presented the case in favour of self-government.

In August a team of three from the select committee visited Niue to assure themselves that the changes were well understood and acceptable to the majority. The proposed constitution had been translated into Niuean and distributed to every household on the island. The select committee team commented on how lively and open the village meetings had been. Although there was some discussion about integration, the overwhelming view was in support of the constitutional proposals.[19] The team paid particular attention to the proposal that the number of assemblymen be increased from 14 to 20; the extra six seats were to be decided by the whole island, on the basis of a common roll. This suggestion had come from Quentin-Baxter as a way of countering the parochial interests of the village representatives.[20] The New Zealand visitors were satisfied the majority of Niueans were comfortable with this idea, and the team left the island confident the New Zealand government was carrying out the wishes of the people.

By the end of August the constitution was ready to be put to the people in a referendum, to be held on 3 September. A team arrived from the UN to observe the referendum that constituted Niue's act of self-determination.[21] Rex later recalled that critical night as the referendum results were broadcast and tension mounted. The first count was 162 in favour of self-government, 148 against. It seemed very close, but with each announcement the gap widened. The final result was 887 in favour, 469 against, with 28 informal votes. There were around 200 who did not exercise their right to vote. Self-government had been accepted. Many people, including Jock McEwen, came to the Rex home in Alofi South to celebrate far into the night.[22] Congratulatory messages began arriving from around the Pacific region. The nineteenth of October was chosen as the day self-government would be granted: this was the day in 1900 when Lord Ranfurly had agreed with King Togia on the annexation of Niue to the British Empire and the Union Jack had been unfurled in Alofi.

News of the referendum on Niue was overshadowed in New Zealand by the sudden death of Norman Kirk on 31 August. He had been prime minister for not quite two years, but in that time he had established himself as a man of great mana and his death was universally mourned, not least in the Pacific, where he was very highly regarded. He would not be at the party in Niue and indeed the party would be subdued because of his absence.

Officials in New Zealand tried to suggest that 19 October might not suit them for a self-government celebration, and that maybe it could be pushed out to November or December. But in Niue they had done their history homework. Lord Ranfurly had issued the proclamation for annexation on 19 October. The proclamation

A second team from the United Nations arrived in Niue to observe the referendum on 3 September 1974. They met with the Executive Committee to discuss the process, then observed the actual voting as Niueans exercised their right to self-determination. Robert Rex is partly obscured but the other three executive members – Young Vivian, Enetama and Frank Lui – are seen in discussion with UN team members. Archives New Zealand, Department of Internal Affairs Te Tari Taiwhenua, ABHS W5310/29

for self-government would also be read on that date. The Assembly asked if a member of the royal family might be able to attend the ceremony, but this was out of the question at such short notice. In Wellington, when it was understood that the Niueans were immovable on the date, arrangements were made to get people there in time. The governor-general, Sir Denis Blundell, would read the proclamation of Niue self-government, and the new Labour prime minister, Bill Rowling, would give an address.

The nineteenth of October 1974 was a Saturday. HMNZS *Tui* arrived a few days before and lay off the coast in Alofi Bay. The now regular Polynesian Airlines flight arrived on Friday afternoon with Pacific leaders from Tonga, Western Samoa and Fiji. This was followed by the arrival of a Ministry of Transport Fokker Friendship carrying the governor-general and party, the prime minister and party, and the prime minister of the Cook Islands, Albert Henry and his wife. An RNZAF Hercules followed with other guests from New Zealand: Island Affairs officials, members of Parliament, former resident commissioners, diplomatic representatives from around the Pacific and from Britain, representatives of the New Zealand Niue community and media representatives. A dance was held on the Alofi wharf on Friday evening and festivities went late into the night, but everyone was gathered in front of the Administration building in Alofi the next morning for the official ceremony.

There was a guard of honour formed by the men of the *Tui*. The governor-general, in full regalia, read the Proclamation of Self-Government, and the New Zealand prime minister and the premier-elect of Niue both gave speeches. Mr Rowling announced that the New Zealand government would build a new parliament, a Fale Fono, for Niue. Rex announced that the Niue government would gift the Residency and the land it was built on at Tapeu to New Zealand. The official ceremony was short and lacked the Kirk touch: Rowling was still feeling his way as prime minister; he was not a natural 'Pacific man'; and he was suffering from a throat infection that threatened to prevent him speaking at all. But it was in many ways a ceremony that would have been familiar to Governor Ranfurly in 1900.

The official self-government ceremony took place in Niue on 19 October 1974, 74 years to the day after Lord Ranfurly had annexed the island to the British Empire. Governor-General Sir Denis Blundell and Lady Blundell, accompanied by the last resident commissioner, Clifford Roberts, arrive for the formal ceremony in Alofi. *Tohi Tala Niue*, 25 October 1974, 12, Alexander Turnbull Library, Wellington, New Zealand

The gift from the New Zealand government to the people of Niue at the time of self-government was a new Fale Fono, parliament building. The government changed in New Zealand in 1976 but the new National government honoured the promise. Prime Minister Robert Muldoon visited Niue in 1977 to unveil the foundation board, here draped in both the New Zealand and the Niuean flags.

Archives New Zealand, Department of Internal Affairs Te Tari Taiwhenua, AAXO 8029 W4742/25

The official party retired to the Residency to change. The focus of activities moved to the Alofi green and the atmosphere relaxed into Niue style. A huge galue, a feast prepared for a special occasion, was arranged on trestle tables on the green and also hung on the traditional wooden fence erected for the purpose. A reporter covering the event noted that the tables sagged under the weight of taro, chicken, pigs, fish, coconuts and other island delicacies, and a wall of food faced the official party. 'Divided into sections for different villages, the *galue* represented the competitions between the villages to provide the most food. Whole pigs, wrapped in leaves, hung alongside bunches of bananas and tuna, mackerel, barracuda and sole marlin.'[23] Kahoa of frangipani had been made for everyone, songs were composed for the occasion, and all afternoon there was feasting and dancing as each village entertained the invited guests. Celebrations moved to the partially completed Niue Hotel in the evening – and the next morning the New Zealand visitors flew out. Niue Island, lying alone in the Pacific Ocean, was self-governing.

Robert (later Sir Robert) Richmond Rex, first premier of Niue from October 1974 until his death in December 1992 at the age of 83. Behind him is the coastline of his beloved island and the bay where he loved to fish. External Aid Division, Ministry of Foreign Affairs, Archives New Zealand, Department of Internal Affairs Te Tari Taiwhenua, AAEG 7398 W4835/3

The official ceremony and the island feasting and dancing had played out on the Alofi green, just as it had done in April 1900 when a British protectorate had been announced, and again in October 1900 when Niue had been annexed to the British Crown. When Basil Thomson sat through the protectorate ceremony, he had gazed out at the people gathered on the Alofi green and had wondered what they made of it all. He had looked beyond the people and he had seen 'the island, lying unchanged and unchangeable through the centuries'. Perhaps that was still the case in 1974. Perhaps that will still be the case a hundred years from now.

Afterword

It is 40 years now since self-government in free association with New Zealand was agreed on by the people of Niue. The relationship is still strong but the movement to New Zealand has not slowed and the population on the island is now at its lowest ebb, somewhere between 1200 and 1500 inhabitants. The hurricane houses are still there, but more and more of them have been boarded up and some have been demolished. On a weekday, when people are away at work or in the bush, there is an eerie silence in many of the villages; the crowing of roosters and the barking of dogs may be all that disturbs it. But late in the day, in that hour before the sun suddenly drops into the Pacific and night falls rapidly, there will once again be activity in the villages: the smell of coconut as people burn the garden rubbish; the sound of voices as people catch up on the day's news; the roar of motorbikes and trucks as people return home; shouting and laughter as the young ones play rugby or cricket on the village green.

There are now satellite dishes beaming in TV from other parts of the world, and the internet links Niueans with the outside world. There is a flight – sometimes two flights – a week of the Airbus A320 into Hanan International Airport from New Zealand. Niueans, now resident in New Zealand and Australia, return home for family reunions or village celebrations, and tourists arrive to explore a little-known island. Plane day is still an important occasion for people from all the villages and is often the biggest gathering of the week.

Life still revolves around the family, the village and the church. The Ekalesia Niue is still central to island life. The Niue government is still the main employer; and when people finish work in the schools, the hospital, the government offices, they still head to the bush to tend their gardens. They still fish from their vaka, shoot the prized peka and lupe and hunt the uga in the forests at night. They still prepare their food in the umu. They still play cricket on the village green, and when they gather to celebrate a family or village event they still share food in the customary way. There is still intense village pride and rivalry.

And life is still hard on Niue. Cyclones still wreak havoc and droughts disrupt the production of food. Although there is now a local supermarket, it too can be short of supplies because of disruptions to shipping. Supplies still have to be brought in to the wharf by lighter from vessels lying out in the bay. And boat day is still worth coming to town for.

Basil Thomson was right: in the end the island is unchanged and unchangeable. James Cook's account of the natural features he saw in 1774 is still accurate today. In the nineteenth century George and Frank Lawes wrote of the people, and their descriptions still resonate today. S. Percy Smith recorded his observations as he travelled around the island in 1901 and it still sounds familiar. Much has changed in the last 200 years, but there is much that is constant. It will be the same in another 100 years. And there will still be Niueans living there, adopting and adapting new ways but still living mahani motu, mahani Niue, the Niuean way.

Glossary

aitu	ghost, spirit
fagai	offering, gift
fiafia	function, entertainment
Fono	council
fono	ban
futi hulahula	plantain banana with reddish-orange flesh
galue	feast for a special occasion
hegakula	*Vini australis*, blue-crowned lory
hiapo	tapa cloth
iki	chief
kafika	*Syzygium inophylloides*, a very strong native timber
kahoa	lei
katoua	a cleaving club
lupe	*Ducula pacifica*, Pacific pigeon
mailē	*Alyxia stellata*, a shrub
magafaoa	extended family
maka	throwing stone
makatea	coral limestone
malē	central meeting space
Mē	annual gathering
ovava	*Ficus prolixa*, Niuean banyan
Pālagi	European
peka	*Pteropus sp.*, flying fox, fruitbat
patu	elder
patuiki	chief of chiefs
puga	coral rock; burnt lime (for building)
takai	journey around the island
telie	*Terminalia catappa*, coastal tree

tī	a small tree, any variety of *Cordyline*
Tiakono	a council of church elders
tīputa	poncho-like garment
ufilei	wild yam
uga	coconut crab
umu	earth oven
umu kai	food prepared in earth oven
umutī	special oven for cooking roots of tī
vaka	canoe; vessel
vaka lotu	mission vessel
vakatāvilivili	helicopter

Historical names for Pacific Islands

Friendly Islands	Tonga
Gilbert Islands	Kiribati
Lagoon Islands	Tuvalu
Navigator Islands	Samoa
New Hebrides	Vanuatu
Sandwich Islands	Hawai'i
Savage Island	Niue
Society Islands	French Polynesia
Sunday Island	Raoul Island
Union Islands	Tokelau

Notes

Abbreviations

AJHR	Appendices to the Journals of the House of Representatives, New Zealand
ANZ	Archives New Zealand
ATL	Alexander Turnbull Library, Wellington, New Zealand
AWMM	Auckland War Memorial Museum, New Zealand
IT	Islands Territories
LMS	London Missionary Society
NZPD	New Zealand Parliamentary Debates
PMB	Pacific Manuscripts Bureau, Canberra, Australia
TN	Tāoga Niue, Niue Museum, Archives and Cultural Centre, Alofi, Niue
WPHC	Western Pacific High Commission

Introduction

1 See Terry Chapman, *Niue: A history of the island*, Institute of Pacific Studies and Government of Niue, Suva, 1982 for more details on precontact history, written by Niuean experts.

2 See Vincent O'Malley, *The Meeting Place: Maori and Pakeha encounters, 1642–1840*, Auckland University Press, Auckland, 2012.

Part A. Early Contacts

Chapter 1. First encounters

1 J.C. Beaglehole (ed.), *The Journals of Captain James Cook*, vol. II, *The Voyage of the Resolution and Adventure 1772–1775*, Hakluyt Society & Cambridge University Press, Cambridge, 1961, 432.

2 Ibid., 432–33.

3 Michael Hoare (ed.), *The Resolution Journal of Johann Reinhold Forster 1772–1775*, vol. III, Hakluyt Society, London, 1982, 535.

4 Georg Forster, *A Voyage Round the World in His Britannic Majesty's Sloop, Resolution, commanded by Captain James Cook*, 1777, London, 163.

5 Ibid., 163.

6 Beaglehole (ed.), *Journals of Captain James Cook*, vol. II, 435.

7 Anders Sparrman, *Voyage Round the World with Captain James Cook in the H.M.S. Resolution*, Robert Hales, London, 1953, 129.

8 Ibid.

9 Forster, *Voyage Round the World*, 163.

10 Hoare (ed.), *Resolution Journal of J.R. Forster*, vol. III, 539.

11 Beaglehole (ed.), *Journals of Captain James Cook*, vol. II, 435.

12 Hoare (ed.), *Resolution Journal of J.R. Forster*, vol. III, 537.

13 Forster, *Voyage Round the World*, 164.
14 Sparrman, *Voyage Round the World*, 129.
15 Forster, *Voyage Round the World*, 165.
16 Quoted by Beaglehole in footnotes of *The Journals of Captain James Cook*, vol. II, 435.
17 John Marra, *Journal of the Resolution's Voyage in 1772, 1773, 1774, & 1775*, F. Newbery, London, 1775, 249.
18 Hoare (ed.), *Resolution Journal of J.R. Forster*, vol. III, 537.
19 Forster, *Voyage Round the World*, 165.
20 Beaglehole (ed.), *Journals of Captain James Cook*, vol. II, 436.
21 Forster, *Voyage Round the World*, 165.
22 Information from Museum of New Zealand Te Papa Tongarewa. So far 11 of these medals have been found in New Zealand. Note the *Resolution* was accompanied by the *Adventure* on this voyage but the two ships became separated in a fierce storm off the east coast of New Zealand in late 1773 and the *Adventure* returned home.
23 Beaglehole (ed.), *Journals of Captain James Cook*, vol. II, 434.
24 Sparrman, *Voyage Round the World*, 130.
25 Beaglehole (ed.), *Journals of Captain James Cook*, vol. II, 437.
26 Ibid., 435.
27 Marra, *Journal of the Resolution's Voyage*, 250.
28 John Elliot & Richard Pickersgill, *Captain Cook's Second Voyage: The journals of Lieutenants Elliott and Pickersgill*, ed. Christine Holmes, Caliban Books, London, 1984, 31.
29 Forster, *Voyage Round the World*, 166–67.
30 Marra, *Journal of the Resolution's Voyage*, 250.
31 See Wolfgang Sperlich (ed.), *Tohi Vagahau Niue: Niue Language Dictionary*, Government of Niue & University of Hawai'i, Honolulu, 1997, 91, under entry for 'Futi hulahula'.
32 Hoare (ed.), *Resolution Journal of J.R. Forster*, vol. III, 538.
33 See Edwin M. Loeb, *History and Traditions of Niue*, Bishop Museum, Honolulu, 1926, 189. The disappearance of the constellation Pleiades over the horizon marked the season of scarcity. Loeb records a Niuean song relating to this.
34 Forster, *Voyage Round the World*, 167.
35 Beaglehole (ed.), *Journals of Captain Cook*, vol. II, 438.
36 Marra, *Journal of the Resolution's Voyage*, 251.
37 Beaglehole (ed.), *Journals of Captain Cook*, vol. II, 514–15.
38 Quoted from Cook Journals vol. I in Nicholas Thomas, *Discoveries: The voyages of Captain Cook*, Allen Lane, London, 2003, 241.

CHAPTER 2. WHALERS

1 J.N. Reynolds, Report to U.S. Congress. September 1828 in *Documents of the Congress of the United States March 1831–June 1836*, vol. IV, *Naval Affairs*, Gale's & Seaton, Washington, 1861.
2 Ship *James Maury*, August 1843, PMB 811.
3 *Sydney Gazette and NSW Advertiser*, Friday 31 Oct. 1828.
4 John Williams, *A Narrative of Missionary Enterprises in the South Sea Islands*, John Snow, London, 1838, 78.
5 John E. Erskine, *Journal of a Cruise among the Islands of the Western Pacific*, John Murray, London, 1853.

6 Ship *Navy*, Dec. 1869, PMB 690.
7 PMB 884; PMB 259; PMB 578.
8 'A Visit to Savage Island', *Boston Daily Advertiser*, 22 Aug. 1840.
9 See Joan Druett, *In the Wake of Madness*, Harper Collins, Auckland, 2003.
10 The survival and preservation of approximately 30 per cent of the New England whaling logbooks provides a rich source of material on whaling activities. Those relating to the Pacific have been microfilmed by PMB and all copies used in this work are available at the Alexander Turnbull Library, Wellington, New Zealand.
11 Ship *William Hamilton*, PMB 726.
12 Ship *Richard Mitchell*, PMB 889.
13 Ship *Newark*, PMB 837.
14 Ship *Neptune*, PMB 689.
15 Ship *James Maury*, PMB 811.
16 Ship *Moctezuma*, log written by Mrs Betsey Tower, wife of master, PMB 302.
17 Ship *Navy*, PMB 814.
18 Ship *Marengo*, PMB 788.
19 Ship *Spartan*, PMB 386.
20 Ship *Oliver Crocker*, PMB 815.
21 Ship *Daniel Wood*, PMB 243.
22 Ship *Napoleon*, PMB 254.
23 Ship *Benjamin Rush*, Around Niue 11 Nov.–31 Dec. 1838 and again in April and August 1839, PMB 216.
24 George Turner, *Nineteen Years in Polynesia: Missionary life, travels and researches in the islands of the Pacific*, John Snow, London, 1861, 467.
25 *Boston Daily Advertiser*, 22 Aug. 1840.
26 Edwin M. Loeb, *History and Traditions of Niue*, Bishop Museum, Honolulu, 1926, 96.
27 Wolfgang Sperlich (ed.), *Tohi Vagahau Niue: Niue Language Dictionary*, Government of Niue & University of Hawai'i, Honolulu, 1997, 200.
28 R. Gerard Ward (ed.), *American Activities in the Central Pacific 1790–1870*, vol. 6, Gregg Press, Ridgewood NJ, 1967, 170–75.
29 Thomas Hood, *Notes of a Cruise in HMS Fawn in the Western Pacific in the Year 1862*, Edmonston & Douglas, Edinburgh, 1863. Hood recounts this story although it is not accurately dated.
30 W.G. Lawes, Journal, 20 May 1863. AU microfilm 2111.
31 *Southland Times*, 16 Dec. 1863; see also *The Mercury*, Hobart, 3 Dec 1863.

CHAPTER 3. MISSIONARIES

1 Niel Gunson, *Messengers of Grace: Evangelical missionaries in the South Seas, 1797–1860*, Oxford University Press, Melbourne, 1978, 344 for individual missionary details.
2 John Williams & Charles Barff, South Seas, 24 May–Sept. 1830, 10. LMS Journals ATL Micro-MS-Coll-02-005. Wherever possible, journals have been used rather than later published works as the latter were often subject to considerable embellishment. The journals have been microfilmed as part of the Australian Joint Copying Project (AJCP).
3 Ibid., 10.

4 Ibid., 10–11.
5 Ibid., 11.
6 Ibid., 11. (Page numbers for Williams' journal refer to typewritten copy; original is in Mitchell Library, Sydney.)
7 John Williams, 'Rarotonga to Navigators on *Olive Branch* 1832–1833', LMS Journals, ATL Micro-MS-Coll-02-005.
8 They were said to have brought the pawpaw from Ra'iatea back to Niue. See S. Percy Smith, *Niue: The island and its people*, Institute of Pacific Studies, Suva, Fiji, 1983, 16.
9 A.W. Murray, 'Pago Pago to Savage Island June 24–July 12 1840', LMS Journals, ATL Micro-MS-Coll-02-007.
10 Ibid.
11 Ibid.
12 Ibid.
13 'Christian missions Savage Island', *Sydney Morning Herald*, 27 Aug. 1853.
14 A.W. Murray, *Missions of Western Polynesia*, John Snow, London, 1863, 361.
15 *Juvenile Missionary Magazine*, 1 Mar. 1853, 64.
16 Murray, *Missions of Western Polynesia*, 361.
17 Described as a coarse cloth made from the bark of the banyan tree and worn as a loincloth.
18 R.G. & M. Crocombe, *The Works of Ta'unga: Records of a Polynesian traveller in the South Seas 1833–1896*, ANU Press, Canberra, Australia, 1968.
19 Ibid.
20 'Christian missions Savage Island', *Sydney Morning Herald*, 27 Aug. 1853.
21 Quoted in Joseph King, *W.G. Lawes of Savage Island and New Guinea*, Religious Tract Society, London, 1909, 19–20.
22 *Sydney Morning Herald*, 27 Aug. 1853.
23 George Turner, *Nineteen Years in Polynesia*, John Snow, London, 1861, 465–66.
24 Ibid., 467.
25 Fifita Talagi, 'Early European contacts', in Terry Chapman (ed.), *Niue: A history of the island*, Institute of Pacific Studies & Government of Niue, Suva, Fiji, 1982, 115.
26 There is a memorial to Peniamina at Makefu, and Peniamina's Day, marking his arrival with the gospel on Niue, is an annual holiday in late October.
27 A.W. Murray & J.P. Sunderland, 29 Apr.–9 July 1852, 37, LMS Journals, ATL Micro-MS-Coll-02-008.
28 Charles Hardie, Samoa, 26 Sept.–24 Nov. 1854, LMS Journals, ATL Micro-MS-Coll-02-008.
29 Ibid.
30 Stallworthy & Gill, 21 May–22 Aug. 1858, LMS Journals, ATL Micro-MS-Coll-02-008.
31 Turner, *Nineteen Years in Polynesia*, 518.
32 See Michael Trotter, 'Niue Island Archaeological Survey', Canterbury Museum, Christchurch, 1979.
33 Edwin M. Loeb, *History and Traditions of Niue*, Bishop Museum, Honolulu, 1926, 90.
34 See John Pule & Nicholas Thomas, *Hiapo Past and Present in Niuean Barkcloth*, Otago University Press, Dunedin, New Zealand, 2005, 62.
35 W.G. Lawes to Rev. Tidman, 10 Nov. 1862. LMS South Seas Letters ATL Micro-MS-Coll-02-043.

36 Turner, *Nineteen Years in Polynesia*, 519.

37 Thomas Hood, *Notes of a Cruise in HMS Fawn in the Western Pacific in the Year 1862*, Edmonston & Douglas, Edinburgh, 1863.

38 Harbutt & Drummond, 7 July–7 Aug.1857, LMS Journals, ATL Micro-MS-Coll-02-008.

39 Ibid.

40 Ibid.

41 See Stallworthy & Gill, 21 May–22 Aug. 1858, LMS Journal, ATL Micro-MS-Coll-02-008.

42 Turner, *Nineteen Years in Polynesia*, 518.

CHAPTER 4. HER BRITANNIC MAJESTY'S SHIPS

1 John E. Erskine, *Journal of a Cruise among the Islands of the Western Pacific*, John Murray, London, 1853, ch. 1.

2 Ibid., 3–4.

3 Ibid., 26–27.

4 Ibid., 27–28.

5 Rod Hay & Ralph Powlesland, *Guide to the Birds of Niue*, SPREP, Apia, Samoa, 1998, 2. See also Wolfgang Sperlich (ed.), *Tohi Vagahau Niue: Niue Language Dictionary*, Government of Niue & University of Hawai'i, Honolulu, 1997, 113.

6 Erskine, *Journal of a Cruise*, 31.

7 Ibid., 3.

8 The reef was referred to as Nicholson's Reef, but this is in fact another name for Minerva, much further to the southwest. The wreck occurred on Beveridge Reef, 240 km to the southeast of Niue, and the name Beveridge is used in some later accounts. See *Lyttelton Times*, 26 Feb. 1853.

9 *Sydney Morning Herald*, 10 Aug. 1852.

10 Ibid. The eventual arrival of these four in Sydney was reported in the *Sydney Morning Herald*, 25 Dec. 1852.

11 *Lyttelton Times*, 26 Feb. 1853

12 Ibid. The existence of gold and silver English coins in the possession of Niueans was also reported to the captain of the *Calliope* as he passed through the Friendly Islands en route to Niue.

13 Ibid.

14 Murray & Sunderland, April–July 1852, LMS Journals, ATL Micro-MS-Coll-02-008, 40.

15 Murray & Sunderland, 20 June 1853–7 Jan. 1854, 37.

16 Ibid., 37–38.

17 *Sydney Morning Herald*, 25 Dec. 1852.

18 *Colonial Times* (Hobart), 17 June 1854, reprint of Carwithen's letter; *Sydney Morning Herald*, 13 June 1854 for Mills' letter.

19 *Sydney Morning Herald*, 13 June 1854.

20 *Empire* (Sydney), 20 June 1854.

21 Ibid.

22 Charles Hardie, 26 Sept.–24 Nov. 1854, LMS Journals, ATL Micro-MS-Coll-02-008, 26.

23 Thomas Hood, *Notes of a Cruise in HMS* Fawn *in the Western Pacific in the Year 1862*, Edmonston & Douglas, Edinburgh, 1863.

24 Ibid., 11. The mat would be hiapo. Dracaena is the tī plant, common throughout the island.

25 Ibid., 12.
26 The Jew's harp is a very small metal musical instrument, placed between the lips and plucked. Niueans returning from working on whaling vessels had introduced them to Niue.
27 Hood, *Notes of a Cruise in HMS* Fawn, 15.
28 Ibid., 25–26.

Part B. Empire

Chapter 5. European settlement

1 G. Lawes to Rev. Cousins, 26 Aug. 1868, Lawes Letterbook, AU microfilm 2111.
2 The American Seventh-day Adventist missionary vessel, the *Pitcairn*, stopped at Niue for one week in 1893 but no attempt was made to leave a missionary on the island. See *Auckland Star*, 28 Aug. 1893.
3 Thomas Hood, *Notes of a Cruise in HMS* Fawn *in the Western Pacific in the Year 1862*, Edmonston & Douglas, Edinburgh, 1863, 15–16.
4 George Lawes, 12 Jan. 1863, Lawes Journal, AU microfilm 2111.
5 Lawes to Rev. Dr Mullins, 6 July 1869, Lawes Journal, AU microfilm 2111.
6 Ibid., Lawes to Rev. Sunderland, 8 July 1869, Lawes Journal, AU microfilm 2111.
7 Hood, *Notes of a Cruise in HMS* Fawn, 26.
8 Joseph King, *W.G. Lawes of Savage Island and New Guinea*, Religious Tract Society, London, 1909, 37–38.
9 George Lawes, 30 Jan. 1863, Lawes Journal, AU microfilm 2111. Fanny had recently given birth to their second son, Frank.
10 W.G. Lawes to sister Joye, 12 July 1868, Lawes letterbook, AU microfilm 2111. Frank Lawes' wife Sarah is referred to as Ally in letters. She had recently given birth to their first son, Alfred. George and Fanny now had three sons, Harry (William), Farani (Frank) and Freddy (George).
11 W.G. Lawes to Rev. Dr Tidman, 20 Oct. 1863, LMS South Sea Letters, ATL Micro-MS-Coll-02-043.
12 George Lawes, 30 Jan. 1863, Lawes Journal, AU microfilm 2111. This and the list of food given relate to a visit to Tavahihi.
13 Ibid., 1 Aug. 1863.
14 At the close of 1884 the 11 stations were Alofi, Avatele, Fatiau, Hakupu, Liku, Makefu, Mutalau, Tamahatokula, Tamakautoga, Tamalagau (Lakepa) and Uhomotu (Tuapa). See John Whitehouse, 'A history of Niue to 1894', manuscript, PMB 149.
15 Lawes to Mullins, 1 Feb. 1870, LMS South Sea Letters, ATL Micro-MS-Coll-02-047.
16 Information on Sionepaea and Manapule from personal communication with Justin Kamupala, Niue, July 2012.
17 Solomona died on Futuna in 1876. His wife and children were brought back to Niue that year, along with Iona.
18 The first teacher, Milani, was sent to Apia in 1872.
19 G. Lawes to Redfern, LMS, 10 Apr. 1868, Lawes Letterbook, AU microfilm 2111.
20 Ibid.
21 Ibid.
22 Ibid.

23 Whitehouse, 'A history of Niue to 1894', 149.
24 Ibid. There was a particularly large contribution in 1873, totalling £877.11.8.
25 Ibid.
26 Ibid.
27 Basil Thomson, *Savage Island: An account of a sojourn in Niue and Tonga*, John Murray, London, 1902, 111.
28 Whitehouse, 'A history of Niue to 1894', 149. Jeremia was at Uhomotu.
29 J.H. Cullen came to Niue to replace Lawes during his furlough. He went on to Mangaia but returned to Niue in 1914 to head the LMS mission. He died on Niue in 1919 and is buried in front of the church in Alofi.
30 V.A. Barradale, *Pearls of the Pacific: Being sketches of missionary life and work in Samoa and other islands in the South Seas*, LMS, London, 1907, 188.
31 Kon-Tiki Makani, 'Ekalesia Niue: An indigenous church in the making', MTheol thesis, Pacific Theological College, Suva, Fiji, 1993. See Appendix for a list of all names.
32 Tamatoa had a young son, Pahetogia, who accompanied his father and stepmother to New Guinea. When his father died, Pahetogia was taken in and raised by George and Fanny Lawes. He became a pastor and served many years in New Guinea and Niue. Information from Rev. Tom Etuata, Wellington, New Zealand.
33 Memo by Sterndale, AJHR 1874 A-3B, 4.
34 There is evidence that the very first trader, a Samoan by the name of Lupo, attempted to set up a store in Avatele in 1865, but the venture failed. However Lupo remained on Niue until his death in 1904. See TN A641 17/6/1 Niue Traders General 1912–1959.
35 William W. Bolton, 'Chronicles of Savage Island, vol. IV', manuscript, Mitchell Library, Sydney, reel 1145, AU microfilm 87-212, 108.
36 Ibid.
37 E.O. Nicholas to F.E. Lawes, 6 Jan. 1881, LMS Records relating to Niue Island 1861–1910, ATL Micro-MS-0471.
38 W.G. Lawes to Rev. Tidman, 8 Oct. 1866, LMS South Sea letters, ATL Micro-MS-Coll-02-045.
39 Ibid.
40 F.E. Lawes to Rev. Mullins, 24 June 1870, LMS South Sea Letters, ATL Micro-MS-Coll-02-047.
41 The plant found to grow best in island conditions was *Gossypium brasiliense*, kidney or sea-island cotton, sometimes known as kapok; its local name is vavae. It is a small tree, still found in most villages.
42 Robert Head's mother came from the Isle of Wight in the south of England, and so did Sarah Lawes.
43 In April 1869 Hayes' agent called at Niue. He collected all the cotton and fungus and left without paying Head his wages or commission. See TN A641 17/6/1 Niue Traders General 1912–1959.
44 Ibid. Head dealt with W. McArthur & Co. Ltd and then with Vines, Utting & Perston.
45 All letters are in ATL Micro-MS-Coll-02-045 LMS South Sea Letters.
46 Lawes to Rev. Dr Tidman, Foreign Secretary, LMS, London, 20 Jan. 1867.
47 Davies to Tidman, 9 Feb. 1867.
48 Chalmers to Tidman, 4 Feb. 1867.
49 Williams to LMS, 8 Feb. 1867.
50 Lawes to Tidman, 13 Apr. 1867.

51 E.O. Nicholas to Frank Lawes, 18 Nov. 1881, LMS Records relating to Niue Island 1861–1910, ATL Micro-MS-0471. Lawes visited the Nicholas family when he was on furlough in England, and several Nicholas children for the next two generations have Lawes as a middle name.
52 Captain William Ross papers, Hocken Library Misc-MS-1043, 135. The May 1889 hurricane had also struck the Samoan Islands, causing devastation in Apia harbour. See *Te Aroha News*, 1 June 1889, 3.
53 Edwin Nicholas and his eldest son George both had children by Niuean women. Llewellyn (Louis) Nicholas married a Niuean woman from Avatele and had four children. See Nicholas family on RootsWeb.com.

CHAPTER 6. THE LABOUR TRADE

1 George Lawes Journal, AU microfilm 2111. The original diary is in the Mitchell Library, Sydney, Australia. Only a small portion remains, mainly covering the visits by the Peruvian slavers in 1863.
2 Ibid. Lawes is quoting from Jeremiah 31:15.
3 H.E. Maude, *Slavers in Paradise: The Peruvian labour trade in Polynesia, 1862–1864*, ANU Press, Canberra, Australia, 1981, 56.
4 Ibid.
5 Lawes quoted in Gill to LMS, 21 Mar. 1863, LMS South Sea Letters, ATL Micro-MS-Coll-02-043.
6 George Lawes, 19 Feb. 1863, Lawes Journal, AU microfilm 2111.
7 Ibid., 9 Mar. 1863.
8 Ibid., 10 Mar. 1863.
9 Ibid., 25 Apr. 1863. Maude in *Slavers in Paradise* gives the spelling as *Adelante* and does not record it calling at Niue, but Lawes gives a lengthy account of the visit.
10 James Cowan, 'The story of Taole the sailor', in *Suwarrow Gold and Other Stories of the Great South Seas*, Jonathan Cape, London, 1936, 49–59.
11 George Lawes, 4 June 1863, Lawes Journal, AU microfilm 2111.
12 G. Lawes to Rev. Sunderland, 22 May 1868, Lawes Letterbook, AU microfilm 2111.
13 G. Lawes to Rev. Cousins, 26 Aug. 1868, Lawes Letterbook, AU microfilm 2111.
14 John Whitehouse, 'A history of Niue to 1894', manuscript, PMB 149.
15 Ibid.
16 Ibid.
17 Basil Thomson, *Savage Island: An account of a sojourn in Niue and Tonga*, John Murray, London, 1902, 82.
18 Some died in Tahiti, some moved on to Queensland or Samoa. A small group, including the daughter of King Togia, were the only ones to return.
19 Quoted in Basil Lubbock, *Bully Hayes: South Sea pirate*, Martin Hopkinson, London, 1931, 147. Miller was the British consul in Tahiti.
20 G. Lawes to Rev. Sunderland, 22 May 1868, Lawes Letterbook, AU microfilm 2111.
21 This company, facing insolvency in 1878, reconstituted its profitable Samoan branch into a new company, the Deutsche Handels und Plantagen Gesellschaft der Sudsee-Inseln zu Hamburg, commonly known as DHPG; by the beginning of the twentieth century it was the biggest trading firm in the South Pacific. See Doug Munro & Stewart Firth, 'Samoan plantations: The

Gilbertese laborers' experience 1867–1896', in B. Lal, D. Munro & E. Beechert, *Plantation Workers, Resistance and Accommodation*, University of Hawai'i Press, Honolulu, 1993, 113.

22 For a more detailed discussion on this, see Trevor Matheson, 'Niuean Land-holdings in Western Samoa', in L. Mason & P. Hereniko (eds), *In Search of a Home*, University of the South Pacific, Suva, Fiji, 1987.

23 For more detail on the German plantations, see Munro & Firth, 'Samoan plantations'.

24 WPHC 110/1886. The names of the three stowaways appear as Arafi, Kaulu and Tafana.

25 Municipal Magistrate to Deputy High Commissioner, Apia, 18 June 1886, ANZ AEND 19678 W3800 WPHC 1W3800 5/1/1/32 Register of Imported Polynesians for use as Labourers 1877–1888.

26 It became common to ship men from Niue to Tonga before signing them on as labourers, so fewer labour contracts exist in the Niue archives. See Captain William Ross papers, Hocken Library Misc-MS-1043.

27 See Albert F. Ellis, *Adventuring in Coral Seas*, Angus & Robertson, Sydney, Australia, 1936, ch. 1 for the first settlement on Hull Island. See also *Auckland Star*, 14 July 1890, 2.

28 J.T. Arundel, Diary, 15 May 1882, Arundel Family Papers, ATL Micro-MS-Coll-08-1227-1 (PMB 1227). Lawes and Arundel met in London. In another diary entry in 1886 Arundel refers to Niue as a 'civilised and Christianised island'.

29 *Otago Daily Times*, 9 July 1892.

30 *Auckland Star*, 9 Jan. 1891.

31 Mouga to Arundel family, 7 Apr. 1887, ATL Micro-MS-Coll-08-1227-2 (PMB 1227/2).

32 She is listed as Linfala Hegafana, unmarried, 46 years old, born on Savage Island. 1881 England census.

33 Captain William Ross papers, Hocken Library Misc-MS-1043, 119.

34 This figure is calculated from average numbers of between 50 and 100 workers at a time going to Malden.

35 All information on living and working conditions on Malden has been compiled from a diary kept by the manager on Malden Island. WPHC 10 Diary of Malden Island 4 Oct 1904–16 May 1910.

36 Whitehouse, 'A history of Niue to 1894', 149. J.T. Arundel also paid for a mission teacher for Flint Island.

37 Ibid.

38 See Arundel family papers, ATL Micro-MS-Col-08-1227-2 (PMB 1227/reel 2). 'The Population of Niue' compiled by Rev. Lawes.

39 For example, Hipa of Hikutavake was said to have gone to Malden with his father as a young lad. He became cook to the European manager and his wife. See William W. Bolton, 'Chronicles of Savage Island, vol. IV 1927', manuscript, Mitchell Library, Sydney, Australia, reel 1145, AU microfilm 87-212, 96.

40 One of R.H. Head's grandchildren gave her place of birth as Hull Island, so her parents were working for J.T. Arundel at the time. ANZ IT11 Box 7 Part 2 JP McMahon-Box 1934–44.

41 See Munro & Firth, 'Samoan Plantations', 106.

42 H.C. Cornwall, AJHR 1909 A-3, 34–35.

CHAPTER 7. THE CALL FOR BRITISH PROTECTION

1 George Turner, *Nineteen Years in Polynesia: Missionary life, travels and researches in the islands of the Pacific*, John Snow, London, 1861, 522.
2 George Lawes, 19 Feb. 1863, Lawes Journal, AU microfilm 2111.
3 Ibid., 16 Mar. 1863.
4 Murray & Sunderland, 1853–54, LMS Journals, ATL Micro-MS-Col-02-008.
5 See Hafe Vilitama, 'Traditional politics', in Terry Chapman (ed.), *Niue: A history of the island*, Institute of Pacific Studies & Government of Niue, Suva, Fiji, 1982, 91–95.
6 *Journal of Commodore Goodenough during his last command as Senior Officer on the Australian Station 1873–1875*, edited by his widow, Henry S. King, London, 1876, 188–90.
7 John Whitehouse, 'A History of Niue to 1894', manuscript, PMB 149.
8 Ibid.
9 British Order in Council, 13 Aug. 1877.
10 G. Lawes to F. Lawes, 1 July 1879, LMS Records relating to Niue Island 1861–1910, ATL Micro-MS-0471.
11 Ibid. *Kaufakalataha mo Peritania* is 'to unite with Britain'. The term *patus* refers to elders.
12 Ibid.
13 WPHC Inward Correspondence 318/1887.
14 Ibid.
15 Lawes to LMS, Apia, 2 Oct. 1868, Lawes Letterbook, AU microfilm 2111.
16 Fataaiki to Sir G. Mitchell, WPHC, 3 Nov. 1887, LMS Records relating to Niue Island 1861–1910, ATL Micro-MS-0471.
17 *Morning Post*, London, 3 Oct. 1888 and 8 Oct. 1888, quoting the *North German Gazette*, Berlin.
18 Fataaiki to Sir J.B. Thurston, 12 Feb. 1895, WPHC Inward Correspondence 172/1895.
19 Fataaiki to Sir J.B. Thurston, 15 Feb. 1896, WPHC Inward Correspondence 88/1896.
20 M.F. Morris, 'The history of Niue-Fekai', MA thesis, University of Auckland, New Zealand, 1933.
21 Togia to Sir G.T.E. O'Brien, 10 Oct. 1899, WPHC Inward Correspondence 222/1899.
22 Basil Thomson, *Savage Island: An account of a sojourn in Niue and Tonga,* John Murray, London, 1902, 4.
23 Ibid., 9.
24 Ibid., 10.
25 The treaty was signed by Togia, Fataaiki (probably the son of the former patuiki), Pahumake and Tavavaitoga.
26 Thomson, *Savage Island*, 41–42.
27 Ibid., 65–66. Thomson refers to Gordon by his peerage, Lord Stanmore.
28 Ibid., 112.
29 This regulation stayed in force for many years. The positions were filled at first by the European traders, and later by Niueans.
30 Thomson, *Savage Island*, 44.

CHAPTER 8. ANNEXATION TO NEW ZEALAND

1 The name Pearse appears with several different spellings; this is the spelling he himself used in a letter of thanks to the premier for photos received after the visit. ANZ ACHW/8633/Seddon 1/13/60 Seddon Papers – Official and other correspondence relating to annexation of the Cook and Other Islands 1900.

2 Edward Tregear, *The Right Hon. R.J. Seddon's Visit to Tonga, Fiji, Savage Island and the Cook Islands, May 1900,* Government Printer, Wellington, New Zealand, 1900, 137.

3 Ibid., 142.

4 Ibid., 153.

5 Ibid., 424. Seddon's speech at Tuapa is copied in full.

6 Niel Gunson, *Messengers of Grace: Evangelical missionaries in the South Seas, 1797–1860,* Oxford University Press, Melbourne, Australia, 1978, 275.

7 Captain William Ross Papers, Hocken Library Misc-MS-1043, 115.

8 'Savage Island by a Trader's Wife, Part II', *Australian Town and Country Journal,* 3 Nov. 1894, 30.

9 E.O. Nicholas to F.E. Lawes, 18 Nov. 1881, ATL LMS Records relating to Niue Island 1861–1910 Micro-MS-0471.

10 Basil Thomson, *Savage Island: An account of a sojourn in Niue and Tonga,* John Murray, London, 1902, 26–27.

11 Ibid., 119.

12 Malcolm Ross, 'The annexation of Savage Island', *Otago Daily Times,* 12 Nov. 1900.

13 Constructed from 1881 to 1915, it halved the time needed to get from the Atlantic to the Pacific.

14 On 1 Jan. 1901, the self-governing British colonies of New South Wales, Queensland, South Australia, Tasmania, Victoria and Western Australia federated to form the Commonwealth of Australia.

15 NZPD, vol. 114, 14 Sept.–9 Oct. 1900, 387.

16 Ranfurly family papers 1896–1913, 148–49, ATL MS-Group-0756 MS Copy Micro 0734-02.

17 Ibid., 149.

18 Malcolm Ross, 'Cruise of the Mildura', *Otago Daily Times,* 12 Nov. 1900, 2.

19 Ibid.

20 Ranfurly family papers, 151. Iki who signed were Niuloa (Alofi), Sosene (Avatele), Kapagahemata (Tamakautoga), Pokihega (Tafiti), Puletagaloa (Hakupu), Tagaloailuga (Liku), Lagahetau (Tamalagau), Kautapu (Mutalau), Hipa (Tamahatokula), Ikenei (Uhomotu) and Matiu (Makefu).

21 See Charles E. Hill-Trevor, album 2. Written and photographic record of the annexation of the Cook Islands and Niue, 26, ATL PAI-f-143.

22 *Otago Daily Times,* 12 Nov. 1900.

23 Ranfurly to WPHC, 2 Nov. 1900, WPHC Inward Correspondence.

24 Sir J. Thurston to Under Secretary of State for Colonies, 26 July 1895, WPHC Archives 22/11/9.

25 F. Lawes to J.T. Arundel, 14 Nov. 1902, Arundel family papers, PMB 1227.

26 Ranfurly to Lawes, 26 Dec. 1900, LMS Records relating to Niue island 1861–1910, ATL Micro-MS-0471.

27 R.H. Head to Premier, 7 Nov. 1901, ANZ ACHW/8633/Seddon 1/13/60 Seddon Papers 1900.

28 Vines, Utting and Perston to Premier, 11 Nov. 1901, ANZ ACHW/8633/Seddon 1/13/60 Seddon Papers 1900.

29 Smith to Ranfurly, 11 Oct. 1901, AJHR 1902 A-03, 31.

30 S. Percy Smith, 18 Sept. 1901, Smith diary, AWMM MS281 (5) Box 3.

31 Ibid. Smith collected the numbers from Rev. Lawes,

32 F. Lawes to J.T. Arundel, 17 Jan. 1901, Arundel family papers, PMB 1227.

33 Smith diary, 22 Sept. 1901.

34 The young couple were Siuea and his wife Hegatogia Alesi. Information from TN.
35 All text from Smith diary, AWMM MS 281 (5) Box 3. Spelling of placenames as in diary.
36 F. Lawes to J.T. Arundel, 17 Jan. 1901, Arundel family papers, PMB 1227.
37 S. Percy Smith, Wed. 2 Oct. 1901, Smith diary, AWMM MS281 (5) Box 3.
38 Ibid., Mon. 7 Oct. 1901.
39 See AJHR 1902 A-3, 33-39, for copies of all five Acts.
40 The terms 'natives' and 'whites' have been used here, as this was the wording in the legislation.
41 S. Percy Smith, Sun. 8 Dec. 1901, Smith diary, AWMM MS 281 (5) Box 3.
42 *Auckland Star*, 2 June 1903. Reporters and photographers from several New Zealand daily newspapers travelled with the parliamentary tour.
43 AJHR 1903 A-3b, Report on the Visit of Members of the General Assembly to the Cook and Other Islands, 27.
44 James Allen in *Otago Witness*, 17 June 1903.
45 'The Island Trade', *Auckland Star*, 9 Apr. 1903, 3.

Part C. New Zealand Administration

Chapter 9. From Rhetoric to Reality

1 Quoted in letter from C.H. Mills to S.P. Smith, 21 Aug. 1903, AJHR 1904 A-03.
2 Maxwell to Mills, 11 June 1904, AJHR 1905 A-03.
3 Maxwell to Mills, 19 May 1904, AJHR 1905 A-03.
4 Maxwell to Mills, 4 Oct. 1904, AJHR 1905 A-03.
5 AJHR 1907 A-3.
6 Ibid. The European petition was signed by Leslie L.R. Rex, R.H. Head JP, Robert D. Head, H. Worsley, George H. Nicholas, A.O. Head, R.T. Jessop, L.H. Gulliver and G.J. Jackson.
7 Ibid.
8 *Auckland Star*, 10 Sept. 1908.
9 *Observer*, 1 Dec. 1917.
10 Cornwall to Cook Islands Dept, 12 Nov. 1907, AJHR 1908 A-3.
11 One boy, Heketaha Uea, did attend St Stephens from 1905 and then Te Aute College in Hawke's Bay from 1911. His fees were paid by his father, Uea, but there was also a grant towards the costs. It was planned for Heketaha to return to Niue and work in the Administration, but he died at Te Aute College in April 1916, possibly as a result of the infantile paralysis (polio) epidemic at that time. See TN Box 12P 7/4/7 Education-Pupils: Overseas training 1904–46.
12 AJHR 1909 A-3.
13 The school is referred to in all correspondence as Tufu until 1918, then by its more usual name, Tufukia.
14 Cornwall to Minister, 1 Dec. 1909, AJHR 1910 A-3.
15 Rev. Smith to Rev. Cullen, 12 Oct. 1913, LMS records Niue 1910–53 ATL Micro-MS-Coll-08-0701-1 (PMB 701).
16 See TN Sunday Labour and LMS records Niue 1910–53, ATL Micro-MS-Coll-08-0701-1 (PMB 701).
17 Correspondence between Cornwall & Smith, 9–11 Jan. 1912, LMS records Niue 1910–53, ATL Micro-MS-Coll-08-0701-1 (PMB 701).

18 The first medical officer, Dr Schumacher, arrived in 1911. The first chief of police, Sergeant Holmes, was transferred from Rarotonga in 1913.
19 This included one island councillor and one magistrate. Some native pastors were also involved.
20 Report of Resident Commissioner for year ended 31 March 1911, AJHR 1911 A-3.
21 Smith to Cullen, 12 Oct. 1913, LMS Records Niue 1910–53, ATL Micro-MS-Coll-08-0701-1 (PMB 701).
22 Niue Island Report for year ended 31 March 1915, AJHR 1915 A-3. Also *Evening Post*, 30 Apr. 1915.
23 A special umu for the three days of cooking needed to render tī roots sweet and edible.
24 The 1911 Census recorded 295 horses on Niue: AJHR 1912 A-3. Captain Ross talks of bringing horses back for returning workers on his vessel: see Captain William Ross papers, Hocken Library Misc-MS-1043.
25 Rev. Cullen to LMS, London, 30 July 1914, LMS Records Niue 1910–53, ATL Micro-MS-Coll-08-0701-1 (PMB 701). Cullen had replaced Smith in early 1914 after ill health had caused Smith's departure.
26 Ibid., 4 Oct. 1914.
27 AJHR 1914 A-3. HMS *Torch* called at Niue to deliver witnesses from Malden Island for a trial involving a Niuean worker on Malden charged with manslaughter: see *Poverty Bay Herald*, 14 Jan. 1914.
28 L. Rex & Y. Vivian, 'New Zealand period', in Terry Chapman (ed.), *Niue: A history of the island*, Institute of Pacific Studies & Government of Niue, Suva, Fiji, 1982, 127.
29 Rev. Smith to LMS, Sydney, 24 Jan. 1914, LMS Records Niue 1910–53, ATL Micro-MS-Coll-08-0701-1 (PMB 701).
30 'Report on Pomare's visit to Niue', *Evening Post*, 29 June 1914.
31 Smith to Cullen, 12 Oct. 1913, LMS Records Niue 1910–53, ATL Micro-MS-Coll-08-0701-1 (PMB 701).
32 Ibid. Cullen to Thompson, London, 10 June 1914.
33 Ibid. Cullen to Lenwood, London, 12 Apr. 1915; he lists several other officials who fell out with Cornwall.
34 Ibid. Cullen to Lenwood, London, 23 Aug. 1917.

CHAPTER 10. INVOLVEMENT IN WORLD WAR I

1 This chapter is based on an earlier work by the author: Margaret Pointer, *Tagi Tote e Loto Haaku, My Heart Is Crying a Little: Niue Island involvement in the Great War 1914–18*, trans. Kalaisi Folau, Institute of Pacific Studies & Government of Niue, Suva, Fiji, 2000.
2 M. Sherwood, 'Racism by omission', *BBC History Magazine*, 29 Dec. 2009.
3 Cullen to Lenwood, 4 Oct. 1914, LMS records Niue 1910–53, ATL Micro-MS-Coll-08-0701-1 (PMB 701).
4 Offer from Niue, 14 Sept. 1914. Quoted in H. Stewart, *France: Official history of New Zealand's effort in the Great War*, vol. II, Whitcombe & Tombs, Auckland, New Zealand, 1921, 9.
5 Holmes to Cornwall, 24 Nov. 1914, LMS records Niue 1910–53, ATL Micro-MS-Coll-08-0701-1 (PMB 701).
6 See Michael King, *Te Puea: A biography*, Hodder & Stoughton, Auckland, New Zealand, 1977 for details of the Waikato anti-conscription movement.

7 See Pointer, *My Heart Is Crying a Little*, 16, for details of names.
8 He was buried at O'Neill's Point Cemetery. Ibid., 22.
9 Margaret Pointer, 'Pacific Islanders in World War I', www.nzhistory.govt.nz.
10 WPHC Archives, British Consul Tonga 1, General Correspondence no. 53.
11 P. Cooke, J.H. Gray & K. Stead, *The Auckland Infantry*, 3rd Battalion Regimental Association, Auckland, New Zealand, 2010, 125.
12 Cullen to Lenwood, 11 Apr. 1917, LMS Records Niue 1910–53 ATL Micro-MS-Coll-08-0701-2 (PMB 701).
13 Christopher Pugsley, *Te Hokowhitu a Tu: The Maori Pioneer Battalion in the First World War*, Auckland, Reed, 1995, 45.
14 Pointer, *My Heart Is Crying a Little*, 48. LMS obituary to Mrs Lawes, Oct. 1917.
15 The headstones in the St Andrew's Church graveyard serve as an enduring link between the tiny 'South Sea island' and the English village. The Niuean team to the Commonwealth Games in Manchester in 2002 was invited to visit Hornchurch and a service was held in the church and at the gravesides to honour the WWI servicemen.
16 Pointer, *My Heart Is Crying a Little*, 32. Information from Nicholas Boyack & Jane Tolerton, *In the Shadow of War*, Penguin, Auckland, New Zealand, 1990, 99, interview with Colin M. Gordon.
17 Mrs Lawes to Rev. Cullen, 1 July 1916, LMS records Niue 1910–53, ATL Micro-MS-Coll-08-0701-1 (PMB 701).
18 *The Imperial Colonist*, Oct. 1916.
19 Pointer, *My Heart Is Crying a Little*. Sixteen men died while enlisted in the NZEF, and at least another 15 died within five years of return from service.
20 *Tohi Tala Niue* vol. 49, no. 14, 8 June 1984.
21 *Thames Star*, 25 Aug. 1916, 2. Vasau and Taleva are both buried at Hornchurch.
22 Lowell Thomas, *The Sea Devil: The story of Count Felix von Luckner, the German war raider*, Heinemann, London, 1928, 263.
23 Ibid.
24 Morris to Minister, Report for year ended 31 March 1919, AJHR 1919 A-3, 19.

CHAPTER 11. THE INTERWAR YEARS

1 Michael Field, *Mau: Samoa's struggle against New Zealand oppression*, A.H. & A.W. Reed, Wellington, New Zealand, 1984, ch. 3.
2 There were, however, deaths among the Niuean community in Tonga and probably also in Samoa and New Zealand.
3 Editorial, 'Our duty: To know our Pacific', *Evening Post*, 6 Aug. 1920, 6.
4 C. Jordan, Secretary Cook Islands Dept. to Minister, 5 Mar. 1918, ANZ file IT11 7, Part 1, McMahon-Box, Joseph Patrick – Treasurer, Niue 1915–33.
5 AJHR 1915 A-3. Reference is to Dr J.P. Cameron.
6 Cornwall to Minister, July 1916, TN Final A List 5/1/1/ Police File. The man was John Seymour-Grahame. It was discovered he had no former police experience whatsoever.
7 NZPD vol. 174, 20 Sept.–4 Oct. 1915, 171.
8 McMahon-Box to Secretary, Cook Islands Dept, 15 Mar. 1929, ANZ file IT11 7, Part 1, McMahon-Box, Joseph Patrick – Treasurer, Niue 1915–33.

9 Island Council to Minister Pomare, 22 Oct. 1917, ANZ IT 1 310 50/1/2 Part 1 Niue Island Council 1910–1932.

10 F.H.L. Lewin, Commander HMS *Veronica* to Commodore Commanding New Zealand Squadron, 6 June 1921, ANZ N1 16/9/4 Minor disturbances-Unrest at Niue-Warship required.

11 Morris to Cook Islands Dept, 27 March 1919, ANZ IT 1 310 50/1/2 Part 1 Niue Island Council 1910–1932.

12 Evison to Minister, 17 May 1921, ANZ N1 16/9/4 Minor disturbances-Unrest at Niue-Warship required.

13 Hotham to Minister of Defence, 25 Oct. 1921, ANZ N1 16/9/4 Minor disturbances-Unrest at Niue-Warship required.

14 Harry Johnson to Editor, *Auckland Star*, 26 Dec. 1922.

15 See *Auckland Star*, 14, 15, 16, 18 & 26 Dec. 1922

16 Island Council to Minister Pomare, 22 Oct. 1917, ANZ IT 1 310 50/1/2 Part 1 Niue Island Council 1910–1932.

17 When Morris returned to Niue he was instructed 'to issue an antedated warrant for whoever has acted in the interim'. Sec. Cook Islands Dept to Morris, 30 Aug. 1922, ANZ IT 11 Box 7/1 JP McMahon-Box.

18 Niue Council to Dr Pomare, 8 Sept. 1921, ANZ ACGA 8290 IT11 8, Morris, Guy N. – Resident Commissioner, Rarotonga, 1917–50.

19 The transfer Rarotonga–Niue was estimated to have cost the Cook Islands Department double the move Niue–Rarotonga.

20 Taylor to LMS, London, Oct. 1931, LMS Records Niue 1910–53 ATL Micro-MS-Coll-08-0701-3 (PMB 701).

21 NZPD vol. 174, 20 Sept.–4 Oct. 1915, 162–91 Legislative Council.

22 Morris to Minister, 7 July 1920, ANZ ACGA 8290 IT11 8, Morris, Guy N. – Resident Commissioner, Rarotonga, 1917–50.

23 TN Final Closed Numbers 16/2/9 Shipping – casual Sunday Work.

24 Ibid., Luckham to Pomare, Sept. 1926.

25 Beharell to Barradale, 24 Aug. 1928, LMS records Niue 1910–53, ATL Micro-MS-Coll-08-0701-4 (PMB 701).

26 Ibid., Pomare to Beharell, 25 July 1928.

27 Ibid., Sec. Cook Islands Dept to Rev. V.A. Barradale, LMS Foreign Secretary, Aug. 1927.

28 AJHR 1925 A-3 Annual Report for Niue for year ending 31 March 1925. The LMS ran schools in 10 villages at this stage, catering for over 450 pupils. Another 300 attended Tufukia and Tuatea.

29 Kofekofe school was opened in Mutalau in Feb. 1940.

30 Taylor to LMS Samoa, 20 Feb. 1940, LMS records Niue 1910–53, ATL Micro-MS-Coll-08-0701-4 (PMB 701).

31 *Auckland Star*, 31 July 1925.

32 Robert Rex interview, Tony Johns 1977, ATL Oral History Collection OHColl-0557/1.

33 LMS Records Niue 1910–1953, ATL Micro-MS-Coll-08-0701-4 (PMB 701). Robert Rex recalled that Avatele won the competition.

34 Information from personal communication on Niue.

35 Cullen to Thompson, 1 July 1914, LMS Records Niue 1910–53, ATL Micro-MS-Coll-08-0701-1 (PMB 701).

36 Evison to Cook Islands Dept, 9 Oct. 1917, ANZ IT 1 310 50/1/2 Part 1 Niue Island Council 1910–32.
37 Ibid., Pomare to Council. 27 Nov. 1917.
38 Ibid., Jordan, Sec. of Cook Islands Dept to Morris, 16 May 1919.
39 NZPD vol. 174, 20 Sept.–4 Oct. 1915, 164.
40 Frances Steel, 'New Zealand's tourism empire in the Pacific 1900–1930', paper presented at the Pacific History Association Conference, Wellington, New Zealand, December 2012.
41 Taylor to Bell, 7 Sept. 1936, LMS records Niue 1910–53, ATL Micro-MS-Coll-08-0701-4 (PMB 701).
42 AJHR 1922 A-3 Annual Report for year ended 31 March 1922.
43 William W. Bolton, *Chronicles of Savage Island Vol. IV* 1927, manuscript, Mitchell Library, Sydney, Australia, reel 1145, AU microfilm 87-212.
44 Sir Maui Pomare died on 27 June 1930 while visiting the United States.
45 Bell to Sec. Admin. W. Samoa, 25 Mar. 1936, ANZ IT 1 213 Ex17/3 Labour-Niuean.
46 Ibid., Bell to Sec. External Affairs, 31 Mar. 1936.
47 Uncle of David Lange, Labour prime minister of New Zealand 1984–89.
48 Dr Lange to Mr J. Thorn, 27 Apr. 1937. ANZ IT1 W2439 12/ 50/12/3 Niue-JW Naea Sulliana-Complaints against administration regarding employment 1937–37.
49 S. Smith, Sec. Ex. Affairs to W.M. Bell, 2 Apr. 1931, ANZ IT11 1, Part 1, Bell, William Moody-Resident Commissioner, Niue 1920–36.
50 Bell to Sec. Cook Islands Dept, 28 June 1932, TN Exec Govt-Personal File- WM Bell 1932–1942.
51 Ibid., Niue Island Council to Sec. Ex. Affairs, 30 Dec. 1941.
52 Ibid., Sec. Ex. Affairs to Jennings, Nov. 1941; quoted in letter from Jennings to Bell.
53 Ibid., Bell to External Affairs, 21 Dec. 1941.
54 Taylor to LMS Samoa, Sept. 1939, LMS records Niue 1910–53, ATL Micro-MS-Coll-08-0701-4 (PMB 701).
55 Tailby to Director, National Services, 11 July 1940, ANZ AD1 1299 312/2/623 Part 1 Recruitment-Tongans, Rarotongans, Niue Islanders, Samoans.
56 Ibid.
57 McMahon-Box to Sec. External Affairs, 28 Jan. 1942, ANZ AD1 1299 312/2/623 Part 2 Recruitment-Tongans, Rarotongans, Niue Islanders, Samoans.
58 Shanahan, Secretary Organisation for National Security, PM's Dept, to Naval Secretary, Chief of the General Staff, Chief of the Air Staff, 2 Mar. 1942, ANZ AD1 1299 312/2/623 Part 2 Recruitment-Tongans, Rarotongans, Niue Islanders, Samoans.
59 Administration of Niue Public Notice, 15 Dec. 1941, LMS records Niue 1910–53 ATL Micro-MS-Col-08-0701-5 (PMB 701).
60 Information from Hine Welsh, Alofi, June 2010.
61 Information from Geoff Harding, Alofi, 1998.
62 Organisation for National Security to Joint Chiefs of Staff and reply, Jan./Feb. 1942, ANZ N2 29 020/14/12.
63 Robert Rex interview, Tony Johns 1977, ATL Oral History Collection OHColl-0557/1.
64 McMahon-Box to External Affairs, 9 Jan. 1943, ANZ AD12 17 28/17 2NZEF reports- Niue Island January 1942–June 1945.
65 Ibid.

66 Army Headquarters to Island Territories, Jan. 1944, ANZ AD1 1299 312/2/623 Part 2 Recruitment-Tongans, Rarotongans, Niue Islanders, Samoans.

CHAPTER 12. ACCELERATING CHANGE

1 *Auckland Star*, 12 Jan. 1944.
2 Tokelau is a non-self-governing territory administered by New Zealand since 1926.
3 Department of Island Territories Act 1943.
4 AJHR 1945 A-3.
5 *Evening Post*, 2 Jan. 1945.
6 'Island peoples better facilities New Zealand's pledge', *Evening Post*, 21 Sept. 1945, 7.
7 ANZ IT11 7, Part 2, McMahon-Box, JP-Treasurer, Niue 1933–44.
8 Ibid.
9 The New Zealand government accepted a moral responsibility to help Dr Hunt and approved a payment of £500. No payment was made to Collins who, as a businessman, knew the risk he was taking.
10 Taylor to Challis, 22 June 1944, LMS records Niue 1910–53, ATL Micro-MS-Coll-08-0701-5 (PMB 701). Reference to detectives is because the New Zealand Police met the *Maui Pomare* on arrival in Auckland and searched McMahon-Box's luggage for official papers and money; none were found.
11 Ibid.
12 Rev. Whyte to Taylor, 28 June 1945, LMS Records Niue 1910–53, Micro-MS-Coll-08-0701-5 (PMB 701).
13 Robert Rex interview, Tony Johns 1977, ATL Oral History Collection OHColl-0557/1.
14 Letters to and from Larsen, TN Box 12P 7/4/7 Education-Pupils-Overseas Training.
15 It is still talked of on Niue as Sunday Island, rather than Raoul Island – its earlier French name and the name generally used today.
16 TN Box 4h 2/27/5 1947 Executive Government Labour Sunday Island.
17 Ibid.
18 TN Archives Final A List 2/27/5 Labour-Sunday Island 1948–55.
19 See 'New Golden Hind sails north', an approximately 19-minute film made by New Zealand National Film Unit in 1949, which shows the Niueans being picked up on Sunday Island and returned to Niue. ANZ ARNZ 25035 200503 Weekly Review no. 417.
20 Quoted in letter from Public Works Department to Air Department Wellington, 10 Mar. 1951, ANZ AAQB W3950 889 Box 188 23/437/7/1 Raoul Island-Niueans employed.
21 Taylor to McMahon-Box, 7 July 1942, LMS Records Niue 1910–53, ATL Micro-MS-Coll-08-0701-5 (PMB 701).
22 Ibid., Larsen to Sec. IT, Wellington, Oct. 1945.
23 Larsen to Beharell, 21 Jan. 1946, LMS records Niue 1910–1953, ATL Micro-MS-Coll-08-0701-6 (PMB 701).
24 Sec IT to Larsen, on leave in Auckland, 4 June 1946, NZ Archives IT1 Box 328 Ex 50/11/1.
25 Empen to Beharell, 11 Apr. 1946, LMS Records Niue 1910–53, ATL Micro-MS-Coll-08-0701-6 (PMB 701).
26 Larsen to Sec. IT, 12 Aug. 1946, NZ Archives IT1 Box 328 Ex50/11/1 Sunday work Niue 1932–1948.

27 Ibid., Larsen to Sec. IT, 9 Sept. 1946.
28 Ibid., Larsen to Sec. IT, 10 Oct. 1946.
29 Ibid., Larsen to Sec. IT, 20 Oct. 1946.
30 Lankshear to Beharell, 20 Oct. 1946, LMS records Niue 1910–53, ATL Micro-MS-Coll-08-0701-6 (PMB 701).
31 Robert Rex interview, ATL OHColl-0557/1. Rex also quoted the words of Larsen.
32 Patrick to Fraser, 30 June 1947, ANZ IT 1 Box 328 Ex 50/11/1 Sunday work Niue 1932–1948.
33 Ibid. Notes of a meeting held at Hakupu 23 July 1947.
34 Ibid. Patrick to Larsen 29 Sept 1947.
35 See letters in 1947 in LMS Records Niue 1910–53, ATL Micro-MS-Coll-08-0701-6 (PMB 701).
36 Ibid., reel 7. Check to Hurst, London, 9 Aug. 1949.
37 Ibid., Check to Hurst, London, 18 Nov. 1949.
38 TN 2/20/5 Final A List Fire at Burns Philp Building.
39 Taylor to LMS, London, Jan. 1942, LMS Records Niue 1910–53, ATL Micro-MS-Coll-08-0701-5 (PMB 701).
40 TN Final A List A398 5/1/1 Police-Chief of Police-General.
41 Ibid.
42 Check to Lankshear, 12 Feb. 1950, LMS records 1910–53, ATL Micro-MS-Coll-08-0701-7 (PMB 701).
43 Ibid., Check to Ennor, 13 Dec. 1950. The Paulo commemoration was held a year late so it was actually 101 years since his arrival.
44 Larsen to IT, Sept. 1950, TN Final A List A398 5/1/1 Police-Chief of Police-General.
45 Check to Rev. Challis, 8 June 1950, LMS Records 1910–53, ATL Micro-MS-Coll-08-0701-7 (PMB 701).
46 Personal Assessment Sept. 1949, 1951, 1952, ANZ IT11 5, Part 1, Larsen, C.H.W. - Resident Commissioner, Niue 1926–1951.
47 Robert Rex interview, ATL OHColl-0557/1.
48 Ibid.
49 AJHR 1951 A-3. Judge of Native Land Court, Rarotonga, spent six weeks on Niue hearing cases.
50 Robert Rex interview, ATL OHColl-0557/1.
51 AJHR 1948 Magistrate sent to hear retrial in rape case. 1951 Judge and counsel sent to hear case of murder and grievous bodily harm. 1952 Judge and counsel sent to hear two cases of rape and incest.
52 W. Frank Ponder, *A Man from the Ministry: Tales of a New Zealand architect*, Wenlock House, Blenheim, New Zealand, 1996, 32.
53 The first female scholarship student was Ofania, daughter of Mokafenoga of Alofi. She went to Waitaki Girls' High School in Oamaru, New Zealand.
54 John Garrett, *Footsteps in the Sea*, Institute of Pacific Studies, Suva, Fiji, 1992, 222.
55 AJHR 1954 A-3.
56 Joye Taylor, *Henry Head of Niue Island*, Department of Island Territories, Wellington, New Zealand, 1965, 36–39.
57 Hickling to Check, 15 Apr. 1952, LMS Records Niue 1910–53, ATL Micro-MS-Coll-08-0701-7 (PMB 701).
58 Public notice, 17 Apr. 1952. Signed H.H. Hickling, Deputy Resident Commissioner, LMS Records Niue 1910–53, ATL Micro-MS-Coll-08-0701-7 (PMB 701).
59 Ottley to Minister IT, 8 Oct. 1952, ANZ IT 1 W2439 43 84/11/4 Part 1 Mormon Mission to Niue.

60 Check to Cocks LMS, 6 May 1952, LMS Records Niue 1910–53 ATL Micro-MS-Coll-08-0701-7 (PMB 701). Picture theatre operator is a reference to Krueger.
61 Ottley to Minister IT, 8 Oct. 1952, ANZ IT 1 W2439 43 84/11/4 Part 1 Mormon Mission to Niue.
62 Ibid. Petition to Hon. Clifton Webb, 1 Aug. 1952.
63 Ibid. Petitioners to Minister, 5 Nov. 1952. The petition was presented to the New Zealand Parliament in 1953 and rejected.
64 Robert Goodman, *Niue of Polynesia: Savage Island's first Latter-day Saint missionaries*, Brookstone Publications, Powhatan, VA, 2002, Larsen to All Departments, Administration 9 Aug. 1952, appendix C, 153.
65 Ibid., 98–99.
66 In October 1951, Larsen applied for the position of resident commissioner in Rarotonga. TN Exec Govt E185 CHW Larsen 1941–52.

CHAPTER 13. AN END TO COMPLACENCY

1 Slaven to Wright, Sec IT TN Exec. Govt. E88 CHW Larsen 1953–54. Wright replied immediately, 'DEEPLY GRIEVED AND SHOCKED AT TERRIBLE NEWS'.
2 At the trial it was suggested that the positioning of the golf course alongside the prison was unfortunate, but it is still like that today.
3 Author interview with Bill (Billy) Larsen, June 2014. Bill said it was the first time he had ever been asked for his account. He could remember nothing else of the night but he did not go back to Tapeu. As a minor, he was not questioned by police, nor did he give evidence. The trial proceedings state that the housegirl, Margaret Jackson, took Billy and went to the doctor but Bill is adamant this was not the case.
4 Account of events from trial proceedings and sworn statements of the three accused, ANZ IT 1 W2439 37 84/7/16, Part 1, Niue Island-Legal-Murder of Resident Commissioner 1953–53.
5 Lack of embalming facilities on the island make burial an urgent priority.
6 Robert Rex interview, Tony Johns 1977, ATL Oral History Collection OHColl-0557/1.
7 Prisoner statements, ANZ IT 1 W2439 37 84/7/16, Part 1, Niue Island-Legal-Murder of Resident Commissioner 1953–53.
8 The people of Fatiau had moved to the new village of Vaiea in Feb 1953.
9 Robert Rex interview, ATL OHColl-0557/1.
10 Ibid.
11 Sec. IT to Powles, Apia, Samoa, 18 Aug. 1953, ANZ IT 1 W2439 37 84/7/16 Part 1, Niue Island-Legal-Murder of Resident Commissioner 1953–53.
12 Ibid., Slaven to Sec. IT, 20 Aug. 1953.
13 Ibid., Wright to Minister, 21 Aug. 1953.
14 Ibid., Quin to Wright IT, 14 Sept. 1953.
15 The Privy Council – a formal body of senior politicians who advise the sovereign – acts as a supreme court of appeal for a number of Commonwealth countries.
16 Quin to Wright IT, 10 Dec. 1953, ANZ IT 1 W2439 37 84/7/16, Part 2, Niue Island-Legal-Murder of Resident Commissioner 1953–54.
17 Ibid., Powles Apia to Wright IT, 10 Dec. 1953.
18 The Howard League had been formed in the 1920s to work for the reform of prison conditions

and was totally opposed to the death penalty. It formed the United Committee to Save the Niue Islanders and funded the appeal to the Privy Council.

19 Editorial, *Auckland Star*, 22 Feb. 1954.

20 *People's Voice*, 23 Sept. 1953; 7 Oct. 1953; 9 Dec. 1953; 16 Dec. 1953.

21 *People's Voice*, 16 Dec. 1953, 4.

22 Confidential affidavit to Appeal Court hearing on 27 Oct. 1953, J.C. Beaglehole Room, Boyd 00025, Victoria University of Wellington. Robert Rex and Jock McEwen both later questioned the role of Check and were less than supportive of him.

23 ANZ IT 1 W2439 37 84/7/16 Niue Island-Legal-Petition number 2.

24 Wellington Committee's full statement to Minister, 27 Apr. 1954. ANZ IT 1 W2439 37 84/7/16 Niue Island-Legal-Petition number 2.

25 Judge Sinclair's report on trial, Sept. 1953, ANZ IT 1 W2439 37 84/7/16, Part 1, Niue Island-Legal-Murder of Resident Commissioner 1953–53.

26 Pleasants to Wright, Sec IT, 17 Sept. 1953. ANZ IT 1 W2439 37 84/7/16, Part 1, Niue Island-Legal-Murder of Resident Commissioner 1953–53.

27 Robert Rex interview, ATL OHColl-0557/1.

28 Powles to Sec IT, 10 Dec. 1953, ANZ IT 1 W2439 37 84/7/16, Part 2, Niue Island-Legal-Murder of Resident Commissioner 1953–54.

29 NZPD vol. 174, 20 Sept.–4 Oct. 1915, Debate in Legislative Council, Hon. Mr Samuel, 170.

Part D. The Road To Self-Government

CHAPTER 14. POLITICAL WILL FOR CHANGE

1 McEwen family private letters. Jock to Mother, 10 Jan. 1954.

2 Based on figures in AJHR 1957 A-3 Niue Revenue and Expenditure.

3 ANZ T1 449 62/19/1 Treasury Papers 1951–1954 Expenditure-Island Territories.

4 McEwen family private letters, Jock to Mother, 12 Sept. 1955.

5 AJHR 1954 A-3 Niue Report.

6 Jock McEwen interview, Rhys Richards 1991, Radio NZ ATL OHInt-0201/1.

7 Mrs Kalia and Mrs Siakimotu, Mrs Patricia Rex and Mrs Malama Head.

8 Fritz van Westerndorp was appointed and proved very successful on Niue. He was responsible for the trial plantations referred to earlier.

9 Jack Roughan, Archie Jacobsen and Ernie Welsh are three who were mentioned frequently in reports back to Wellington. All married Niuean women.

10 McEwen family private letters, Jock to Mother, 19 Oct. 1955.

11 McEwen to Sec. IT, Aug. 1954, ANZ IT-Niue 1/1, Confidential reports to Department of Island Territories 1953–63.

12 AJHR 1956 A-3.

13 McEwen to Sec. IT, Sept. 1954, ANZ IT-Niue 1/1, Confidential reports to Department of Island Territories 1953–63.

14 McEwen to Sec. IT, 6 Sept. 1954, ANZ IT 1 W2439 44 Niue-Catholic Mission.

15 McEwen to Sec. IT, Feb. 1954, ANZ IT-Niue 1/1, Confidential reports to Department of Island Territories 1953–63.

16 McEwen to Sec. IT, 6 Sept. 1954, ANZ IT 1 W2439 44 Niue-Catholic Mission.

17 Ibid.

18 Ibid., Report from Resident Commissioner to IT, 5 Oct. 1954.
19 Ibid., Minister of IT, T.L. McDonald, to Niue Island Council, 18 Jan. 1955.
20 McEwen to Sec. IT, Sept. 1955, ANZ IT-Niue 1/1, Confidential reports to Department of Island Territories 1953–63.
21 Ibid., Feb. 1954.
22 Ibid., Nov. 1954.
23 H. Belshaw & V.D. Stace, *A Programme for Economic Development in the Cook Islands*, Department of Island Territories, Wellington, New Zealand, 1955.
24 McEwen to Sec. IT, Nov. 1954, ANZ IT-Niue 1 1, Confidential reports to Department of Island Territories 1953–63.
25 J.B. Wright would later become high commissioner in Western Samoa in the lead-up to independence in 1962.
26 Some IT officials suggested it should be named Department of Niue Affairs. Jock McEwen interview, Rhys Richards 1991, Radio NZ ATL OHInt-0201/1.
27 Robert Rex interview, Tony Johns 1977, ATL Oral History Collection OHColl-0557/1.
28 Heatley to Sec. IT, Mar. 1959, ANZ IT-Niue 1/1, Confidential reports to Department of Island Territories 1953–63.
29 Interview by author with Selwyn Wilson, July 2010.
30 Ibid.
31 Ibid.
32 Information from Cecily Wilson, July 2010.
33 W. Frank Ponder, *A Man from the Ministry: Tales of a New Zealand architect*, Wenlock House, Blenheim, New Zealand, 1996, 90.
34 Mathison to Heatley, 15 Apr. 1959, ANZ IT11 4, Part 2, Heatley, David W.R. – Resident Commissioner, Niue 1955–70.
35 Heatley to Sec. IT, Dec. 1959, ANZ IT-Niue 1/1, Confidential reports to Department of Island Territories 1953–63.
36 Ibid., Heatley to Sec. IT, Jan. 1960.
37 Robert Rex interview, ATL OHColl-0557/1.
38 Springford to Sec. IT, March 1960, ANZ IT-Niue 1/1, Confidential reports to Department of Island Territories 1953–63.
39 Robert Rex interview, ATL OHColl-0557/1.

CHAPTER 15. A TIMETABLE FOR CHANGE

1 New Zealand Cabinet Meeting, 18 June 1962, ANZ AAFD 807 W3738/27 CM(62)25.
2 Ibid.
3 Ibid.
4 Ibid.
5 Ibid.
6 Robert Rex interview, Tony Johns 1977, ATL Oral History Collection OHColl-0557/1.
7 *Niue Newsletter*, 3 May 1962. Article by Lyle Shanks, resident commissioner.
8 Ibid.
9 Shanks to Sec. IT, July 1962, ANZ IT-Niue 1/1, Confidential reports to Department of Island Territories 1953–63.

10 Ikimotu, member for Avatele, at Niue Assembly meeting, 18 Jan. 1965 ANZ ACIE 8805 W2492 EAW2492 2/82. One of the reasons for the delay had been a serious illness for McEwen in 1964.
11 Assembly meeting, 19 Jan. 1965, ANZ ACIE8805 W2492 EAW2492 2/81.
12 Public meeting, 21 Jan. 1965. Quoted in Terry Chapman, *The Decolonisation of Niue*, Victoria University Press, Wellington, and NZIIA, 1976, 22.
13 Assembly meeting, 22 Jan. 1965, ANZ ACIE 8805 W2492 EAW2492 2/79.
14 Statement in Plenary session of UN General Assembly by NZ Representative, N. Farrell, 19 Dec, 1967. ANZ ABHS 6942 W5399 178/ API307/4/1 part 2, The Pacific-NZ Island Territories-Niue [12/1966-03/1973].
15 Rex attended the South Pacific Conference as the Niue representative in the Cook Islands delegation in 1950.
16 WHO and UNICEF signed agreement with New Zealand Government Sept. 1967, AJHR 1968.
17 Saulaina Sale of Alofi. Information from TN.
18 Words from song composed by Tahafa Talagi for opening of Radio Niue. Translation and information from Hima Douglas.
19 See Kon-Tiki Makani, 'Ekalesia Niue: An indigenous church in the making', MTheol thesis, Pacific Theological College, Suva, Fiji, Sept. 1993. The LMS changed its name to Congregational Council for World Missions.
20 AJHR 1967 A-3 Report for Niue.
21 AJHR 1971 A-3 Report for Niue.
22 The site at Laucala Bay was handed over for the new University of the South Pacific, which began offering degree courses in 1969.
23 NZ Cabinet, 16 Mar. 1967, ANZ AAFD 811 W3738 1365/ CAB402/5/1 NZ Island Territories-Niue Island-General.
24 Information from Selwyn Wilson, resident commissioner at the time.
25 Terry Coe was brought in as a mechanic for the heavy machinery. He married locally, became an assemblyman in 1993 and is still in the Niue Assembly. Information from author interview with Selwyn Wilson.
26 E.K. Fisk, *The Island of Niue: Development or dependence for a very small nation*, ANU Press, Canberra, Australia, 1978.
27 Ibid. Fisk is quoting Brian Pollard, University of Auckland, New Zealand, 1975.
28 A.C. Walsh, Niue Migration Study, Massey University, New Zealand, 1972.
29 Assembly meeting, 18 Jan. 1965, ANZ ACIE 8805 W2492 EAW2492 2/82.
30 They were Mrs Marion McQuoid, Mr Lagi Tuhega and Mr Lagi Sipeli. Assembly meeting, 20 Jan. 1965, ANZ ACIE 8805 W2492 EAW2492 2/80.
31 Wilson to Sec. Island Affairs, March 1969, ANZ IT-Niue 1 1/3, Confidential monthly reports to Secretary of Maori and Island Affairs 1968–74.
32 R.Q. Quentin-Baxter, Report to the Niue Island Assembly, AJHR 1971 A-4, 10.
33 Wilson to Sec. Island Affairs, Jan. 1970, ANZ IT-Niue 1 1/3, Confidential monthly reports to Secretary of Maori and Island Affairs 1968–74.
34 Ibid., Jan. 1970.
35 Jock M. McEwen, *Niue Dictionary*, Department of Maori and Island Affairs, Wellington, New Zealand, 1970.
36 Wilson to Sec. Island Affairs, Apr. 1972, ANZ IT-Niue 1 1/3, Confidential monthly reports to Secretary of Maori and Island Affairs 1968–74.

CHAPTER 16. THE FINAL STEPS

1 McEwen confidential notes on the UN visit to Niue, June 1972, ANZ ABHS 6942 W5399 Box 178/ API 307/4/1 part 2 The Pacific-NZ Territories-Niue [12/1966-03/1973].
2 Ibid.
3 In October 1973 the first Niuean speaker, Sam Tagelagi, was appointed. The speaker is not an elected member of the Assembly and has no voting rights.
4 Report of the UN Visiting Mission to Niue, 19 July 1972, ANZ ABHS 6942 W5399 178/ API 307/4/1 part 2 The Pacific-NZ Territories-Niue [12/1966-03/1973].
5 Ibid.
6 Select Committee of Niue Island Legislative Assembly Report Nov. 1972, ANZ ABHS 6942 W5399 178/ API 307/4/1 part 2 The Pacific-NZ Territories-Niue [12/1966-03/1973].
7 Cables between Wellington and Apia, Feb. 1973, ANZ ABHS 6942 W5399 178/ API 307/4/1 part 2 The Pacific-NZ Territories-Niue [12/1966-03/1973].
8 This position would become secretary to Government and Terry Magaoa Chapman would take up the role in November 1974.
9 Rex spoke very warmly of Alison Stokes, first secretary at the New York office, and Malcolm Templeton, 'a fine gentleman', permanent representative at the UN.
10 Robert Rex speech to Special Committee on Decolonisation, *NZ Foreign Affairs Review*, vol. 23, no. 11, Nov. 1973, 56–61.
11 Robert Rex interview, Tony Johns 1977, ATL Oral History Collection OHColl-0557/1.
12 Ibid.
13 Noel Holmes, 'Independent Niue? It's just not practical', *Auckland Star*, 10 May 1973, 8.
14 C.A. Roberts to Sec. IA, June and Oct. 1973, ANZ IT-Niue 1 1/3, Confidential monthly reports to Secretary of Maori and Island Affairs 1968–74. Clifford Roberts was the last resident commissioner, serving from early 1973 until November 1974.
15 McEwen to Wilson, 2 June 1972, ANZ ABHS 6942 W5399 178/ API 307/4/1 part 2 The Pacific-NZ Territories-Niue [12/1966-03/73].
16 'Prime Minister's visit to Niue', *NZ Foreign Affairs Review*, vol. 24, no. 3, Mar. 1974, 35–38.
17 An old name for Niue.
18 Articles appeared in the *Dominion* and *Evening Post*, 23, 24 July 1974.
19 Report on Visit to Niue of Island Affairs Select Committee 5–9 Aug. 1974, ANZ ABGX 16127 W3706 76/ Island Affairs Committee-Administration-Minutes 1974.
20 This meant each elector would have two votes, one for the village representative and one for the common roll seats.
21 The UN team comprised representatives from Ethiopia, Iran and Venezuela along with UN Secretariat staff.
22 Robert Rex interview, ATL OHColl-0557/1.
23 Phillip Melchior, 'Feasting and dancing on Niue as Premier proclaims "Best of both worlds"', *Evening Post*, 21 Oct. 1974, 18.

Bibliography and resources

Manuscripts and unpublished works

Alexander Turnbull Library, National Library of New Zealand, Wellington

Arundel Family Papers, ATL Micro-MS-Coll-08-1227 (PMB 1227)

Grice, Sumner & Co Papers, ATL MS-Papers-6524

LMS Journals, ATL Micro-MS-Coll-02-005

LMS Samoan District Administration Records 1851–1973, ATL Micro-MS-Coll-08-1278/9 (PMB 1278/9)

LMS Records relating to Niue Island 1861–1910, ATL Micro-MS-0471

LMS Records Niue 1910–1953, ATL Micro-MS-Coll-08-0701 (PMB 701)

LMS South Seas Letters, ATL Micro-MS-Coll-02-046

Martin, A.W., Reminiscences of voyages in the Pacific Ocean 1850s, 1860s, ATL Micro-MS-Coll-08-1342 (PMB 1342)

McEwen interview, Rhys Richards 1991 Radio NZ, ATL OHInt-0201/1

New England Whaling Project, ATL Micro-MS-Coll-08 (PMB, 420 reels of microfilm). Used in conjunction with Robert Langdon (ed.), *Where the Whalers Went* (see 'Published works')

Ranfurly family papers 1896–1913, ATL MS-Group-0756 MS Copy Micro 0734-02

Robert Rex interview, Tony Johns 1977, ATL Oral History Collection OHColl-0557/1

Tohi Tala Niue, Niue newsletter, Alofi, Office of Resident Commissioner, 1953–1966 (PMB 467)

Townsend, Charles & H.F. Moore, 'Ethnographic Notes on South Sea Islands 1899–1900. Albatross Cruise', ATL Micro-MS-Coll-08-0121 (PMB 121)

Whitehouse, John, 'A history of Niue and the Loyalty Islands to 1894', manuscript, ATL Micro-MS-Coll-08-0149 (PMB 149)

Archives New Zealand, Wellington

AAEG Ministry of Foreign Affairs

AAFD Cabinet Office

AAQB R Corporation (Works and Development Services Corporation)

AAYS (AD) Army Department

AAYT (N) Navy Department

ABEP Ministry of Education

ABHS Ministry of Foreign Affairs and Trade

ABGX Office of the Clerk of the House of Representatives

ABKK Works Consultancy Services

ACGA (IT) Island Territories Department

ACHW Rt. Hon. Richard John Seddon

ACIE Department of External Affairs

ADRK (T) Treasury

AECO Prime Minister's Department

AEND Western Pacific High Commission

University of Auckland Library Special Collections

George Lawes Journal and Letterbook, AU Microfilm 2111 (Original in Mitchell Library, Sydney)

Western Pacific High Commission Archives

William W. Bolton, 'The Chronicles of Savage Island', vol. IV, manuscript, Mitchell Library, Sydney, reel 1145, AU microfilm 87-212 (See online version below)

Auckland War Memorial Museum Tāmaki Paenga Hira

Stephenson Percy Smith diary MS281 (5) Box 3

Beaglehole Room, Victoria University of Wellington

Mary Boyd papers

Hocken Library Uare Taoka o Hākena, University of Otago, Dunedin

Captain William Ross papers Misc-MS-1043

Mallard family papers MS-0107

Official publications

Appendices to the Journals of the House of Representatives (AJHR), New Zealand

New Zealand Foreign Affairs Review, New Zealand Ministry of Foreign Affairs, 1970–1988

New Zealand Parliamentary Debates (NZPD)

Tāoga Niue, National Museum and Cultural Centre, Niue

New Zealand Administration Files, 1901–1959

Theses

Makani, Kon-Tiki, 'Ekalesia Niue: An indigenous church in the making', MTheol thesis, Pacific Theological College, Suva, Fiji, 1993

Morris, M.F., 'The history of Niue-Fekai', MA thesis, University of Auckland, 1933

Ryan, Thomas F., 'Narratives of encounter: The anthropology of history on Niue', PhD thesis, University of Auckland, New Zealand, 1993

Websites and online articles

Nineteenth-century UK Periodicals – online website of historical publications, including missionary magazines. Available to search at National Library of New Zealand Te Puna Matauranga o Aotearoa. Magazines accessed:
Juvenile Missionary Magazine (LMS)
The Juvenile: A Magazine for the Young (LMS)
The Missionary News (LMS)
Chronicle of the LMS

Bolton, William Washington 1927, 1931. Part II, *The Chronicles of Savage Island*, in *The Writings of William Washington Bolton* (3rd edn, 2013), ed. Timothy Adair Lawson, www.mediafire.com/download/a4faerq59b7mhh2

Papers Past – New Zealand newspapers online: paperspast.natlib.govt.nz

Trove – Australian newspapers online: trove.nla.gov.au

Published books and articles

Akeli, Safua & Pasene, Shane, 'Exploring "The Rock": Material culture from Niue Island in Te Papa's Pacific Cultures Collection', *Tuhinga*, vol. 22, Museum of New Zealand Te Papa Tongarewa, Wellington, 2011, 101–24

Barradale, V.A., *Pearls of the Pacific: Being sketches of missionary life and work in Samoa and other islands in the South Seas*, London Missionary Society, London, 1907

Beaglehole, J.C. (ed.), *The Journals of Captain James Cook*, vol. II, *The Voyage of the Resolution and Adventure 1772–1775*, Hakluyt Society & Cambridge University Press, Cambridge, 1961

Belshaw, H. & V.D. Stace, *A Programme for Economic Development in the Cook Islands*, Department of Island Territories, Wellington, New Zealand, 1955

Brenchley, Julius, *Jottings during the Cruise of H.M.S. Curaçao among the South Sea Islands in 1865*, Longmans, Green, London, 1873

Chapman, Terry, *The Decolonisation of Niue*, Victoria University Press & NZIIA, Wellington, 1976

Chapman, Terry (ed.), *Niue: A history of the island*, Institute of Pacific Studies & Government of Niue, Suva, Fiji, 1982

Cowan, James, *Suwarrow Gold and Other Stories of the Great South Seas*, Jonathan Cape, London, 1936

Crocombe, R.G. & M. Crocombe, *The Works of Ta'unga: Records of a Polynesian traveller in the South Seas 1833–1896*, ANU Press, Canberra, 1968

Druett, Joan, *In the Wake of Madness: The murderous voyage of the whaleship Sharon*, Harper Collins, Auckland, 2004

Ellis, Albert F., *Adventuring in Coral Seas*, Angus & Robertson, Sydney, 1936

Erskine, John E., *Journal of a Cruise among the Islands of the Western Pacific*, John Murray, London, 1853

Field, Michael J., *Mau: Samoa's struggle against New Zealand Oppression*, A.H. & A.W. Reed, Wellington, 1984

Fisk, E.K., *The Island of Niue: Development or dependence for a very small nation*, ANU Press, Canberra, Australia, 1978

Forster, Georg, *A Voyage Round the World in His Britannic Majesty's Sloop, Resolution, commanded by Capt. James Cook*, London, 1777

Garrett, John, *To Live among the Stars: Christian origins in Oceania*, World Council of Churches & Institute of Pacific Studies, Geneva & Suva, Fiji, 1982

Garrett, John, *Footsteps in the Sea: Christianity in Oceania to World War II*, Institute of Pacific Studies, Suva, Fiji, 1992

Goodenough, J.G., *Journal of Commodore Goodenough during his last command as Senior Officer on the Australian Station 1873–1875*, edited by his widow, Henry S. King & Co., London, 1876

Goodman, Robert, *Niue of Polynesia: Savage Island's first Latter-day Saint missionaries*, Brookstone Publications, Powhatan, VA, 2002

Grimshaw, Beatrice, *In the Strange South Seas*, Hutchinson, London, 1911

Gunson, Niel, *Messengers of Grace: Evangelical missionaries in the South Seas, 1797–1860*, Oxford University Press, Melbourne, Australia, 1978

Hay, Rod & Powlesland, Ralph, *Guide to the Birds of Niue*, South Pacific Regional Environmental Program, Apia, Samoa, 1998

Hoare, Michael (ed.), *The Resolution Journal of Johann Reinhold Forster 1772–1775*, vol. III, Hakluyt Society, London, 1982

'Hoisting the Flag in a Savage Isle', by 'an Official who was Present', in *The Wide World Magazine*, vol. VI, Jan. 1901

Holmes, Christine (ed.), *Captain Cook's Second Voyage: The Journals of Lieutenants Elliott and Pickersgill*, Caliban Books, London, 1984

Hood, Thomas, *Notes of a Cruise in HMS Fawn in the Western Pacific in the Year 1862*, Edmonston & Douglas, Edinburgh, 1863

Jones, John D., *Life and Adventures in the South Pacific, by a Roving Printer*, Harper & Bros, New York, 1861

King, Joseph, *W.G. Lawes of Savage Island and New Guinea*, Religious Tract Society, London, 1909

Langdon, Robert (ed.), *Where the Whalers Went: An index to the Pacific ports and islands visited by American whalers, and some other ships, in the 19th century*, Pacific Manuscripts Bureau, Canberra, Australia, 1984

Liverpool, C.G.S.F., *Three Years on the Australian Station*, Hatchard, London, 1868

Loeb, Edwin M., *History and Traditions of Niue*, Bishop Museum, Honolulu, 1926

Lowell, Thomas, *The Sea Devil: The story of Count Felix von Luckner, the German war raider*, Heinemann, London, 1928

Lubbock, Basil, *Bully Hayes: South Sea pirate*, Martin Hopkinson, London, 1931

Marra, John, *Journal of the Resolution's Voyage in 1772, 1773, 1774, & 1775*, F. Newbery, London, 1775

Matheson, Trevor, 'Niuean land-holdings in Western Samoa', in L. Mason & P. Hereniko (eds), *In Search of a Home*, University of the South Pacific, Suva, Fiji, 1987

Maude, H.E., *Of Islands and Men: Studies in Pacific history*, Oxford University Press, Melbourne, 1968

Maude, H.E., *Slavers in Paradise: The Peruvian labour trade in Polynesia, 1862–1864*, ANU Press, Canberra, 1981

Moss, Frederick J., *Through Atolls and Islands in the Great South Seas*, Sampson, Low, Marston, Searle & Rivington, London, 1889

Munro, Doug & Firth, Stewart, 'Samoan plantations: The Gilbertese laborers' experience 1867–1896', in B. Lal, D. Munro & E. Beechert (eds), *Plantation Workers, Resistance and Accommodation*, University of Hawai'i Press, Honolulu, 1993

Munro, Doug & Thornley, Andrew (eds), *The Covenant Makers: Island missionaries in the Pacific*, Pacific Theological College & Institute of Pacific Studies, Suva, Fiji, 1996

Murray, A.W., *Missions of Western Polynesia: Being historical sketches of these missions, from their commencement in 1839 to the present time*, John Snow, London, 1863

O'Malley, Vincent, *The Meeting Place: Māori and Pākehā encounters, 1642–1840*, Auckland University Press, Auckland, New Zealand, 2012.

People's Voice, People's Voice Press, Auckland, New Zealand, 1939–1966. (Hard copy available in ATL.)

Philbrick, Nathaniel, *Sea of Glory: The Epic South Seas expedition 1838–1842*, Harper, London, 2005

Pointer, Margaret, *Tagi Tote e Loto Haaku: My Heart is Crying a Little: Niue Island involvement in the Great War 1914–18*, trans. Kalaisi Folau, Institute of Pacific Studies & Government of Niue, Suva, Fiji, 2000

Ponder, W. Frank, *A Man from the Ministry: Tales of a New Zealand architect*, Wenlock House, Blenheim, New Zealand, 1996

Powell, Thomas, *Savage Island, a brief account of the island of Niue, and of the work of the gospel among its people*, John Snow, London, 1868

Pugsley, Christopher, *Te Hokowhitu a Tu: The Maori Pioneer Battalion in the First World War*, Reed, Auckland, New Zealand, 1995

Pule, John & Thomas, Nicholas, *Hiapo Past and Present in Niuean Barkcloth*, Otago University Press, Dunedin, New Zealand, 2005

Reynolds, J.N., 'Report to U.S. Congress. September 1828 'in *Documents of the Congress of the United States March 1831–June 1836*, vol. IV, *Naval Affairs*, Gale's & Seaton, Washington, 1861

Salesa, Damon, 'New Zealand's Pacific', in Giselle Byrnes (ed.), *The New Oxford History of New Zealand,* Oxford University Press, Melbourne, Australia, 2009

Salmond, Anne, *The Trial of the Cannibal Dog: Captain Cook in the South Seas*, Penguin Books, Auckland, New Zealand, 2004

Scott, Dick, *Years of the Pooh-Bah: A Cook Islands history*, Hodder & Stoughton, Auckland, New Zealand, 1991.

Scott, Dick, *Would a Good Man Die? Niue Island, New Zealand and the late Mr Larsen*, Southern Cross Books & Hodder & Stoughton, Auckland, New Zealand, 1993

Skogman, Carl J.A., *Erdumsegelung der Konigl. Schwedischen Fregatte Eugenie; in den Jahren 1851 bis 1853*, Otto Janke, Berlin, 1856

Smith, S. Percy, *Niue: The island and its people*, Institute of Pacific Studies, Suva, Fiji, 1983

Sparrman, Anders, *Voyage Round the World with Captain James Cook in the H.M.S. Resolution*, Robert Hales, London, 1953

Sperlich, Wolfgang (ed.), *Tohi Vagahau Niue: Niue Language Dictionary*, Government of Niue & University of Hawai'i Press, Honolulu, 1997

Stevenson, Mrs Robert Louis (Fanny), *The Cruise of the 'Janet Nichol' among the South Sea Islands,* Chatto & Windus, London, 1915

Stewart, H., *The New Zealanders in France: The official history of New Zealand's effort in the Great War,* vol. II, Whitcombe & Tombs, Auckland, New Zealand, 1921

Sykes, W.R., *Contributions to the Flora of Niue*, Department of Scientific and Industrial Research, Christchurch, New Zealand, 1970

Talagi, Maru, *Politics, Propositions and Perspectives: Niue nationhood*, Solomua Press, Niue, 2013

Taylor, Joye, *Henry Head of Niue Island: A story of the South Seas*, Islands Education Division of the Department of Education, New Zealand, for the Department of Island Territories, Wellington, New Zealand, 1965

Thomas, Nicholas, *Discoveries: The voyages of Captain Cook*, Allen Lane, London, 2003

Thomas, Nicholas, *Islanders: The Pacific in the age of Empire,* Yale University Press, New Haven CT & London, 2010

Thompson, Ralph Wardlaw, *My Trip in the 'John Williams'*, London Missionary Society, London, 1900

Thomson, Basil, *Savage Island: An account of a sojourn in Niue and Tonga*, John Murray, London, 1902

Tregear, Edward, *The Right Hon. R.J. Seddon's visit to Tonga, Fiji, Savage Island and the Cook Islands, May 1900,* Government Printer, Wellington, New Zealand, 1900

Trotter, Michael, *Niue Island Archaeological Survey*, Canterbury Museum, Christchurch, New Zealand, 1979

Turner, George, *Nineteen Years in Polynesia: Missionary life, travels and researches in the islands of the Pacific*, John Snow, London, 1861

Ward, R. Gerard (ed.), *American Activities in the Central Pacific 1790–1870*, vol. 6, Gregg Press, Ridgewood NJ, 1967

Williams, John, *A Narrative of Missionary Enterprises in the South Sea Islands*, London, John Snow, 1838

Index

*Page numbers in **bold** refer to illustrations.*